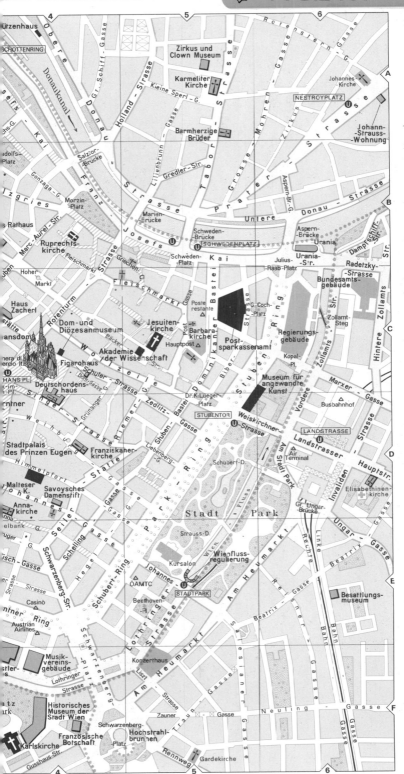

The Ring at the beginning of the
20th century, with the State Opera
to the right.

The ferris wheel at the Prater in the 1930's.
It was later made famous by Carol Reed's film,
The Third Man (1949).

The Graben c. 1900. The Fountain of St Leopold is in the foreground, with the Plague Column (Pestsäule) beyond.

Vienna. English
Vienna / [Gallimard editions].
p. cm. -- (Knopf guides) --
Includes bibliographical references and index.
ISBN 0-679-75068-1 : $25.00
1. Vienna (Austria) -- Guidebooks.
I. Gallimard (Firm) . II. Title.
III. Series.
DB849.V4813 1994
914.36'130453—dc20
CIP 94–1526

First American Edition

NUMEROUS SPECIALISTS AND ACADEMICS HAVE CONTRIBUTED TO THIS GUIDE:
AUTHORS: Pierre Crisol, Philippe J. Dubois, Dominique Fernandes,
Jean-François Frémont, Jean-Louis Gaillemin, Jean-Claude Klotchkoff,
Pierre de Lagarde, François de Lannoy, Laurence Lesage, Jean-Louis Poitevin,
Andreas Ranner.
ILLUSTRATORS: Cent Alantar, Michel Aubois, Philippe Biard, Vincent Brunot,
Vincent Brunot, Jacqueline Candiard, Jean-Philippe Chabot,
Jean Chevallier, Paul Coulbois, François Desbordes, Hugh Dixon,
Jean-Yves Duhoo, Claire Felloni, Frédéric Hillion, Jean-Michel Kacédan,
Catherine Lachaux, Cyrille Mallié, Jean-Marc Lanus, Alban Larousse,
Caroline Picard, Maurice Pommier, Pascal Robin, Michel Simier, John Wilkinson.
LOCAL CORRESPONDENT: Catherine Polsterer.
PHOTOGRAPHERS: Philippe Bénet, Matthias Cremer, Renata Holzbachovà,
Kathrin Leithner.

WE WOULD ALSO LIKE TO THANK:
Christian Brandsätter, Ferdinand Fellinger (Historischesmuseum der Stadt Wien),
Edwin Hofbauer (Österreichische Nationalbibliothek), Traudl and Eric Lessing,
Andreas Ranner (Österreichische Gesellschaft für Vogelkunde),
Richard Schmitz and Sonia Schmitz.

TRANSLATED BY ANTHONY ROBERTS;
EDITED AND TYPESET BY BOOK CREATION SERVICES, LONDON.
PRINTED IN ITALY BY EDITORIALE LIBRARIA.

VIENNA

KNOPF GUIDES

CONTENTS

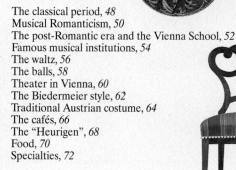

I Innere Stadt II Leopoldstadt III Landstraße IV Wieden V Margareten VI Mariahilf VII Neubau VIII Josefstadt IX Alsergrund X Favoriten XI Simmering XII Meidling XIII Hietzing

XIV Penzing XV Rudolfsheim-Fünfhaus XVI Ottakring XVII Hernals XVIII Währing XIX Döbling XX Brigittenau XXI Floridsdorf XXII Donaustadt XXIII Liesing

HOW TO USE THIS GUIDE

The page shown below is from the guide to Venice

The symbols at the top of each page refer to the different parts of the guide.

■ NATURAL ENVIRONMENT

● UNDERSTANDING VIENNA

▲ ITINERARIES

◆ PRACTICAL INFORMATION

The itinerary map shows the main points of interest along the way and is intended to help you find your bearings.

The mini-map locates the particula itinerary within the wider area covered by the guide.

THE GATEWAY TO VENICE ★

The star symbol signifies that a particular site has been singled out by the publishers for its special beauty, atmosphere or cultural interest.

●▲■◆
The symbols alongside a title or within the text itself provide cross-references to a theme or place dealt with elsewhere in the guide.

At the beginning of each itinerary, the suggested means of transport to be used and the time it will take to cover the area are indicated:

🚤 By boat
🚶 On foot
🚲 By bicycle
⏱ Duration

THE GATEWAY TO VENICE ★

PONTE DELLA LIBERTA. Built by the Austrians 50 years after the Treaty of Campo Formio in 1797 ● *34,* to link Venice with Milan. The bridge ended the thousand-year separation from the mainland and shook the city's economy to its roots as Venice, already in the throes of the industrial revolution, saw

🚶 Half a day

BRIDGES TO VENICE

NATURE

■ PARKS AND GARDENS

The park at Schönbrunn ▲ *284* has plenty of broad open spaces, perfectly adapted for birds foraging for worms and field insects.

From the tiniest shady square to the magnificent Schönbrunn Park, Vienna's green areas shelter a surprising variety of wild creatures. The city is still a favorable environment for woodland bird species such as the tawny owl, the stock dove and various woodpeckers (including the rare Syrian woodpecker, Vienna being the westernmost point of its range). There are forest trees everywhere, such as beech and moss-capped oak. Even the shy pine marten may sometimes be seen at Schönbrunn.

A panoply of species, most of them common to the forests of Central Europe, make Schönbrunn a true woodland park.

CARRION AND HOODED CROW
Vienna is one of the points in Central Europe where these two sub-species appear to co-exist. The carrion crow is thought to be expanding its territory eastward, at the expense of its close relative.

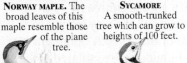

NORWAY MAPLE. The broad leaves of this maple resemble those of the plane tree.

SYCAMORE A smooth-trunked tree which can grow to heights of 100 feet.

LIME TREE. Delicious honey can be made from lime blossom.

HORSE CHESTNUT Some of Vienna's parks have chestnut avenues that are hundreds of years old.

GREEN WOODPECKER This large woodpecker often feeds on the ground.

MIDDLE SPOTTED WOODPECKER. This is rare in cities but is common in Vienna.

GREAT SPOTTED WOODPECKER. This is common in Vienna's parks and gardens.

NUTHATCH The nuthatch is easily identified by its "tuit, tuit, tuit" call.

BLACKBIRD The blackbird can be seen foraging everywhere in the grass parks of Vienna.

BLACKCAP This migratory species reappears in Vienna's parks in April.

RED SQUIRREL The red squirrels at Schönbrunn are so confident and inquisitive that one can almost touch them.

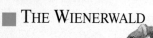

THE WIENERWALD

BEECH TREE

PINE MARTEN. The pine marten's usual diet consists of rodents and small birds, but it will also eat berries and wild fruit.

The Wienerwald (Vienna Forest), a good example of Central European woodland, stretches all the way from the gates of the city to the foothills of the Alps. A dominant tree species is the beech, which favors humid, well-ventilated soil. The oak family is also strongly represented, with several trees many centuries old, and also the Norwegian pine, which often grows in companionship with the oak. Red deer, fallow deer and wild boar abound in the Wienerwald, where they still occupy the old imperial game preserves, while woodpeckers and flycatchers (both red-breasted and white-collared) are the commonest birds.

EUROPEAN RED DEER
The more distant and protected areas of the forest shelter large numbers of deer.

Female

Male

Male

RED-BREASTED AND COLLARED FLYCATCHERS
These two species of flycatcher, characteristic inhabitants of the great forests of Central Europe, are strongly represented in the Wienerwald. They appear in the older beech and oak plantations in about mid-May.

WOOD WARBLER
This bird is very common in the groves of older trees.

RAMSON
The undergrowth of the Wienerwald is carpeted with this plant in May.

SPOTTED SALAMANDER
This reptile is found in wet areas of the woods, especially at dusk.

EURASIAN WILD BOAR
This shy creature steers well clear of human beings.

■ THE DANUBE

In former times, the Danube at Vienna was a maze of branch streams and side-channels, much prone to flooding. This explains the Viennese preoccupation with the movements of the river.

The first attempt to regulate the river was made after a flood in 1501, but this came to nothing since the Danube continued to overflow its banks. The canal acquired its present appearance during the 18th century, when a dam was erected draining several major side channels. A terrific flood in 1787 demolished many new dikes. In the late 19th and especially in the 20th century, permanent regulatory measures were undertaken: these were completed in 1972, with the creation of the 13-mile New Danube Canal and the Donauinsel Island. Wild fauna settled on this artificial island, and the site is now heavily populated with ducks throughout the winter.

GREAT CORMORANT
The cormorant is on the increase throughout Europe; it winters on the banks of the Danube and is often seen in the center of Vienna.

BLACK-THROATED DIVER
Like its cousin the red-throated diver, this bird is a rare visitor to the Danube in winter; most divers spend winter in coastal waters.

Although it is artificial and surrounded by buildings, the canalized Danube attracts large numbers of water birds in winter on account of its abundant food sources.

male   female

POCHARD
A few hundred of this diving duck visit the Vienna area from November to March.

CARP
Carp thrive in all the Danube's quieter backwaters, living on mollusks, worms and vegetable debris.

male   female

TUFTED DUCK
This winter-visiting diving duck lives on the tiny mussels which thrive in Vienna's waterways.

CATFISH
A transplant from North America, the catfish competes successfully with indigenous fish species.

GREEN TOAD
This can be found right in the heart of Vienna.

EUROPEAN KINGFISHER
The concrete banks of the river do not suit this bird as a nesting site, but it can easily spend all winter along the Danube Canal.

Winter   Summer

BLACK-HEADED GULL
The black-headed gull enlivens the river with its swooping, graceful flight.

THE LOBAU

PENDULINE TIT
This shy species builds its elaborate ball-shaped nest on willow boughs.

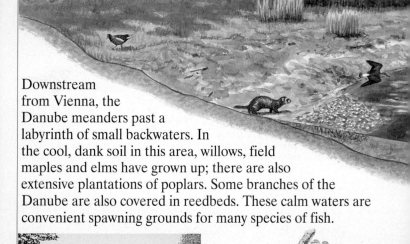

Downstream from Vienna, the Danube meanders past a labyrinth of small backwaters. In the cool, dank soil in this area, willows, field maples and elms have grown up; there are also extensive plantations of poplars. Some branches of the Danube are also covered in reedbeds. These calm waters are convenient spawning grounds for many species of fish.

The Lobau is made up of riverside woodlands penetrated by still backwaters, more or less directly connected to the main stream.

EUROPEAN BEAVER
This species was on the brink of extinction and has now been successfully reintroduced both here and in other regions of Europe.

male   female

ICTERINE WARBLER
The grating, mimicking cry of this warbler echoes among the willows along the river.

RIVER WARBLER
The song of this brown-colored oriental species resembles the sound of an elderly sewing machine.

REED BUNTING
The smallest patch of swamp is colonized by the humidity-loving reed bunting.

GOLDEN ORIOLE
The song of the oriole can be heard in the tallest poplars and willows.

WILLOWS AND POPLARS
These are the two commonest tree species around the Danube backwaters.

GRAY HERON
The heron feeds on amphibians and fish in the quieter backwaters.

COMMON GRASS SNAKE
This relentless predator of frogs, newts and small rodents lives by the waterside.

COMMON FROG
This wood-dweller only visits the marsh area in early spring to lay its eggs.

EUROPEAN POND TURTLE
These aquatic tortoises, menaced elsewhere by pollution and land drainage, may still be found in the Lobau.

PIKE
This freshwater superpredator is very common in the Lobau, where it comes to spawn.

ROACH
The roach, which can live in relatively polluted waters, may be found in every creek of the Lobau.

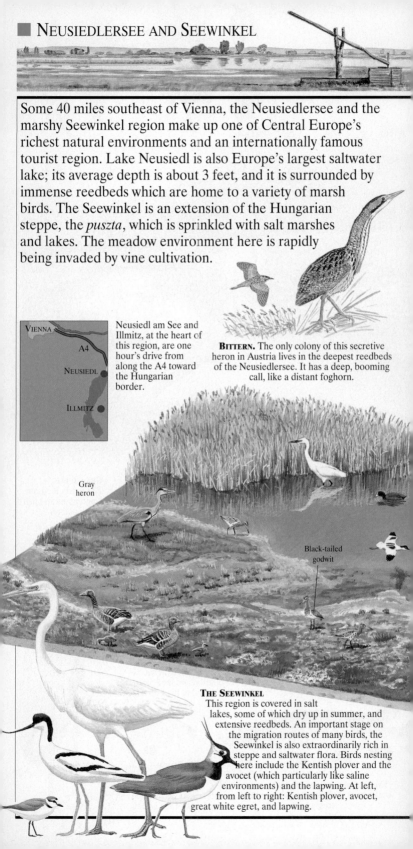

NEUSIEDLERSEE AND SEEWINKEL

Some 40 miles southeast of Vienna, the Neusiedlersee and the marshy Seewinkel region make up one of Central Europe's richest natural environments and an internationally famous tourist region. Lake Neusiedl is also Europe's largest saltwater lake; its average depth is about 3 feet, and it is surrounded by immense reedbeds which are home to a variety of marsh birds. The Seewinkel is an extension of the Hungarian steppe, the *puszta*, which is sprinkled with salt marshes and lakes. The meadow environment here is rapidly being invaded by vine cultivation.

Neusiedl am See and Illmitz, at the heart of this region, are one hour's drive from along the A4 toward the Hungarian border.

BITTERN. The only colony of this secretive heron in Austria lives in the deepest reedbeds of the Neusiedlersee. It has a deep, booming call, like a distant foghorn.

Gray heron

Black-tailed godwit

THE SEEWINKEL
This region is covered in salt lakes, some of which dry up in summer, and extensive reedbeds. An important stage on the migration routes of many birds, the Seewinkel is also extraordinarily rich in steppe and saltwater flora. Birds nesting here include the Kentish plover and the avocet (which particularly like saline environments) and the lapwing. At left, from left to right: Kentish plover, avocet, great white egret, and lapwing.

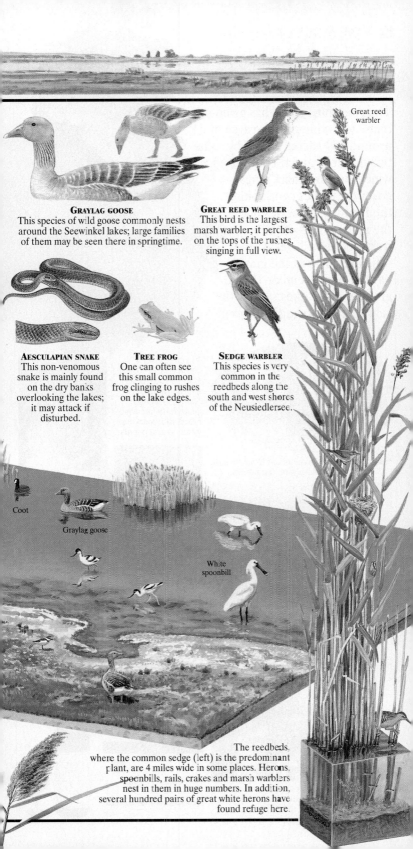

GRAYLAG GOOSE
This species of wild goose commonly nests around the Seewinkel lakes; large families of them may be seen there in springtime.

GREAT REED WARBLER
This bird is the largest marsh warbler; it perches on the tops of the rushes, singing in full view.

Great reed warbler

AESCULAPIAN SNAKE
This non-venomous snake is mainly found on the dry banks overlooking the lakes; it may attack if disturbed.

TREE FROG
One can often see this small common frog clinging to rushes on the lake edges.

SEDGE WARBLER
This species is very common in the reedbeds along the south and west shores of the Neusiedlersee.

Coot

Graylag goose

White spoonbill

Graylag goose

The reedbeds, where the common sedge (left) is the predominant plant, are 4 miles wide in some places. Herons, spoonbills, rails, crakes and marsh warblers nest in them in huge numbers. In addition, several hundred pairs of great white herons have found refuge here.

The Austrian capital has given its name to a wine growing area of around 1800 acres owned by some two hundred and fifty different wine growers, whose vines cover the slopes overlooking the Danube. Wineries line the main streets of the surrounding villages; at the official closing of the grape harvest on November 11, the growers invite guests to try the year's new vintage (*Heuriger*).

"HEURIGEN" ● *68.* Some of the *Heurigen* have become full-blown wine restaurants.

"WIENER TRILOGIE"
One of the few Viennese red wines, this is a blend of cabernet sauvignon, pinot noir and the local fruity Zweigelt grapes.

SCHWARZENBERGPLATZ These vine stalks are a symbolic reminder that the vineyards reached right into the center of town in former days.

Viennese wine is considered drinkable at every stage of its vinification, as *Most*, *Sturm* or *Heuriger*. *Gespritzt* (white wine mixed with sparkling water) is also popular.

WIENINGER
Wiener Trilogie
1991

Weingut Wieninger, 1210 Wien, Stammersdorfer Straße 78
Qualitätswein mit staatlicher Prüf-Nr. S 8420/93, 12,0% vol
ÖSTERREICH trocken ℮ 0,75 l

EIGENBAUWEINE   NATURELASSEN
**Ruster
Großlage Vogelsang**
BLAUFRÄNKISCH
ERICH KARASSOWITSCH
℮ 0,7 l

1992
Grüner Veltliner
Kabinett
Ried Schenkenberg · Gutsabfüllung
alc. 11,0% vol   trocken 0,75 l N

The principal grape varieties are the Grüner Veltliner (top of the page) and the Neuburger, in addition to one or two indigenous vines (above, the Blaue Portugiese). Much the commonest is the Grüner Veltliner, which yields a light, fruity wine. As a rule, the Viennese prefer Riesling ● *69*, which is more elegant, or Chardonnay, which is more woody.

HISTORY

The Venus of Willendorf,
c. 750–25 BC
(Hallstatt civilization).

334–30 BC
Conquest of the Persian Empire by Alexander the Great.

264–122 BC
Roman conquest of the Mediterranean Basin.

Vienna was founded at the meeting of two great highways: one which crossed Europe following the Danube, and the other which linked the Baltic to Italy. From 500 to 15 BC the site of Vienna was a small town occupied by a Celtic tribe, the Vendi.

VINDOBONA UNDER THE ROMANS

31 BC
Battle of Actium.

AD 29
Octavius founds Imperial Rome.

AD 395
Partition of the Roman Empire (Western and Eastern).

At the close of the 1st century AD, the Romans made Vienna (Vindobona, then Flaviana Castra) a frontier fortress to watch the Danube upstream from Carnuntum, capital of Pannonia. In 180, following the invasions of the Quadi and the Marcomanni, Vindobona was destroyed. In 213 the city gained the status of a municipality and began a period of prosperity; at the end of the same century, Emperor Probus authorized the legionaries stationed at Vindobona to cultivate their own vines.

Hercules, pre-4th-century vase. The Hoher Markt (right).

476
Western Roman Empire collapses.

800
Charlemagne crowned Emperor of the West.

THE GREAT INVASIONS. In 365 the Barbarians finally succeeded in crossing the Danube. In 400 Vindobona was destroyed again. In the 6th century it was occupied by the Lombards, then by the Avars; between 630 and 660, the Avars founded the Slavic kingdom of Samo. In 795 Charlemagne defeated the Avars, forced their submission and joined Ostmark (the Eastern Marches) to his empire. In 881, the Moravians under Prince Svatopluk (870–94) invaded the town, which by then bore the Slavic name of Wiena. The Hungarians were defeated by Otto I at the battle of Lechfeld (955); Otto received the imperial crown in 962 and founded the Germanic Holy Roman Empire. In 974 Emperor Otto II fortified the Eastern Marches of Bavaria.

"WIENNE" UNDER THE BABENBERGS

863
Preaching by the Byzantine monks Cyril and Methodus.

962
Coronation of Otto I, first Holy Roman Emperor.

1054
Greek Schism.

1099
The crusaders take Jerusalem.

In 976 Otto II named Leopold of Babenberg hereditary Margrave (*Mark-Graf*, or Lord of the Marches) of Ostmark. In 996, the name Ostarrichi first appears, and in 1030 Wienne. At that time Wienne was the second largest town north of the Alps, after Cologne. The Babenbergs enlarged their landholdings (bordering the Leitha by 1043) and made Vienna their capital and place of residence in 1135. The first Romanesque church of St Stephen was consecrated in 1147. In 1156 Emperor Frederick I Barbarossa gave Henry Jasormigott the title of Duke of Austria, and the latter left his castle, Leopoldberg, to establish his court just outside the walls at Am Hof. From 1160, Henry set about rebuilding St Stephen's. In 1192 the King of England, Richard Coeur de Lion, was arrested at Erdberg and his eventual ransom was used to build new walls

"BELLA GERANT ALII, TU FELIX AUSTRIA NUBE."
"LET OTHERS MAKE WAR:
THOU, HAPPY AUSTRIA, MAKEST MARRIAGES."

MATTHIAS CORVINUS

for Vienna, which were completed in 1200. More building went on around the Kärntnerstrasse, the Kohlmarkt and the Graben. In 1221 Leopold IV granted municipal and commercial privileges to Vienna, notably the monopoly of trade with Hungary. In 1246 Frederick II the Warlike, last Duke of Babenberg, was killed at the victorious battle of the Leitha against the Hungarians. Ottokar II of Bohemia and Bela IV of Hungary both claimed his throne, causing the great interregnum in the Holy Roman Empire.

1270
Seventh and last crusade: death of St Louis at Tunis.

1357
The Ottomans gain their first foothold in Europe.

VIENNA AS THE SEAT OF THE HOLY ROMAN EMPIRE

From 1250 to 1273, the popes and the Germans engaged in a ferocious struggle, and Austria passed into the hands of Ottokar II of Bohemia, who built the Hofburg.

THE HABSBURGS. The interregnum came to an end in 1273, when Rudolph von Habsburg (1218–91), the overlord of German Switzerland, was elected King of the Romans because "he bore a grudge against no man". Rudolph immediately claimed Austria and demanded the homage of Ottokar II. He finally succeeded when, in 1278, Ottokar died at the Battle of Marchfield, after having seized Vienna in 1276. In 1282 Rudolph I gave Austria and Styria as fiefs to his sons Albert I and Rudolph II; but the Viennese rebelled against Rudolph when he tried to take away their privileges, forcing him to grant them a municipal charter: henceforth the city was administered by its own mayor. The Habsburgs went on to complete the Schweizertrakt of the Hofburg, begun by Ottokar II, and encouraged the development of the aristocratic quarter (Herrenviertel). In 1298 Albert I von Habsburg was elected King of the Romans. From 1303 to 1340, the dynasty built the choir of St Stephen's (1330–9), the Church of the Augustines (from 1330 onward), the Church of Maria Stiegen and a new St Stephen's Cathedral. The founder of the cathedral, Duke Rudolph IV, created a university in 1365 to rival that of Prague, founded in 1348. After clashes between the Austrian and Jewish communities, the Jewish quarter was demolished in 1421. In 1433 the spire of St Stephen's Cathedral was completed. In 1437 Duke Albert V of Austria (1401–39) became King of Bohemia and Hungary and was subsequently elected Emperor, as Albert II. The title remained with the Habsburgs until 1806 (except for the years 1742–5). In 1462, following a quarrel between Frederick III (1443–93) and his brother Albert, the people laid siege to the sovereign and his family in the Hofburg for two months. Vienna became a bishopric in 1469. In 1485 Matthias Corvinus, King of Hungary, occupied the city after a four-month siege. He died in the Hofburg in 1490; Archduke Maximilian, the "last chevalier", then retook Vienna. He became Holy Roman Emperor Maximilian I (1493–1519); Philip, his son, married Jeanne of Castile, daughter of Ferdinand and Isabella, the heiress to Castile and Aragon. Maximilian himself founded the choir of the court in 1498. In 1515, the cathedral was the scene of the wedding of Maximilian I's grandson

Rudolph II (1552–1612).

1378
The Great Schism in the West.

1440
Invention of the printing press at Gutenberg.

1453
The fall of Constantinople.

Maximilian I (1459–1519) by Dürer.

Charles V (1500–58)
and Ferdinand I (1503–64).

1517
Luther begins to preach reform.

1520–66
Reign of Suleyman the Magnificent: height of the Ottoman Empire.

Prince Eugène (1663–1736).

1535
Calvin publishes his "Institutes of the Christian Religion".

1545–63
The Council of Trent heralds the start of the Counter-Reformation.

Maximilian II (1527–76) and his family.

1555
The Peace of Augsburg: victory of Lutheranism in Germany.

1571
The Holy League triumphs over the Turks at Lepanto.

1689–1725
Peter the Great builds Russia into a great power.

Charles and granddaughter Mary with the children of Ladislas, King of Hungary and Bohemia. This double marriage launched the Spanish and Austrian branches of the Habsburg dynasty. In 1522 Charles V (1519–58) entrusted the administration of Austria to his brother Ferdinand. In 1526 Louis II Jagellan, King of Hungary and Bohemia, was killed fighting the Turks at the battle of Mohács and Ferdinand was elected to succeed him. Ferdinand I (1521–64) abolished Vienna's privileges and executed Burgomeister Martin Siebenbürger, along with other critics of the imperial authority. In 1529 half of Vienna was destroyed by fire, but in the same year Ferdinand I chose Vienna as his residence. In 1553 he concentrated the administration of all his subject states (Alsace, Southern Germany, Austria, Hungary and Bohemia) in the city.

The Turks. In 1529 Sultan Suleyman I's army was at the gates of Vienna, but the resistance of the Count of Salm and persistent heavy rain saved the city from this first siege. Ferdinand I, King of the Romans since 1531, became Emperor in 1558, succeeding his brother Charles V. The completion of the city wall (1560) took up most of the available resources, so there are few Renaissance buildings in Vienna. Ferdinand's son Maximilian II was a Protestant; after 1570 close to 80 percent of the Viennese had converted to the new religion. He founded the Spanish Riding School in 1572; his successor Rudolph II (1570–1612) left Vienna and moved to Prague in 1582.

Triumph of the Counter-Reformation. In the first half of the 17th century, Catholic monastic orders installed themselves in Vienna at the behest of Cardinal Khlesl to fight heresy: the Carmelites and the Hospitallers of the Brotherhood of Grace moved into Leopoldstadt, the Paulaner installed themselves on the Wieden, and the Augustines built their Church of Saint Roch on the Landstrasse. The flowering of the first wave of Viennese Baroque architecture, created by Italian architects and artists, was a manifestation of the Counter-Reformation, which produced the churches of the Franciscans, Dominicans, Capuchins and Jesuits, in addition to the Baroque Scots monastery. Ferdinand II (1619–37) was a highly effective adversary of Protestantism; it was he who gave Leopoldstadt to the Jewish community in 1625 (they were to be expelled again in 1670). From 1618 to 1648 the Thirty Years' War ravaged Germany and Bohemia; in 1619 the Czechs rebelled and threatened Vienna. Then at the battle of the White Mountain near Prague in 1620, the Catholics defeated the Protestants and confirmed the power of the Habsburgs. The Protestants were driven from Bohemia and Moravia; the Counter-Reformation had triumphed. However the Peace of Westphalia (1648) confirmed the partial failure of religious universalism by establishing the principle of *cuius regio, eius religio* (whoever is king, that is the religion). The Emperor, though master of his own fief, was forced to recognize Germanic liberties in the rest of the Holy Roman Empire, which by then had fragmented into a series of

principalities. The plague epidemic of 1679 preceded the second siege of Vienna by the Grand Vizier Kara Mustafa (1683). The arrival of the King of Poland, John Sobieski, and Charles, Duke of Lorraine, finally relieved the defenders, who were commanded by the Count of Starhemberg. Charles of Lorraine and Max-Emmanuel of Bavaria undertook the reconquest of Hungary: Buda and Pest were liberated in 1686 and the Peace of Karlowitz followed. In 1699, the Turks evacuated Hungary.

The Church of St Charles; Leopold I (1640–1705) (left); the Battle of Wagram (1809) (above).

VIENNA, CAPITAL OF THE ARTS. Under Leopold I (1658–1705), Vienna became the European center of music and theater. From late 17th to mid-18th centuries, the Baroque style continued to dominate, represented by Fischer von Erlach (St Charles' Church) and Hildebrandt (the Belvedere). In 1704, during the War of the Spanish Succession (1701–14), ramparts were built around the new environs of Vienna to protect them from Hungarian rebels. During the reign of Maria Theresa (1740–80) the population of Vienna increased from 88,000 to 175,000. In 1740 war broke out against Frederick of Prussia, a conflict that was to afflict Europe for more than twenty years. Two years later, the imperial crown passed to the royal family of Bavaria; this lasted until the 1745 election of Francis of Lorraine, Maria Theresa's husband since 1736, who became Emperor Francis I (1745–65). The Schönbrunn Palace was completed in 1769. After 1750, the Baroque style gave way to Rococo. The collapse of the 1756 alliances (hastened by the new relationship between Austria and France) led to the 1770 marriage of the Empress' daughter Marie-Antoinette with the future Louis XVI of France. Joseph II (1780–90) began to centralize the Austrian monarchy. The principal reforms, or "Josephism", were established by the Edict of Toleration (1781), the abolition of serfdom (1781), the suppression of many monasteries, and a trend toward "Germanization".

1762–96
Reign of Catherine II in Russia.

1773
Suppression of the Jesuits (founded in 1534).

1783
American Independence confirmed by the Treaty of Versailles.

1804
Beginning of the Serbian revolt against the occupying Turks.

1805
Battle of Trafalgar.

1809
Napoleon annexes the Papal States.

1825
The first railway is built in England.

1835
Industry starts to use steam power.

The people of Vienna assisting the French wounded, 19th-century engraving.

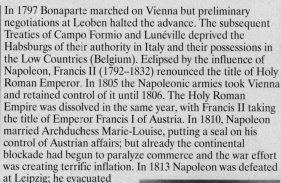

Francis I
(1768–1835).

THE AUSTRIAN EMPIRE

Prince von
Metternich
Winneburg
(1773–1859); right, a
Vienna café scene.

1862
*Bismarck's accession
to power.*

1871
*Proclamation of the
German Empire.*

Franz-Joseph
(1830–1916).

In 1797 Bonaparte marched on Vienna but preliminary negotiations at Leoben halted the advance. The subsequent Treaties of Campo Formio and Lunéville deprived the Habsburgs of their authority in Italy and their possessions in the Low Countries (Belgium). Eclipsed by the influence of Napoleon, Francis II (1792–1832) renounced the title of Holy Roman Emperor. In 1805 the Napoleonic armies took Vienna and retained control of it until 1806. The Holy Roman Empire was dissolved in the same year, with Francis II taking the title of Emperor Francis I of Austria. In 1810, Napoleon married Archduchess Marie-Louise, putting a seal on his control of Austrian affairs; but already the continental blockade had begun to paralyze commerce and the war effort was creating terrific inflation. In 1813 Napoleon was defeated at Leipzig; he evacuated Germany, and in 1814 the Austrians and their allies occupied the French capital. After the peace concluded at Paris, Napoleon went into exile on the island of Elba. The Holy Alliance between Austria, Prussia and Russia was then established at the Congress of Vienna.

THE BIEDERMEIER ERA. The period between 1815 and 1848, under the government of Prince Metternich, was Vienna's golden age. As the city grew more industrialized, its cultural life was distinguished by a bourgeois lifestyle known as "Biedermeier". At this time the first neo-classical buildings were constructed in Vienna; the bastions, which had been dismantled by the French in 1809, were converted into gardens (Volksgarten and Burggarten). By 1817 the old ramparts had become a public promenade. Vienna flourished again as a capital of music, poetry and literature. The Biedermeier epoch came to an end with the bombardment of Vienna by Prince Windischgrätz in 1848, the Year of Revolutions. In that year Ferdinand I (1835–48), brother of Francis I, was forced to abdicate in favor of his nephew, Franz-Joseph I. The simultaneous Hungarian revolution was crushed with the help of Russian forces.

THE REIGN OF FRANZ-JOSEPH (1848–1916). In 1849 Austria, which had lost none of its power and influence as a result of the revolution, thwarted a concerted Prussian attempt to unify Germany (the retreat of Olmütz). Ten years later war broke out in Italy; disastrous Austrian reverses at Magenta and Solferino were followed by the loss of Lombardy and Milan. Now the German question returned to the forefront. The defeat at Sadowa (Königgrätz) in 1866 had serious repercussions, with the loss of the Veneto and Austria's withdrawal from the Germanic Confederation, thenceforward dominated by Prussia. In 1867, the Empire was transformed by the installation of an Austro-Hungarian double monarchy, which enabled Franz-Joseph to reconcile Austria with Hungary. By 1850 Vienna had expanded as far as Gürtel and had a total of eight districts, with 431,000

> **"AND AT THE VERY MOMENT WHEN THE FÜHRER'S MOTOR ESCORT BEGAN ITS PARADE THROUGH THE ANCIENT CITY OF THE HABSBURGS, ALL THE CHURCH BELLS BEGAN TO RING OUT IN OBSCENE JUBILATION."**
>
> GEORGE CLARE

inhabitants. In 1857 the Emperor ordered the destruction of the ramparts and their replacement by the Ring, and later the Danube flood of 1862 led to the construction of the Donaukanal (1870–5). The State Opera was completed in 1869; its inaugural performance was *Don Giovanni* by Mozart. The Vienna World's Fair of 1873 was a huge success, despite the fact that it was held in the midst of a stock market crash and a cholera epidemic. The metro system was constructed between 1894 and 1900. In 1891 the 11th to 19th districts were incorporated into the city, and in 1904 the 20th and 21st districts on the other side of the Danube were absorbed.

Scene from the 1848 Revolution.

1912–13
The Balkan Wars.

1933
Hitler becomes Chancellor of the Third Reich.

1945
Conference at Yalta and destruction of Hiroshima.

VIENNA, CAPITAL OF AUSTRIA

By 1910 Vienna, with a population of two million, was the fourth largest city in Europe after London, Paris and Berlin. It had residents of the many nationalities (a dozen in all) which made up the Austro-Hungarian Empire. In 1914 Archduke Franz-Ferdinand, heir apparent to Franz-Joseph, was assassinated at Sarajevo; Austria declared war on Serbia, after which the conflict spread to the rest of Europe. Charles I, Franz-Joseph's nephew, succeeded him in 1916. After an unsuccessful attempt to sue for peace in 1917, Austria found itself, in 1918, on the defeated side. After October in that year, the Empire was broken up with the tacit approval of the Allies. In 1919, the Treaty of Saint-Germain reduced Austria to the Ostmark established by Charlemagne and forbade its union with Germany. Vienna became the capital of a republic of 6 million people living in an area of 52,000 square miles, whereas before it had ruled 52 million in an area of 435,000 square miles. A Socialist government dominated municipal affairs in Vienna until 1934, grappling with the economic crisis that followed World War One. A new social policy was introduced; by 1927 Socialists and Christian Democrats were fighting pitched battles in the streets. After riots in 1934, Chancellor Dollfuss set up an authoritarian regime and sought a rapprochement with Mussolini's Italy. By 1938 Austria had aligned itself with Germany (the "Anschluss"). By the end of World War Two, when Soviet troops entered Vienna in 1945, the city had been heavily bombed. After the war Austria was divided into four zones and occupied by the Allies. Vienna, in the Soviet zone, was consigned to a four-power administration. In 1955, by the Belvedere Treaty, Austria regained its sovereignty and became a neutral state. Today Vienna contains the headquarters of several United Nations agencies, as well as OPEC; it has also hosted a series of disarmament conferences. In 1986 Kurt Waldheim, UN Secretary General, became President of the Austrian Republic, but did not seek a second term in 1991.

1968
Prague Spring.

1989
Fall of the Berlin Wall: end of the Cold War.

1990
War in Yugoslavia.

Kurt von Schuschnigg (1897–1977).

Viennese in front of a cinema destroyed in the 1940's.

1991
Breakup of the Soviet Union.
1993
Partition of Czechoslovakia.

● THE TURKS AT THE GATES OF VIENNA

John Sobieski ● *31*,
King of Poland, relieves Vienna.

After crushing the Hungarians at Mohács in 1526 and occupying Budapest, Suleyman I encamped under the walls of Vienna in 1529 with an army of 120,000. But the 20,000 defenders under the Count of Salm, and the early onset of winter, saved the eastern bastion of Charles V's Empire from this first siege. In 1682 Imre Thököly, leader of the Hungarian rebellion against the Habsburgs, asked the Turks for assistance; they sent him 200,000 men commanded by Grand Vizier Kara Mustafa. The imperial family fled. The second siege began on July 14, 1683, but the Count of Starhemberg enlisted the aid of Polish forces; they appeared on the heights of Kahlenberg and put the Turks to flight.

SULEYMAN I (1494–1566)
When the tide of battle turned against him, Suleyman ● *30*, signed a truce which allowed him to carry his arms to Asia and North Africa; this he did to such effect that by the end of his reign he dominated almost the entire Islamic world. Suleyman I, who raised the Ottoman Empire to the height of its influence by his conquests, was known in Europe as Suleyman the Magnificent.

KARA MUSTAFA (1634–83)
The Grand Vizier and commander-in-chief Mustafa "The Black" ● *31* suffered such a humiliating defeat at Vienna that he was put to death in Belgrade on December 25, 1683, on the orders of Sultan Mehmet IV.

34

THE TURKS DRIVEN FROM EUROPE
In 1683 Leopold I took advantage of the unexpected triumph at Vienna to send Duke Charles of Lorraine into battle against the Turks. Charles reconquered all of Hungary and pushed his campaign to Belgrade (1688), after liberating Budapest in 1686. In 1697, Prince Eugène of Savoy ▲ 247 defeated the Ottomans at Zenta: this allowed him to impose the Peace of Karlowitz (1699), whereby the Turks ceded Hungary entirely. In a subsequent campaign Prince Eugène won a decisive victory at Belgrade.

A SERIOUS ENEMY
The Ottoman forces, which used classic weapons and light cavalry, were capable of sustaining long sieges with artillery powerful enough to breach the strongest ramparts. The bell of St Stephen's Cathedral in Vienna, known as the Pummerin ▲ 134, was cast of metal from cannons captured from the Turks.

● MARIA THERESA AND JOSEPH II

SCHÖNBRUNN ▲ *274*. The imperial couple and their sixteen children conducted their private family life amid the Rococo décor commissioned by Maria Theresa.

When Crown Prince Leopold died in 1716, Emperor Charles VI von Habsburg had no male heir. He nominated his eldest daughter, Maria Theresa, to be his heir, so that the younger (Caroline) branch of his family could retain the throne. Backed by the Pragmatic Sanction, the edict by which he regulated his succession, Charles VI pleaded his cause with all the great courts of Europe: these, in exchange for considerable financial and territorial advantages, eventually recognized Maria Theresa as the heir to the throne. Everything was called back into question after the Emperor's death in 1740; this sparked off the War of Austrian Succession (1740–8), in which a young woman of twenty-three successfully defended her cause against most of the rest of Europe.

MARIA THERESA (1717–80) ▲ *158, 260*
Maria Theresa secured the throne of Hungary in 1740 and in 1745, she engineered her husband Francis of Lorraine's election to the imperial throne. The Treaty of Aix-la-Chapelle (1748) restored peace, and the Empress undertook a series of reforms. Reducing the power of the aristocrats, she established Vienna as the capital of a centralized state. Her administrators were trained at the School of the Theresanium ▲ *244*. The professions of justice, education and medicine were over-hauled, new factories built, industry was protected by high import tariffs and roads were improved.

FRANCIS I (1708–65)
Maria Theresa distanced her husband from real power. Francis I was a poor adviser and soldier, much happier with his science specimens than with affairs of state.

JOSEPH II ▲ 292 AND CATHERINE OF RUSSIA
On the death of his father, Archduke Joseph joined his mother as co-regent. When she died in 1780, he succeeded her, continuing her work of centralization, reinforcing the role of the administration and police force, and encouraging industry and the arts.

JOSEPH II (1741–90)
"Josephism" ▲ 291 severely curtailed the power of the Roman Catholic Church in the Habsburg states by abolishing the religious orders and confiscating church property. By his Edict

THE SEVEN YEARS' WAR ▲ 260
In 1756 Austria took up arms to recapture Silesia from Prussia, thus starting a war which embroiled all of Europe. Thanks to the wily diplomacy of Count Kaunitz, the Empress contrived to upset the previous system of alliances. She became reconciled with France, Austria's traditional enemy, after her former British allies made a pact with the Prussians; she also obtained the support of Sweden, of some of the German princes and of Russia. The Prussians were eventually crushed at Kunersdorf in 1759, and the Treaty of Paris, signed in 1763, brought peace to a Europe which had been bled dry by warfare.

of Toleration (1781) Joseph also granted freedom of worship to all other religions in Vienna.

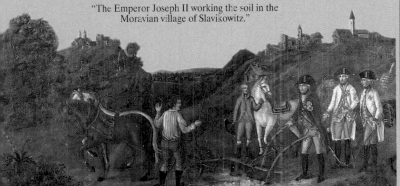

"The Emperor Joseph II working the soil in the Moravian village of Slavikowitz."

● THE COLLAPSE OF THE HOLY ROMAN EMPIRE

At the ball in the
Redoutensäle.

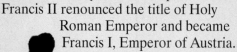

Archduke Charles
▲ *261* defeated
the French
at Aspern
(1809).

In 1792 a general war began against Revolutionary
France, but in 1797 Napoleon advanced
northward as far as Leoben. The Treaties of
Campo Formio (1797) and Lunéville (1801)
confirmed the defeat of the Habsburgs. In
1804 Napoleon's coronation compromised
the authority of the Habsburg emperor in
Germany, and the creation of the
Confederation of the Rhine, followed by the
Treaty of Pressburg (1805) sounded the death
knell of the Holy Roman Empire. In 1804
Francis II renounced the title of Holy
Roman Emperor and became
Francis I, Emperor of Austria.

THE RETURN OF THE EMPEROR
This fresco in the Museum of Art History ▲ *208*
shows the return of Francis I to Vienna in 1809,
after its occupation by Napoleon. Since he was
opposed to revolutionary ideas, Francis joined
the coalition against France. But his
policies did not bear fruit until 1813,
with the defeat of Napoleon at
Leipzig and the evacuation of
Germany ● *32*.

The Congress of
Vienna continued
throughout 1814
and 1815.

"The Congress doesn't work, it dances." (Prince de Ligne)

At the ball in the Redoutensäle, a ballroom and banquet hall in Josefsplatz, 6,000 people turned up instead of 3,000, because the doormen resold the invitations as soon as they were handed in. A total of 1,500 vermeil spoons vanished with the departing guests.

TALLEYRAND (1754–1833) ▲ *147*
A powerful presence at the Congress of Vienna, France's Minister for Foreign Affairs tried to curb the demands of the Allies but Napoleon's return in March 1815 ruined his efforts.

The Czar of Russia, Alexander I ▲ *180*, bragged that he had danced for forty consecutive nights while the Congress was in progress. The party ended with the formation of the Holy Alliance between Russia, Prussia and Austria.

● THE REVOLUTION OF 1848

A caricature showing Metternich in flight during the revolution.

The period preceding the 1848 revolution, known as the Vormärz, was an era of prosperity and cultural expansion for Vienna, which saw the construction of the first neo-classical buildings and the start of the industrial revolution. A steamship company opened on the Danube in 1823, gas was first used in 1828 and the country's first railway line was built in 1837. The Vormärz and the Biedermeier epoch came to a definitive end on March 13, 1848, when a huge demonstration took place in front of the Landhaus (the diet or parliament of Lower Austria). The crowd demanded reforms; the armed forces opened fire and killed some of their number, which led to a general uprising.

The Viennese plundered the arsenal and murdered the Minister of War, Count Latour (above). Prince Metternich, who had been chancellor since 1815, fled the city.

The execution of the parliamentary deputy Robert Blum on November 9, 1848. Blum had taken part in the October uprising.

THE UNIVERSITY GUARDS
The university was one of the main battle areas during the revolution; the students formed an "academic legion" of their own.

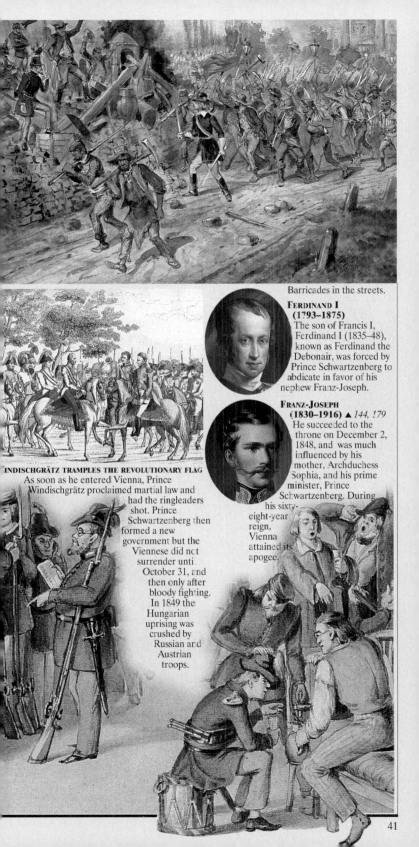

Barricades in the streets.

FERDINAND I (1793–1875)
The son of Francis I, Ferdinand I (1835–48), known as Ferdinand the Debonair, was forced by Prince Schwartzenberg to abdicate in favor of his nephew Franz-Joseph.

FRANZ-JOSEPH (1830–1916) ▲ *144, 179*
He succeeded to the throne on December 2, 1848, and was much influenced by his mother, Archduchess Sophia, and his prime minister, Prince Schwartzenberg. During his sixty-eight-year reign, Vienna attained its apogee.

INDISCHGRÄTZ TRAMPLES THE REVOLUTIONARY FLAG
As soon as he entered Vienna, Prince Windischgrätz proclaimed martial law and had the ringleaders shot. Prince Schwartzenberg then formed a new government but the Viennese did not surrender until October 31, and then only after bloody fighting. In 1849 the Hungarian uprising was crushed by Russian and Austrian troops.

● THE DESTRUCTION OF VIENNA

With the fall of the Habsburgs in 1918, the empire collapsed and a republic was proclaimed. The 1920's brought a serious economic crisis; the Socialists, who were in a minority in the country, dominated political life in Vienna. At the 1930 elections, the Nazi party was moderately successful, and then Chancellor Dollfuss, who was hostile to Hitler's ambitions, was assassinated in 1934. The country found itself squeezed

by Nazi Germany; in March 1938 "Anschluss" (union) was proclaimed in Vienna, and Hitler entered the city in triumph. Austria subsequently entered World War Two on the German side. In 1945, the Soviets attacked the German troops who had retreated to Vienna by bombarding the city. After this, Austria was occupied by the Allies for a decade.

Vienna's situation became more difficult after 1944. Apart from the Allied bombings, which had begun in 1943, the city was seriously short of food, relying on a fast-developing black market. In August 1944, the theaters and public areas were closed and the working week lengthened to sixty hours. In October a mass recruitment (*Volksturm*) of all males between 16 and 60 years old was proclaimed. At the same time Vienna became a refuge for deserters and opponents of the Nazi regime. Finally, in 1945, Austrian patriots assisted in the liberation of the city.

"THE THIRD MAN" ▲ *192, 267* This 1949 film starring Orson Welles remains a record of post-war Vienna in ruins.

THE REINSTALLATION OF THE PUMMERIN

The cathedral ▲ *132*, renovated section by section, was finally restored to use in 1948. At the end of the 1950's the spire was rebuilt and the recast Pummerin ● *35*, ▲ *134* was hoisted onto the unfinished North Tower, since the shaky spire was no longer capable of bearing its weight.

DESTRUCTION AND HUMAN LOSS

The bombings killed 12,000 people and wrecked 20 percent of the buildings in Vienna; a further 270,000 Viennese were made homeless. In 1945, Vienna's recorded death rate was the highest in Europe.

"FOUR MEN IN A JEEP"

Military policemen from the four occupying powers (America, Russia, Britain and France) driving around the city in the same vehicle, an incident which was immortalized on film.

THE RUINED CATHEDRAL

The entire roof of St Stephen's collapsed, while the towers were burning.

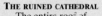

POSTER FOR SUBSCRIPTIONS

The post-war period was devoted to raising the nation from its ruins. The reconstruction of the cathedral, which had burned down in 1945, took more than ten years. The Opera ▲ *223* reopened in 1955, a few months after the Treaty which restored Austria's sovereignty.

● THE VIENNESE DIALECT

"The cook, the cellarmaster, and the Croatian canvas-seller in Vienna" *(Die Köchinn, der Vullnermeister und der croatische Leinwandhändler in Wien).* Watercolor by J. Opitz from the collection "Viennese Types" (c. 1810).

Three Jews in discussion.

❝Obviously the Slovenes, the Galicians, the Ruthenes from Poland, the Jews in caftans from Boryslaw, the cattle dealers from the Bacska, the Muslims of Sarajevo, the chestnut-sellers from Mostar, all sing the Emperor's anthem. But the students of Brno and Eger, the dentists, chemists, waiters, barbers and photographers from Linz, Graz, Knittelfeld, the men with goitres from our Alpine valleys, all sing the *Wacht am Rhein.* Gentlemen, this allegiance of Nibelungen Teutons will be the death of Austria.❞

Joseph Roth, *The Crypt of the Capuchins*

Germans from the north, arriving in Vienna for the first time, take it for granted that the language spoken here will be identical to their own, so they are rather taken aback to find that the Viennese do indeed speak German, but in a completely different manner. The consonants are run together, the vowels have a chanted quality; the language sounds sweeter, livelier, more cheerful. In this unexpected music, the northerner tends to perceive a betrayal of what he considers to be the pure, authentic German language. Such tiny variations and differences, which do not affect the linguistic structures, make it clear that we are listening to a dialect. German is a language which has grown from a mosaic of dialects and patois, such as Swabian or Bavarian; not until

Coachmen and boatmen on a craft going up the Danube. Watercolor by J. Opitz.

Luther and the Gutenberg press was there any kind of uniformity to it. While all the dialects of the north eventually bowed to the model imposed by Prussia, the southern countries, Bavaria and the different regions of Austria, held out stoutly, with a view to affirming their individuality. All language conveys and expresses both a character and an outlook on life. Hence, in a manner of speaking, the Viennese are the equivalent of the Geordies of the UK's Tyneside.

VIENNESE GERMAN: A GALAXY OF SOURCES

When Vienna was an imperial capital, all the languages of the empire were spoken there; Viennese popular speech owes many of its characteristics to this influence. The court itself was not averse to using the local dialect. On the other hand, Viennese slang was evolved less in the salons of the aristocracy than in the streets; until recently it accurately reflected the complex mosaic of this most cosmopolitan of cities. Social classes and castes, provincials and foreigners came to live in particular quarters and made their contributions to the development of the language. Vienna is definitely not a German city, in the sense that at least two-thirds of its population hail from non-German-speaking origins. There were, first of all, the Turks who remained behind after the siege of the city. Then there were always plenty of Slavs and Hungarians. Even today, Vienna attracts these ethnic groups, as it does Slovenes, Croats and Czechs. Viennese German was shaped by such immigrants. Therefore the task of finding the origins of certain words and expressions can often be extremely complicated. For example, the name for the delicious Viennese pancakes, *Palatschinken*, comes from the Hungarian, but the Hungarians got it from the Romanians, who had themselves slightly altered it from the old Latin word for cake, *placenta*. Again in the food line, the Viennese word for "maize" originates in the Balkans, but was first filtered through Serbo-Croat before alighting in Vienna as *kukuruz*. The apricot, *aprikose* in German, became *marille* in Vienna. This word comes from Latin, via Italian. Finally, the word for "tomatoes" comes from India by way of French; in Vienna they are called *paradeiser*, because the new fruit was compared to the golden apple of Paradise, *pomodoro* in Italian, shortened to *paradise* in Austria. Mostly it is cooking terms which show the traces of the various ethnic influences, but other, rarer examples confirm the wealth of the mixtures which have shaped this language and with it the soul of Vienna.

FRENCH AND THE VIENNESE DIALECT. Although the French share no frontier with the Austrians, France has played a prominent role in Austria's history. Even more surprising is the contribution of the French language to Viennese. For example, card games are very much colored by French. The

❝Where could she hail from? Vienna? Never. And since she was smiling... German? Perhaps, given the correctness of her pronunciation. On the other hand, those dark eyes full of promise, that black hair... Now he knew it: she was Italian. Catching Thérèse's distracted eye, the young man burst out laughing and reassured her. He knew now she was from Vienna, her accent betrayed her in spite of herself, but as for her race, he could have sworn there was southern blood in her veins.**❞**

Arthur Schnitzler, *Thérèse*

"Die Kleine Poste" (the little post office).

❝What makes the difference between the Austrian and the German is the language they share.**❞**
Karl Kraus

Sleeve of a record
by Karl Ambros
(1979).

LIVE
W. Ambros

Along with classical music, jazz, rock and *Schrammelmusik*, the Viennese "chanson" is sung by a few local celebrities (Falco, below, has been internationally famous for ten years or more) and contributes to the survival of the Viennese dialect.

word *coupiern* (*couper*) is used for "cut"; *trèfle*, *coeur*, *carreau* and *pique* (meaning club, heart, diamond and spade) are borrowed directly. Many words adopted in Viennese from French have also made their way into English usage. Dressmaking has borrowed *fasson* from *façon* meaning fashion and *frack* from *froc*, a dress; in the newspaper world, the Viennese talk of the *journal* and the *presse*. The kitchen features prominently, as one might expect, with *consommé*, *kotelett*, *petits fours* and *meringues*. The Viennese use the word *flair* just as both French and English speakers do; likewise the word *bordell* (chaos), which came to Vienna from old French by way of Dutch, and the inevitable *rendez-vous*, which was formerly a military command.

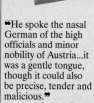

KLEINES CAFÉ

FALCO
NACHTFLUG

THE AESTHETICS OF SUFFERING AND THE PHILOSOPHY OF HUMOR

The Viennese dialect has its peculiarities, which are shared by all Viennese, and to them the city owes much of its rich flavor. The Viennese have a certain relish for pleasure blended with fatalism, irony and insolence. This mixture of optimism and despair, with the latter carefully distilled so as not to be quite unbearable, may be found in the writing of Karl Kraus and in the contemporary poetry of H.C. Artman or E. Janal. It is the constant receptiveness of the Viennese language to all influences which has enabled it to dance around the quicksand of linguistic standardization. Viennese is a spoken tongue: anyone attempting to formalize it or transcribe it is doomed to failure. Some words are easy to transcribe: I in English, which is *Ich* in German, becomes *I* again in Viennese. Once you get into complete sentences, things become more complicated. Nowadays, linguistic standardization has produced irreversible effects elsewhere, and yet the dialect of Vienna still remains an inexhaustible living archive of the city, or rather of its citizens' unconscious; a treasure chest in which all can delve for their lost roots, or find the strength to reaffirm their uniqueness as inhabitants of Vienna. "A rhythmical philosophy, laced with humor" is how Peter Wehle has described the Viennese way of speaking. It shows, if nothing else, that a single language can give expression to many different facets of the human soul, and in that sense they speak a language very different from ordinary German in Vienna.

❝ He spoke the nasal German of the high officials and minor nobility of Austria...it was a gentle tongue, though it could also be precise, tender and malicious. **❞**
Joseph Roth,
The Radetsky March

"THE GOLDEN CROWN"
Originally called "Das Elephantenhaus"; since 1690 "Zur Goldenen Krone". Notice the Fountain of St Leopold ▲ *138* on the Graben in this pre-1866 photo.

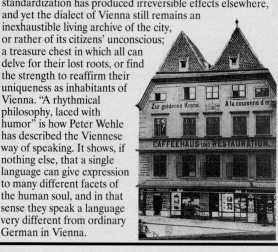

ARTS, CRAFTS AND TRADITIONS

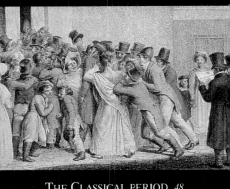

In the 18th century, Vienna reached the high water mark of its musical history. The removal of the Turkish threat allowed the city to regain its former prosperity and, in the first fifty years of the century, to endow itself with churches and Baroque palaces. Its musical life, already rich, developed fast around a group of Italian composers and performers (Bononcini, Caldara, Conti, Metastasio and Porpora). The Viennese appetite for opera was insatiable, and the city became one of the centers of musical classicism as exemplified by Gluck, Haydn and Mozart.

WOLFGANG AMADEUS MOZART (1756–91) ▲ *106, 147*
Mozart was writing musical notes before he could shape the letters of the alphabet. At the age of six he performed at Schönbrunn ▲ *281*; in 1768 he returned to Vienna to compose his first "opera buffa" (*La finta semplice*) and his first "Singspiel" (*Bastien and Bastienne*). In 1773, during a third stay in the city, he heard Haydn's Quartets and under their influence composed six of his own, which confirmed his independence of the Italian style.

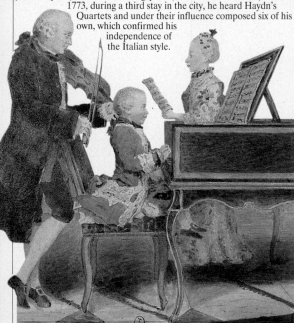

CHRISTOPH WILLIBALD GLUCK (1714–87)
Gluck was the son of a gamekeeper; at the end of his life he was one of the richest and most famous operatic composers of his time. From 1755 he was musical director at the court of Vienna; thereafter he toured Europe with his many operas, which he adapted to the tastes of the various capitals. At sixty years old, acclaimed all over Europe, Gluck achieved his crowning triumph in Paris, invited by his former pupil Marie-Antoinette. In 1779 he returned to Vienna, where he died of apoplexy in 1787.

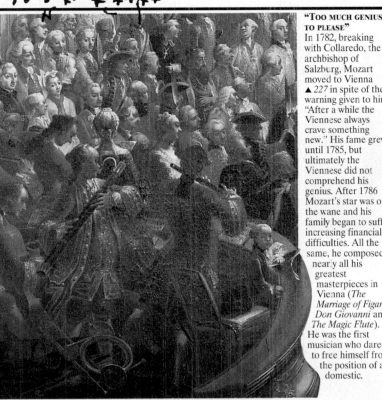

THREE PRINCES
Haydn spent thirty years in the service of Paul Antony, Nicolas the Magnificent and Nicolas II Esterházy ▲ 162.

GLUCK THE REFORMER
After his training in Italy, Gluck set out to establish Italian opera as a serious art. In the end, however, he laid the groundwork for the German opera which began with Mozart and ended with Wagner and the post-Romantics.

JOSEPH HAYDN (1732–1809)
Haydn's career began with the cathedral choir ▲ 152, 162 after which he remained for thirty years in the service of the Esterházy family. His frequent visits to Vienna kept him in contact with the musical life of the city; in 1785 he established a close friendship with Mozart, based on mutual admiration.

glückig van

Classicism's swan song was dominated by two titanic figures: Haydn and Mozart. Two other personalities, Beethoven and Schubert, confirmed Vienna's musical preeminence in the first two decades of the 19th century. A new wind was blowing through the world of the arts, yet these composers personified the enduring fascination of Vienna for artists. Beethoven, though not Vienna-born, could never leave the place once he had adopted it as his home; Schubert was a true Viennese who lived there all his life.

FRANZ SCHUBERT (1797–1828)

At the age of twelve, Schubert was composing works for his family quartet, but his true genius was for *Lieder*. His six hundred *Lieder*, nearly all of them masterpieces, demonstrate a sure sense of drama that goes right to the heart of the subject.

Schubert's musical training was much more serious than legend has it. As a boy he sang in the imperial chapel choir and worked with Antonio Salieri. But his fame hardly spread beyond the circle of friends who gathered to hear his latest works (the *schubertiades*▲ 227). Since he had no regular income, Schubert shared his friends' lodgings and was an habitué of the cafés and *Heurigen* ● 68. From 1822 onward his health began to fail, but he produced a lot of work in his last years.

He died with the name of Beethoven on his lips and was buried near the master ▲ 262.

> "AFTER BEETHOVEN, I TRULY WONDER IF THERE IS ANYTHING LEFT TO DO."
>
> FRANZ SCHUBERT

Beethoven

JOHANNES BRAHMS (1833–97)
Having come to Vienna to "drink the wine Beethoven drank", Brahms remained for the rest of his life and gave the city a musical luster which it had lost through its obsession

with the waltz ● *56*. His caring classicism delighted the Viennese; Brahms, the most classical of the German Romantics, stands midway between Beethoven and Schubert ▲ *262*. The one taught him Germanic rigor, the other Viennese charm.

A TORMENTED GIANT
A hirsute, miserly, short-tempered man, Beethoven was stone deaf from 1819 onwards ▲ *298*; nevertheless in his music he created the coherence that was lacking in his life. He came to Vienna for the first time in 1792. By the end of his life he had written nine symphonies, all of them masterpieces of emotional expression so complete that both Wagner and Debussy considered it impossible to write others after him. After the unexpected triumph of his opera *Fidelio* in 1814, Beethoven engrossed himself in the creation of sixteen quartets, the last five of which bore no relation to the other written works of this genre and showed extraordinary genius.

LUDWIG VAN BEETHOVEN (1770–1827)
Born in Bonn, Beethoven narrowly missed taking lessons with Mozart in 1787; in the end Haydn brought him to Vienna. In his early career he was supported by noble families.

The admirers of Richard Wagner, Anton Bruckner (for whom the discovery of *Tannhäuser* was a revelation), Gustav Mahler and Hugo Wolf, were succeeded by the three members of the "Vienna School". This title

ANTON BRUCKNER (1824–96)

was given to the group Arnold Schönberg formed with his two most famous disciples, Alban Berg and Anton von Webern, and refers to the teachings of Schönberg at Vienna between 1904 and 1924. The three were not only close friends, but also closely aligned in their work.

BRUCKNER: "HALF GENIUS, HALF CRETIN" (MAHLER)

Bruckner first heard Wagner at Linz, near his birthplace. In 1868 he was appointed court organist and a teacher at the conservatory of Vienna. His life in the city was much like that of Brahms but the two avoided each other. Bruckner's social gaffes are legendary: one of the worst was when he slipped some money to Hans Richter, after the maestro had conducted one of his eleven symphonies.

A GREAT CONDUCTOR

Mahler was the greatest conductor of his time, lavishing care on scenery and staging, and selecting singers for their ability to fill particular rôles. From 1897 he directed the Vienna Opera for ten years, before departing for New York. There he fell sick and asked to be taken home to Vienna, where he died five days after his return.

HUGO WOLF (1860–1903)

Expelled from the conservatory and highly unpopular because of his pro-Wagner articles and attacks on Brahms in the *Wiener Salonblatt*, Wolf failed in all his attempts to gain recognition. After 1888 he found success with his *Lieder* (three hundred in all) which led him to compare his work with Schubert's.

GUSTAV MAHLER (1860–1911) ● *54*

Mahler was Wolf's fellow-disciple, sharing his apartment and his admiration for Wagner. Wagner thought it impossible for anyone to write a symphony after Beethoven; but Mahler applied Wagner's own aesthetic dictum to his work: for him, to write a symphony was "to build a world, using all the technical resources available to a musician". As the last true Romantic (along with Richard Strauss), Mahler joined the Secessionist coteries ● *86*, ▲ *232* and defended the early works of Schönberg.

Arnold Schönberg, by Egon Schiele ▲ 252.

ARNOLD SCHÖNBERG (1874–1951)

At an early stage, Schönberg was influenced by the writings of Brahms and the chromatics of Wagner and Richard Strauss; later, he distanced himself from the traditional musical language. He dedicated his famous treatise on Harmony, *Harmonielehre*, to his friend Mahler.

Großer Musikvereinssaal

Montag, 31. März, ½8 Uhr abends

Großes Orchester=Konzert

Schönberg
Dirigent

Das Orchester des Wiener Konzertvereines
Gesang: A. Bornttan, Margarete Bum, Maria Freund

Schönberg: Kammersymphonie. Mahler: Kindertotenlieder
Werke von Alban Berg, Anton v. Webern u. A. v. Zemlinsky
Wagner: Tristan-Vorspiel

Karten bei Kehlendorfer

...gerstraße 3 und an der Konzertkassa Canova...

GESELLSCHAFT FÜR GRAPHISCHE IND. STRIE, WIEN VI.

THE VIENNA SCHOOL

With Schönberg, music ceased to be a "figurative" art. In 1908 he eliminated all precedence of one sound over another; then he perfected dodecaphonics, a way of organizing the twelve semi-tones in a series governed by the absence of any functional relationship between sounds, without the possibility of repeating one of them before all the others have been heard. Dodecaphonics proved to be one of the crucial stages in the development of 20th-century music.

ANTON VON WEBERN (1883–1945)

He worked with Schönberg until 1910. Passing through Germany and Prague before the war, he later rejoined his master in Vienna. His works are characterized by brevity, abstraction and dodecaphonic rigor. He retired after 1933 and was killed accidentally by an American bullet near Salzburg.

ALBAN BERG (1885–1935)

Berg (seen here in a painting by Schönberg) was the only one of the trio whose poetic sense proved stronger than his intellectualism. After investigating atonality in the opera *Wozzeck*, 1922, he adopted a series technique of composition (first used in his *Lyric Suite* for string quartet, 1925). This led to the opera *Lulu* and his violin concerto. "*In memory of an angel*", 1935.

● FAMOUS MUSICAL INSTITUTIONS

The concert in celebration of the marriage of Joseph II and Isabella of Parma. Painting by Martin Meytens (1695–1770) ● 98.

Vienna is a city steeped in tradition, where life still revolves around music and most of the great Viennese musical institutions are very much alive. The most famous is the Vienna Boys' Choir (*Wiener Sängerknaben*), whose origins go back to the 12th century and which was attached to the Hofmusikkapelle, created by Maximilian I. The collapse of the monarchy forced the municipal authorities to reorganize the choir around concert tours. After World War Two, the choir school moved to the Augarten Palace, where it is to this day. One hundred and fifty children attend it, receiving comprehensive musical and vocal training in addition to a general education. The choir sings mass at the Hofburgkapelle on Sundays and feast days, except in July and August.

CHOIRS OF VIENNA
The two principal amateur choirs, the *Singakademie* and the *Sing Verein*, which date back to the great days of Romanticism, still dominate Viennese choral life. The former performs at the Konzerthaus and the latter at the Musikvereinsgebäude.

"WIENER PHILHARMONIC"
In 1842 the Prussian conductor Otto Nicolai decided to give two symphony concerts every year with the orchestra of the Vienna State Opera. The word "philharmonic" was used for the first time to describe the second of these concerts; until the departure of Nicolai in 1847, these events were a regular feature of musical life in Vienna. They were organized by the Opera musicians themselves, who shared the profits. The Philharmonic attained its final form in 1860 with the

CELEBRATED CONDUCTORS
The world's greatest conductors came one after another to the Wiener Philharmonic, among them Hans Richter, Gustav Mahler ● 52, ▲ 232, 301 (right) and many guest conductors. In 1908 Felix Weingartner began his nineteen-year reign, which was followed by that of Wilhelm Furtwängler, who presided over the most outstanding period in the orchestra's history.

election of Otto Dessoff, who spent the next fifteen years turning it into a Music Society (the Musikverein) housed in the Music Society Building (the Musikvereinsgebäude ▲ 242, ◆ 326) which recently acquired a new auditorium with 2,000 seats and perfect acoustics.

BAROQUE MUSIC. In 1952 the *Concentus Musicus*, created by Nicolaus Harnoncourt and instrumentalists from the Wiener Symphoniker, initiated a fresh approach to 17th- and 18th-century music. A Viennese tradition formed in Harnoncourt's wake, with the *Musica Antica, Capella Academica* and *Clemencic Consort*

CHAMBER MUSIC

Chamber music is very much a part of life in Vienna. Young instrumentalists come from all over the world to deepen their knowledge of the styles of the different Viennese composers, notably Haydn, Mozart and Beethoven, whose traditions of performance have been handed down intact from the 18th century. In the last few decades, many new ensembles have emerged, most of them short-lived despite enormous success. The Alban Berg Quartet, founded in 1971 and supported by the Alban Berg Foundation, is today one of the world's most renowned ensembles.

More recently, younger groups such as the Hagen and Artis quartets have been acclaimed as the foremost of their generation.

● THE WALTZ

The Austrian general Franz Freiherr von Uchatius
(1811–81) was also a part-time inventer.
Right, his "phenakistiscope",
a kind of magic lantern.

The terms *walzen* (to turn around) or *walzerisch tanzen* (to dance turning round) appeared in the mid-18th century, when used to describe the final set of the *Ländler* (a popular dance in triple time derived from the court minuet). First the aristocracy, then the bourgeoisie were attracted by the new dance, which was found to be far less rigid than the minuet. The Congress of Vienna (1814–15) was accompanied by a frenetic round of balls and waltzing, after which the craze spread like wildfire all over Europe. The waltz was soon accepted in society everywhere; it reached its apogee after the 1848 revolution, with the reign of Johann Strauss the Younger, the "Waltz King" (1825–99).

STRAUSS AND LANNER
In 1819, Johann Strauss the Elder (1804–49) joined the orchestra of Joseph Lanner (1801–43). Their relationship quickly soured after Lanner published some of Strauss' compositions under his own name. Strauss formed his own orchestra, the Strauss Kapelle, and in 1829 signed a contract to play in the *Zum Sperl*, the smartest café in Vienna. Liszt, Wagner and Chopin came to hear the

Strauss repertoire, which quickly became symbolic of the Viennese style. In addition to waltzes, Strauss churned out galops, polkas and quadrilles by the score. After 1883 the Strauss Kapelle toured all over Europe with its waltz melodies.

When dancing the waltz, one leads with the left foot. To complicate matters, the Viennese also dance what they call the *Linkerwalzer*, a reverse waltz with the right foot leading.

STRAUSS AND SON
Rivalry between the two Johann Strausses, father and son, began with the triumph of the son's new orchestra. In 1848 the father celebrated the victory of the Austrian forces over the Italian rebels with his *Radetzky March*; at the same time the son was composing *Barricadenlieder* and a *Revolution March*. On the death of his father, the younger Strauss ▲ 227 took over the Strauss Kapelle and continued its seasonal concerts and international engagements.

THE GLISSADE
The swing which gives the waltz its special impetus is produced by anticipating the second step and holding back on the third.

The proliferation of ballrooms with slippery parquet dance floors instead of hardened clay led to the evolution of the glissaded step, as opposed to the skipped step; this in turn reduced the breadth of the movements involved.

FRENETIC COMPOSITION
Johann Strauss composed 200 waltzes, 140 polkas, 70 quadrilles and 50 marches. In 1863 he handed his orchestra over to his brothers and devoted himself to operettas ● 60, ▲ 140. Josef Strauss died in 1870 leaving Eduard to run the orchestra alone. It was dissolved in 1901.

● THE BALLS

JOINING THE DANCE
Colonel Willy von Vestenbrugg-Ellmayer taught young
Viennese how to dance in the early 1900's. His method
was as strict as the one used by the trainers at the
imperial stables: he tolerated no error.

Kaiser Walzer

The ball, a
tradition for many
centuries in the courts of
Europe, is still a popular
feature of Viennese life. The
ball season, from mid-January
to mid-February, exactly
corresponds to the period of
Carnival preceding Lent. Right
from its beginnings in the 19th
century, the waltz was danced
as often in the emperor's
palace as in the dance halls
of the workers and the
bourgeoisie; the latter,
modeled on the great
ballrooms of Paris, were
introduced to
Vienna by the
Strauss family.

WIENER OPERNBALL
27. Februar 92

THE INSTITUTIONAL WALTZ

The balls of Vienna
did not escape class
divisions; they may
even have deepened
them. Every region of
Austria would hold its
own ball; so too
would every
profession. Balls were
even given by such
esoteric groups as the
"Association of
Workers and
Employees of the
Administrative
Section of the
Conservative Party".
The wholesalers and
retailers of sweets
and sweetmeats had a
Zuckerbäckerball, and
the pharmacists had
an *Apothekenball*.
The name indicated
who would be
present. The ball
was a party; but the
guests wanted to be
among people of
their own kind. To
this day, the balls
remain the most
apt expression of
the soul of Vienna,
with its appetite for
fun which, paradoxically,
may only be expressed
within a rigid framework.

THE EMPEROR'S BALL

The ball season opens on December 31 with the *Kaiserball* at the Hofburg ▲ *175*. The most famous ball is the one at the State Opera – the *Opernball* ▲ *223* (above) – created for the court in 1877. Nowadays, the Austrian aristocracy has opened its doors to the internationally wealthy, but tradition is still strictly observed. The daughters of rich and titled Austrian families make their debuts at the *Opernball*.

TRADITIONS

Costume balls are rare in Vienna. Evening clothes for men and long dresses for women are the norm; the national costume – the *Tracht* and the *Dirndl* ● *64* – may also be worn, but guests are expected to show that they know and respect the rules of etiquette. Above: the Police Ball, the Hunters' Ball and the *Opernball*. At the Hunters' Ball – the *Jägerball* – the atmosphere is more relaxed.

The curtain of the former
Josephstadt Theater (below);
the Staatsoper (right) ▲ *223*.

The theater has a more important role in Vienna than in any
other city. Ever since the Baroque period and the emergence of
popular theaters the Viennese have tended to view dramatic
fiction as more credible than the current events
described by newpapers. Satire, romantic comedy and
social criticism are the main ingredients of a
theatrical tradition which has always had a
popular dimension, and has renewed itself by
drawing on this source. An example of this is the
archetypal Viennese anti-hero Hans Wurst, a
peasant who first appeared in the 18th century and
who is still present in 20th-century plays.

THE OPERETTA
Franz von Suppé, Johann
Strauss the Younger ● *57*, ▲ *140, 227*,
Karl Millöcker, Carl Zeller, Karl-Michael
Ziehrer and Franz Lehár ▲ *299* were the
principal creators of this genre, which
blended French humor and Viennese wit.

NESTROY'S "DER TALISMAN"
The plays of contemporary Austrian writers such
as Bernhard, Handke and Horváth are regularly
staged abroad, but the great 19th-century classics
by Raimund, Nestroy and
Grillparzer have yet to
be revived.

The Burgtheater does not confine itself to a classical repertoire but features some controversial modern works: in 1988 there was uproar over the Thomas Bernhard play *Heroes' Square*.

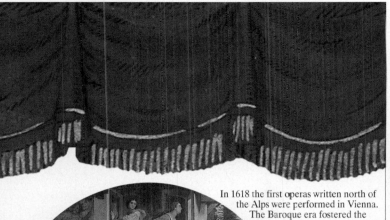

In 1618 the first operas written north of the Alps were performed in Vienna. The Baroque era fostered the idea of a work of art uniting all the arts, as later conceived by Richard Wagner ▲ 224: at that time music was inconceivable without ballet, given its roots in carnival traditions.

Vienna has produced several playwrights and composers of genius. Lunettes of the operas *Der Freischütz* by Weber (above) and *The Magic Flute* by Mozart ● 48, ▲ 147, 281 (left) designed by Moritz von Schwind are shown.

THE BURGTHEATER. Founded by Maria Theresa in 1741, the original Burgtheater was on St Michael's Square. On Joseph II's birthday ● 37, ▲ 291 February 12, 1797, Haydn ● 49, ▲ 152, 162, 164 conducted a choir and orchestra there in the first performance of the anthem which was to become the Emperor's Hymn, later adopted as Austria's national anthem.

The present Burgtheater on the Ring ▲ 204, opposite the City Hall, was opened on October 14, 1888, with an inaugural performance of Franz Grillparzer's ● 62, ▲ 147 *Esther*. In addition to a group of statues by Carl Kundmann (*Apollo and the Muses of Tragedy and Comedy*) above the portal, the wings of the theater contain Art Nouveau frescoes by Franz Matsch and the brothers Gustav ▲ 227, 234, 250 and Ernst Klimt.

● THE BIEDERMEIER STYLE

Between 1815 and 1848 ● *40* there was peace
throughout Europe. In Austria, the start of the
Industrial Revolution was accompanied by a new style
of living that became known as the Biedermeier style.

Biedermeier, the "worthy Meier" (an imaginary hero), personified a return to bourgeois values. Everyone from the emperor to the man in the street decorated his home with deliberate simplicity. It was an era of domestic contentment, when families played music together. People frequented the *guinguettes* (taverns) at the Prater and in the Weinerwald. The Theater an der Wien (1831–45) was packed out for Grillparzer's dramas and the boulevard plays of Nestroy and Raimund.

UNCLUTTERED COMFORT
The Biedermeier style, the forerunner of modern design, produced a number of functional, quietly elegant domestic objects and decorative features. Simple desks and chairs like these were as much in demand at the emperor's court as in ordinary Viennese bourgeois households.

A VIENNESE INTERIOR
The bourgeois comfort and simplicity of this interior are characteristic of the Biedermeier style. It is a long way from the grandiose "antique" décor in favor at the beginning of the 19th century.

"WIENER ZIMMER" (1837)
The Biedermeier style of painting glorified genre scenes of bourgeois family life. The painter Ferdinand Georg Waldmüller ● *100* is considered the master of Biedermeier style.

● TRADITIONAL AUSTRIAN COSTUME

Viennese fashion has always been influenced by local costumes, combined with a taste for what was stylish in Paris. During the Secession era, the School of Applied Arts opened a fashion department; its best-known member was Emilie Flöge, Gustav Klimt's muse, who designed all her own clothes. In 1909 the stylist Gertrud Pesendorfer created the modern *Dirndl* from old patterns, and after World War One there was a general revival of interest in traditional costumes.

The Vienna School of Fashion is based in Schloss Hetzendorf (Hietzing, 13th District ▲ *286*).

EVERYDAY "DIRNDL" AND PARTY "DIRNDL"
The color, shape and embroidery of the *Dirndl* vary, from region to region. The one worn at Bozn, in Italy's Southern Tyrol (left), is blue and red, with black facings.

The woman's garment called a *Dirndl* consists of a *Dirndlbluse*, a short blouse cut off under the bosom; the *Dirndl* itself, which is a skirt sewn to a bodice worn over the *Dirndlbluse*; and an apron to protect the skirt.

The women wear black deerskin shoes decorated with silver buckles and fringes. The men wear ankle boots. Hats and head coverings vary from region to region.

MATERIALS AND MOTIFS

The *Dirndl* is often made entirely of cotton, though the bodice can be linen or velvet. The patterns of the skirts tend to be garlands of little flowers, or geometrical motifs forming stripes, or else simple stripes.

In Vienna, traditional costumes (*Trachten*) are now only worn on special occasions: weddings, shooting parties, hunters' balls (*Jägerball* ● 59), and the Salzburg Festival. They are also worn by waiters in some restaurants.

The skirts are embroidered; the socks and stockings ● 72 are of lace.

WINTER "DIRNDL"

In winter, women prefer to wear the bodice, a woolen brocade skirt and a silk taffeta apron.

Men wear scarves, thick stockings and generously ruffled shirts.

HUNTING COSTUME

This includes leather trousers, short for boys and long for men, and a knitted jacket of loden or linen, which is usually brown or gray-green in color.

● THE CAFÉS

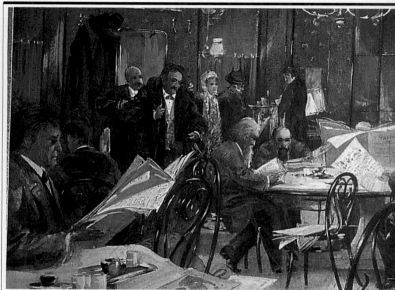

An Armenian immigrant named Johann Diobato was Vienna's first coffee-maker. In 1685 he obtained the right to prepare and serve "the Turkish beverage in the form of coffee" from the Imperial Aulic Council. Within a very short time many other coffeehouses had opened: people went to them to read the first newspapers and to play the game of billiards, which had hitherto been restricted to the aristocracy. Some cafés became the haunts of chess and card players; others were known for their musical programs. Johann Strauss the Elder, for example, began his career in the cafés. From its earliest origins, the Viennese café has always been much more than an establishment in which assorted coffees and drinks are served. Its cosy, comfortable atmosphere has made it a regular meeting place for artists, journalists and politicians.

The *Café Central* (above) ▲ *160.*

The *Sacher Hotel* (below) ▲ *140.*

"THE FIRST CAFÉ IN VIENNA"
Legend has it that a Polish spy named Kolschitzky, shown here in Moorish costume in a painting by Franz Schams (1862), stole sacks of coffee beans from the Turks. The beans were at first thought to be camel fodder. The Pole, who knew the secret of coffee-roasting, is said by some to have opened Vienna's first café.

The *kleiner Schwarzer* (small black coffee), the *Melange* (coffee with hot milk), the *Kapuziner* (black coffee with a little cream), or the *Einspänner* (black coffee with whipped cream) invariably come with a glass of water, a croissant (*Kipfel*, another souvenir of the Turkish siege) and a newspaper. All cafés serve pastries, most of them topped with a helping of whipped cream.

ROUND TABLES

Viennese cafés were at their most popular at the beginning of the 20th century, when they became the focus of intellectual life in the city. Every group had its appointed café. At the *Café Central* one was sure to see Karl Krauss, Peter Altenberg (the man with the hat at the top of the page, seen here at the *Griensteidl*), Egon Friedell and Alfred Polgar.

Herman Bahr, Arthur Schnitzler and Hugo von Hofmannsthal usually met at the *Café Griensteidl*. In the 1920's, Robert Musil, Hermann Broch, Franz Werfel and Joseph Roth frequented the *Herrenhof*, while Gustav Klimt, Egon Schiele and Oskar Kokoschka had their tables at the *Museum*. Otto Wagner and Adolf Loos, the Art Nouveau architects, also spent many hours here: Loos designed the interior in 1899.

"THE PASSION FOR NEWSPAPERS"

A cartoon from the Biedermeier era ● *62*. Reading the newspapers, smoking and talking have always been the principal occupations of café-goers. In Vienna, the rooms are quiet and spacious, and you can spend a whole day for the price of a *kleiner Schwarzer*.

● THE "HEURIGEN"

The vineyards of Nussdorf and Heiligenstadt on the hillsides of Nussberg produce a Riesling wine of very high quality ● 72.

The arrival of each year's new wine *(Heuriger)*, announced by the hanging of a pine branch over the door, is a cause for celebration in the *Heurigen* *(guingettes* or small taverns) of Vienna's suburbs. This wine, typical of the Vienna region, is a light, white wine that should be served chilled. It is made from a blend of grapes from the vineyards of the Wienerwald along the hillsides of Kahlenberg, Bisamberg and Nussberg that surround the city. The cultivation of vines in "Germania" (as well as in Gaul and Spain) was first authorized by the Roman Emperor Probus in the 3rd century, with a view to supplying the legions garrisoning those countries with their own sources of wine.

As well as wine, the *Heurigen* serve country dishes such as lentils and bacon, roast pork, local ham and pastries.

The new wine *(Heuriger)* is served in quarter-liter bottles and is often a blend of the best produce of the Vienna region.

The Viennese taste the new wine in a festive atmosphere, shaded by birches and hazels in courtyards and gardens that often have fine views across the Danube Valley.

Today, the vines are cultivated by about seven hundred winegrowing families in the ring of villages ■ 26 (Nussdorf, Heiligenstadt, Grinzing, Sievering and Neustift) that surround Vienna.

> "In the Wienerwald, the violets were flowering blue and the couples were trysting. In our favorite café we joked, laughed, and played chess, teetotum and the tarot."
>
> Joseph Roth

"SCHRAMMELMUSIK"

The *guinguettes* are famous for their typical *Schrammelmusik*. Joseph Schrammel (1850–93) gave this music its distinctive form by putting together a quartet of two violins, a guitar and a small clarinet (later replaced by an accordion). To the repertoire of older songs, some of them dating from the 18th century, Schrammel added compositions of his own. His *Wien bleibt Wien!* remains a favorite popular Viennese melody.

THE BEST WINES

The winegrowing villages produce more than 792,500 gallons of wine a year, the most popular of which are the Sylvaner of Grinzing, the Riesling of Nussberg, the muscats of Sooss and the red wines from Vöslau which include the *Goldeck von Schlumberger*.

At the emperor's table, etiquette required that the emperor should be served first; he immediately began to eat. Franz-Joseph was said to be so frugal that he finished his food before most of the guests could begin, so the luckless young officers who were placed at the bottom of his table got nothing to eat. For this reason they went afterward to dine at the *Sacher Hotel*, where they enjoyed a *Tafelspitz* ("table end") cut of beef. The *Sacher* still serves the best beef in town.

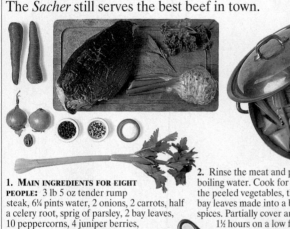

1. MAIN INGREDIENTS FOR EIGHT PEOPLE: 3 lb 5 oz tender rump steak, 6¼ pints water, 2 onions, 2 carrots, half a celery root, sprig of parsley, 2 bay leaves, 10 peppercorns, 4 juniper berries, 1–1½ teaspoons lovage seeds.

2. Rinse the meat and place in a pan of boiling water. Cook for 30 minutes, then add the peeled vegetables, the celery, parsley and bay leaves made into a bouquet garni, and the spices. Partially cover and simmer for another 1½ hours on a low flame. Pierce the meat with a knife: if the blade comes out cleanly, the meat is ready.

3. GARNISH: 2 lb 3 oz potatoes, 1 diced onion, salt, pepper, oil, lump of butter, pinch of cumin.

4. Boil the potatoes in their skins, allow to cool and peel. Sauté the onions in a pan with a few spoonfuls of oil. Cut the potatoes into thin rounds and place in the pan, add salt and pepper to taste, and fry until golden. Add a little butter and some cumin to refine the taste before serving.

5. APPLE AND HORSERADISH SAUCE: 4 peeled apples, ½ pint white wine, 1–1½ teaspoons sugar, finely chopped horseradish.

6. Peel the apples, remove seeds and dice.

"In regard to 'garnishes', as the Germans of the Reich call them, I could wish next time that what you call horseradish were not steeped for quite so long. It shouldn't be allowed to lose its aroma in the milk."

Joseph Roth

7. Soften the apples by simmering them in the white wine and sugar, strain off the wine, then reduce to a purée.

8. Put back a little wine for better consistency if necessary. Add the finely chopped horseradish.

10. Drain the bread well and chop finely, blend with the hard-boiled eggs.

9. Chive sauce: 2 hard-boiled eggs, 3 slices white bread soaked in milk, 2 egg yolks. ⅓ oz salt, ½–¾ teaspoon sugar, 1–1½ teaspoons vinegar or juice of half a lemon, chopped chives, 5 oz oil.

11. Add the egg yolks, salt, sugar and vinegar or lemon juice, mixing well.

12. Beat the mixture to a mayonnaise, adding the oil very slowly. Add chives and season to taste with salt and lemon juice.

13. Cut the boiled beef into slices about ½ inch thick (on the bias). Garnish with the vegetables from the stock chopped into small pieces; then moisten with a little stock. Serve the potatoes and horseradish sauce either in separate dishes or directly on the plates if you prefer. Serve the chive sauce separately.

● SPECIALTIES

GLASSWORKS. The *Lobmeyr* glassworks was founded in Vienna in 1823. Horejce (design above) and Loos (wine service below) designed patterns here. *Lobmeyr* manufactured the chandeliers for the Kennedy Center (1971), for the Metropolitan Opera (1966), and for the Vienna Opera (1955).

PORCELAIN
The factory, which moved to the Augarten Palace in 1923, was founded in 1718. Right, Augarten's most famous product, the *Maria-Theresia* pattern.

SPARKLING WINE
Johann-Kattus (1857) is based at the oldest house in Vienna, on the Am Hof.

BREAD
There are said to be as many different types of bread in Vienna as there are days in the year. For breakfast, and for making sandwiches, the Viennese favor the *Semmel*, a small, round, white roll.

STOCKINGS
Since 1946 *Wolford* has built its reputation on quality, softness and durability.

CONFECTIONERY. Vienna produces *bonbons* (miniature chocolates) by the boxful. The *Altman & Kühne* confectionery shop was designed by Otto Wagner; its wrapping paper design dates from the 1900's. *Demel* is famous for its pastries.

COFFEE. *Julius Meinl*, a coffee-exporting house since 1862, is now a large chain of grocery stores.

72

ARCHITECTURE

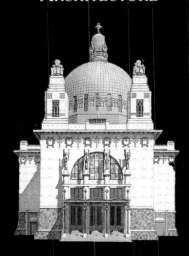

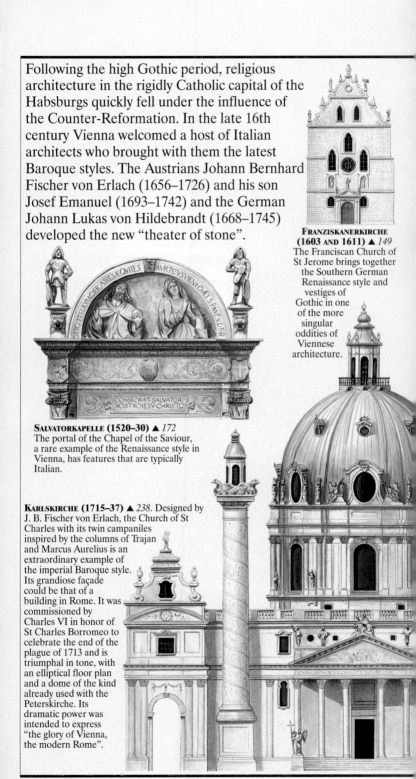

Following the high Gothic period, religious architecture in the rigidly Catholic capital of the Habsburgs quickly fell under the influence of the Counter-Reformation. In the late 16th century Vienna welcomed a host of Italian architects who brought with them the latest Baroque styles. The Austrians Johann Bernhard Fischer von Erlach (1656–1726) and his son Josef Emanuel (1693–1742) and the German Johann Lukas von Hildebrandt (1668–1745) developed the new "theater of stone".

FRANZISKANERKIRCHE (1603 AND 1611) ▲ *149*
The Franciscan Church of St Jerome brings together the Southern German Renaissance style and vestiges of Gothic in one of the more singular oddities of Viennese architecture.

SALVATORKAPELLE (1520–30) ▲ *172*
The portal of the Chapel of the Saviour, a rare example of the Renaissance style in Vienna, has features that are typically Italian.

KARLSKIRCHE (1715–37) ▲ *238*. Designed by J. B. Fischer von Erlach, the Church of St Charles with its twin campaniles inspired by the columns of Trajan and Marcus Aurelius is an extraordinary example of the imperial Baroque style. Its grandiose façade could be that of a building in Rome. It was commissioned by Charles VI in honor of St Charles Borromeo to celebrate the end of the plague of 1713 and is triumphal in tone, with an elliptical floor plan and a dome of the kind already used with the Peterskirche. Its dramatic power was intended to express "the glory of Vienna, the modern Rome".

RUPRECHTSKIRCHE (740) ▲ 154
The Church of St Rupert is the oldest in Vienna. Its Romanesque nave was built between 1130 and 1170; the choir, belltower and doorway date from the 14th and 15th centuries.

KARMELITENKIRCHE (1623) ▲ 269
The Carmelite Church of St Joseph offers a less conventional version of the classic Roman façade, not unlike the one chosen by the Dominicans for their church. The three levels of the façade, narrowing from base to summit, create a strong vertical tension. This is emphasized by the lines of the pilasters and by the various decorative elements, which also accentuate each projecting angle of the composition. The relative economy of decorative effects lends a certain austerity to the structure.

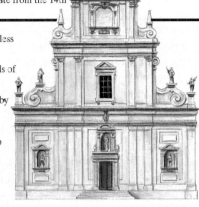

DOMINIKANERKIRCHE (1631–34) ▲ 152
The Church of the Dominicans, a project shared by the architects Spatz, Biasino and Canevale, was closely copied from the Church of Gesù in Rome. The façade (1666–74) is in the same vein: its broad lower story is succeeded by a narrower one, flanked by upside-down corbels and topped with a triangular pediment.

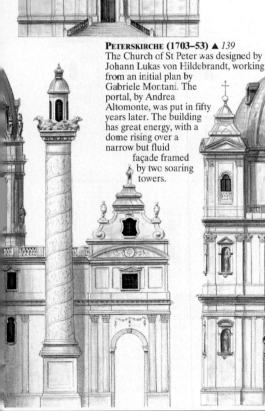

PETERSKIRCHE (1703–53) ▲ 139
The Church of St Peter was designed by Johann Lukas von Hildebrandt, working from an initial plan by Gabriele Montani. The portal, by Andrea Altomonte, was put in fifty years later. The building has great energy, with a dome rising over a narrow but fluid façade framed by two soaring towers.

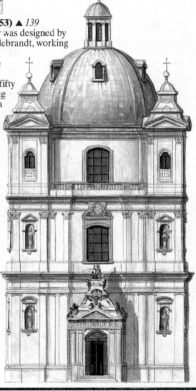

The churches within the original city walls are usually part of groups of buildings and are often situated in courtyards, or *Höfe*. There are very few planned perspectives to set off the diverse façades and belltowers. Almost as if they were torn between the Italian dome and the Gothic spire, the Viennese architects resorted to a wealth of combinations, spawning a number of charming hybrids such as the basic "onion" and "pumpkin" shapes.

ANNAKIRCHE ▲ *146* AND **STIFTSKIRCHE** *(Mariahilfer Strasse 24).* The Baroque churches of St Anne (1630–1715) and the Abbey (1739) are both powerful and graceful.

The belltowers of Vienna add a note of fantasy to some of the city's otherwise pretentious and conventional Italianate façades.

EVANGELISCHE KIRCHE *(Dorotheergasse 16)* ▲ *138* The belltower (1887) of the Protestant Reform Church is a clever pastiche adding a flourish to the church built by Nigelli in 1784.

SERVITENKIRCHE (1651–77) ▲ *293* The clocktowers of the Church of the Servites, rebuilt in 1754 to a design by F. S. Rosenstingls, emphasize the straightforward Baroque style of the façade.

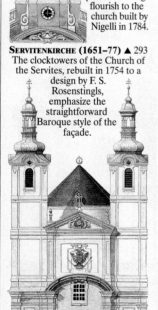

SCHOTTENKIRCHE (12th–17th century) ▲ *163* Between 1643 and 1648, the Italians Silvestro Carlone and Andrea Felice d'Allio gave the venerable Scottish church ▲ *163* the Baroque features it has today. The bulb-domed main belltower, isolated behind the chevet, provides a pleasant counterpoint to the simple lines of the façade and the two towers on either side.

JESUITENKIRCHE (1627–1705) ▲ *151*
The façade of the Jesuit Church carries the imprint of each of its architects. Carlo Antonio Carlone reinstated the building's original proportions in 1531, bringing together the many differing features of its design in a single unified composition.

MARIAHILFER KIRCHE
(Mariahilfer Strasse 55)
This church was built between 1686 and 1689, probably by Sebastiano Carlone. In front of the church you can see a monument dedicated to Joseph Haydn ● *49*, which was unveiled in 1887.

THE JESUITENKIRCHE'S TWO BELLTOWERS
The towers soar above a horizontally conceived façade in a structure that dominates Dr Ignaz Seipel Platz.

MINORITENKIRCHE ▲ *161*
The Church of the Minorite Friars (1339) was damaged during the siege of Vienna and was later "improved" with Baroque elements; it was then restored to its original form by the architect Johann Ferdinand Hetzendorf von Hohenberg in 1717–19. The chevet of this very Germanic church-cum-hall is flanked by two apses, with a tall octagonal belltower between them reminiscent of the campaniles of Northern Italy. Nevertheless Gothic is the dominant style here.

In Vienna, houses of the bourgeois are often almost indistinguishable in style from aristocratic mansions. Rich bourgeois tradespeople and craftsmen copied and adapted the formal and figurative repertoires of the palaces in four- to six-floor buildings, which were often inhabited by several different families and mostly concentrated along the narrow streets of the inner city (Innere Stadt). As tastes changed, the oldest bourgeois houses dating from the 15th and 16th centuries were successively revamped to suit the Baroque, neo-classical and Biedermeier fashions; the bright colors of their façades contrast strongly with pure white or gray-beige ornamentation.

CORNER BUILDING ▲ *139*
(Naglergasse 13–15)
Large bourgeois houses, mostly dating from the 15th and 16th centuries, overlook Naglerstrasse, a street that runs along the old Roman ramparts. This 15th-century building was given a classical façade in 1700 and, during the 18th century, further ornamented with a colored relief of the coronation of the Virgin.

THE BOW WINDOW
(Naglergasse)
Projections such as these are a familiar feature of 17th- and 18th-century Viennese buildings.

DREIMÄDLERHAUS (1803)
▲ *166 Schreyvogelgasse* 10
The "House of the Three Maidens" is an example of bourgeois Viennese neo-classical style.

"ZUM BLAUEN KARPFEN" ▲ *146*
(Annagasse 11)
"The Blue Carp" is an 18th-century building altered in 1814 by the architect Ehmann, who turned it into a subtle neoclassical composition incorporating arabesque motifs and cameo figures.

BAROQUE WINDOW
▲ *168 (Kurrentgasse 12)*
An ogee arch lends further dynamism to the already lively colors.

BIEDERMEIER REFINEMENT ● *62*
A powerful frieze by the sculptor J. Klieber does not detract from the extraordinary delicacy of the colors on this façade. It is an example of the classic Biedermeier style which took Vienna by storm in the early 19th century.

BIEDERMEIER WINDOW
(Nestroyplatz)
A tracery of friezes and balustrades punctuates the formality of the design.

KURRENTGASSE 6–8
The buildings along this narrow thoroughfare form a classic 18th-century urban ensemble. The first floor is characterized by continuous reliefs; above, the four floors gradually diminish in height, with identical and regular bay windows on each level. Nos. 6 to 8 offer a variation on the basic five-tier design. The details of the distribution and the choice of decorative motifs – the double bays and pediments, for example – give variety to the rhythms of the façades.

● BAROQUE PALACES

The palaces of the many great magnates who converged on Vienna to attend the court, or to serve in the government or army, were built around the Hofburg, the imperial residence. The façades of these noble residences influenced the style of public buildings, which were constructed to look like palaces, with pediments sporting the imperial two-headed eagle. These great houses were usually adorned with sculptures whose purpose was to emphasize the contrasts between the other architectural features. There were gods and giants, caryatids and Atlantes, together with symbols of glory and trophies of war. Neo-classicism was to bring a calmer note to the palaces of Vienna, though there was another brief period of exuberance during the era of the Ring.

Heraldic eagle on the façade of the Arsenal.

THE STATE CHANCELLERY (HOFBURG) (1726–30) ▲ *175* Wing designed by J. B. Fischer von Erlach.

THE ARSENAL (1731) ▲ *258*. A building constructed by Anton Ospel. The rich statuary by Lorenzo Mattielli offsets the otherwise extreme regularity of the composition.

THE OLD UNIVERSITY (1735–55) ▲ *151* The Aula (Main Hall) of the university was built in an eclectic European style in which Baroque principles began to be supplanted by neo-classical ones.

THE TRAUTSON PALACE (1702–5) Oedtl built this palace to plans by J. B. Fischer von Erlach. The clear structure of the wings, together with the exaggerated importance of the central part, echoes the 16th-century Palladian style.

THE BELVEDERE (1714–22). The original concept of the twin Belvedere Palaces, which are connected by a garden, came from the close collaboration between the architect, Johann Lukas von Hildebrandt, and his client, Prince Eugene of Savoy. The Lower Belvedere (above, left-hand page) served as a summer residence; the more ceremonial Upper Belvedere (this page, above) was used for balls and receptions.

PORTAL OF THE LOBKOWITZ PALACE Added in 1710 by J. B. Fischer von Erlach to the palace built by Tencala, this portal copies the high altar of the Church of the Franciscans at Salzburg.

THE KINSKY PALACE (FORMERLY THE DAUN PALACE) (1713–16) ▲ *164*. The opulence of this palace's stunning façade, constructed by Hildebrandt, is only a prelude to its highly original interior.

CARYATIDS Young girls sculpted by Franz Anton Zauner at the Pallavicini Palace.

THE BATTHYANY-SCHÖNBORN PALACE (1698–1706) ▲ *165* This palace, designed by J. E. Fischer von Erlach, is based on originals by Bernini in Rome. Its façade was modified in the 19th century when the central coping of its attic story was removed.

THE PALLAVICINI PALACE (1783–4) ▲ *192* In this neo-classical construction, Ferdinand von Hohenberg simplified the flamboyant rhythms of the traditional façade.

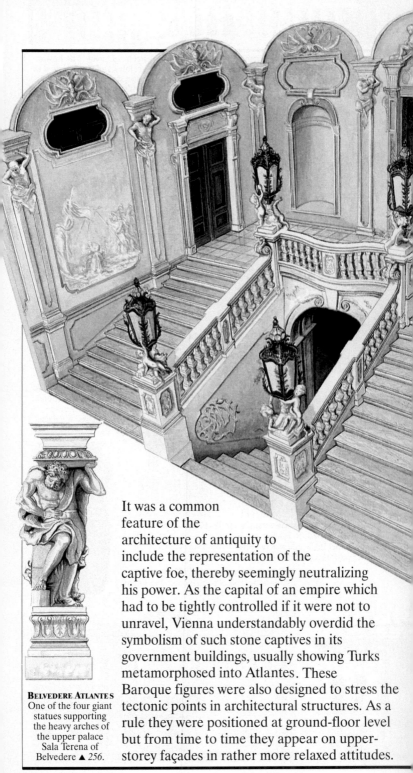

BELVEDERE ATLANTES
One of the four giant statues supporting the heavy arches of the upper palace Sala Terena of Belvedere ▲ 256.

It was a common feature of the architecture of antiquity to include the representation of the captive foe, thereby seemingly neutralizing his power. As the capital of an empire which had to be tightly controlled if it were not to unravel, Vienna understandably overdid the symbolism of such stone captives in its government buildings, usually showing Turks metamorphosed into Atlantes. These Baroque figures were also designed to stress the tectonic points in architectural structures. As a rule they were positioned at ground-floor level but from time to time they appear on upper-storey façades in rather more relaxed attitudes.

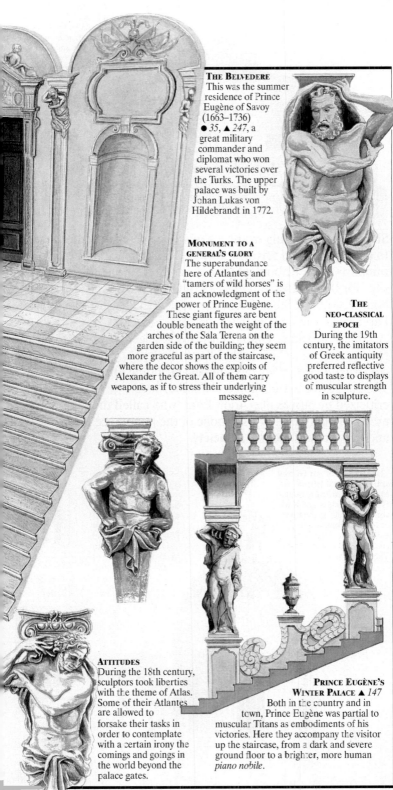

THE BELVEDERE
This was the summer residence of Prince Eugène of Savoy (1663–1736) ● *35*, ▲ *247*, a great military commander and diplomat who won several victories over the Turks. The upper palace was built by Johan Lukas von Hildebrandt in 1772.

MONUMENT TO A GENERAL'S GLORY
The superabundance here of Atlantes and "tamers of wild horses" is an acknowledgment of the power of Prince Eugène. These giant figures are bent double beneath the weight of the arches of the Sala Terena on the garden side of the building; they seem more graceful as part of the staircase, where the decor shows the exploits of Alexander the Great. All of them carry weapons, as if to stress their underlying message.

THE NEO-CLASSICAL EPOCH
During the 19th century, the imitators of Greek antiquity preferred reflective good taste to displays of muscular strength in sculpture.

ATTITUDES
During the 18th century, sculptors took liberties with the theme of Atlas. Some of their Atlantes are allowed to forsake their tasks in order to contemplate with a certain irony the comings and goings in the world beyond the palace gates.

PRINCE EUGÈNE'S WINTER PALACE ▲ *147*
Both in the country and in town, Prince Eugène was partial to muscular Titans as embodiments of his victories. Here they accompany the visitor up the staircase, from a dark and severe ground floor to a brighter, more human *piano nobile*.

83

● THE RINGSTRASSE

THE BURGTHEATER (1874–88) ▲ *204*
Detail of the dome over the main hall
and the balustrade above the façade.
This theater was constructed by
Gottfried Semper and Karl von
Hasenauer.

Since it was suffering from lack of space, Vienna decided
to demolish its old fortifications in 1860. In place of the
ramparts majestic boulevards were created, along with
sites for the palaces and temples of the new
bourgeoisie: the Stock Exchange, the City Hall, the
Parliament, the universities, museums, Fine Arts
Academy and State Opera. The joyous eclectism of
the Ringstrasse, which looks like an adult
construction set in which architects including Otto
Wagner strove to outshine one another, was
criticized by purists like Adolf Loos, who called the
area a "Potemkin City", symbolic of the impotence
and hypocrisy of industrial society.

The Museum of Art History
and the Natural History
Museum ▲ *207* were built by
Gottfried Semper and Karl
von Hasenauer in the form
of two half-Renaissance,
half-Baroque palaces, facing
each other across the Maria-
Theresien-Platz.

THE RATHAUS
(1872–3) ▲ *205*
Friedrich von
Schmidt's City Hall is
a symbol of municipal
freedom directly
confronting the old
town. It aimed to
rival the lavishness of
the imperial court.

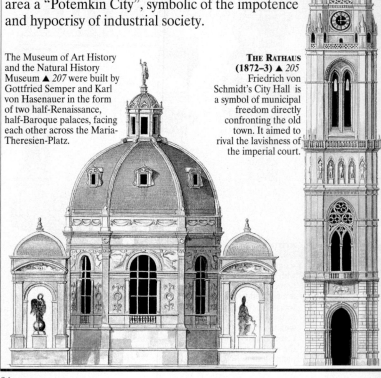

ATHENEBRUNNEN BY THE PARLIAMENT BUILDING (1874–83)
Theophil von Hansen designed the Parliament in neo-Grecian style in homage to the land where democracy was born. The white-marble Athena Fountain, surrounded by allegories of the virtues and of the great rivers of the empire, has a gilded helmet and shield. This statue, designed by Hansen and completed by Carl Kundmann in 1902, is modeled on the gold and ivory statue of Athena by Phidias at the Parthenon in Athens.

THE TODESCO PALACE (1861–4) ▲ 223
Built on the Kärntnerstrasse in front of the Opera by Ludwig von Förster and Theophil von Hansen, the Todesco Palace was one of the first buildings of its kind to be built for a bourgeois businessman. Its neo-Renaissance style was intended to evoke the splendor of the Medicis.

A RESIDENTIAL BUILDING
On the corner of Grillparzerstrasse ▲ 203 and Rathausstrasse, this apartment block demonstrates the skill of turn-of-the-century architects in concealing floors in order to achieve the tripartite pattern of Italian Renaissance palaces. A rustic overlay links the first three floors, while the attic windows are camouflaged in the ornamented cornices.

THE VOTIVKIRCHE ▲ 203
Drawing on the great 13th-century cathedrals of France for inspiration Heinrich von Ferstel could not resist introducing a certain rationalist emphasis on the basic elements of Gothic architecture, particularly in the design of the graceful main façade.

The Vienna Secession (1897–1907) was an association formed by artists to break with academic art conventions. In architecture it was dominated by Otto Wagner (1841–1918), who began the transition from the neo-Renaissance eclecticism of the Ring epoch to a form of rigorous but ornamental Art Nouveau (known in Vienna as Jugendstil, 1894–1914) which was rimmed with steel, covered in ceramic, and embellished with aluminum and copper ornaments. Well before 1900, Secessionist architecture had developed the kinds of straight lines that were later to fuel French Art Deco. Josef Hoffmann (1870–1956) set his cubist outlines within lavish corner designs, and delighted in reversing the values of classical proportion on decorated structures. Adolf Loos (1870–1933), a dandy and a provocateur, pushed his own style of iconoclastic purism to the brink of the surreal.

THE ANKERHAUS (1893–5) ▲ *138*
This house on the Graben by Otto Wagner contrasts the light metal structure of its ground floor and mezzanine and the glass of its terraces, with the stone of its rich façade.

THE SCHÜTZENHAUS (1906–7)
The Lock House, also by Otto Wagner, is all that remains of the Kaiserbad dam installation, part of a scheme for regulating the Danube which (like the Metro) was a major feature of Vienna in 1900. A plinth of granite, plaques of white marble attached with rivets, and blue porcelain tiles combine to form a frieze which goes well with the Schützenhaus' technical function. The building is very elegant, given its utilitarian purpose.

**LEOPOLDKIRCHE
(1905–7)** ▲ *288*

The icily sumptuous church of St Leopold was a neo-Byzantine version of the Karlskirche ▲ *238* and a triumphant beacon on the hill above the new Steinhof lunatic asylum.

**THE KARL LUEGER MEMORIAL CHURCH
(1908–10)** ▲ *262*. This building is a much more eclectic, academic version of the one at the Steinhof. It is dedicated to the memory of Karl Lueger ▲ *227*, a populist mayor during the last years of the empire.

SECESSION (1897–8) ▲ *222, 232*. Although he went on to pay tribute to the extravagant international Art Nouveau style, Joseph Maria Olbrich (1867–1908) produced his best work in the Secession Pavilion, a shrine to the various artists of the Secession movement. The archaic rigor and oriental lavishness of this edifice evoke the palace of a Salome figure dressed by Klimt ▲ *227, 250* and Koloman Moser ▲ *235*. Outrageous in its useless luxury, the empty dome covered in triumphal laurel leaves was intended to echo that of the Karlskirche on the far side of the Wien.

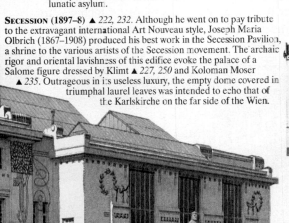

**THE HOUSE OF
DR VOJCSIL (1900–1)**
Designed by O. Schöntha, this house displays the Jugendstil trend of affixing Mannerist ornaments to classical structures.

**KARLSPLATZ METRO
STATION (1898–9)**
▲ *223, 240*

A classic Jugendstil creation by Otto Wagner. The technical concept was revolutionary, with prefabricated metal elements covered in colored ceramic panels.

**THE MEDALLION
HOUSE** ▲ *237*
Otto Wagner constructed three rental apartment blocks (1898–9), including the Medallion House. Its floral motifs evoke the pages of the review *Ver Sacrum*, as do those of its neighbor, the Majolikahaus.

THE BEGINNINGS OF MODERNISM:
OTTO WAGNER'S POSTSPARKASSE

Tubular heating vent ▲ 228

During the period of artistic renewal that took place between 1890 and 1900, Otto Wagner proposed a novel architectural concept which took account of modern techniques and extolled the individual freedom of the artist, outside the mainstream styles of history. Wagner stripped his buildings of all decorative formalism, and instead accentuated surface effects. Sculpted motifs were replaced by flat ornamentation, producing a more highly colored, dark-on-light result with lines whose sole purpose was to stress decorative perfection. The first building of this type on the Ringstrasse, the Postsparkasse (Post Office Savings Bank, 1904–6) perfectly illustrates Wagner's theory, which was to become one of the fundamental tenets of the modern movement.

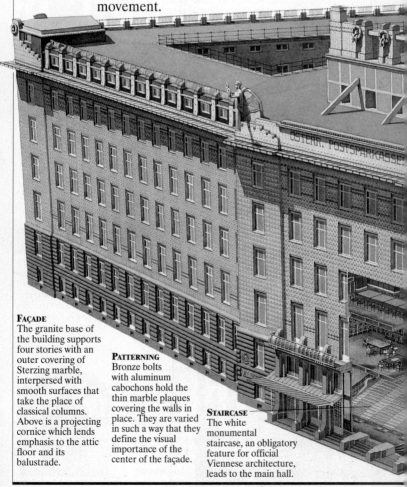

FAÇADE
The granite base of the building supports four stories with an outer covering of Sterzing marble, interspersed with smooth surfaces that take the place of classical columns. Above is a projecting cornice which lends emphasis to the attic floor and its balustrade.

PATTERNING
Bronze bolts with aluminum cabochons hold the thin marble plaques covering the walls in place. They are varied in such a way that they define the visual importance of the center of the façade.

STAIRCASE
The white monumental staircase, an obligatory feature for official Viennese architecture, leads to the main hall.

FLOOR PLAN. A regular polygon whose symmetry exalts functional character and mastery of the latest modern building techniques.

WINGED VICTORIES These cast aluminum figures were designed by Othmar Schimkowitz.

The systematic division of the floor plan into parallel cells reveals the use of a metal framework.

SCULPTURE
While rejecting merely decorative features, Wagner was very partial to monumental sculpture – for example, these figures which punctuate the upper parts of his building.

MATERIALS
Otto Wagner had a clear preference for industrial materials that looked artificial – steel, glass and cement, for example – and was extremely interested in metal-framed constructions. The features that show are used as decor and as pretexts for abstract geometrical compositions in which the architect skillfully creates a range of material effects with mat, shiny, smooth or grainy surfaces.

THE MAIN HALL
The marriage of form and technological necessity is expressed here without any stylistic go-between. The hall's functional purpose is immediately made clear, with structures and technical installations transformed into furnishings which illustrate Wagner's dictum "Necessity is the only criterion for Art".

VAULTING OF THE MAIN HALL
The system of construction used for the Main Hall is drawn from naval architecture (with tie-beams and narrow columns of fluted metal), and comes together to remarkable effect in a thin, curved layer of glass and steel, a technical tour de force. It allows light to flood into the hall.

89

THE WITTGENSTEIN HOUSE (1926–8) *(Kundmanngasse 19)*
Paul Engelmann and Ludwig Wittgenstein invested a large amount of money in this beautifully conceived and executed minimalist construction.

After the bourgeois neo-classicism of the Biedermeier epoch, the Industrial Revolution produced a horde of newly rich Viennese who built large Italianate villas on the hills surrounding the city. Otto Wagner, who began by designing luxurious houses of this sort, adopted Secessionist principles. Adolf Loos carried this purism to its logical conclusion without, however, attaining Wittgenstein's degree of philosophical rigor, and Josef Hoffmann used wit and subtle classical allusions to redefine the Biedermeier style.

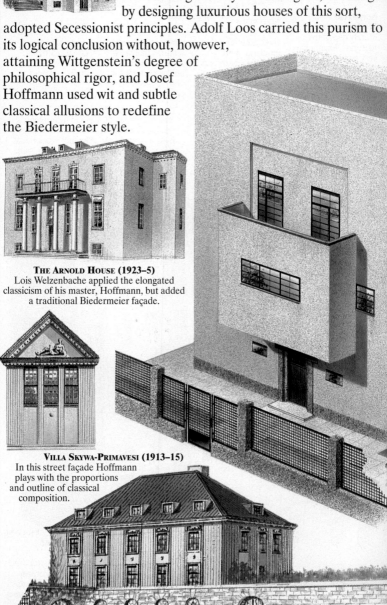

THE ARNOLD HOUSE (1923–5)
Lois Welzenbache applied the elongated classicism of his master, Hoffmann, but added a traditional Biedermeier façade.

VILLA SKYWA-PRIMAVESI (1913–15)
In this street façade Hoffmann plays with the proportions and outline of classical composition.

FLOORPLAN OF THE VILLA WAGNER I (1886–8)
(Hüttelbergstrasse 26)
A terrace site, two wings with columns, and majestic flights of steps
leading in – Wagner's first villa exhibits Palladian influences redefined
in the light of turn-of-the-century symbolism.

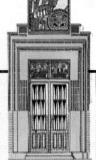

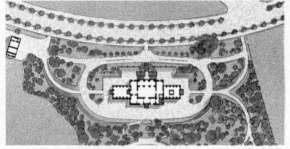

The greatest single source of inspiration was Arnold Böcklin's
Seaside Villa, which effectively took Viennese
architecture beyond the limits of the
Italian model.

**VILLA WAGNER II
DOORWAY.** Leopold
Forstner's Warrior
Athena over the
doorway marries with
the rest of the design
because of its stylistic
character and formal
three-part casing.

VILLA WAGNER II (1912–13)
(Hüttelbergstrasse 28)
The disciplined geometrical use of ornament
and archaic coloring are part of the architect's
evolution toward a form of monumental
austerity, encompassing both the Secessionist
and Weiner styles.

**HAUS MOLLER
(1927–8)**
Designed by Adolf
Loos a year after
Tristan Tzara's
house in
Montmartre.
The façade is
anthropomorphic, its ironic
mask surreptitiously reintroducing
the ornamentation and axial emphasis
so admired by the architect's modernist
disciples.

THE HOFFMANN HOUSE (1930–2)
Built specially for the Werkbund exhibition,
this project for a working man's home
blends economy of materials, comfort and
functional effectiveness; the handling of
space, particularly that of the glassed-in
entrance, is remarkable.

VILLA AST (1909–11) *(Steinfeldgasse 2)*
In this last of the Hohewarte houses,
Josef Hoffmann expresses his view of
classicism in the form of solid, foursquare
buildings. Even so, his ornamental
details go directly against the grain of
traditional values.

THE MOLL HOUSE (1906–17)
(Steinfeldgasse 8). It blends well with the neo-
Biedermeier buildings that surround it.

● "RED VIENNA"

After the breakup of the empire and the proclamation of the Austrian Republic in 1918, Vienna ceased to be an international capital. The serious economic downturn which ensued caused wholesale migrations and a huge increase in the population of Vienna, which created a severe shortage of housing. In 1919 the socialist triumph at the municipal elections transformed the city, which by then was a "state within a state", into a testing ground for a workers' democracy. The great working-class building projects *(Hof)*, constructed between 1919 and 1933, are an impressive reminder of the ambitions of socialist Vienna, in both the sociopolitical and the architectural spheres.

KARL-SEITZ-HOF
(1926–7) ▲ 297
This refined complex by Hubert Gessner is built around a monumental semicircle.

KARL-MARX-HOF
(1927–30) ▲ 295
This majestic structure by Karl Ehn (more than a half mile long, containing 1,600 apartments), extends around six central towers built over 40-foot arches. The ensemble has the look of a great triumphal archway.

RESIDENTIAL COMPLEX (1924–5) (PHILLIPSGASSE 8)
With an astounding strap-work façade, stone harps at the corners, triangular bow windows and a variety of apertures, this building by Siegfried Theiss and Hans Jaksch seems to be an attempt to enliven the monotony of the urban environment.

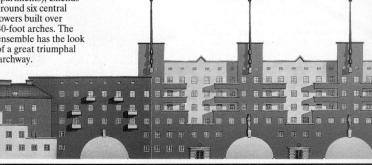

REUMANNHOF (1924–6) ▲ 297
In order to give his massive Reumannhof a palatial appearance,
Gessner grouped large numbers of bow windows in the central part of
the building, in the ground-floor arcades, and at the attic levels.

DOOR AT KLOSEHOF
(1924). This has all
the elegance of
Hoffmann's classic
modernism ▲ 235.

LIEBKNECHTHOF (1926)
In this building Karl Krist's expressionist and constructivist instincts
subtly modify the historical elements, such as the ogival arch and the
gabled turrets of bow windows, inspired by Gothic antecedents.

**DOOR AT
SANDLEITENHOF
(1924–8)**
Hoppe, Schönthal,
Matuschek, Theiss,
Jaksch, Krauss and
Tölk: a litany of
architects for a
complex in which
everyday motifs are
handled with superb
imagination.

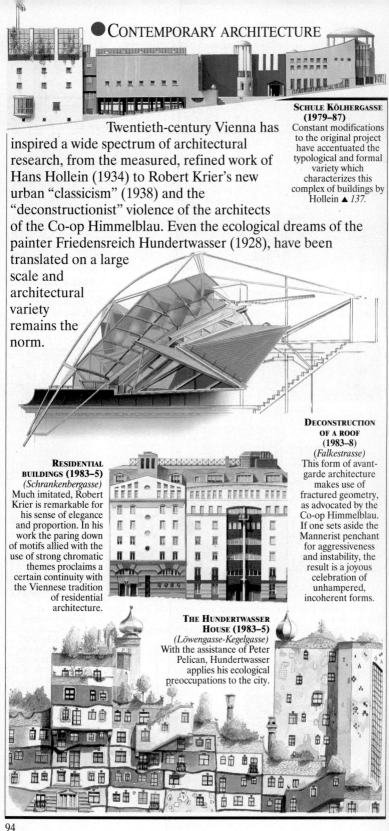

● CONTEMPORARY ARCHITECTURE

SCHULE KÖLHERGASSE (1979–87)
Constant modifications to the original project have accentuated the typological and formal variety which characterizes this complex of buildings by Hollein ▲ 137.

Twentieth-century Vienna has inspired a wide spectrum of architectural research, from the measured, refined work of Hans Hollein (1934) to Robert Krier's new urban "classicism" (1938) and the "deconstructionist" violence of the architects of the Co-op Himmelblau. Even the ecological dreams of the painter Friedensreich Hundertwasser (1928), have been translated on a large scale and architectural variety remains the norm.

DECONSTRUCTION OF A ROOF (1983–8)
(Falkestrasse)
This form of avant-garde architecture makes use of fractured geometry, as advocated by the Co-op Himmelblau. If one sets aside the Mannerist penchant for aggressiveness and instability, the result is a joyous celebration of unhampered, incoherent forms.

RESIDENTIAL BUILDINGS (1983–5)
(Schrankenbergasse)
Much imitated, Robert Krier is remarkable for his sense of elegance and proportion. In his work the paring down of motifs allied with the use of strong chromatic themes proclaims a certain continuity with the Viennese tradition of residential architecture.

THE HUNDERTWASSER HOUSE (1983–5)
(Löwengasse-Kegelgasse)
With the assistance of Peter Pelican, Hundertwasser applies his ecological preoccupations to the city.

VIENNA AS SEEN
BY PAINTERS

As the pupil and sometime copyist of his uncle Antonio Canal, otherwise known as Canaletto, Bernardo Belloto (1720–80) suffered for many years from unfair comparison with his master. Yet he was wise enough to leave Venice at an early age and travel through the rest of Italy, after which he went to Dresden at the invitation of the Elector of Saxony, the then king of Poland Augustus III. Enchanted by the Elbe Valley, Belloto began painting the romantic canvases which established his reputation at the courts of Munich, Vienna and Warsaw. He was invited to Vienna by Empress Maria Theresa, where he produced a series of portraits of the city in which detail and charm were matched with genuine poetry. In his *View of Vienna from the Upper Belvedere* (above, 1722) Belloto depicts the overlapping gardens of the Salesian monastery and the Belvedere, along with the Belvedere's orangery and the gardens of the Schwartzenberg Palace. The domes of the churches of St Charles and of the Salesians frame the composition, and in the distance is the old city, a thicket of towers dominated by the spire of St Stephen's; beyond is the undulating Wienerwald. In this picture Belloto contrasts the wordly atmosphere of the Belvedere with the romantic garden of the Schwarzenbergs. The *Freyung at Vienna* (opposite) shows a square in the old town. Side by side with bourgeois buildings stand (on the left) the Harrach, Kinsky and Batthyány-Schönborn palaces, while the people milling around the street stalls are drawn from all social classes.

"'But all the same I am the guardian at the art museum, and a state official,' he said. 'In the evening, after six o'clock has struck, I lock up not criminals but works of art: I turn the key on Rubens and Belloto.'" OLD MASTERS

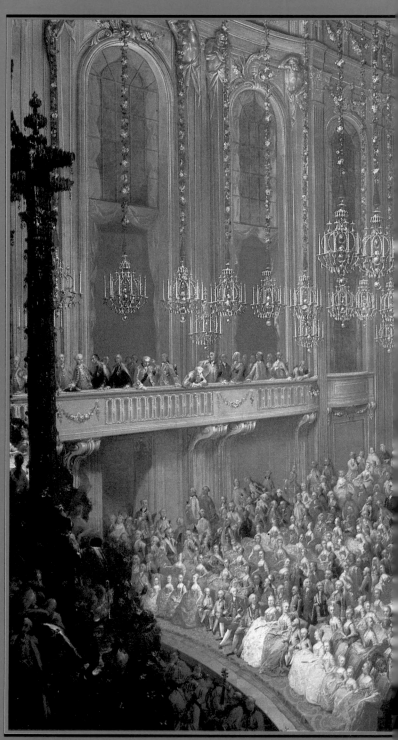

Some painters owe their posthumous reputations less to artistic talent than to the quality of their contemporary observation: among these are Longhi in Venice, Van Mour in Constantinople, and Martin van Meytens (or Mytens) in Vienna. Meytens (1695–1770) was of Dutch origin but was raised in Stockholm, where his father was court painter. After studying in Holland and England, he settled in Paris where, as the protégé of the Duke of Orléans, he painted the French king's portrait and forty miniature portraits for Peter the Great. After visiting the courts of Dresden and Vienna, Meytens traveled to Italy to study the Venetians before returning to the imperial capital. There, in 1730, he was appointed official court painter and, twenty-nine years later, became Director of the Fine Arts Academy. Today the interest in his work lies mainly in the glimpse of 18th-century dress and, in his badly composed larger canvases, the rich period detail. An example is the series of paintings commissioned by Maria Theresa ● 36 for the marriage of her son, the future Joseph II, to Isabella of Parma, in 1760. The painting at the top depicts the wedding procession on its way to the Augustinian Church; the one to the left shows a concert given at the Burgtheater before the imperial family on the same occasion.

The hills of the Wienerwald ■ *18* have always been a favorite walking place for the Viennese; for painters, their attraction lay in the romantic views they afforded of the city and the villages around it. These included Nussdorf, Grinzing and, as here, Mödling (1848 and 1849, above) as depicted by Ferdinand Georg Waldmüller (1793–1865). An advocate of realism who was hostile to academic art, Waldmüller left one of the most complete visual descriptions of Viennese society during the Biedermeier epoch ● *62*. His court portraits, and scenes of rural life, portray a society that is still patriarchal at the dawn of industrialization. His landscapes, which are particularly famous, are bathed in a hard light which breaks up the silhouettes of the trees and lends an unearthly sharpness to perspectives. Instead of including scenes of Italy like so many other neo-classical landscape painters, he took care to paint his landscapes realistically, preferring to attack them from close up, thus circumventing the tyranny of "good composition". An example is his view of the Prater (opposite), where at that time the meadow was still mown by locals. In his most poignant landscapes Waldmüller conveyed a sense of the hard existence that lay behind the peasants' colorful traditional costumes.

THE RENDEZVOUS TOOK PLACE AT NOON THE NEXT DAY, AT THE SIGN
OF THE BLUE STAG. THIS WAS A GRINZING TAVERN WHERE, IN
SUMMER, THEY USED TO COME WITH SAUSAGE AND HAM TO DRINK
HE NEW WINE; AND SO THEY DINED UNDER THE ACACIA, AMONG THE
BARRELS WITH THEIR SIXTEEN HOOPS." PAUL MORAND

Portrait of
Franz Alt.

The best-known members of the Alt family were Franz and Rudolf, the sons of Jacob Alt of Frankfurt. An itinerant landscape painter, Jacob painted watercolors of every part of the empire, including several of Vienna (below, 1817). Rudolf, the "Viennese Canaletto", carried the same genre to new heights before concentrating on interiors; he eventually earned his keep supplying the imperial nobility with albums of their residences. The studio below (main picture) is that of Hans Makart, a neo-Renaissance artist who painted portraits of Ringstrasse ladies.

103

After a period of rapid economic expansion, by 1900 Vienna was suffering from social unrest. The avant-garde showed little interest, but naturalist painter Joseph Engelhardt (1864–1941) set about portraying contemporary Vienna in paintings such as *An Evening at the Sophienbad* (right). (The Sophienbad was popular with the middle class during the winter season.) A more attentive observer than Engelhardt, Carl Moll (1861–1945) ▲ *255* viewed social reality with the rational view of the Dutch painters (above, the *Muttel Fabrik*).

VIENNA AS SEEN
BY WRITERS

FIRST IMPRESSIONS

A SMALL TOWN

William Lithgow (1582–1645?) passed through Vienna during his travels across Europe, but was disappointed to find that it did not live up to its reputation.

❝Being arrived at Vienne, I found the Towne, and the flying fame of it far different, either for greatnesse, strength, or wealth; for the Towne rising upon a moderat height circular, is but of small compasse without, not passing two English miles.

The suburbs round about, being twice as great as the Towne; and the strength of it is no way comparable to a hundred Cities that I have seene, neither is it for wealth so much to be admired, being depraved of Seas, shipping, and navigation, having onely the needfull prosperity of dry land Townes.❞

WILLIAM LITHGOW, *RARE ADVENTURES AND PAINFULL PEREGRINATIONS*,
1614–32, PUB. JAMES MACLEHOSE & SONS,
GLASGOW, 1906

A CHRISTIAN WELCOME

Peter Tolstoi (1645–1729), the Russian ambassador to Vienna, was very impressed to see the care given in a hospital which he visited in 1698.

❝I was at a *shpital* (Ger. *Spital*), that is, a hospital or a house for the ill. This hospital is built outside the city of Vienna in a suburb, on the other side of a tributary of the river Danube; in this hospital is a very long room, and in this room, opposite the doors, a man's bones are placed beneath glass in an icon-case, arranged into a likeness [of a man] and held together with brass wire. These are the bones of the man who first began to build this hospital. In this same room around the walls are placed many beds of fine joiner's work, and around each bed is placed a green curtain, and on each bedstead is placed good bedding. They are covered with white sheets, and on each bed is a good blanket. On these beds lie the sick, and by the head of each sick person is a tankard with a drink, and the tankards are all pewter; each sick person also has a white towel. This hospital is just being built by the imperial treasury. Alongside of this hospital is a good pharmacy for the drugs for those sick people, and doctors are attached to it; and the druggists and chemists in this pharmacy are assigned to it, and all are kept at the emperor's expense. In the middle of that long room in which the sick people lie is a *kaplica*, that is, a small church, where the Roman monks conduct a Mass for the sick daily early in the morning. And here they have set the tables on which the sick eat; and on the other side of this long room is a small garden, and placed in it are grapes, and this is why they built it: when a sick person begins to recover from his illness, he may stroll in this garden because of its coolness. They accept into this hospital the sick of every rank without cost; they only inquire if the sick person has no means of his own, and these they accept into this hospital, and they rest and are treated with great care; they also admit into this hospital traveling foreigners who fall ill, and they keep these sick people in this place until they are completely cured; and when they are completely healthy, they are free to go wherever they wish without paying; no one takes anything from anyone in this hospital, and they do this because of the Christian faith and for the saving of souls.❞

THE TRAVEL DIARY OF PETER TOLSTOI, 1697,
TRANS. MAX J. OKENFUSS,
PUB. NORTHERN ILLINOIS UNIVERSITY PRESS, 1987

VIENNESE APARTMENTS

Lady Mary Wortley Montagu (1689–1762) was the wife of the British ambassador to Constantinople, so spent much time overseas. She soon became known in society for her eloquent and incisive letters, which were first published in 1837 after her death. The following letter, to her sister the Countess of Mar, was written on September 8, 1716, and describes the living accommodation available in Vienna at the time.

❝This town, which has the honour of being the emperor's residence, did not at all answer my ideas of it, being much less than I expected to find it; the streets are very close, and so narrow, one cannot observe the fine fronts of the palaces, though many of them very well deserve observation, being truly magnificent, all built of fine white stone, and excessive high, the town being so much too little for the number of the people that desire to live in it, the builders seem to have projected to repair that misfortune, by clapping one town on the top of another, most of the houses being of five, and some of them six stories. You may easily imagine, that the streets being so narrow, the upper rooms are extremely dark; and, what is an inconveniency much more intolerable, in my opinion, there is no house that has so few as five or six families in it. The apartments of the greatest ladies, and even of the ministers of state, are divided but by a partition from that of a tailor or a shoemaker; and I know nobody that has above two floors in any house, one for their own use, and one higher for their servants. Those that have houses of their own, let out the rest of them to whoever will take them; thus the great stairs (which are all of stone) are as common and as dirty as the street. 'T's true, when you have once travelled through them, nothing can be more surprisingly magnificent than the apartments. They are commonly a *suite* of eight or ten large rooms, all inlaid, the doors and windows richly carved and gilt, and the furniture such as is seldom seen in the palaces of sovereign princes in other countries – the hangings the finest tapestry of Brussels, prodigious large looking-glasses in silver frames, fine japan tables, beds, chairs, canopies, and window curtains of the richest Genoa damask or velvet, almost covered with gold lace or embroidery. The whole made gay by pictures, and vast jars of japan china, and in almost every room large lustres of rock crystal.❞

THE LETTERS AND WORKS OF LADY MARY WORTLEY MONTAGU
EVERYMAN'S LIBRARY, LONDON 1993

UNQUALIFIED ADMIRATION

Anton Chekhov (1860–1904), the Russian dramatist and short-story writer, visited Vienna in 1891 and was impressed by all aspects of the city. The following letter was written on March 20, 1891, soon after his arrival.

❝Oh, my friends, if you knew how wonderful Vienna is! It cannot be compared to any of the cities I have seen in my whole life – wide streets, exquisitely paved, a multitude of boulevards and plazas, all the houses six and seven stories high, and stores – they are not stores but sheer vertigo, reveries! Billions of ties alone in the windows! What amazing articles made of bronze, porcelain, leather! Enormous churches, yet they do not oppress you by their bulk, but caress the eyes because they seem to be woven of lace. The Cathedral of St Stephen and the *Votivkirche* are especially admirable. They are not edifices but tea biscuits. The Parliament, the City Hall, the University, are magnificent. Everything is magnificent, and only today and yesterday I understood fully that architecture is really an art. And here art is offered not piecemeal, as with us, but it stretches in belts for miles. Many monuments. In every side street, without fail, a bookshop. In their windows you notice Russian books too, but alas, they are not by Albov or Barantzevich or Chekhov, but by all kinds of anonymous authors writing and printing abroad. I saw Renan and *The Secrets of the Winter Palace*, etc. Oddly enough, here everyone may read and say whatever he pleases.

Know, ye natives, what manner of cabs are here, deuce take them. No buggies, but only brand-new, pretty carriages drawn by one or, more frequently, two horses. The horses are wonderful. On the box sit dandies in short coats and top hats, reading newspapers. Civility and courtesy.

Dinners are good. There is no vodka, they drink beer and tolerable wine. One thing is objectionable: they charge for bread. Before handing you the check they ask, *Wieviel Brodchen?* i.e. how many rolls did you gobble? And they charge for each roll.

The women are beautiful and elegant. And in general everything is deucedly elegant. **99**

LETTERS OF ANTON CHEKHOV,
PUB. VIKING PRESS, NEW YORK, 1973

SIGHTSEEING

Djuna Barnes (1892–1982), the American novelist, illustrator and short-story writer, is best remembered for her novel, "Nightwood", published in 1936 with a preface by T. S. Eliot. It describes a nightmare world of troubled characters and has, according to Eliot, "a quality of horror and doom very nearly related to that of Elizabethan tragedy".

66He took her first to Vienna. To reassure himself he showed her all the historic buildings. He kept saying to himself that sooner or later, in this garden or that palace, she would suddenly be moved as he was moved. Yet it seemed to him that he too was a sightseer. He tried to explain to her what Vienna had been before the war; what it must have been before he was born; yet his memory was confused and hazy, and he found himself repeating what he had read, for it was what he knew best. With methodic anxiety he took her over the city. He said, 'You are a *Baronin* now.' He spoke to her in German as she ate the heavy *Schnitzel* and dumplings, clasping her hand about the thick handle of the beer mug. He said: '*Das Leben ist ewig, darinliegt seine Schonheit.*' They walked before the Imperial Palace in a fine hot sun that fell about the clipped hedges and the statues warm and clear. He went into the *Kammergarten* with her and talked, and on into the *Gloriette*, and sat on first one bench, and then another. Brought up short, he realized that he had been hurrying from one to the other as if they were orchestra chairs, as if he himself were trying not to miss anything; now, at the extremity of the garden, he was aware that he had been anxious to see every tree, every statue at a different angle. 99

DJUNA BARNES, *NIGHTWOOD*, 1936,
PUB. FABER & FABER, LONDON, 1958

MUSIC

STREET MUSICIANS

Dr Charles Burney (1726–1814) was an organist, musical historian and minor composer who wrote accounts of his travels in Europe collecting material for his master work, a four-volume "General History of Music" published in 1776–89. Here he describes the music heard in the streets and lodging houses of Vienna.

66[One] night two of the poor scholars of this city sung, in the court of the inn where I lodged, duets in *falsetto, soprano* and *contralto*, very well in tune, and with feeling and taste. I sent to enquire whether they were taught music at the Jesuits' college, and was answered in the affirmative. Though the number of poor scholars, at different colleges, amounts to a hundred and twenty, yet there are at present but seventeen that are taught music.

After this there was a band of these singers, who performed through the streets a kind of glee, in three and four parts: this whole country is certainly very musical. I frequently heard the soldiers upon guard, and sentinels, as well as common people, sing in parts. The music school at the Jesuits' College, in every Roman Catholic town, accounts in some measure for this faculty; yet other causes may be assigned, and, among these, it should be remembered, that there is scarce a church or convent in Vienna, which has not every

morning its *mass in music*: that is, a great portion of the church service of the day, set in parts, and performed with voices, accompanied by at least three or four violins, a tenor and bass, besides the organ; and as the churches here are daily crowded, this music, though not of the most exquisite kind, must, in some degree, form the ear of the inhabitants. ...

There was music every day, during dinner, and in the evening at the inn, where I lodged, which was the Golden Ox; but it was usually bad, particularly that of a band of wind instruments, which constantly attended the ordinary. This consisted of French horns, clarionets, oboes, and bassoons; all so miserably out of tune, that I wished them a hundred miles off.

In general I did not find that delicacy of ear among the German street musicians, which I had met with in people of the same rank and profession in Italy. The church organs being almost always out of tune here, may be occasioned by the parsimony or negligence of the clergy, bishop or superior of a church or convent; but the being, or stopping, in or out of tune, among street musicians, must depend on themselves, and on their organs being *acute* or *obtuse*. **99**

> Dr Charles Burney's Continental Travels (1770–1772),
> Compiled by Cedric Howard Glover,
> Pub. Blackie & Son, Glasgow, 1927

Outdoor entertainment

Hans Christian Andersen (1805–75), the Danish writer, recalls hearing the waltzes of Johann Strauss performed outdoors on a visit to Vienna.

66 'We are in Volcksgarten!' – Gentlemen and ladies stroll under the green trees in lively conversation; the waiters fly in all directions to procure ices. The tones of a whole orchestra spread through the garden. In the midst of the musicians stands a young man of dark complexion; his large brown eyes glance round about in a restless manner; his head, arms, and whole body move; it is as if he were the heart in that great musical body, and, as we know, the blood flows through the heart, – and here the blood is tones; these tones were born in him; he is the heart, and all Europe hears its musical beatings; its own pulse beats stronger when it hears them:– the man's name is – Strauss. **99**

> Hans Christian Andersen, *A Poet's Bazaar*,
> Trans. Charles Beckwith, Pub. Richard Bentley, London, 1846

Mozart's lodgings

Wolfgang Amadeus Mozart (1756–91) moved to Vienna in 1781, and the following year he married Constanze Weber. The last nine years of his life saw an astonishing outpouring of masterpieces in every musical genre, but yet he was beset by constant financial hardships. The following extracts are from letters to his father on August 22, 1781, and then on May 3, 1783.

66 I cannot let you know the address of my new lodging, as I have not yet got one. But I am bargaining about the prices of two, one of which I shall certainly take, as I cannot stay here next month and so must move out. It appears that Herr von Auernhammer wrote and told you that I had actually found a lodging! I had one, it is true, but what a habitation! Fit for rats and mice, but not for human beings. At noon I had to look for the stairs with a lantern. The room was a little closet and to get to it I had to pass through the kitchen. In the door there was a tiny window and although they promised me to put up a curtain inside, they asked me at the same time to draw it back as soon as I was dressed, for otherwise they would not be able to see anything either in the kitchen or in the adjoining rooms. The owner's wife herself called the house the rats' nest. ... **99**

66 I simply cannot make up my mind to drive back into town so early. The weather is far too lovely and it is far too delightful in the Prater today. We have taken our lunch out of doors and shall stay on until eight or nine in the evening. My whole

company consists of my little wife who is pregnant, and hers consists of her little husband, who is not pregnant, but fat and flourishing. ... I must ask you to wait patiently for a longer letter and the aria with variations – for, of course, I cannot finish them in the Prater; and for the sake of my dear little wife I cannot miss this fine weather. Exercise is good for her. So today I am only sending you a short letter to say that, thank God, we are both well and have received your last letter. Now farewell.**

THE LETTERS OF MOZART AND HIS FAMILY,
MACMILLAN PRESS, LONDON, 1985

THE DEATH OF MOZART

Mozart had been in poor health for some time and became bedridden about two weeks before his death on December 5, 1791. The following account of his last days was written by Sophie Haibel to her elder sister's husband Georg Nikolaus von Nissen.

**I thought to myself, 'How I should love to know how Mozart is.' While I was thinking and gazing at the flame, it went out, as completely as if the lamp had never been burning. Not a spark remained on the big wick and yet there wasn't the slightest draught – that I can swear to. A horrible feeling came over me. I ran to our mother and told her all. She said: 'Well, take off your fine clothes and go into town and bring me back news of him at once. But be sure not to delay.' I hurried along as fast as I could. Alas, how frightened I was when my sister, who was almost despairing and yet trying to keep calm, came out to me, saying: 'Thank God that you have come, dear Sophie. Last night he was so ill that I thought he would not be alive this morning. Do stay with me today, for if he has another bad turn, he will pass away tonight. Go in to him for a little while and see how he is.' I tried to control myself and went to his bedside. He immediately called me to him and said: 'Ah, dear Sophie, how glad I am that you have come. You must stay here tonight and see me die.' I tried hard to be brave and to persuade him to the contrary. But to all my attempts he only replied: 'Why, I have already the taste of death on my tongue.' And, 'if you do not stay, who will support my dearest Constanze if you don't stay here?' 'Yes, yes, dear Mozart,' I assured him, 'but I must first go back to our mother and tell her that you would like me to stay with you today. Otherwise she will think that some misfortune has befallen you.' 'Yes, do so,' said Mozart, 'but be sure and come back soon.' Good God, how distressed I felt! My poor sister followed me to the door and begged me for Heaven's sake to go to the priests at St Peter's, and implore one of them to come to Mozart – a chance call, as it were. I did so, but for a long time they refused to come and I had a great deal of trouble to persuade one of those clerical brutes to go to him. Then I ran off to my mother who was anxiously awaiting me. It was already dark. Poor soul, how shocked she was! ... I then ran back as fast as I could to my distracted sister. Süssmayr was at Mozart's bedside. The well-known Requiem lay on the quilt and Mozart was explaining to him how, in his opinion, he ought to finish it, when he was gone. Further, he urged his wife to keep his death a secret until she should have informed Albrechtsberger, for the post should be his before God and the world[1]. A long search was made for Dr Closset, who was found at the theatre, but who had to wait for the end of the play. He came and ordered *cold* poultices to be placed on Mozart's burning head, which, however, affected him to such an extent that he became unconscious and remained so until he died[2]. His last movement was an attempt to express with his mouth the drum passages in the Requiem. That I can still hear. 99

THE LETTERS OF MOZART AND HIS FAMILY,
MACMILLAN PRESS, LONDON, 1985

1 As Mozart intended, Albrechtsberger, the court organist, succeeded him as assistant to the Kapellmeister at St Stephen's Cathedral, Leopold Hofmann.
2 Mozart died at 55 minutes past midnight on December 5, 1791.

SCHUBERT'S EVENING WALK
On the evening of June 14, 1816, Franz Schubert (1797–1828) described the following walk in his diary. Währing and Döbling were northwestern urban districts of Vienna, easily reached from the Himmel-fortgrund. The cemetery they passed was the general one of Währing, just outside the Nussdorf gate in the outer ring of fortifications bounding the suburbs of Vienna.

66 I took an evening walk for once, as I had not done for several months. There can be scarcely anything more agreeable than to enjoy the green country on an evening after a hot summer's day, a pleasure for which the fields between Währing and Döbling seem to have been especially created. In the uncertain twilight and in the company of my brother Karl, my heart warmed within me. 'How beautiful,' I thought and exclaimed,

standing still delightedly. A graveyard close by reminded us of our dear mother. Thus, talking sadly and intimately, we arrived at the point where the Döbling road divides. And, as from the heavenly home, I heard a familiar voice coming from a halting coach. I looked up – and it was Herr Weinmüller, just alighting and paying us his compliments in his cordial, honest voice. – In an instant our conversation turned to the outward cordiality of people's tone and language. How many attempt vainly to show their upright disposition by means of cordial honest language; how many would thus only expose themselves to derision. Such a thing may not be

regarded as an acquisition, but only as a natural gift.**"**

SCHUBERT'S DIARY, QUOTED IN SCHUBERT – A DOCUMENTARY BIOGRAPHY
BY OTTO ERIC DEUTSCH, PUB. J.M. DENT & SONS, LONDON, 1946

VIENNESE STYLE

THE RINGSTRASSE

Hermann Bahr (1863–1934) was a poet, essayist and art critic. Here he writes about the "artistic deceit" of the architecture of the Ringstrasse epoch.

"If you walk across the Ring, you have the impression of being in the midst of a real carnival. Everything masked, everything disguised … Life has become too serious for that sort of thing. We want to look life in the face. This is what we mean when we talk of 'realist architecture', that is, that the building must not only serve its intended purpose, but must also express, not conceal, that purpose. … To disguise it behind borrowed forms is both silly and ugly. Earlier, people used to require that a building should 'look like something'; we demand that it should 'be something'. We, the working people of today, should be ashamed to live in the style of the princes and patricians of yesterday. That we think of as a swindle. From the appearance of a house, we should be able to judge what is its purpose, who lives in it and how. We are not of the age of the Baroque, we don't live in the Renaissance, why should we act as if we did? Life has changed, costume has changed, our thoughts and feelings, our whole manner of living has changed, architecture must change too. … These demands have now become audible, and will no longer be stifled.**"**

HERMANN BAHR, SECESSION, VIENNA, 1900

ADVICE ON THE WIENER WERKSTÄTTE

Charles Rennie Mackintosh (1868–1928), the Scottish architect and designer, wrote to Fritz Wärndorfer on March 17, 1903, two months before the foundation of the Wiener Werkstätte. Mackintosh traveled to Vienna on several occasions and was a great admirer of the city.

Arthur

❝If one wants to achieve an artistic success with your programme ... every object which you pass from your hand must carry an outspoken mark of individuality, beauty and most exact execution. From the outset your aim must be that every object which you produce is made for a certain purpose and place. Later ... you can emerge boldly into the full light of the world, attack the factory-trade on its own ground, and the greatest work that can be achieved in this century, you can achieve it: namely the production of objects of use in magnificent form and at such a price that they lie within the buying range of the poorest. ... But till then years of hard, serious, honest work are still needed. ... First the 'artistic' (pardon the word) scoffers must be overcome; and those who are influenced by these scoffers must be taught... that the modern movement is not a silly hobby-horse of a few who wish to achieve fame comfortably through eccentricity, but that the modern movement is something living, something good, the only possible art – for all and for the highest phase of our time.

Yes – the plan which Hoffmann and Moser have designed is great and splendidly thought through, and if you have the means for it you are not taking any risk, and all I can say is: begin today! – If I were in Vienna, I would assist with a great strong shovel!**❞**

E. SEKLER, *MACKINTOSH AND VIENNA*,
PUB. IN *ARCHITECTURAL REVIEW*, LONDON 1968.

THE FASHION IN DRESS

Martha Wilmot (1771–1873) was the wife of a chaplain at the British Embassy in Vienna. She wrote regularly to her friends in English society and particularly her sister Alicia.

❝I must tell you that in expences we are disappointed – everything except luxuries is as dear as in England: dress, dearer, worse and a year behind us in fashion; *Tay* and *sugar* enormous. *However* there are glass konvaniences to be had in abundance, and fruit and flowers dirt cheap – parqué flours – Carpits if you chuse to give a daughters dowery for them, and if you do, the *Moths* eat them up to riddles in the summer. We happened luckily to bring a few knives with us which are invaluable, as is a small *tayput* – but the bedding!! No tongue can tell it, and as for a *double* bed, there is but one in Vienna ... and that is Ld Stewart's, so English Turtle doves place two together to make believe tis one, and we have purchased *leather* sheets, exquisite things, one to serve as an under, the other as an upper blanket, for a blanket is not to be had for gold and precious stones. O had you seen Arnold cheapening said leather sheets! taking them on and off our bed, ballyragging in German! and finally beating the poor man down 15 florins on the pair! Such a thing as a bed curtain is not known, but then the turn out on the Prater of a Sunday Eve is Magnificent – 4, 6, 8 horses to *shell* like little carriages, footmen with streaming feathers. The Emperour and all his Court, young Napoleon (Wm saw a *child* in the Imperial Carriage), in fact from the Emperour to the Scavenger all turn out finer than butterflys. Not a *drab* of a Hussy that has not better broderie about her tail than *my best* and parterres of artificial flowers round her head. And à propos of dress, while I was in London I did my best to procure you a patinet *half* handkerchief and could not, such a thing was not to be had; well, in the Prater I saw *scores* on the trollops! How is this to be accounted for I beg to know? English

Schnitzler

second rate dress is so common here that every milk maid has our prints, our ginghams, our muslins, even our tabinets, but *stuffs* are rare (I have *not* one), ribbons are dear, and as for shawls, or eyes are sickened of what looks like Turkish ones, but what is in reality Cotton. "

MORE LETTERS FROM MARTHA WILMOT,
EDITED BY THE MARCHIONESS OF LONDONDERRY,
MACMILLAN PRESS, LONDON, 1935

CONVERSATION

Henry Reeve was a doctor who lived in Vienna in the winter of 1805–6 and wrote about his experiences in a journal. The work was published posthumously by his son.

"The Germans take very little for breakfast; a dish of coffee and a bit of bread suffices till dinner; many eat nothing at all. The usual hour of dinner is from one to three o'clock among all classes of people. They do not sit long at table; coffee is usually served in another room, and the company separate at six o'clock, when most people pay visits or go to the opera or to the theatre. The pleasures of social discussion and the gay fireside are quite unknown. The conversation is for the most part dull, languid, and uninteresting, often, in what is called *la bonne compagnie*, indecent and licentious. The married women are always expecting to be in love, and to have young men *faire la cour* to them; and the young misses are corrupted by what they hear, and are left to amuse themselves. With regard to literature, arts, and sciences, Vienna is far behind other towns even of Germany. Reading is in a manner forbidden by the Government not allowing the free circulation even of classical books; and many a man with a smattering of knowledge has a reputation of being a savant without being able to keep up a conversation for half-an-hour without betraying his gross ignorance. Literary men are not respected as at Paris, and it is one of the slowest ways to eminence to write a book. "

HENRY REEVE, *JOURNAL OF A RESIDENCE IN VIENNA AND BERLIN,*
LONGMANS, LONDON 1877

FREUD IN VIENNA

Sigmund Freud (1856–1939), the creator of psychoanalysis, practiced for many years in Vienna until Hitler's invasion of Austria drove him to London, where he died. The following piece is from a memoir written by his son Martin.

"My father began work at eight every morning and it was not uncommon for him

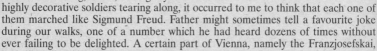

to work through until perhaps three o'clock the following morning, with breaks for luncheon and dinner, the former extended to include a walk which nearly always took in the full circle of the Ringstrasse, although sometimes he shortened it by cutting across the inner city to collect, or deliver, proofs at his publishers. However, it must not be imagined that these excursions took the form of leisurely promenades designed to enjoy the beauty of the Ringstrasse and its flowering trees in springtime. My father marched at terrific speed. The Italian bersaglieri are celebrated for the speed of their marching; when, during my travels I saw these highly decorative soldiers tearing along, it occurred to me to think that each one of them marched like Sigmund Freud. Father might sometimes tell a favourite joke during our walks, one of a number which he had heard dozens of times without ever failing to be delighted. A certain part of Vienna, namely the Franzjosefskai, had, like all cities, its share of chimney-pots and other jutting-up adornments. My father often explained this phenomenon by telling us the story of the coffee party given by the devil's grandmother. It seems that this old lady for some reason or other was flying over Vienna with an enormous tray upon which she had put her very best coffee service, a large quantity of pots, jugs and cups and saucers of devilish design. Something happened, my father never explained just what, but I expect she entered an air pocket: at any rate the great tray turned over and the coffee service was distributed on to the roofs of Vienna, and each piece stuck. My father always enjoyed this joke as much as we did. ...

I am not convinced that Sigmund Freud's often-expressed dislike of Vienna was either deep-seated or real. It is not difficult for a London man, or a New York man, both devoted to their respective home cities, to say: 'How I hate London: how I loathe New York.' They are speaking the truth of a day, of an hour or of a moment: not necessarily a fixed attitude. And my own feeling is that sometimes my father hated Vienna, and that sometimes he loved the old city, and that, in a general sense, he was devoted. He could have left Vienna at any time during the many secure years before the Hitler shadow began dimming the city's gay sky; but he never did, nor did he, so far as I know, ever seriously contemplate emigrating. And even at the end, when every consideration compelled him to leave, he left with great reluctance and only after strong persuasion.**

MARTIN FREUD, *GLORY REFLECTED*,
ANGUS & ROBERTSON, LONDON, 1957

FOOD AND DRINK

INTERNATIONAL INFLUENCES

Paul Hofmann wrote a very insightful guide to the Viennese, which was published in the US in 1988. The following piece examines the origins of some traditional Viennese dishes.

Like the dialect, the cuisine of Vienna is the result of many influences from various directions. Take the schnitzel, considered the epitome of Danubian cooking. Actually, the Viennese way of breading and frying veal cutlets was copied from the Milanese when Lombardy was under Habsburg rule in the eighteenth and nineteenth centuries. The *scaloppina alla milanese* had been imported by the Spaniards, who were in control of the northern Italian city before the Austrians were, and the Spaniards had probably learned to fry meat in bread crumbs from the Byzantines at the eastern end of the Mediterranean. The strudel – thin dough rolled and filled with apples or other fruits, curds, poppyseeds, or chopped cabbage – was probably brought from Hungary, as surely was goulash. Bohemia contributed dumplings and other farinaceous dishes to the Viennese tables; from Germany and Poland came a passion for sausages. Wieners are a Viennese staple but are always called frankfurters. Other popular sausage types are named after the cities of Cracow, Debrecen, and Paris. The sweet tooth of the Viennese, satisfied by their many kinds of torte and other rich desserts and by their indulgence in whipped cream, seems to be a very old characteristic of the city, one probably enhanced by its many contacts with the Turks. … **99

PAUL HOFMANN, *THE VIENNESE – SPLENDOR TWILIGHT AND EXILE*,
DOUBLEDAY, NEW YORK 1988

THE SCENTS OF THE CITY

William Sansom (1912–76), the English novelist and travel writer, describes here his sensual impressions of Vienna.

FÁCKEL

66 Whiffs of incense, hot plaster, and Egyptian-smelling cigarettes seem to be the prevalent smells. Coffee, whipped cream, hockish white wine paprika and, curiously, boiled beef (*Beinfleisch*) are the tastes. (The Schnitzel, as we know, hardly tastes of anything, unless it is a Kaiserschnitzel, larded with ham and Emmentaler cheese.) Mix into these colours and smells the rumble of motor traffic and the grinding of trams, and the sound of the last piece of music, great or small that you heard in this most musical city of *Eroica* or *Schmaltz*; add the omnipresence of glittering gaswork-heavy baroque Prunk; place these impressions against miles and miles of pavement and caryatid-encrusted nineteenth century building, and sprinkle with the sense that although few people are rich there is a feeling somewhere of ease in most pockets – at least wine and beer and black coffee are cheap – and you will begin to feel some of the quality of this monstrously pleasant mirage. *Prunk* is a nice word, used for a show-room in a palace; 'pride' and 'hunk'

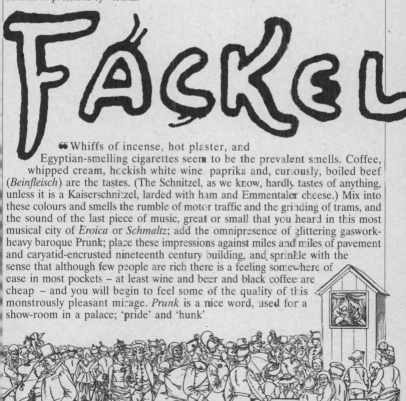

combine in our ear to give a phonetically exact description of baroque.**99**

WILLIAM SANSOM,
BLUE SKIES, BROWN STUDIES, 1960

COFFEE HOUSES

John Gunther (1901–70), a prolific and renowned travel writer, here describes the customs in Viennese coffee houses.

66Coffee houses, which continue to be the unalterable vital center of Viennese life, are everywhere. The visitor – or citizen – can sit for hour after hour over a single cup of coffee, which costs about 25 cents, while reading magazines and newspapers from all over the world, supplied free. Coffee exists in twenty or thirty different forms, from Mokka (jet black) to Weissen Ohne, which contains milk but is not topped by Schlagobers.

I had forgotten some piquant items in Viennese coffee-house lore and other customs, but they were quickly restored. In a café you normally get *two* glasses of water side by side – I don't know why – with your coffee; this drinking water is the best in Europe, coming from the Styrian hills ice-cold on even the hottest day. If you have a meal in a coffee house – or in a restaurant, for that matter – you must tell the headwaiter how many pieces of bread you have had when you are paying your bill, and these are charged for. Three different waiters must be tipped; 50 percent of the whole tip to the *Herr Ober*, who counts up the bill but does nothing else; 40 percent to the man who actually serves; 10 percent to the bus boy. This rule holds good even in the most humble cafés. Lightning mathematics is required.**99**

JOHN GUNTHER, *TWELVE CITIES*,
HAMISH HAMILTON,
LONDON, 1969

THE TURKS

Patrick Leigh Fermor (1915–), the English traveler, soldier and writer, journeyed on foot to Constantinople from the Hook of Holland in 1933 and passed through Vienna on the way. This part of his account relates the sole effect of Turkish influence on the city.

66I had never understood till now how near the Turks had got to taking Vienna. Of the first siege in Tudor times there were few mementoes in the museums. But the evidence of the second, more than a century later, and of the narrow escape of the city, was compellingly laid out. There were quivers and arrows and quarrels and bow-cases and tartar bows; scimitars, khanjars, yataghans, lances, bucklers, drums; helmets damascened and spiked and fitted with arrowy nasal-pieces; the turbans of janissaries, a pasha's tent, cannon and flags and horsetail banners with their bright brass crescents. Charles of Lorraine and John Sobiesky carocoled in their gilded frames and the breastplate of Rüdiger v. Starhemberg, the town's brave defender, gleamed with oiling and burnishing. (When John Sobiesky of Poland met the Emperor on horseback in the fields after the city was saved, the two sovereigns conversed in Latin for want of a common tongue.) There, too, was the mace of Suleiman the Magnificent, and the skull of Kara Mustafa, the Grand Vizir strangled and decapitated at Belgrade by Suleiman's descendant for his failure to take Vienna: and beside it, the executioner's silken bowstring. The great drama had taken place in 1683, eighteen years after the Great Fire of London; but all the corroborative detail, the masses of old maps, the prints and the models of the city, turned it into a real and a recent event. ... It had been a close run thing. What if the Turks had taken Vienna, as they nearly did, and advanced westward? ... Martial spoils apart, the great contest has left little trace. It was the beginning of coffee-drinking in the West, or so the Viennese maintain. The earliest coffee houses, they insist, were kept by some of the Sultan's Greek and Serbian subjects who had sought sanctuary in Vienna. But the rolls which the Viennese dipped in the new drink were modelled on the half-moons of the Sultan's flag. The shape caught on all over the world. They mark the end of the age-old struggle between the hot-cross-bun and the croissant.**"**

PATRICK LEIGH FERMOR,
A TIME OF GIFTS,
JOHN MURRAY, LONDON, 1977

THE VIENNESE

INTERNATIONAL INFLUENCES
Washington Irving (1783–1859), the American journalist and essayist, wrote to his sister on November 10, 1822, about the array of nationalities to be met in Vienna.

"This is one of the most perplexing cities that I was ever in. It is extensive, irregular, crowded, dusty, dissipated, magnificent, and to me disagreeable. It has immense palaces, superb galleries of paintings, several theatres, public walks, and drives crowded with equipages. In short, everything bears the stamp of luxury and ostentation; for here is assembled and concentrated all the wealth, fashion, and nobility of the Austrian empire, and every one strives to eclipse his neighbour. The gentlemen all dress in the English fashion, and in walking the fashionable lounges you would imagine yourself surrounded by Bond Street dandies. The ladies dress in the Parisian mode, the equipages are in the English style though more gaudy; with all this, however, there is a mixture of foreign costumes, that gives a very motley look to the population in the streets. You meet here with

Greeks, Turks, Polonaise, Jews, Sclavonians, Croats, Hungarians, Tyroleans, all in the dress of their several countries; and you hear all kinds of languages spoken around you . . . here the people think only of sensual gratifications. **99**

WASHINGTON IRVING, LETTER TO HIS SISTER, FROM *THE TRAVELLERS' DICTIONARY OF QUOTATION*, ED. PETER YAPP, ROUTLEDGE & KEGAN PAUL, LONDON, 1983

STATELY AND COURTEOUS

Richard Bassett's impression of the Viennese is that far from living up to their reputation for gaiety, they are a cynical and lethargic people, with the "past centuries of absolutist rule weighing down from high grey façades".

66The people of Vienna are completely different from western and Alpine Austrians, with a different set of morals and attitudes from the rest of the country. They regard their city as incomparable – as indeed it is, after a fashion. No European capital has such a stately, imperial air – despite decades of Socialist rule, the double-headed eagle still broods overhead wherever you go – and no other European capital has such delightful surroundings. On a Sunday afternoon, wandering among the deserted cobbled streets around the Minorites Church, one can almost hear Castlereagh's footsteps marking the way from the Palais Dietrichstein, where he was lodged, to the Ballhausplatz during the Congress of Vienna. Close by, the chancery gates still seem firmly closed to the 1848 mob eager for Metternich's blood, while across the grass the vast megalomaniac pile of the New Hofburg, with its balcony overlooking the Heldenplatz, inevitably conjures up that day in 1938 when Austrians stood roaring with delight at the only man ever to have addressed them from this vantage point – Adolf Hitler. Through the Hofburg, in the Michaelerplatz, Adolf Loos flaunts his concept of streamlined architecture, free from 'the crime of ornament', in his bleak, classical Goldman and Salatch House. Through an arch on the right, the Palais Pallavicini still seems to resound to Orson Welles' footsteps and the Harry Lime theme.

In all these places time seems to have stood still. Elsewhere, however, in the Café Zartl in the Rasumofskystrasse on a late winter's evening, or in the Gmoa Keller on the Heumarkt, smoky, shabby and run by two ancient Hungarian ladies whose wit, manners and charm, like their rooms, have remained unchanged for decades, one encounters a different Vienna. Beneath the appearance of gaiety among the habitués there is evidence of much hard work; beneath the superficial politeness there is much real courtesy; alongside the childishness, a great shrewdness and knowledge of mankind; and amid scepticism and carelessness, a fabulous wealth of talent.**99**

RICHARD BASSETT, *THE AUSTRIANS – STRANGE TALES FROM THE VIENNA WOODS*, FABER & FABER, LONDON, 1988

A FINAL WORD

The British television presenter and writer Alan Whicker sums up his impressions succinctly.

66The nostalgic city with a streak of gentle hopefulness, where Freud discovered sex. Baroque Vienna knows that an illusion which makes you happy is better than a reality which makes you sad.**99**

ALAN WHICKER, FROM *THE BEST OF EVERYTHING*, ED. WILLIAM DAVIS, LONDON, 1980

A journey
through Vienna

▲ The Prater, encircled by the Danube and the Danube Canal.

▼ The Danube Canal, alongside Morzinplatz...

▼ View of the 16th District (Ottakring).

...between the Salztorbrücke and Marienbrücke.

The *Café Sperl,* on Gumpendorfer Strasse.

The celebrated patisserie, *Demel,* on the Kohlmarkt.

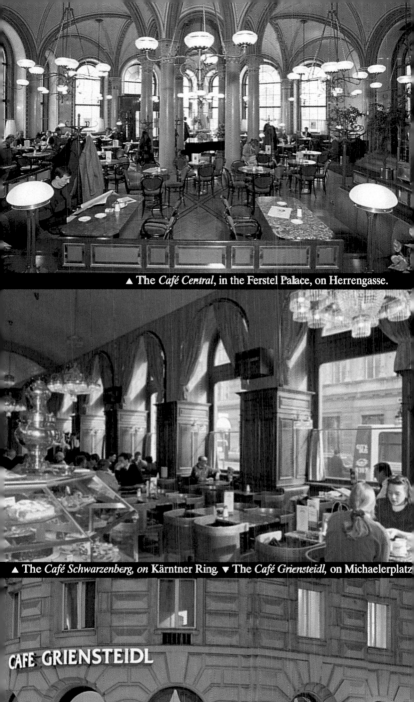

▲ The *Café Central*, in the Ferstel Palace, on Herrengasse.

▲ The *Café Schwarzenberg, on* Kärntner Ring. ▼ The *Café Griensteidl,* on Michaelerplatz

▲ The Lobau Park. ▼ TheTiergarten, a zoological garden in the Schönbrunn Park.

▼ The Augarten Palace and Gardens.

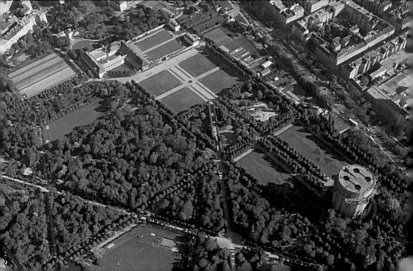

▲ The palace and the park of Schönbrunn, with the Naïad fountain in the center.

▲ The Belvedere Gardens. ▼ View of Schörbrunn Park to the west of the parterres.

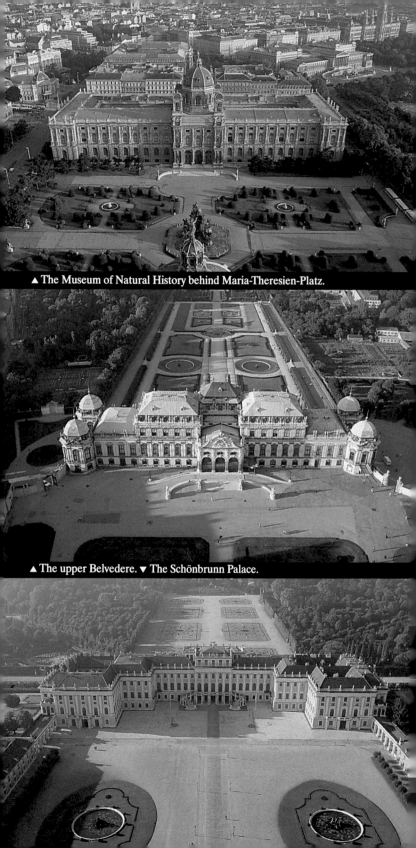

▲ The Museum of Natural History behind Maria-Theresien-Platz.

▲ The upper Belvedere. ▼ The Schönbrunn Palace.

THE CITY CENTER

THE SPIRE of ST STEPHEN'S CATHEDRAL
"When one sees Vienna from one of the hills adjoining the city, the Cathedral of St Stephen's appears to stand at its center, with buildings spreading in a circle about it. The spire of the cathedral is an indication of its majesty ... from this distance, wherefrom one may not discern either the city itself or the main body of the cathedral, the spire soars upward in one's sight like a blue shadow, a vague line drawn on the horizon, or a poplar at dusk."
Adalbert Stifter,
Vienna and the Viennese

STEPHANSDOM

St Stephen's Cathedral (Stephansdom) is at once the center of Vienna and its principal symbol. Its 390-foot spire is visible from all parts of the city and strikingly so from many miles away along the route of the old Budapest highway. The Viennese nickname for it is Stiffl, a diminutive of Stephan.
AN UNFINISHED MASTERPIECE. A 12th-century Romanesque basilica once stood on the site of the cathedral, built at the behest of the margraves of Babenberg ● 28 ● 302. After being ravaged by two fires, this basilica was completely rebuilt and consecrated in 1263 in the reign of Ottokar II of Bohemia. When the Habsburgs became Holy Roman Emperors in 1273 ● 29, Vienna – which already enjoyed the status of a free imperial city – aspired to become a bishopric. In anticipation of this, a worthy sanctuary was built, although Vienna did not get its bishop until the end of the 15th century. The first work on the cathedral was the construction of a Gothic choir, extending the old Romanesque basilica, between 1330 and 1339. The original church was demolished on the accession of Rudolph IV (1339–65), who was known as the founder because he financed the bulk of the new building. The only part that was preserved was the west façade (the Giant's Portal and the Pagans' Towers) which was framed by two Gothic chapels. The nave (1359) and the spire were built in the next century. Of the many architects and sculptors who took part in the construction of the cathedral, only those

🦥 Half a day

COLORED TILES.
Under restoration for
several years following
the 1945 fire, the high
roof of St Stephen's is
decorated with the
Habsburg emblem: a
two-headed eagle,
bearing the imperial
crown and a golden
fleece.

**A REMINDER OF THE
1451 CRUSADE
AGAINST THE TURKS**
From this pulpit,
overlooked by a statue
of St Francis
trampling on a Turk,
the Italian Franciscan
St John Capistrano
(1386–1458), apostolic
legate of Pope Nicolas
V in Bavaria, Silesia,
Poland and Austria,
called for the
Crusade.

involved in the final stages are remembered: Hans von
Prachatitz completed the spire in 1433 and Hans Puchsbaum
worked on the vaulting and the nave. The latter also
attempted to add a second tower to the cathedral, but at the
start of the 16th century the Viennese were concerned about a
threatened Turkish invasion and were keener to invest in
fortifications than in churches ▲ *198* . The north tower
remained unfinished and was crowned with a Renaissance
dome in 1578. In 1490, during the reign of Matthias Corvinus,
King of Hungary ● *29*, the roof was covered with diamond
patterns of polychrome tiles, and in 1511 the works were
finally considered finished. St Stephen's was bombarded by
the Turks in 1683 (a cannonball fired in that year may
still be seen lodged in the wall above the sacristy)
● *34*, and again by the French in 1809 ● *31*. But
neither of these sieges caused anything like the
catastrophic damage of 1945 ● *42*.

THE RIESENTOR. On the west façade, the two
PAGANS' TOWERS, (Heidentürme) which are the
only vestiges of the old Romanesque basilica, and
two GOTHIC CHAPELS with rose windows in a
delicate tracery of stone, frame the main entrance.
To enter the building you have to go through the
Giant's Portal (Riesentor) on the north side, so
called because the tibia of a mammoth dug up on
this spot when the cathedral was under construction
was thought at the time to be the shinbone of a
giant drowned during the Flood. The tympanum
over the portal and the columns on either side of
it are covered with Romanesque sculptures
representing Christ in glory, flanked by two
angels and surrounded by innumerable saints
and mythical creatures.

BISCHOFSTOR. If you walk round the
cathedral's north side, you pass in front of
the Bishop's Portal (Bischofstor), a Gothic
feature which for many years was the entrance
reserved for women. On the column is a statue
of the *Virgin in a Mantle*.

Interior of
St Stephen's
Cathedral.

**THE MIRACULOUS
ICON**
The icon of the Virgin
of Potsch, in Hungary,
hangs beneath a
marble baldachin
(right). Real tears are
said to have poured
from its eyes in 1696,
during Prince
Eugène's campaign
● *35,* ▲ *147, 247*
against the Turks.
Leopold I acquired
the icon in 1697.

THE ADLERTURM. Continue along the line of the builder's
lodgings to the Eagle's Tower (Adlerturm), or North Tower,
which is unfinished. Since 1957, this tower has served as the
belltower for the celebrated Pummerin ● *43* on special
occasions; for example, its chimes at midnight are the signal
for the New Year's celebrations to begin. At the foot of the
tower is a warren of catacombs containing the bones of many
thousands of Viennese. Most of these were originally buried
in the cemetery surrounding the cathedral, before this was put
out of commission in the 18th century.
THE DUCAL CRYPT. At the center of the catacombs is the Ducal
Crypt, set up here during the reign of Rudolph IV; this
contains several bronze caskets and urns filled with viscera of
many of the Habsburgs ● *29* ▲ *143, 144–5, 176, 280*. A
baldachin, attributed to the master Puchsbaum, arcs over the
EAGLE PORCH (Adlertor) or Tower Porch. In the Middle Ages,
anybody who grasped the sanctuary ring sealed into one of
the columns, through this act, automatically came under

church jurisdiction and could escape the officers of the civil law. On the far east side of the cathedral stands a statue of Christ known colloquially as "Our Lord of the Toothache".

THE SPIRE ★. On the south side one can climb up 418 steps inside the spire to a platform, which offers a magnificent view over the city. During the siege of 1683 ● *34*, the Count of Starhemberg watched the Turkish forces from this lookout and sent up his rockets to summon the King of Poland and the Duke of Lorraine.

SINGERTOR. The Singer's Portal (Singertor), which was for centuries the men's entrance to the cathedral, has a 14th-century tympanum decorated with sculptures that represent scenes from the life of St Paul. All around are Gothic statues of saints.

MEISTER PILGRAM'S PULPIT ★. The interior of the cathedral, with tall columns that support the transept's ogival vaulting, is planned as a Latin cross with three naves of equal size. The choir is lower than the main nave because it was built first, as an extension of the original Romanesque basilica. At first sight the Stephansdom appears to be a Gothic cathedral of great splendor. Then one begins to notice 17th-century Baroque additions, such as the altars backing on to the columns of the nave or nestling in side chapels, and above all the high altar: all are loaded with statues and ornamentation in colored marble. The principal attraction, on the left of the central nave, is a Gothic feature – the great pulpit sculpted in 1500 by the master stone-carver Anton Pilgram.

THE EMPEROR'S TOMB. Other marvels of Gothic sculpture may be seen all over the cathedral: the foot of the organ loft (by Pilgram) on the lower left-hand side of the nave; the *Wiener Neustädter Altar*, an altar screen from 1447 that shows the Virgin between St Catherine and St Barba, in the left-hand chapel of the choir; the tomb of Frederick III in the chapel to the right of the choir, designed by the late 15th-century sculptor Nicolas of Leyden, among others; and finally the fonts (1481) in the chapel of St Catherine at the foot of the spire. A Gothic stone baldachin to the right of the entrance shelters the *Virgin of Potsch* and a statue of the *Virgin, Patroness of Servant Girls*. This

statue is said to have come to the aid of a girl accused of stealing, by miraculously revealing the gem which her mistress had lost. Some of the medieval stained-glass windows were restored after World War Two and may now be seen in the collections of the choir (the remainder have been deposited in the Museum of Decorative Arts and the Vienna City Museum). They represent the Passion in a blaze of color dominated by red, yellow and green.

SELF-PORTRAITS
The man poking his head through the window of the pulpit

and the man at the foot of the organ (above) are both portraits of the Meister Pilgram, the sculptor, and carved by his own hand.

MEISTER PILGRAM'S PULPIT
In Vienna during the 16th century, the Gothic style was in its last flamboyant stage prior to the Renaissance; the sculptor decorated his pulpit with rosettes, perforated balustrades and ornaments in the form of stalactites, flames and foliage. The salamanders and toads pursuing one another along the hand rail symbolize good driving out evil.

135

"At the Stefankirche, in the stone, there are lodged cannonballs fired by the Turks during the siege of Vienna; there is also the cage in which pagan idols were imprisoned, and the chapel of the Black Madonna where our servants go to pray; I prayed there too; I felt the soul of a chambermaid within me...**"**

Paul Morand,
Fleur-du-Ciel

"DER MOOR"
The *Moor* marks the site of the former grocery store *Meinl* on St Stephen's Square. A bank of the same name has replaced the store (which has its shop-front on the Kohlmarkt ▲ *158*). Nevertheless the statue has been left in place.

THE DIKES
The Graben, which today is a long, very elegant square, was originally no more than a deep dike (*Graben*) which was a part of the fortifications of the Roman camp of Vindobona. This small settlement extended into a rectangle enclosed by the Danube to the north, the Ottakring River to the northwest (now filled in), the Graben to the south, and another dike (which passed across the cathedral site) to the east. In the Middle Ages, Vienna spread beyond the limits of the original camp. In 1255 all the dikes were filled in, including the Graben, which became a fairground.

STEPHANSPLATZ ★

In the Middle Ages the immediate vicinity of the cathedral was crammed with houses and street vendors, with a cemetery occupying what little space remained. At the close of the 18th century, after several epidemics of the plague, it was feared that the corpses buried so hastily there were a breeding ground for disease, so the cemetery was cleared and the bones transferred into the cathedral catacombs. The area was laid out as Stephansplatz and is now a pedestrian precinct.

VIRGILKAPELLE. The 13th-century Virgilkapelle was unearthed during the construction of the metro in the 1970's and 1980's. The remains of it are displayed behind a large plate-glass window inside the Stephansplatz metro station (in the 1st District).

ERZBISCHÖFLICHES PALACE. Directly on the square is the episcopal palace, housing the CATHEDRAL AND DIOCESAN MUSEUM (Dom- und Diozesanmuseum). The cathedral treasure is on display here (notably the reliquary of St Andrew, a reliquary cross dating from the 14th century, a Carolingian version of the Gospels, and an 18th-century monstrance), along with religious sculptures dating from the Middle Ages to the 19th century.

ST MARY MAGDALENE
This chapel on the south side of the
square was used for funeral
ceremonies; it was destroyed by fire in
1781. Its floor plan is commemorated
today with lines of red paving stones.

STOCK-IM-EISEN-PLATZ

This small square at the junction of Stephansplatz, the
Graben and the Kärntnerstrasse is in a way an antechamber
to the many pedestrian streets in this area. It owes its name to
the "post set in iron" into which apprentice locksmiths
traditionally drove a nail on their way through Vienna while
touring the area.
THE HAAS HAUS. When it opened in 1990, this shopping
center designed by Hans Hollein ● 94 caused a scandal
because of its total lack of harmony with the cathedral.
Nevertheless from the DOME BAR inside it there is a superb
view of the cathedral and Stephansplatz from above.

THE GRABEN

**MODERN DESIGN AND
OLD GOTHIC**
The Haas Haus
shopping center,
covered in plate glass,
never fails to make an
impact.

The Graben and Stephansplatz together form a right angle,
with Stock-im-Eisen-Platz at its junction. Since the filling of
the dike (Graben), every form of trade has been pursued
here, especially prostitution: in the 18th century the "nymphs
of the Graben" were a notorious feature of Vienna. The
Habsburg court ▲ 144 organized major entertainments here,
since the Graben was one of the most attractive open
spaces in the inner city. Today, at the least sign of
sunshine, café tables ● 66 invade the square. The Graben
also boasts a string of luxury stores; all in all it is one of
Vienna's most elegant thoroughfares and a favorite haunt
of window-shoppers. Many of the Graben boutiques
are designed by famous architects – for example,
the *Knize* clothes shop (1913) is by Adolf Loos
● 86, 91, ▲ 236, 287 and the
Schullin jewelry shop
(1982) is by Hans
Hollein.

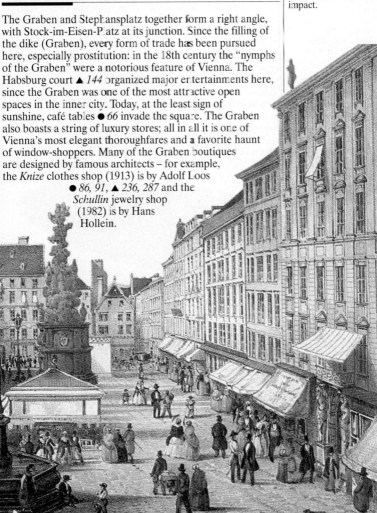

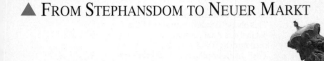

LEOPOLDSBRUNNEN AND JOSEPHS-BRUNNEN. The statue of Margrave Leopold (1096–1136, right) dominates the Fountain of St Leopold ● 46 , as does Joseph the fountain bearing his name. Both fountains have lions' masks (above) and stand beside the Graben.

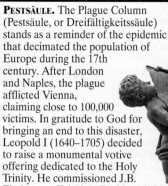

PESTSÄULE. The Plague Column (Pestsäule, or Dreifältigkeitssäule) stands as a reminder of the epidemic that decimated the population of Europe during the 17th century. After London and Naples, the plague afflicted Vienna, claiming close to 100,000 victims. In gratitude to God for bringing an end to this disaster, Leopold I (1640–1705) decided to raise a monumental votive offering dedicated to the Holy Trinity. He commissioned J.B. Fischer von Erlach ● 74, 80, ▲ 147 in 1686; von Erlach had just returned from Rome, where he had been influenced by the Baroque sculptor Borromini, a rival of Bernini. The scrolls of sculpture winding upward around the column show the figure of the emperor on his knees before the Trinity; the ragged crone being thrust down to Hell by an angel symbolizes the plague. To one side of the column stands a statue of St Leopold, the patron saint of Lower Austria.

OTTO WAGNER – EARLY WORK. Most of the buildings along the Graben belong to the 1900 style; two of them, however, stand out as examples of Otto Wagner's early work ● 86, ▲ 228, 233, 237, 294. Between 1870 and 1880 Wagner was influenced by neo-Renaissance architecture, and at this time he tried his hand at the neo-classical GRABENHOF (nos. 14–15)

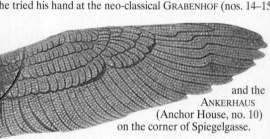

and the ANKERHAUS (Anchor House, no. 10) on the corner of Spiegelgasse.

SPIEGELGASSE

Number 9 Spiegelgasse was the house of Franz von Schobert, where he lodged his friend Franz Schubert ● 50, ▲ 166, 227, 262. Schubert composed his *Unfinished Symphony* (No. 8) here in 1822, completing only two movements.

DOROTHEERGASSE

This street leading into the Graben is the preserve of Vienna's antique dealers; it is also the site of the DOROTHEUM, an auction house with several rooms, open daily. In the same street is the CAFÉ HAWELKA ★, formerly a well-known meeting-place for the intelligentsia ● 67, which is now jammed with students until 2am. This is where Vienna's artists come for their coffee at opening time every morning.

CAFÉ LEOPOLD HAWELKA

> "IN THE MIDDLE STANDS A MCNUMENTAL COLUMN THAT LOOKS
> VERY MUCH LIKE A DICE TUMBLER."
>
> GÉRARD DE NERVAL

TUCHLAUBEN

During the 1980's, when the house at no. 19 Tuchlauben (Drapers' Street) was being restored, a series of FRESCOES was discovered under a layer of rendering. Originally painted at the behest of a wealthy 15th-century draper, Michael Menschein, these frescoes are clearly inspired by the work of Neidhart von Reuenthal (1190–1241), who introduced themes from country life into the medieval poetry of courtly love and chivalry (*Minnesang*). The house at no. 13 Naglergasse is decorated with an 18th-century bas-relief of *The Crowning of the Virgin*.

IN DIESEM HAUSE WOHNTE IM JAHRE 1840
CONRADIN KREUTZER
(1780 – 1849)
KOMPONIST UND KAPELLMEISTER
AM KARNTNERTOR-THEATER
GESTIFTET VON DR.H. SCHINDLER
FREIBURG(BREISGAU) 1968

PETERSKIRCHE ★

On the cramped ST PETER'S SQUARE (Petersplatz), set back from the Graben, stands the church of the same name (Peterskirche) which, for lack of horizontal space, was constructed mainly skyward. The entrance is a fine Baroque porch by Andreas Altomonte. The oval dome is well lit by eight large windows, decorated with a fresco of the Assumption by Johann Michael Rottmayr ▲ 293, and the altarpiece of the second chapel to the right is dedicated to St Francis de Sales. On the left of the choir, the Baroque pulpit designed by Matthias Steinl matches a Baroque ornamental altar by the sculptor Lorenzo Mattielli which is dedicated to St John Nepomuceno, confessor of the Queen of Bohemia, who was martyred in 1393 for refusing to betray his oath of confession to Wenceslas IV.

THE CHOIR. The choir with its trompe l'oeil dome was decorated by Antonio Galli-Bibiena. The high altar, by Santino Busti, has a screen by Martino Attomonte and a painting by Leopold Kupelwieser, *The Immaculate Conception*. Above, the Habsburg eagle ▲ 144 rises over one of two balconies. According to tradition, Empress Sissi ▲ 143, 144, 178 used to come incognito to one of these balconies late at night to pray.

THE KREUTZER SONATA. In the Dorotheergasse there is a plaque to the violinist Rodolphe Kreutzer, to whom Beethoven dedicted his *Ninth Sonata For Piano and Violin*.

ENGEL-APOTHEKE A Jugendstil ● 86 fresco adorns the façade of the Angel Pharmacy on Bognergasse.

THE CHURCH OF ST PETER'S. It was built in the early 18th century by Gabriele Montani and Lukes von Hildebrandt ● 75, 81 on the site of the first church in Vienna (4th century) which was destroyed by fire.

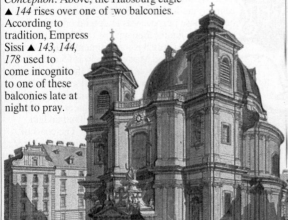

Kärntnerstrasse has a casino, a series of bookshops, travel agencies and souvenir shops (one of which sells *Sachertorte* ▲ *141*, ◆ *324*).

THE ORDER OF ST JOHN OF MALTA
In 1530, Charles V ceded the island of Malta to the Knights of St John in perpetuity. The Saracens and Turks had driven the Knights successively from Jerusalem, Acre, Cyprus (12th–13th centuries) and Rhodes (1522).

THE FLEDERMAUS CABARET
Built during the Secession period ● *86*, ▲ *232*, this cabaret is named after the operetta *Die Fledermaus* (1874) by Strauss the Younger ● *56*, a work popular with the Viennese.

HALLOWED RELICS.
The curious reliquaries on the altars on either side of the choir contain the skeletons of saints martyred at Rome – in particular that of St Benedict – covered in spangles and false precious stones. During the Counter Reformation, Baroque art ● *74, 82* was used as a weapon against heresy; the relics of saints, usually decorated and displayed as in this church, were also pressed into service for the cause.

KÄRNTNERSTRASSE ★

The pedestrian Kärntnerstrasse (Carinthia Street) in the center of the inner city is one of the two liveliest shopping streets in Vienna. The other is the Graben. People linger here throughout the day, to stare at the window displays and the street performers and sip coffee on the café terraces. The bustle continues at night, long after the smart shops, restaurants and terrace cafés have closed.

MALTESERKIRCHE. On the left going down Kärntnerstrasse from St Stephen's Cathedral toward the Ring stands the church of the Order of St John or the Knights of Malta (Malteserkirche), a Gothic building given a neo-classical façade during the 19th century. Founded in Jerusalem at the time of the Crusades, this order of hospitalers was originally intended to look after pilgrims during their sojourn in the Holy Land. In the 12th century, the Knights of St John became a military order whose purpose was to defend pilgrims, first against the Arabs, then against the Turks. Inside their Vienna Church is a monument to Jean de la Valette, the Grand Master who in 1565 defended Malta from the fleet of Suleyman the Magnificent; thereafter Malta remained the order's head-quarters until 1793. It is no accident that this great victory is commemorated in Vienna, seeing that in 1529 the forces of the selfsame sultan had laid siege to the capital of Austria ● *34*. The coats of arms of most of the families belonging to the order hang in the Malteserkirche. Just before the street joins the Ring ▲ *197* it is entered from the right by Philharmonikerstrasse, the street containing the State Opera ● *59* ▲ *223* and the *Sacher Hotel*.

THE "SACHER" HOTEL. The *Sacher* has been a Viennese institution since its founding in 1876 ● *66*, when its plush salons became the haunt of men of letters such as Arthur Schnitzler ▲ *141* ◆ *324*; since then it has been a favorite of the world's celebrities, royalty, diplomats and musicians. Many of the *Sacher*'s famous guests have sampled the celebrated *Sachertorte*, a recipe which was invented during the Congress of Vienna (1814–15) by an anonymous chef. Anna Sacher, the widow of the hotel's founder, was the first to serve this dish to her clients at the end of the 19th century. Among the latter were the *Sacherbuben*, hard-up members of good Viennese families who came to the hotel not so much for the *Torte* as for the cash loans extended to them by Frau Sacher, who eventually became the city's principal moneylender.

NEUER MARKT ★

The Neuer Markt (New Market Square) is linked to Kärntnerstrasse by Donnergasse. Its name is no longer

appropriate, since the flour market which was opened there in the 13th century has long ceased to exist. Nevertheless the Neuer Markt is one of the city's finest squares, today congested with traffic.
DONNERBRUNNEN. In the middle of this square is Vienna's most graceful fountain, the Donnerbrunnen. It owes its name to the sculptor Georg Raphael Donner ▲ *170, 256, 304*, who designed it at the beginning of the 18th century; the statue of Providence on a plinth crowded with putti is its principal feature. Allegories representing each of the four tributaries of the Danube in Austria (the Traun, the Enns, the Ybbs and the March) used to stand at the fountain's corners. Maria Theresa thought the statues immodest, so they were removed. In the 19th century the Donner pieces, which had been cast in lead, were replaced by bronze copies. (The originals are now displayed in the Museum of Baroque Art ▲ *256* in the lower Belvedere.) A number of fine buildings stand around the square: at no. 18, the 18th-century Baroque façade of the former RAUCHMILLER PALACE can be seen, while nos. 10 and 11, festooned with floral reliefs,

MARCO D'AVIANO
In a niche of the façade of the Capuchin Church is a statue of the Capuchin Marco D'Aviano, papal legate to the army of Charles of Lorraine. It was he who celebrated mass at the top of Mount Kahlenberg on the morning of the battle against the Turks.

A SHAMELESS STATUE
To revenge himself on an erstwhile patron, Donner had one of his statues display its buttocks in front of his window!

THE TOMBS OF ELIZABETH-CHRISTINE AND CHARLES VI (detail) The tombs of both Maria Theresa and her father were sculpted by Balthasar Ferdinand Moll. Notice the crowned death's heads on the corners.

FRANZ-JOSEPH
"The Emperor was an old man. He was the oldest emperor in the world. Around him, death had cut circle after circle and swathe after swathe. Already the field was entirely bare and only the Emperor still stood, like a forgotten stalk, waiting. For many years his clear, hard eyes had been trained on the vague distance. His pate was bald like a desert. His side-whiskers were as white as two snowy wings. The lines in his face were an impenetrable undergrowth in which the years nestled by the score."
Joseph Roth,
The Radetsky March

have an overhanging triangular projection). No. 2 was the lodging of Joseph Haydn ● *49*, ▲ *152, 162, 164* from 1795 to 1796, when he is supposed to have composed the quartet which was later to become the anthem of Imperial Austria.
AMERICAN BAR. On the north side of the Neuer Markt is the Kärntnerdurchgang, which overlooks the Kärntnerstrasse and the Seilergasse. This shopping street contains the *American Bar,* a jewel of modern architecture designed by Adolf Loos ● *86, 91*, ▲ *137, 174, 236, 287* in 1908 and a classified historical monument since 1959. Today it is a private club.
KAPUZINERKIRCHE. The Church of the Capuchins (Kapuzinerkirche), which fronts on to the Neuer Markt, is not much to look at, though the aesthetics of this 17th-century church do succeed in reflecting the outlook of the mendicant Capuchins, which was closely akin to that of the Franciscans. Indeed it was the rigorous austerity of the Kapuzinerkirche which led Emperor Matthias (1557–1619) and Empress Anne to select it as the Habsburg crypt. Members of the family have been buried here since 1633.
KAPUZINERGRUFT. About ten emperors, fifteen empresses and a hundred archdukes lie in the imperial vault (Kaisergruft) of the Capuchin crypt (Kapuzinergruft). Before each funeral, it was customary for the heart of the deceased to be taken out, placed in a casket and carried to the crypt of the Church of the Augustines, while the remaining viscera were moved to the crypt of St Stephen's Cathedral ▲ *132*. The official ceremonies only began after the body had been dressed in state robes, laid in a coffin and covered with flowers. The coffin would be displayed in the Assumption Chapel of the Palace so the public could pay its last respects (this was notably the case for the "Aiglon"▲ *283*, son of Napoleon, and for Archduke Rudolph ◆ *323*). Then came the full state funeral at St Stephen's Cathedral, with the coffin finally coming to rest in the crypt of that cathedral, after the father superior had asked it the question: "Who art thou? Who asks to be admitted here?" The Great Chamberlain would reply, "I am His Majesty the Emperor of Austria, King of Hungary." "I know him not. Who asks to be admitted here?" "I am the Emperor Franz-Joseph, Apostolic King of Hungary, King of Bohemia, King of Jerusalem, Prince of Transylvania, Grand Duke of Tuscany

and Cracow, Duke of Lorraine..." "I know him not. Who asks to be admitted here?" And at this point the Great Chamberlain knelt and answered humbly. "I am Franz-Joseph, a poor sinner, and I implore the Mercy of Our Lord God." "Then thou mayst enter."

MARIA-THERESIA-GRUFT. The imperial burial vault is made up of ten underground halls. In the first, which is the smallest, lie Emperor Matthias and the Empress Anne. Throughout these rooms, which are laid out in chronological order, there is a noteworthy contrast between the more lavish tombs and the simpler ones. The tomb of Maria Theresa (1717–80) and of her husband Francis of Lorraine (1708–65) ● *36*, designed by Balthasar Ferdinand Moll, is in the form of a huge state bed on which the two sovereigns are stretched out face-to-face. In addition to its generally Baroque style, this tomb is decorated with a series of bas-reliefs representing the coronation of the imperial couple. The tomb of Joseph II is in simple but direct contrast to that of his parents.

A GUEST FROM OUTSIDE THE FAMILY. Although she was not of royal blood, Countess Fuchs-Mollardt was buried in the imperial vault because of her friendship with Maria Theresia, whose governess she had been. Marshal Radetsky nearly – but not quite – attained a similar honor at the request of Franz-Joseph, who greatly admired his achievements.

ABSENT HABSBURGS. All the Habsburgs ● *29*, ▲ *144-5, 176, 280* before Matthias were buried in places other than Vienna; most notably Charles V (1500–58) is interred at the Escorial in Spain. Among the other absentees are Marie-Antoinette, the wife of Louis XVI (who was buried on the spot in Paris after her execution), Napoleon's son, the "Aiglon" (the Germans transferred his ashes to the Invalides in Paris in 1940), the Archduke Ferdinand and his wife, and finally Charles I (who is buried at Funchal, Madeira).

The tombs of Joseph I, Ferdinand and Charles VI (top). An early 19th-century engraving (above).

THE HABSBURG PANTHEON
In the crypt are buried Marie-Louise, Empress of the French, her nephew Franz-Joseph and Empress Elizabeth ● *119*, ▲ *144, 178* (left), in mourning for her son Rudolph whose death mask is shown (above). Maximilian I of Mexico lies in the "new crypt". Like the tomb of Empress Sissi, this is permanently covered in flowers in the national colors of Hungary (green, white and red).

SALVATOR. The Archduke Salvator, nephew of Franz-Joseph, disappeared on his way to South America after breaking with his family and taking the name of Johann Orth in order to marry a girl from the Viennese bourgeoisie.

Guillotined in 1793, Marie-Antoinette, the daughter of Maria Theresa, was the first member of the Austrian royal family to come to a tragic end. A century later, misfortune seemed to afflict the last of the Habsburgs and their relatives, confirming Franz-Joseph's bitter comment "I have been spared nothing". By the end of his reign, in 1916 during World War One, the Emperor was living as a virtual recluse in his apartments at the Hofburg and Schönbrunn. It is said that when a member of the Habsburgs was approaching his end a woman in white – the White Lady of the Habsburgs – appeared.

FRANZ-JOSEPH (1830–1916) AND ARCHDUKE OTTO (1912)
The 68-year reign of Franz-Joseph ● *41*, ▲ *142, 178* saw the change from absolute monarchy to a parliamentary system. His great-nephew Charles I (1887–1922), the last Emperor of Austria, succeeded him from 1916 to 1918. Then in 1919, Charles went into exile in Switzerland. After two attempts to return he was banished to Madeira, where he died of tuberculosis.

ELIZABETH (1837–98)
The Empress Elizabeth ▲ *142, 178*, who married Franz-Joseph in 1854, turned the court of Vienna into one of the most brilliant in Europe; but later she suffered from mental disorders after a series of bereavements. She traveled widely and, during a tour of Switzerland she was stabbed to death by Italian anarchist, Luigi Luchini.

MAXIMILIAN I (1832–67)
This archduke, the younger brother of Franz-Joseph, became Emperor of Mexico and was shot by part sans led by Benito Juárez in 1867. His wife Carlotta, daughter of Leopold I, King of the Belgians, subsequently went mad.

FRANZ-FERDINAND (1863–1914)
On June 28, 1914, the assassination of Archduke Franz-Ferdinand (the nephew of Franz-Joseph and heir to his throne since the death of Rudolf, and his wife Sophie in Sarajevo was the event that sparked off World War One.

FRANZ-FERDINAND'S TUNIC
The Army Museum ▲ 258 still displays the Archduke's bloodstained jacket (below).

RUDOLPH (1858–89)
In 1889, Archduke Rudolph, heir to the throne of Austria-Hungary, killed his mistress Marie Vetsera and himself at the hunting lodge of Mayerling, south of Vienna. This episode has been a favorite topic for literature and the press ever since. The coffin of Marie Vetsera was later stolen from the convent which Franz-Joseph had built for it at Mayerling.

THE DAUPHIN'S PARTING FROM HIS FAMILY, JULY 3, 1793
Louis XVII, Duke of Normandy, the second son of Louis XVI and Marie-Antoinette, became Dauphin (heir to the French throne) on the death of his older brother in 1789. He was locked up in the Temple prison after the King's execution and died of scrofula on June 8, 1795.

"Annakirche in the Snow". A painting (right) by Hanz Götzinger (1914).

"All of Austria, complete with the problems and contradictions which went unresolved until the collapse of 1918, is reflected in the work of Grillparzer, in his sensitivity and creative power.**"**
Claudio Magris,
Le Mythe et l'Empire

The Blue Carp
The Blue Carp House (*Haus zum blauen Karpfen*, above) at no. 14 is one of the most singular buildings in Annagasse. The early 19th-century façade is decorated with frescoes and bas-reliefs, one of which represents a blue carp.

Annagasse

Lavish palaces. Leading eastward from halfway along the Kärntnerstrasse, St Anne's Street (Annagasse) has a number of fine buildings. Most notable are the Esterházy Palace ▲ *162* (no. 2) built in the 17th century and restored in the 18th; the Kremsmünsterhof (no. 4) with its elegant 17th-century façade; the Baroque Herzogenburgerhof (no. 6); the Deybelhof, or Täuberlhof (no. 8), built in the 18th century to plans by Hildebrandt ● *75, 81*, ▲ *147, 247*; the 19th-century Haus zum blauen Karpfen (Blue Carp House, no. 14); and the Roman Emperor's House (no. 18).

Annakirche. The Annakirche ● *76*, a French parish church belonging to the congregation of lay brothers of St Francis de Sales, faces on to Annagasse. The building was constructed in the 15th century, and rebuilt in the Baroque style during the 18th century. The ceiling inside is decorated with a series of frescoes by Daniel Gran (1694–1757). Also look for the sculpted 15th-century group representing St Anne with the Virgin and Child, attributed to Veit Stoss (1448–1533), as well as the Baroque reliquary which is said to contain the hand of the saint.

JOHANNESGASSE

URSULINENKIRCHE UND KLOSTER

Johannesgasse runs parallel to Annagasse; on it stands the church and convent of the Ursulines (Ursulinenkirche und Kloster), built in the 18th century by the Ursuline teaching order which was then established in about thirty countries. According to legend, their patroness, St Ursula, went to Cologne accompanied by eleven thousand virgins and was martyred there by the Huns who sacked the town because she had refused to marry their king. In one wing of the church there is a small MUSEUM OF RELIGIOUS FOLK ART.

IN JOHANNESGASSE. Opposite, at no. 15, stands the FOUNDATION FOR NOBLE LADIES (Savoyisches Damenstift). The IMPERIAL HOUSEHOLD RECORDS OFFICE (Hofkammerarchiv) is at no. 16; stretching back in the direction of Annagasse, this building's two wings date from the 18th and 19th centuries respectively. Franz Grillparzer was its director at one time. Near the Kärntnerstrasse is the QUESTENBERG-KAUNITZ PALACE, built in the 18th century, which was the residence of the brilliant French diplomat Talleyrand.

HIMMELPFORTGASSE

PRINCE EUGÈNE'S WINTER PALACE ★. This palace dominates Himmelpfortgasse, a small street running parallel to Johannesgasse. The conqueror of the Turks ● 34 built himself several palaces in Vienna (most notably the Belvedere ▲ 246) which he filled with works of art. The prince used the greatest architects of his time, Johann Bernhard Fischer von Erlach and Johann Lukas von Hildebrandt, and did much to foster the rivalry between these two. For instance, Fischer von Erlach worked on the Winter Palace from 1697 to 1698 and Hildebrandt took over from 1702 to 1724. The former ● 74, 80, ▲ 138, 155, 164, 169, 275, 302 was responsible for the FORMAL STAIRCASE, which is remarkable for its Atlas figures acting as caryatids, and the FOUNTAIN OF HERCULES on the landing. Hildebrandt gave fluidity to the façade with a system of fluted pilasters. Prince Eugène died in this palace in 1736; since 1848 it has been occupied by the Ministry of Finance.

THE ERODÖDY-FÜRSTENBERG PALACE. Opposite Prince Eugène's Winter Palace is the Baroque Erodödy-Fürstenberg Palace, whose early 18th-century façade has a magnificent portal ornamented with atlantes.

RAUHENSTEINGASSE

MOZART'S DEATH. In 1847 a new building replaced the dwelling at no. 8 Rauhensteingasse where the debt-ridden Mozart ● 48, 110 ▲ 150, 281 had moved on his return from

FRANZ GRILLPARZER
The son of a Viennese lawyer, Franz Grillparzer (1791–1872) is considered Austria's greatest playwright. His plays feature figures from classical antiquity such as Sappho, Medea and Leander, as well as Libuse, the founder of the city of Prague. A room at the Imperial Household Records Office is devoted to Grillparzer, who was its director from 1832 to 1856.

"I have reached the end before I could use my talent to the full. Life has been so beautiful, my career began under such happy auspices ... yet no-one can alter his own destiny. One must resign oneself to whatever shall be, for that is the will of Providence. So I am completing my song of mourning, which I must not leave unfinished behind me."

Mozart, September 1791

Mozart and Beethoven. The only meeting between the two geniuses took place in the house on Rauhensteingasse: at the time Beethoven ● 50 was seventeen and Mozart was thirty-one. Mozart singled out the younger man, telling his friends to "Watch that one; one day he will set the world talking about him".

Franciscan Church This was built between 1603 and 1611 in South German Renaissance style.

Prague in 1787. It was here that he composed many of his greatest masterpieces, notably *Don Giovanni, Cosi fan tutte, The Magic Flute* and the *Requiem*, which was unfinished at the time of his death. Mozart's star was on the rise until 1788, with the support of Joseph II himself; but after that date things grew increasingly difficult for him financially. Mozart was only thirty-five in November 1791 when he was forced to

take to his bed with a high fever; by the 28th his condition was desperate, and he died on the night of 4th to 5th December. On the following day the undertakers carried his coffin to the entrance of the cathedral catacombs for a final blessing ▲ *134*, and thence to St Mark's cemetery ▲ *262*.

Ballgasse. A small alley, the Ballgasse, leads through a vaulted passage from midway along Rauhensteingasse to Franziskanerplatz.

Franziskanerplatz ★

The Moses Fountain. This pretty square has its own little church and fountain, as well as a number of fine old houses. The Fountain of Moses was designed by Johann Martin Fischer in 1798.

Detail of
the Fountain of
Moses.

FRANZISKANERKIRCHE. The Franciscan Church of St Jerome
(Sankt Hieronymus, or Franziskanerkirche ● 74) belonged to
the Order of St Francis and was the only place of worship in
Vienna to receive a Renaissance façade at the beginning of
the 17th century. The Baroque interior includes a fine
high altar (1707) by Andrea Pozzo and an organ (1643)
sculpted by J. Wöckerd.

"KLEINES CAFÉ". Although it was built in the 1970's, the Art
Deco *Kleines Café* (Little Café) on the square has nothing
jarring in its décor. It was designed in retro style by the
architect Hermann Czech.

SINGERSTRASSE

BAROQUE PALACES. North of Franziskanerplatz is
Singerstrasse, a long thoroughfare which comes out at Stock-
im-Eisen-Platz ▲ 137. In this street are the ROTTAL PALACE
(no. 17–19), built according to plans by Hildebrandt, which is
now the PUBLIC DEBT BANK; and the NEPAUER-BREUNER
PALACE (no. 16, below), likewise an 18th-century building,
with a monumental doorway held up by figures of Atlas.

THE TEUTONIC ORDER IN VIENNA. The order of Teutonic
Knights (Deutschorden) moved in the 14th century into a
cluster of houses which included the Gothic Church of St
Elizabeth. Originally an order of hospitalers, the Order's
history dates back to the earliest crusades and it had its
first base in the Holy Land at Acre. Later it became a
military organization which fought against the Muslims.
By the 13th century the Grand Master was no longer
resident in the Holy Land but at Marienburg in Poland,
from where he launched a crusade in central Europe.
This campaign enabled the Order to colonize Prussia,
Lithuania and Estonia, to such effect that by the 14th
century they ruled over a sovereign state with about
twenty provinces.

SCHATZKAMMER DES DEUTSCHEN ORDENS. Several rooms
within
the Order's
headquarters are
used to display its
treasures
(Schatzkammer des
Deutschen Ordens).
These consist of
coins, medals, and
the rings and chains
of the grand masters, as well as sundry ceremonial swords,
holy objects, clocks and astronomers' instruments. These
relics commemorate some great stages in the history of the
Teutonic Knights, who were a major power in northern
Europe during the Middle Ages. But their war with Poland,
which allied itself with the aristocracy and bourgeoisie of the
Prussian cities to thwart the Knights' growing influence, led to
the Order's destruction during the 15th century.

DEUTSCHORDENSKIRCHE SANKT ELIZABETH. Built in the
Gothic style during the 14th century and altered to some
extent in the 18th century, the Church of Saint Elizabeth
(Deutschordenskirche Sankt Elizabeth) possesses a fine 16th-
century Dutch altarpiece. Mozart ● 48, ▲ 147, 150, 262, 281

DEUTSCHORDEN
Sergei Eisenstein's
film *Aleksandr Nevsky*
(1938, below)
presents the Teutonic
Knights as fanatical
soldier-monks.

In reality, the work of
Germanization
undertaken by the
Teutonic Order
eclipsed the influence
of the Orthodox
Russian religion.
Ultimately, the states
of northern Europe
united against them.
After a series of
military disasters in
the 15th century and
the secularizations of
the 16th century, the
Order forfeited all its
territories and fell
back on its hospital
vocation. In 1809 the
Order was dissolved
by Bonaparte, but was
resurrected in Austria
in 1840; since 1929 it
has been limited to
charitable functions.

149

Plaque on the Figarohaus.

The Figarohaus.

lived in one of the Order's houses during one of his periods in Vienna, in the spring of 1781. Maria Theresa *36*, ▲ *158, 291* had just died and the Prince-Archbishop of Salzburg, Colloredo, had brought the Mozart family to Vienna for her funeral. At the same time Mozart's *Idomeneo*, written in Munich in January 1781, received acclaim in Vienna. A plaque commemorates the composer's brief residence here.

DOMGASSE

Blutgasse leads off Singerstrasse to the narrow Domgasse (Cathedral Street), which continues to Schulerstrasse in the vicinity of St Stephen's Square ▲ *132, 136*.

FIGAROHAUS ★. Mozart moved to no. 5 Domgasse in the autumn of 1784. There he composed chamber music with his friends including Haydn ● *48*, and at the end of 1785 he worked on one of his greatest operas, *The Marriage of Figaro*, with a libretto by Lorenzo da Ponte (1749–1838) who had already written the text for *Cosi fan tutte*. The *Marriage* was only a qualified success in Vienna, where it opened in May 1786, but it triumphed at Prague in the following year, when Mozart was given a hero's welcome on arriving to conduct it. On his return to Vienna, however, Mozart found himself heavily in debt and was obliged to move from his fine house on Domgasse to much more modest lodgings on Rauhensteingasse ▲ *147*. Today there is a museum at no. 5 Domgasse (the only one of Mozart's various residences to have survived). The house is known as the Figarohaus, and has a collection of objects, paintings and musical scores that belonged to the composer.

HAUS "ZUM ROTEN KREUTZ". Vienna's first café opened in 1683 at no. 6 Domgasse ● *66*. Rebuilt in the 18th century, this building now bears the insignia of the Red Cross (Haus *zum roten Kreutz*).

FÜRSTENBERG PALACE. On the corner of Domgasse and Grünangergasse stands the 18th-century Fürstenberg Palace, with its magnificent façade and imposing sculpted staircase. The small streets in the vicinity of the cathedral are connected by a warren of underground passages, some of which contain shops and restaurants.

BÄCKERSTRASSE ★

After two shopping streets – Schulerstrasse (which owes its name either to a school for jurists established here in 1389, or to St Stephen's School, founded in 1237) and Wollzeile – one

FIGLMÜLLER

reaches Bäckerstrasse (Baker Street). Here there are several places of interest, notably the courtyard of the SCHWANENFELD HOUSE (no. 7). Opposite stands the 18th-century SEILERN PALACE (no. 8), where Madame de Staël (1766–1817), author of the essay *On Germany* and a precursor of Romanticism in France, stayed in 1808. Farther along is the ALT WIEN café. Bäckerstrasse has several popular cafés, in particular OSWALD & KALB, and the KIX, decorated with work by contemporary artists.

ALTE UNIVERSITÄT. At its western end, Bäckerstrasse looks on to LUGECKPLATZ, where there is a statue by Gutenberg and several pleasant cafés and restaurants are sited, and to ROTENTURMSTRASSE, a major shopping street. At its other end it leads into DR-IGNAZ-SEIPEL-PLATZ, where the Alte Universität used to be. This building was reconstructed during the reign of Maria Theresa ● *36* by the French architect Nicolas Jadot de Ville-Issey (1753–5), who was brought here from Lunéville by Francis of Lorraine ▲ *280*. Under Ferdinand (1847) ● *41* the building became the seat of the

ACADEMY OF SCIENCES (Akademie der Wissenschaften). **JESUITENKIRCHE.** In front of the academy stands the Jesuit Church (known as Jesuitenkirche or Universitätskirche) ● *77*. Ferdinand II gave this order a monopoly on the teaching of philosophy and theology in the university, a task it fulfilled until Maria Theresa's reforms in

"**FIGLMÜLLER**"
This inn, located in a passage at the beginning of Bäckerstrasse, takes pride in its *Wiener Schnitzels*, reputedly the largest in Vienna.

THE SCHWANENFELD HOUSE
The courtyard of this house, which is surrounded by galleries and arcades, is the only Renaissance construction of its type in Vienna. The rarity of Renaissance architecture is attributable to the Turkish threat: for several decades, any spare money was spent on ramparts. F. von Amerling, the 19th-century Habsburg portraitist, lived in this house, which now contains a collection of wrought ironwork; the best pieces may be seen in the courtyard.

Robert Schumann

THE ACADEMY OF SCIENCES
The old university building (the Academy of Sciences since 1847) has an imposing Baroque façade and a huge hall, in which a number of great composers (among them Beethoven ● *50* and Haydn ● *48*) played their own compositions.

1761 ▲ *291*. Built in the 17th century by an anonymous architect, it looks rather dreary from the outside, but the Baroque interior is magnificent, devised in the early 18th century by the Italian Andrea Pozzo (1642–1709). Pozzo, a Jesuit lay brother, was a great painter who specialized in Baroque trompe l'oeil frescoes, with which he decorated the ceilings of many Italian churches (notably the one at San Ignatius, in Rome). While in Vienna, he worked on the Liechtenstein Palace, now the Museum of Modern Art, at no. 9 Fürstengasse ▲ *292*, and on the ceiling of the Jesuit Church, where the trompe l'œil cupola is a major achievement. Don't miss the magnificent PULPIT OF TRUTH, which is encrusted with mother-of-pearl and decorated with encrustation of Baroque sculpture.

POSTGASSE

DOMINIKANERKIRCHE UND KLOSTER.
Beyond the Jesuit Church is the Postgasse, site of the Dominican monastery and church (Dominikanerkirche und Kloster). This church, also known as the Rosary Basilica, is built on the foundations of

Violine.

several earlier sanctuaries, the first of which was constructed by the Dominicans in 1237. Destroyed by fire, this was replaced by a Gothic church, which was in turn demolished during the siege of 1529 ● *34.* Today's Baroque church dates from the 17th century and is inspired by Roman

HAYDN AND "THE CREATION"
The oratorio *The Creation* was included in the last concert attended by Haydn. It was played in the old university's great hall on March 27, 1808, a year before the composer's death. Aged sixty-seven and unable to move, Haydn went to the event in a wheelchair and was greeted with drum rolls and a blare of trumpets by his many admirers and pupils, among them Princess Esterházy. Overwhelmed, he was obliged to leave the hall before the end of the concert: it was the old master's final public appearance. He died on May 31, 1809, a few days before the French army entered Vienna ● *32, 38*.

SCHUMANN IN VIENNA
Robert Schumann (1810–56) stayed in Vienna on two occasions, in 1838 and 1846. Clara, his wife, had learned the piano there, and Robert was looking for a publisher for his review *Die neue Zeitschrift für Musik*. Vienna inspired the composer, even though he disapproved of the city's moral climate and felt that the Viennese did not understand his music.

styles. The frescoes of the ceiling in the nave are by Matthias Rauchmiller. The CHAPEL OF ST THOMAS AQUINAS has an altarpiece dating from 1638.

SANKT BARBARA KIRCHE. The small 17th-century Ukrainian church of St Barbara has an interesting collection of old icons.

SCHÖNLATERNGASSE ★

This street, which begins opposite the Dominican church, owes its name to the lantern on the front of the HOUSE OF THE BEAUTIFUL LANTERN (Haus zur schönen Laterne) at no. 6 (this is a copy; the original was long ago moved to a museum).

HEILIGENKREUZERHOF. At no. 5, a covered passage leads through to a courtyard (Heiligenkreuzerhof) surrounded by buildings

belonging to the monastery of Heiligenkreuz to the southwest of Vienna. Constructed in the middle of the 17th century and restored in the 18th, this complex includes the abbot's residence, the monks' lodgings and the CHAPEL OF ST BERNARD, whose Baroque interior is decorated with an altarpiece by Martino Altomonte (1657–1745).

BASILISKENHAUS. The Basiliskenhaus, at no. 7, is a 13th-century bakery; it is easily recognizable by a sandstone block which resembles the mythical basilisk.

ALTE SCHMIEDE. The composer Robert Schumann (1810–56) lived in the house next door, at no. 7a. On the same street are the museum of wrought iron (Alte Schmiede, no. 9) and the *WUNDER BAR* (1976). Schönlaterngasse leads back to SONNENFELSGASSE, a street full of cafés ● 66.

FLEISCHMARKT ★

Via the Meat Market (Fleischmarkt), a street that was formerly the center of the butchers' district, one reaches the extreme north side of the inner city (Innerstadt). This is very much a night-time district, peopled by young Viennese and foreign tourists. Known as the 'Bermuda Triangle', it lies between the Danube Canal, the

THE BASILISK
This mythical animal, believed to emerge from a serpent's egg hatched by a toad, could kill with a single glance. The basilisk poisoned a well with its breath and was slain by an intrepid baker, who held up a mirror to it.

"DER LIEBER AUGUSTIN"
*"O, du lieber Augustin,
's Geld is hin,
's Mensch is hin,
O, du lieber Augustin,
alles is hin!"*
("Oh, my darling Augustin, there's no money, there are no more people, Oh my darling Augustin, there's nothing more!"). This song, written in 1679 at the height of the plague epidemic, gave courage to the sick and to the survivors. In the song, Augustin gets drunk and falls into a mass grave, but he is so sodden with alcohol that he is safe from infection. The melody was later borrowed by Mozart and Schönberg (*Second Quartet*).

THE BISHOP OF SALZBURG. Ruprecht, the patron saint of Bavaria (650–718), was Bishop of Worms in Germany before coming to Salzburg where he founded the Abbey of St Peter. Vienna's oldest church is dedicated to him.

Church of Our Lady and Franziskanerplatz. The more fashionable restaurants here tend to be grouped around Ruprechtskirche and the synagogue.

GRIECHENKIRCHE. The Greek Orthodox Church of St George on the Fleischmarkt is of greater interest for its religious ceremonies than for its architecture, which is an amalgam of the 18th and 19th centuries. The orthodox services here are very beautiful, with the priest in his miter and brocaded chasuble, the clouds of incense, the deep-voiced choir, and the icons glimmering in the candlelight.

"GRIECHENBEISL". Formerly a haunt of such luminaries as Mark Twain, Johannes Brahms ● *51*, Johann Strauss ● *56* and Franz Grillparzer ▲ *147*, the *Greek Tavern* (*Greichenbeisl*) next to the Greek Orthodox Church is best known for the legendary piper, hero and composer of the folk song *Der Lieber Augustin*, who is commemorated on its façade.

RUPRECHTSKIRCHE. Built on a former defensive bastion, the Church of St Rupert (Ruprechtskirche) ● *75* overlooks Franz-Joseph Wharf ▲ *200, 229, 230* and the Danube Canal ▲ *229*. It is the oldest religious edifice in Vienna, reputedly founded in 740, at which time the site lay just to the north of the Roman camp of Vindobona. A Romanesque church was later constructed on the ruins of the original chapel in the

12th century. More changes were made in the 13th and 15th centuries, and today the Ruprechtskirche's only authentic Romanesque elements are its nave and the base of its belltower. This is traditionally the French parish church in Vienna; inside, above the choir, there is a 13th-century window, and above the altar stands a statue of the Black Virgin who protected the Viennese from invading Turks and the ravages of the plague.

A REMINDER OF THE GREAT SIEGE
This plaque retains three cannonballs fired into the city by its Turkish besiegers ● 34. There are similar grim mementos all over Vienna. A cannonball may still be seen embedded in the façade of St Stephen's Cathedral.

THE HOHER MARKT ★

The Hoher Markt is Vienna's oldest marketplace and was originally the forum of the Roman camp of Vindobona. It is very probable that Marcus Aurelius died here of plague in 180 AD (facing no. 6 in nearby MARC AUREL STRASSE there is a statue of this emperor, who was a friend of Seneca and celebrated for his own philosophical writings). Roman remains have been excavated here (access is by way of no. 3); these consist of the ruins of two houses occupied by Roman officers belonging to the garrison of Vindobona in the first centuries AD. During the ascendancy of the Babenbergs, and later under the Habsburgs in the Middle Ages, the Hoher Markt was used for public executions (hangings) and for the markets after which it is named.

VERMÄHLUNGSBRUNNEN. The sinister tools of torture that used to stand here have today given way to much pleasanter monuments to look at. Leopold I (1640–1705) prayed that his son, the future Joseph I, should return safe and sound from the siege of Landau in 1702; when this prayer was granted, the emperor commissioned a first votive column of wood (Josephssäule), which was raised in the center of the square by J. B. Fischer von Ehrlach ● 74, 80, ▲ 138, 147, 164, 169, 302, in 1706. This was replaced in 1732 by the Betrothal Fountain (Vermählungsbrunnen), also known as Joseph's column, in marble and bronze, which was created by Fischer von Erlach's son, Josef Emanuel ● 74, 80, ▲ 302, and sculpted by the Italian Antonio Corradini.

ANKERUHR ★. The anchor clock (Ankeruhr) by Franz von Matsch, which has long adorned the headquarters of the insurance company of the same name, somehow survived the bombardment of the square in 1945 ● 42. On the stroke of every hour, one of a number of different figurines appears: Marcus Aurelius, Charlemagne, Maria Theresa, Rudolph I

THE HOHER MARKT
The gallows remained in the Hoher Markt until the beginning of the 18th century, and the pillory until the 19th. The latter was used to punish bad bakers, who were locked in an iron cage and dunked three times in the Danube.

155

Detail of the synagogue's exterior.

THEODOR HERZL
As correspondent of the liberal newspaper *Neue Freie Presse*, Theodor Herzl (1860–1904) attended the trial of Dreyfus in Paris. Shocked by the injustice of the verdict, he began to call for the foundation of a Jewish state in Palestine. Initially he was ridiculed, but in time he was able to organize the first Zionist congress at Basel in 1897. There he predicted the foundation of a Jewish state within the next half century.

He was only off by one year: the state of Israel came into being in 1948.

Walter von der Vogelweide and Prince Eugène are some of them. At noon, the whole cast troops forth. A scene from the film *The Third Man* ● *42*, ▲ *192, 267* was set at the foot of this celebrated clock.

Beyond the Hoher Markt

To the north of the square, one can make one's way back along Judengasse to Ruprechtskirche. Heading eastward, one reaches the huge Rotenturmstrasse which leads to St Stephen's Cathedral ▲ *132*. To the west of the square, Tuchlaubengasse leads to the Graben ▲ *137*.

SYNAGOGUE. The quiet synagogue in Seitenstettengasse obeys to the letter the rules established by Joseph II in his Edict of Toleration (1781) that all non-Catholic denominations could practice freely, provided that they did not flaunt their differences. Outwardly similar to any other ordinary building, the great synagogue was able to survive the Fascist pogroms of the post-Anschluss years ● *42*, during which the forty-odd other Jewish temples in Vienna were systematically burned to the ground. Inside, a small JEWISH MUSEUM (Judenmuseum) has been set up.

THE JEWS IN VIENNA. The Jews were tolerated by the Habsburgs through to the end of the 19th century. At the beginning of Franz-Joseph's reign, new laws were passed to suppress all discrimination against them. Policies of economic liberalism after 1860, coupled with the growth of the empire, created a need for capital; moreover a number of official projects, including the grandiose new building projects on the Ring ▲ *197,* required heavy financing. The crucial rôle played in this by the bourgeois Jewish families of Vienna led the emperor to ennoble some of them; but the stock exchange collapse of 1873 brought about a wave of anti-Semitism and certain politicians (notably the mayor of Vienna, Karl Lueger ● *87,* ▲ *227,* founder of the Social Democratic Party, and Georg von Schönerer, the Pan-Germanist and nationalist) used this sentiment as a vehicle to power. Ultimately, it was an Austrian who had lived in Vienna, Adolf Hitler, who committed the ultimate outrage. Of Vienna's two hundred thousand Jews, a quarter emigrated and most of the remainder eventually perished in death camps.

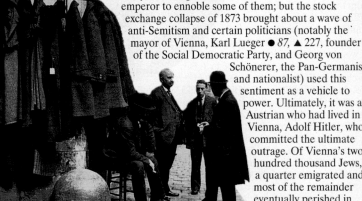

> "THE BAROQUE, IMPERIAL POMP OF VIENNA COMES LESS
> FROM THE EXALTATION OF POWER THAN FROM
> AWARENESS OF ITS INSTABILITY."
>
> GUY HOCQUENGHEM

BAROQUE CARYATIDS AND FIGURES OF ATLAS
"To be worthy of the Ring, a building had to display all the caryatids and other figures, all the urns, and all the motifs and small embellishments imaginable, in the decoration of its façade. As to the government buildings, these outclassed the private ones in their sheer opulence and in the proliferation of their styles."

George Clare,
The Last Waltz in Vienna

✻ Half a day

THE LAST ROMANTIC
As a Prussian high
official, Joseph von
Eichendorff
(1788–1857) visited
Vienna several times,
where his literary
talents were much
admired. Known as
"the last Romantic
knight", he
approached nature as
a mystical theme.

For many years the
Sacher Hotel ● 66,
▲ 140 and the *Café
Demel* have been
disputing the right to
sell the *Original
Sachertorte*, *Demel*
maintaining that the
chef who invented it
left the *Sacher* to
work for *Demel*. The
Fellini window at
Demel
(below).

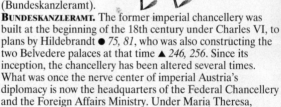

KOHLMARKT

Kohlmarkt is one of the most elegant
streets in Vienna. *Kohl* means cabbage, and
Kohle, coal, but since its recent restoration
there is no sign of either cabbage or
anthracite. There are only the façades of
noble buildings and a line of shop windows,
with the white-and-gold imperial palace
(Hofburg) in the background.
"CAFÉ DEMEL" ★. At the Hofburg ▲ 173
end of Kohlmarkt is *Café Demel*, a tearoom
and supplier of confectionery to the
imperial court for more than two centuries.
Founded in 1785 and taken over by
Christoph Demel in 1857, this is one of
Vienna's major gastronomic institutions
● 66, ◆ 324. The waitresses wear black and
white uniforms and address clients in the
third person as they bring them delicious
pastries on beautiful china.
THONET. Farther along on the same side of
the street is the Thonet furniture
manufacturer's shop. The *Café Central*
● 66 ▲ 160 is furnished
throughout by Thonet.

BALLHAUSPLATZ

West of the Hofburg is the
Ballhausplatz, dominated
by the Federal Chancellery
(Bundeskanzleramt).

BUNDESKANZLERAMT. The former imperial chancellery was
built at the beginning of the 18th century under Charles VI, to
plans by Hildebrandt ● 75, 81, who was also constructing the
two Belvedere palaces at that time ▲ 246, 256. Since its
inception, the chancellery has been altered several times.
What was once the nerve center of imperial Austria's
diplomacy is now the headquarters of the Federal Chancellery
and the Foreign Affairs Ministry. Under Maria Theresa,
Chancellor Kaunitz ● 37, worked here to upset the European
alliances and gain the friendship of France, Austria's
traditional foe. This change enabled Maria Theresa ● 36
▲ 291 to wage the Seven Years' War (1756–63) against
Prussia and marry her daughter Marie-Antoinette to the
future King of France, Louis XVI, in 1770. Kaunitz also
served Joseph II and Leopold II. Participants in the
Congress of Vienna ● 38 at the time of Prince
Metternich met in the building. Finally, on February
25, 1934, four years before the Anschluss ● 44 which
united Austria and Germany, Chancellor Dollfuss
was assassinated here.

HERRENGASSE

This street owes its name to the many fine
houses lining it, all of which were built by
members of the Lower Austrian aristocracy

THONET
WIEN.

Over forty million copies of Thonet's bistro chair have been sold worldwide. Michael Thonet (1796–1871), a native of the Rhineland, discovered a process for bending beechwood and created his first chair patterns in 1841. Thonet arrived in Vienna in 1842 and was immediately successful; his arrival coincided with the height of the Biedermeier period ● *62* when Viennese taste was for simple and comfortable furniture.

(Herren) who wished to set themselves up in palaces close to the Hofburg. From St Michael's Square ▲ *174* to the Freyung, Herrengasse boasts every style of Austrian architecture from the Renaissance to our own time.

THE WILCZEK AND MODENA PALACES. The Wilczek Palace, at no. 5, was built in the early 18th century to plans by Anton Ospel; between 1810 and 1812 it was the home of the German Romantic poet Joseph von Eichendorff (1788–1857) and from 1812 to 1813, that of the Austrian playwright Franz Grillparzer ▲ *147*, who was working at the imperial court library at the time. The Modena Palace at no. 7 was rebuilt in 1811 and is now the Interior Ministry.

NIEDERÖSTERREICHISCHES LANDESMUSEUM. Built at the end of the 17th century, the MOLLARD-CLARY PALACE at no. 9 has been converted into the Lower Austria State Museum (Niederösterreichisches Landesmuseum). The collections on the first and second floors are devoted to prehistory, natural science and the traditions of Lower Austria. On the third floor, several rooms have been transformed into a GALLERY OF AUSTRIAN ART. Here are displays of a number of fine altarpieces and Gothic wood carvings, some Baroque works by Maulbertsch, Altomonte and Rottmayr ▲ *139, 293*, and several paintings by Oskar Kokoschka ▲ *254*.

THE MURDER OF DOLLFUSS
Engelbert Dollfuss (1892–1934) became Chancellor of Austria

in 1932; National Socialists favoring Anschluss with Germany arranged his assassination.

159

THE FAÇADE OF THE FERSTEL PALACE
The Ferstel Palace was built in the mid-19th century by Heinrich von Ferstel (architect of the Votive Church) combining Romanesque and Renaissance elements.

VIENNA SEES RED
"...that morning Franz Tunda appeared on the crowded, sunny side of the Graben in the same clothes he had worn at the Moscow consulate, causing a sensation. He looked exactly like what a chemist (standing in the doorway of his odorous shop) described as a 'bolshevik'."
Joseph Roth,
The Endless Flight

LANDHAUS. The façade of no. 13, the Liechtenstein Palace (one of several of the same name in Vienna ▲ *161, 292*) is decorated with half a dozen pilasters; the building was formerly the seat of the Diet of Lower Austria. Today, it is the headquarters of the administration of Lower Austria and has retained its title of Landhaus. Originally built in the 16th century with funds contributed by the nobility, it was entirely reconstructed between 1837 and 1848 by Aloïs Pichl. Concerts were given here by Beethoven, Schubert and Liszt, and several important political events took place here: for example the riot preceding the 1848 revolution ● *40* began in the courtyard, while the main hall was the scene of the proclamation of the Republic on October 21, 1918, following the abdication of Charles I ● *33*, ▲ *144, 180*.

FERSTEL PALACE ★. This palace, with a labyrinthine interior of staircases and corridors, was once the site of the Vienna Stock Exchange and the headquarters of the Bank of Austria. It has now been beautifully renovated and serves as a conference center, with one or two high-class shops.

"CAFÉ CENTRAL". You can reach the magnificent *Café Central* ● *66* (left) through the corridors of the Ferstel Palace, or by way of the Herrengasse. The café has been a meeting place for Viennese intellectuals for more than 100 years. Stefan Zweig used to come here to meet his friends, among them the exiled revolutionary Lev Davidovitch Bronstein, otherwise known as Leon Trotsky.

PORCIA PALACE. Among Vienna's many Baroque and neo-classical palaces, the Porcia Palace at no. 23 stands out as a building from an earlier age. It was constructed around 1646.

PREMONITION
"Who will make the Russian revolution? Herr Bronstein at the *Café Central*, perhaps?", wrote a diplomat in the margin of a dispatch announcing the 1917 Soviet Revolution.

BANKGASSE

BAROQUE PALACES ★. Bankgasse, a narrow street running off Herrengasse, contains several fine Baroque palaces ● *80, 82*. These include the BATTHYANY PALACE (no. 2) built at the close of the 17th century in the style of J. B. Fischer von Erlach ● *74, 80, 138, 147* and the joined TRAUTSON and

CENTRAL

GASSE ECKE STRAUCHGASSE
W. PRÜCKEL.

STRATTMANN-WINDISCHGRÄTZ PALACES (at nos. 4 and 6), redesigned by von Erlach's rival, Johann Lukas von Hildebrandt ● 75, 81, ▲ 147, 247. The latter palaces were formerly occupied by the chancellery of the Kingdom of Hungary, and now house the Hungarian Embassy.

STADTPALAIS LIECHTENSTEIN. Right at the end of the street, near the Volksgarten and the Burgtheater ▲ 204 stands one of the many residences which the princes of Liechtenstein (a small state which Charles VI created as a principality in 1719) built for themselves in Vienna: this one is a winter palace constructed between 1694 and 1706. Like the Liechtenstein summer palace ▲ 292 of the same date, it was built by Domenico Martinelli (1650–1718) and modeled on the Baroque palaces of Italy. The pilasters and statues of the majestic façade are particularly striking.

MINORITENPLATZ

MINORITENKIRCHE. In the center of Minoritenplatz stands the Church of the Minor Friars, the first order founded by St Francis of Assisi (1182–1226). The original monastery was destroyed at the beginning of the 20th century to make way for the ARCHIVE BUILDING at no. 1. Flanked by a small bellturret, the triangular façade has a broad entrance embellished by a handsome Gothic sculpture of *The Crucifixion*, by a Franciscan friar, Jacques de Paris. At the rear of the church, several apses are clustered around the high octagonal tower (right), which is as slender as a chimneystack.

"THE LAST SUPPER". The principal curiosity of this church is a mosaic of twelve massive blocks which reproduces Leonardo da Vinci's *Last Supper* at Milan. This is the work of Giacomo Raffaelli; it was commissioned by Napoleon Bonaparte, who wished to take the original back to the Louvre, leaving this copy in Milan as a replacement. Bonaparte fell before this scheme could be carried out; and the mosaic was bought by the Austrian government, which

PORTAL OF THE MINORITENKIRCHE
This church was originally a chapel, built shortly after the death of St Francis. Later destroyed by fire, it was rebuilt in the Gothic style during the 14th century and altered several times in later years as a result of damage caused by the Turks ● 34. Every rebuilding was done in the spirit of the original Gothic style.

METASTASIO
Pietro Trapassi, known as Metastasio (1698–1782), was a native of Rome who made his name in Naples, where he wrote the texts of ariettas, melodramas, oratorios and cantatas for musicians. In Vienna he wrote a number of melodramas using themes from antiquity; some served later as librettos for opera composers.

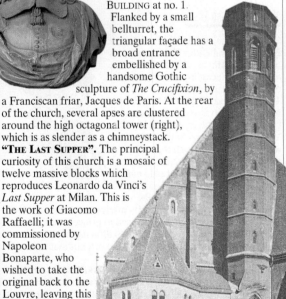

The Esterházy Palace.

NICHOLAS THE MAGNIFICENT
(1765–1833)
The Hungarian prince Nicolas II Esterházy ● *49* (below) was made an imperial marshal in 1770. He was a lover of luxury and the arts, who preferred his country castle of Eisenstadt, a copy of Versailles, to Vienna.

had it transferred to the Minoritenkirche in the mid-19th century. Note also the tomb of the Italian poet Pietro Trapassi (known as Metastasio, 1698–1782) and Rosselino's 18th-century bas-relief of the *Virgin*. The success of Metastasio's *Dido Abandoned* (1724) brought him to the attention of Charles VI, who invited him to his Viennese court. In 1750, the Italian met Joseph Haydn ● *49*, then living in the same building.

THE DIETRICHSTEIN AND STARHEMBERG PALACES. Also on Minoritenplatz are the 17th-century Dietrichstein Palace (no. 3) altered in the 18th century, and (no. 5) the 17th-century residence (also renovated) of Count Ernst Rüdiger Starhemberg, Vienna's defender in 1683 ▲ *31*.

WALLNERSTRASSE

Wallnerstrasse, which begins at the Kohlmarkt and enters Herrengasse near the Landhaus, can also boast some fine palaces; in particular those of the Esterházy clan.

THE ESTERHÁZY PALACE. The palace at no. 2 Wallnerstrasse was the second built by the Esterházy princes in Vienna, after that of Annagasse ▲ *142*. Imposing though they are, the two buildings cannot compare in magnificence with the castle built in the late 18th century at Lake Neusiedl ■ *24* by Prince Nicolas Esterházy. After distinguishing themselves in the war against the Turks, the Esterházys were raised to princely rank following the siege of Vienna ● *34*. Skillful diplomats and military leaders, the Esterházys lived in ostentatious luxury in times of peace.

JOSEPH HAYDN
(1732–1809, right)
"Here I am now in my desert, abandoned like a poor orphan, almost without the company of human beings, full of precious memories of days past – alas, long past! And who knows when they will return?. ... Here at Estoras, nobody asks me 'Would you like some chocolate? With or without milk? Coffee, perhaps? Black coffee or café Liegois? What can I offer you, my dear Haydn? Would you care for an ice-cream? Vanilla or pineapple?' "
Letter from Joseph Haydn

HAYDN IN THE SERVICE OF THE ESTERHÁZYS. The Esterházys were great lovers and patrons of music, as well as of architecture. Musical performances were always an important feature at the lavish entertainments held at their palaces. They maintained a private orchestra, which was led by Joseph Haydn from 1762 to 1790, the year of his death. The great musician suffered agonies of boredom at the Esterházy country residence at Eisenstadt and longed for his employers to return to Vienna, where he could be reunited with his pupils, and his friends and admirers. Among his friends was Mozart ● *48, 110* ▲ *147, 281*, twenty-four years his junior; and among his pupils was the young Beethoven ● *51*, ▲ *262, 298*.

> "ONE DAY IN THE THIRTY-FOURTH YEAR OF MY VAGABOND EXISTENCE, I WAS SITTING AT THE CAFÉ CENTRAL IN HERRENGASSE IN VIENNA, IN ONE OF THOSE GILDED CHAIRS IN THE ENGLISH STYLE."
>
> PETER ALTENBERG

THE CAPRARA-GEYMÜLLER PALACE. On the same side of the street as the Esterházy Palace stands the 17th-century Caprara-Geymüller Palace, altered in the 18th century, which has a fine Baroque doorway framed by two figures of Atlas ● 82, ▲ 157. After the Treaty of Campo Formio (1797) which ended Bonaparte's Italian campaign against the Austrians, the Directoire government in France installed General Bernadotte (1763–1844) in this palace as ambassador. (Jean Bernadotte, a sergeant under Louis XVI, became an imperial marshal under Napoleon and ended his life as King of Sweden.) On his arrival in April 1798, the new ambassador raised a Revolutionary tricolor flag on the building so huge that it hung to the ground; the Viennese, who were still smarting from Austria's defeats in Italy and from the execution of Marie-Antoinette, immediately tore it down, and Bernadotte left the city in disgrace. The small street linking Wallnerstrasse to Herrengasse is called Flag Street (Fahnengasse).

FREYUNG

This triangular-shaped square is one of the biggest in Vienna, along with the Graben ▲ 137, Am Hof ▲ 166 and Hoher Markt ▲ 155. Its name (*frei* means "free") evokes the right of asylum which was accorded strangers and thieves – but not to other criminals – who took refuge in the Scottish convent.
AUSTRIABRUNNEN. In the middle of the square is the Austria Fountain (1846), made by the German Ludwig Schwanthaler. Its various sculptures represent the principal rivers which crossed the Austrian Empire: the Elbe, the Danube ● 20-1, ▲ 230, 271, the Vistula and the Po.
SCHOTTENKIRCHE. The buildings known respectively as the Scottish Church and the Scottish Monastery (Schottenkirche and Schottenstift) were actually founded by Irish Benedictine monks at the beginning of the 12th century. This confusion may be explained by the fact that the great Irish missionary organization founded by St Columba in the 6th century originated on the island of Iona off the northwest

THE AUSTRIA FOUNTAIN
Goethe's grand-daughter ▲ 222 is said to have posed for the statue of Austria (above). The story has it that the sculptor hid contraband tobacco in the fountain's hollow figures but arrived too late to remove it: so that it is there to this day!

The Freyung ● 96, painted by R. Bernt (1906).

163

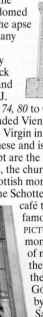

THE SCHOTTENSTIFT SCHOOL
"Whenever I meet a man with the slightly nasal, slightly snobbish accent of the old Schotten-gymnasium, I am rather attracted to him, in spite of myself."

Konrad Lorenz,
On Aggression

THE DEATH OF HAYDN
A mass was said on June 15, 1809, in memory of Haydn ● *49*, ▲ *152, 162*, who died on May 31 and was buried a few days later; Vienna, under siege by the French army, had just capitulated ● *38*. This event overshadowed the death of the great composer in the eyes of the Viennese, but the French remembered that Haydn had been a corresponding member of the Institut Français and insisted that homage be accorded him. As an officer with the French army, Henri Beyle (the future Stendhal) took part in the Austrian campaign and attended this memorial service, which inspired him to write one of his first literary works, *Letter on Haydn*, in 1814.

coast of Scotland. From Iona a large number of missionaries spread out all over Europe, including these Benedictines, who stopped a while at Ratisbon in Germany before being summoned to Vienna by the Babenberg Duke Henry II Jasomirgott. The religious buildings of the Schottenkirche started off in Romanesque style and were then altered in the 14th, 15th and 17th centuries to the Gothic and Baroque styles. With its white and yellow rendering, the church we see today seems very sober for a Baroque building, with the exception of the onion-domed belltower soaring over the apse ● *76*. Inside there are many handsome works of art, notably two 17th-century altarpieces by Tobias Pock and Joachim Sandrart, and a Baroque memorial by J. B. Fischer von Erlach ● *74, 80* to Count Rüdiger von Starhemberg, who defended Vienna against the Turks ● *31* ▲ *142*. The statue of the Virgin in the church is venerated as miraculous by the Viennese and is the oldest Madonna in the city (c. 1250). In the crypt are the tombs of Duke Henry II Jasomirgott and his wife, the church's founders.

SCHOTTENSTIFT. The Scottish monastery is laid out around a large shady courtyard, the Schottenhof, which is shared by café terraces, restaurants, and a famous private school. The PICTURE GALLERY in this monastery possesses a number of masterpieces ranging from the 15th to the 19th centuries; the star exhibit is a large GOTHIC ALTARPIECE painted by Tobias Pock and Joachim Sandrart at the end of the 15th century.

FRANZ LISZT'S HOUSE. The house in which the Hungarian musician Franz Liszt (1811–86) stayed when he visited Vienna for concerts and piano recitals also looks out onto the SCHOTTENHOF, which, like the Gothic-vaulted CAFÉ HAAG, is a real haven of peace.

THE DAUN-KINSKY PALACE. Johann Lukas von Hildebrandt ● *75, 81*, who was to build the Belvedere ▲ *246, 256* shortly afterward, constructed one of his most beautiful buildings, the Daun-Kinsky Palace, on the Freyung in 1716. The façade is particularly refined, with a multitude of decorated pilasters and statues in addition to windows with carefully sculpted pediments. The porch, which resembles a triumphal arch with its high columns and figures of atlantes ▲ 157, 163 leads through to an oval vestibule with a fine staircase and statues, and then to more courtyards.

THE HARRACH PALACE. On the corner of Freyung and the Herrengasse is the Ferstel Palace: next to it stands the Harrach Palace, which dates from the 17th century.

KUNST-FORUM. An extension of the Schottenkirche is the former monastery PRIORY built at the end of the 18th century; this is nicknamed the "commode" on account of its shape. Opposite stands the Kunst-Forum, a recently converted gallery which regularly stages exhibitions of contemporary art. Its décor is inspired by the Secession style ● 86, 88, ▲ 232.

RENNGASSE

THE BATTHYÁNY-SCHÖNBORN PALACE. In Renngasse, which begins between the "commode" and the Kunst-Forum, stands the handsome Batthyány-Schönborn Palace, converted by J. B. Fischer von Erlach ● 80, ▲ 147, 247. This mansion with its imposing sculpted façade used to be the Vienna residence of the great Hungarian Batthyány family, one of whose members, Charles-Joseph (1698–1772), served as a general under Prince Eugène ● 35, ▲ 147, 247 and subsequently commissioned this palace. Franz Schubert ● 50, ▲ 227 very rarely gave concerts, but one of them was at the former *Roman Emperor* Hotel across the street from the Batthyány-Schönborn Palace. Schubert, who was only twenty-one at the time, played the *Complaint of the Shepherd*, inspired by a text from Goethe.

HOHENSTAUFENGASSE. This street, which crosses the Renngasse, heads westward to the vicinity of the Stock Exchange ▲ 201, cutting across the Schottenring. The street contains two remarkable buildings: the LANDERBANK, built in 1882 by Otto Wagner ● 86, 88, ▲ 228, 237, 240, 294 and the LAW FACULTY (Juridicum), an imposing construction dating from the 1970's.

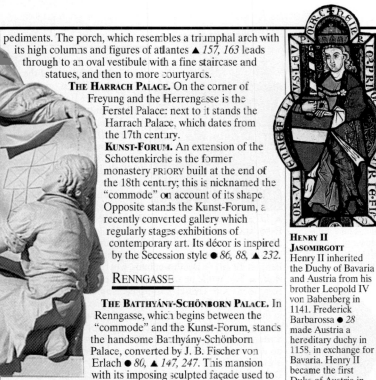

HENRY II JASOMIRGOTT
Henry II inherited the Duchy of Bavaria and Austria from his brother Leopold IV von Babenberg in 1141. Frederick Barbarossa ● 28 made Austria a hereditary duchy in 1158 in exchange for Bavaria. Henry II became the first Duke of Austria in 1156, and founded the Scottish monastery in the same year.

THE FREYUNG
Fêtes and popular entertainments were held on the Freyung ● 96, ▲ 163, as well as the executions of traitors, who were drowned face down in a barrel of water.

The Three Maidens
Schubert's love life was almost as enigmatic as Beethoven's. At the age of twenty he was smitten with a passion for Theresa Groger, the singer who performed his first lieder, but he finally lost her to a baker – probably because he was so poor. If Schubert had other loves, only his music speaks of them, and there is no evidence to suggest that he was an habitué of the House of the Three Maidens, as has been rumored.

Adalbert Stifter
(1805–68)
The painter and novelist Stifter's early education was at the monastery at Krems, in the mountains, which gave him a lasting love of nature. Much of his life was spent in Vienna, where he attended the university and later was a preceptor and adviser at court. After 1840 he wrote a number of stories (*The Great Woods...*) and novels (*St Martin's Summer, Witiko*) in which he described the natural beauty of Austria. They established him as one of the greatest writers in the German language. Marriage problems and the suicide of his adopted daughter darkened his last years; he killed himself in 1868.

Mölkerbastei

Melker Hof. The Melker Hof, the Vienna residence of the Abbots of Melk, is on Schottengasse. It was built in the 15th century and altered in the 18th, and includes a 16th-century CHAPEL adorned with frescoes by Johann Bergl ▲ *180, 278* and a painting by Kremser Schmidt. It also has a *Weinstube* which serves wines from Melk. Across the end of Schottengasse runs the Ring ▲ *202*, with the Schottentor at the intersection.

Pasqualatihaus ★. Dominating the Ring is the Mölkerbastei, a remnant of the old ramparts ▲ *198* which includes two or three outstanding buildings, especially the Pasqualatihaus or Beethovenhaus, where Beethoven lived ● *51*, ▲ *298*. While he was here (between 1804 and 1815) the composer wrote several masterpieces, among them the opera *Fidelio* and the *Fourth* and *Fifth Symphonies*. A small museum in this building displays scores, drawings and engravings from this period. Another major Viennese personality, Adalbert Stifter resided in the building after Beethoven; examples of his drawings and manuscripts are kept in a small separate museum.

Dreimäderlhaus. West of the Mölkerbastei, adjoining the Pasqualitihaus in the little Schreyvogelgasse, stands the handsome House of the Three Maidens (Dreimädlerhaus), a Biedermeier ● *62* building in the early 19th-century neo-Renaissance style. The windows of the façade are embellished with garlands, as is the doorway with its twin sculpted columns.

Am Hof

Am Hof is the largest square in central Vienna. This "Royal Court" square earned its name in the 12th century when the Eastern Marches (Ostmark) were transformed into the Duchy of Austria by Emperor Frederick Barbarossa ● *28*. When the first Duke, the Babenberg Henry II Jasomirgott, moved to Vienna ▲ *165* with his court, he constructed a palace on this square. Today there is no trace of the original Babenberg residence, even though extensive remains of the Roman camp that once stood here have been discovered in the course of archaeological excavations.

MARIENSÄULE AND KIRCHE AM HOF. In the center of the square is the Virgin's Pillar (Mariensäule), sculpted with small angels battling against the four scourges of mankind: the plague (a basilisk), heresy (a serpent), war (a lion) and famine (a dragon). The Kirche Am Hof, the great Church of the Nine Choirs of Angels (zu den neun Chören der Engel), dominates the square. Built by the Carmelites during the 14th and 15th centuries in the Gothic style, the church today has a Baroque façade heavily influenced by Rome. It was altered in the 17th century by the Italian architect Carlo Antonio Carlone ● 77 at the request of the Jesuits who eventually took it over from the Carmelites. Carlone belonged to a family of Genoese sculptors and painters who had worked on the decoration of several different churches in Rome (including the Gesú). Joseph II appeared on the balcony of this church to announce the end of the Holy Roman Empire in 1806 ● 38, ▲ 176, 179; he thus became the first hereditary Emperor of Austria, with the title of Joseph I. Inside the church the best features are a magnificent organ loft, some fine frescoes by Franz Anton Maulbertsch (1724–96), J. J. Daringer's altarpiece at the high altar, and the ceiling of the chapel of St Ignatius painted by the Italian Jesuit Andrea Pozzo (1642–1709) ▲ 149, 152, 292, who also decorated the Jesuit, or University Church.

COLLALTO PALACE. To the north of the Am Hof square, on the same side as the Kirche Am Hof and linked to it by a buttress stands the 17th–18th century Collalto Palace. Mozart held his first concert here in 1762, at the age of six ● 48, ▲ 147, 281.

BÜRGERLICHES ZEUGHAUS ★. This thoroughly eccentric, lavishly decorated fire station occupies the northwest corner of the square. The firemen based here are quartered in the old town arsenal (Bürgerliches Zeughaus), built in the 16th century and converted to the Baroque style ● 80, 82 by Anton Ospel at the beginning of the 18th century. Apart from the firemen's quarters and the fire-engine garage, the barracks contain an interesting FIREFIGHTING MUSEUM (Feuerwehr-museum).

ROMAN REMAINS. In the building next to the fire station (no. 9) one can see remains of the Roman camp of Vindobona, the original city of Vienna ● 29.

MÄRKLEINNISCHES HAUS. The original Babenberg castle was sited at what is now no. 7 Am Hof Square. After its demolition, the Märkleinnisches Haus was built here to plans by Johann Lukas von Hildebrandt ● 75, 81, ▲ 147, 247.

THE FIRE STATION
The Baroque-style fire station with a Greek pediment is decorated with sculptures by Lorenzo Mattielli.

MOZART AT THE COLLALTO PALACE
Leopold Mozart, father of Wolfgang, organized a European tour to "show the world a miracle". The little prodigy, Wolfgang Amadeus, left his native town of Salzburg with his sister Nannerl and his father in 1762. After passing through Ips, Passau and Linz, the Mozarts came to Vienna, where they gave a concert at the Collalto Palace and were received at Schönbrunn ▲ 274.

JUDENPLATZ
A long time before World War Two, Vienna's Jewish community had been subjected to a series of brutal pogroms. The pogrom of 1421 removed all the buildings formerly occupied by Jews – their shops, schools, synagogue and the rabbi's house – from the Judenplatz (right). This occurred during the reign of Archduke Albert V the Illustrious, Holy Roman Emperor and the first Habsburg to assume the crown of Hungary.

Another example of this architect's particular style can be seen at no. 12.

SCHULHOF

The tiny Schulhof square behind the Kirche Am Hof is connected to Am Hof square by a covered passageway.
OBIZZI PALACE. This superb 17th-century mansion takes up the whole south side of the square. A CLOCK MUSEUM (Uhrenmuseum) and more recently a DOLL AND TOY MUSEUM (Puppen- und Spielzeug-Museum ◆ *332*) have been established here. In the former, the entire recent history of the clock is recounted through a display that covers several floors. Among other things, you can see the old cathedral clock, a 17th-century astronomical wall clock, small traveling clocks, painted and automatic timepieces, cuckoo clocks, wristwatches and precious fob watches, and several chiming clocks.

BEYOND THE SCHULHOF. Vienna's oldest restaurant, the GOLDEN DRAGON (*Haus zum Güldenen Drachen*), has been at no. 4 Steindlgasse since the 16th century. Steindlgasse leads on to Tuchlauben and Milchgasse, which in turn leads to Peterskirche ▲ *139*. Kurrentgasse, a small street frequented by horse-drawn carriages and lined by 18th-century buildings, leads to the Judenplatz.

JUDENPLATZ

The Judenplatz is a small, narrow and particularly calm square that retains no traces of its days as the center of the Jewish ghetto.

"HE HAD A TASTE FOR JEWISH STORIES AND TOLD THEM WITH
WICKED GLEE. THE PREFECT DIDN'T UNDERSTAND THEM,
BUT STILL HE SAID:
'VERY GOOD, VERY GOOD INDEED!'" JOSEPH ROTH

HAUS ZUM GROSSEN JORDAN. To commemorate the
auto-da-fé that took place during the 1421 pogrom, a bas-
relief of the Baptism of Christ was carved on the House of the
Great Jordan (Haus zum grossen Jordan), a house built on
the ghetto ruins. At no. 8 stands the HOUSE OF THE TAILORS'
GUILD, while no. 11 is one of the façades of the former
Chancellery of Bohemia, the entrance to which is on
Wipplingerstrasse.

A house in
Kurrentgasse.

JORDANGASSE

The tiny Jordangasse connects
Judenplatz with Wipplingerstrasse.
The great Baroque architect Johann
Bernhard Fischer von Erlach ● 74, 80,
▲ 147, 155, 164, 169, 275, 302 died at
no. 5.

WIPPLINGERSTRASSE

EHEMALIGE BÖHMISCHE HOFKANZLEI★.
The former Chancellery of Bohemia
(Ehemalige Böhmische Hofkanzlei) at
no. 7 Wipplingerstrasse (built 1708–14)
was one of J.B. Fischer von Erlach's
major triumphs. After its enlargement
by Matthias Gerl in 1750, all that
remained of the original building was its
superb façade (1708) in a classical,
almost Palladian style interwoven with
French and Italian Baroque motifs.
ALTES RATHAUS. Facing the Bohemian Chancellery, the old
City Hall (Altes Rathaus) is yet another piece of magnificent
Baroque architecture. The original building here, which dated
from the Middle Ages, was given to the municipal authorities
by Frederick II the Handsome, Duke of
Austria (1286–1330), after it had been
confiscated from Otto Heims for his part in
the assassination plot against Albert I,
Duke Frederick's father. Reconstructed
at the beginning of the 18th century, the
Rathaus served as Vienna's City Hall
▲ 204 until 1883, when it was relocated
to a new building.
FREDERICK THE HANDSOME. Son of the
Habsburg Duke Albert I of Austria,
Frederick II the Handsome succeeded his
brother Rudolph II the Debonair in
1307. On the death of the Holy Roman
Emperor, Henry II of Luxembourg, in
1313, Frederick stood for election to his
throne, eventually resorting to arms to
defeat his rivals. He was finally defeated
at the battle of Mühldorf, where Ludwig IV
of Bavaria, who subsequently reigned as Emperor from 1314
to 1347, took him prisoner. After swearing on oath to cause
no more trouble, Frederick was reconciled with Ludwig, who
released him and even nominated him his deputy when he
went on a trip to Italy in 1326.

**TWO HOUSES
ASSOCIATED WITH
MOZART**
Mozart lived for a
time in nos. 3 and 4
Judenplatz: in the
former in 1783, a few
months after his
marriage to
Constanze Weber;
and in the latter from
1789 to 1790, the year
before his death ● 48,
▲ 110, 147, 281.

**THE BAPTISM OF
CHRIST**
(At no. 2 Judenplatz)
"By baptism in the
Jordan, the body is
washed clean of all
sin. Even secret
thoughts of sin
disappear. In 1421, a
thirst for vengeance
gripped the city, that
the Hebrew dogs
might expiate their
frightful crimes. Once
upon a time the world
was purified by the
flood: this time, the
evil was carried away
by fire."
Inscription on the
Haus zum grosse
Jordan

THE BOHEMIAN CHANCELLERY
J. B. Fischer von Erlach installed dozens of ornamental features on the façade of this building (at top), including statues (figures of Atlas on either side of doors and windows) and ironwork (a wrought iron balcony is located above the doorway). All the statuary is by Lorenzo Mattielli ● *80*.

THE OLD CITY HALL
The Altes Rathaus was built in 1699 by an unknown architect. The façade is in the style of J.B. Fischer von Erlach, with handsome doors framed by columns and allegorical figures of Justice and Bounty, by Johann Michael Fischer. These lead through to the courtyard (entrance at no. 8). A detail of the exterior is shown (right).

MUSEUM OF THE RESISTANCE. Several rooms inside the old City Hall are used as an archive center and record details of the Austrian resistance before and during World War Two. This museum sheds light on a number of little-known episodes in modern Austrian history. From 1934 onward, under the authoritarian rule of Engelbert Dollfuss and Kurt von Schuschnigg, numerous Austrians of every political and ethnic persuasion joined together to form a patriotic front, a kind of union against the German takeover of their country. It was this union that forced Schuschnigg to organize the referendum on Austrian independence, which enraged Hitler and led him to unleash "Operation Otto", the military invasion of Austria and the proclamation of the Anschluss in March 1938 ● *42*. During the war, the resistance went underground to organize acts of sabotage against the occupying Germans and guerrilla operations in the mountains of Styria, Carinthia, the Tyrol and Salzburg. With the help of Tito's Yugoslav partisans, they fought tenaciously against the divisions of the German "SS" and at the end of the war took possession of most of Austria's cities (with the exception of Vienna, which was occupied by the Soviet Army), thus thwarting the scorched-earth tactics of the SS. Nevertheless Austria paid a heavy price during the war: 3,000 resistance members were executed, 17,000 Austrians were taken hostage or killed in Gestapo prisons across Europe, and 140,000 others, particularly Jews, perished in concentration camps. If the total is taken to include all the soldiers who were killed fighting for the Wehrmacht and the large numbers of civilians killed by bombs, more than 600,000 Austrians lost their lives during World War Two.

ANDROMEDABRUNNEN ★. In the courtyard here stands a minor masterpiece of Baroque sculpture: the Fountain of Andromeda (Andromedabrunnen) by Georg Raphael Donner ▲ *141, 304*, which dates from 1741 (three years after the Fountain of Providence on the Neuer Markt, also by

Donner ▲ *141*). The Fountain of Andromeda represents Andromeda delivered by Perseus from the sea monster. A master of Baroque sculpture, Donner was trained in Italy before going to work in Strasbourg, Bratislava and Vienna. In addition to the Fountain of Andromeda and the Neuer Markt Fountain, he created several groups of statues which are now on display at the Museum of Baroque Art ▲ *249* in the Lower Belvedere.

TIEFER GRABEN

In Roman times, Vindobona was a small square of land surrounded on three sides by moats filled with water and on

Framed by small
angels perched on
columns and with its
own wrought iron
balcony is a niche
containing a sculpted
group by Georg
Raphael Donner
(1693–1741).
Andromeda was
rescued by Perseus
from the sea monster
that was going to eat
her. Cassiopeia, wife
of Cepheus, King of
Ethiopia, had
proclaimed that she
and Andromeda were
more beautiful than
the Nereids. Poseidon
in fury created a
monster that began to
ravage the coasts. To
make an example of
Andromeda, he
ordered that she
should be tied to a
rock in the monster's
path. Once rescued,
she married her
savior.

THE ALSBACH
On the wall of a
house on the
Heidenschuss, a little
square south of the
Tiefer Graben, a
plaque over the figure
of a mounted Turk
marks the place
where the Alsbach
was once forded.

**MOZART AND
BEETHOVEN**
Mozart ● *48*, ▲ *147,
281* lived at no. 18
Tiefer Graben with
his father Leopold
during their third visit
to Vienna. Then age
seventeen, the
composer had come
from Salzburg to try
for the position of
music master of the
court chapel. His
candidacy failed, but
Mozart used the time
in Vienna to write six
string quartets and a
serenade. Beethoven
● *51,* ▲ *298* lived at
nos. 8 and 10 at
various times.

the fourth by the Danube. One of these moats was the
Graben ▲ *137*, which connected with the Tiefer Graben (the
"Deep Moat") through which flowed the Alsbach, a small
tributary of the Danube. This river has been filled in since the
Middle Ages, and today the Tiefer Graben is a
broad thoroughfare which starts at the Freyung
and continues past the Church of Maria
am Gestade.

HOHER BRÜCKE. The metal Upper
Bridge (Hoher Brücke) across the
Tiefer Graben is a graceful
Jugendstil ● *86* work of art,
embellished with a number of
elegant floral garlands that
are in that style. Designed
by Joseph Hackhofer
and Karl Christl, the
bridge was completed
in 1903.

MARIA AM GESTADE ★.
The spire of the church of
Maria am Gestade, one
of Austria's loveliest
Gothic buildings, towers
over the Tiefer Graben.
Known as Our Lady of
the Steps (Maria

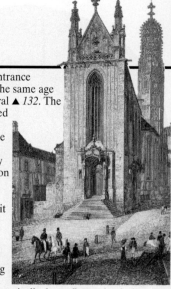

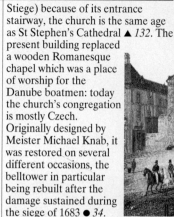

Stiege) because of its entrance stairway, the church is the same age as St Stephen's Cathedral ▲ 132. The present building replaced a wooden Romanesque chapel which was a place of worship for the Danube boatmen: today the church's congregation is mostly Czech.

Originally designed by Meister Michael Knab, it was restored on several different occasions, the belltower in particular being rebuilt after the damage sustained during the siege of 1683 ● 34.

The façade, which rises vertically, has a fine stained-glass window, a pediment and two slender sculpted pinnacles. The doorway is crowned by a stone baldachin and enlivened by a bas-relief representing John the Evangelist and John the Baptist. The interior of the church is surprisingly narrow, while the nave is set at an angle to the choir, because the builders were obliged to adapt themselves to the cramped urban conditions of the Middle Ages. The church, which is lit by 14th-century stained-glass windows, possesses several Gothic altarpieces (SAINT CLEMENT-MARIA CHAPEL), a fine organ case, and a Renaissance altar (ST JOHN'S CHAPEL). An anonymous painting of *The Annunciation* ★, dating from the 14th or 15th century, is alone worth the detour to Maria am Gestade.

THE PORTAL OF THE SALVATORKAPELLE
The two statues of knights in arms here are copies: the originals are kept in the Art History Museum ▲ 208.

SALVATORGASSE

This small street links Maria am Gestade with the Hoher Markt ▲ 155. The doorway of the SALVATORKAPELLE ● 74, at no. 5, built in 1530, is one of the very few examples of the Renaissance style in Vienna.

THE HOFBURG

THE MICHAELERTOR
Baroque and
neo-classicism
are the dominant
architectural styles
of the Hofburg.

MICHAELERKIRCHE
The portal statues by
the early 18th-century
Baroque sculptor
Lorenzo Mattielli
● 80 represent the
Fall of the Angels.

HERCULES IN COMBAT
WITH THE NEMEAN
LION
The Michaelertor is
embellished with
columns, balconies
and statues depicting
the labors of
Hercules. Like
those on the
Michaelerkirche,
the statues are by
Mattielli.

MICHAELERPLATZ

St Michael's Square (Michaelerplatz) stands at the intersection of Vienna's two most elegant streets, Kohlmarkt ▲ 158 and Herrengasse ▲ 159. The square leads to the entrance of the Imperial Palace (the Hofburg). Roman archeological remains excavated recently stand as evidence of the earliest human occupation of this site, though they also disfigure it to some degree.

MICHAELERKIRCHE. Acting as a foil to the Loos House, the Church of St Michael (Michaelerkirche) has none of the latter's stylistic unity. Initially a Romanesque building, it was subsequently given a Gothic choir and belltower, a Baroque portal and a stark neo-classical façade, with the only ornament provided by pilasters. Inside the church, where the imperial court once worshiped, there is a Baroque high altar, as well as vestiges of Romanesque frescoes and a Gothic painting of Christ scourged (*Ecce Homo*, 1430). Also here is the tomb of the Italian poet Metastasio ▲ 161, who was a friend of Haydn ● 49, ▲ 152, 162, 164 and Mozart's librettist ● 48, ▲ 147, 281.

AN OSSUARY. The crypt of the church is somewhat macabre: the whole area is strewn with bones and there are several hundred coffins, several of which are open.

LOOSHAUS. No building in Vienna has provoked as much controversy as the Looshaus, completed in 1911 at no. 3 Michaelerplatz. Franz-Joseph thought it so ugly that he had the curtains drawn in all the windows of his palace looking out on to the square! Nevertheless the simple, functional style that Adolf Loos (1870–1933) launched with this building was destined to take the world by storm. The building clashes less than its critics would claim with the rest of the architecture on the square; using fine materials such as green marble, Loos constructed a colonnade which matched those of the church and

"THE EMPIRE IS BUILT IN THE STYLE OF ITS HOUSES
– UNINHABITABLE, BUT PRETTY."

KARL KRAUS

St Michael's Gate. What is new about the building – apart
from its deliberately austere outline – is the clear division of
its functions. The ground floor and the mezzanine, which are
in colored marble, were designed to contain shops and offices,
while the four bare, white floors above were intended for
apartments. As one becomes more familiar with the
Looshaus, one gradually comes to appreciate the harmonious,
muted tones of its façade. The use of veined marble in its
lower portion gives it a discreet mobility to what would
otherwise appear squat and foursquare.

"CAFÉ GRIENDSTEIDL". The *Café Griensteidl* recently
reopened at no. 2 Michaelerplatz, having closed in 1897.
Along with the *Central* ▲ *160* and the HERRENHOF, the café
used to be a favored haunt of the great writers Arthur
Schnitzler, Hugo von Hoffmannsthal, Herman Broch and
Karl Kraus. To these "theaters of life", as Peter Altenberg ●
67 called them, came the musicians Hugo Wolf, Arnold
Schönberg and Alban Berg ● *52*, the architect Loos, and even
the revolutionary Leon Trotsky, all determined to remake the
world. Most of the time, these were no more than "café
revolutions". The new *Café Griensteidl* offers a discreet,
genteel atmosphere, far from the smoky ambience of the time
of Kraus's "joyous apocalypse".

MICHAELERTOR. The emperor and his family entered their
private apartments, as well as the formal rooms of the palace,
by way of the monumental Michaelertor ▲ *180*. The *dome*
▲ *174, 181* atop this gate forms a golden band above the entry
porch. Beyond the door is a vestibule in the shape of a
rotunda from which stairways lead to the imperial apartments
and to the court collection of china and silver ▲ *186*.

THE HOFBURG

The buildings of the Imperial Palace (the Hofburg) seem to
be laid out in no particular order. After the construction of
the first palace by Rudolph I in the 13th century, his
successors enlarged it without any coherent plan, tending at
the same time to make alterations in the styles of their own
times. Nevertheless, the architecture here is
predominantly Baroque and
neo-classical.

THE LOOSHAUS ● *86,
90,* ▲ *174, 236* "A
building without
eyebrows!" was the
verdict of the
Viennese on the
Looshaus. Karl Kraus
said of it, "That's not
a house he has built
for us, but a thought."

MICHAELERTOR
Built like a Roman
triumphal arch, the
Michaelertor was the
main entrance to the
Hofburg Palace in
Habsburg times,
guarded by soldiers
who kept the public
out. A superb
wrought iron awning
spreads over the
porch. Inside are
allegorical statues of
the imperial mottoes:
"Justice and
Clemency" (Maria
Theresa) ● *36*, "By
Courage and
Example" (Joseph II
● *36*), "By United
Strength"
(Franz-Joseph ● *41*).

▲ THE HOFBURG

PERIODS OF CONSTRUCTION

■ Middle Ages

■ 16th century

■ 17th century

■ 18th century

■ 1800–50

▫ After 1850

RUDOLPH I
Already lord of several fiefs in Alsace and Switzerland, Rudolph von Habsburg (1218–91) presented no threat, and was therefore elected Emperor in 1273, in preference to the powerful Ottokar II. This brought the great twenty-year interregnum, during which no emperor had gained election, to an end. Rudolph I defeated and killed Ottokar II at the Battle of Marchfeld (1278), earning for himself most of the fiefs of the Kingdom of Bohemia, including the Duchy of Austria. He set up this Duchy as a hereditary fiefdom for his sons Albert and Rudolph, thereby founding a dynasty which reigned until 1918.

A COMPLEX LAYOUT. The Michaelertor leads through to a first group of buildings which includes ST MICHAEL'S WING (Michaelertrakt), the Chancellery Wing and the Winter Riding School. These buildings are among the most recent in the Hofburg, since St Michael's Wing, begun in the 18th century, was only completed at the close of the 19th. Joined to it is the CHANCELLERY WING (Reichskanzleitrakt) which contained Franz-Joseph's apartments. Those of Empress Elizabeth were in Empress Amelia's Palace (Amalienburg), built in the 16th century but several times altered (in 1764, for instance, Nicolas von Pacassi gave it a small tower with a bulb dome). The other buildings are in effect an extension of the Amalienburg.

IN DER BURG. This first group of buildings is joined to the Leopold Wing and the Old Palace, forming a courtyard (In der Burg). Horse races were organized here during the reign of Maximilian II (1527–76), and later parties, concerts and even executions took place on this site. In the center of the courtyard stands a statue of Francis I ▲ *38*.

LEOPOLDINISCHERTRAKT. Facing the Chancellery Wing is Leopold Wing (Leopoldinischertrakt), now the official residence of the President of the Austrian Republic. This was built by Emperor Leopold in the

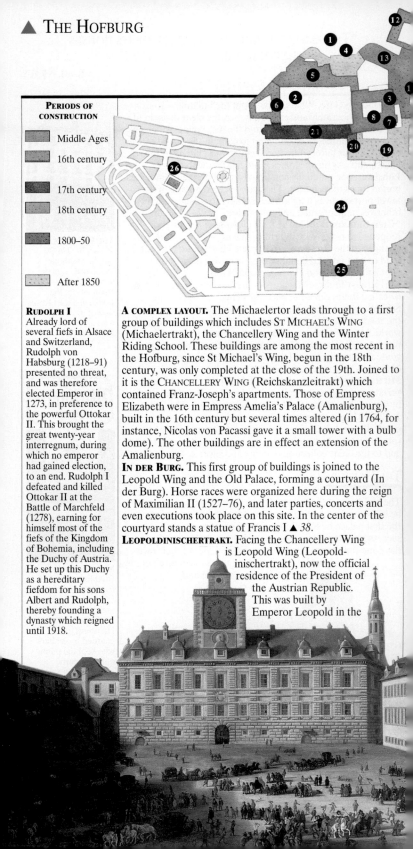

🏃 Half a day

Baroque style at the end of the 17th century. His granddaughter Maria Theresa lived here.

ALTE BURG. This palace, originally a stronghold, has been substantially altered. Several monarchs stayed there and, in the 19th century, the apartments were converted for the use of important guests, including Marshal Radetzky ▲ 143, 179. One passes from here through the SWISS COURTYARD (Schweizerhof) to the Palace Chapel of the Assumption (Burgkapelle) and treasury. The old palace is here extended by a group of buildings which includes the BALLROOM WING (Redoutensaaltrakt), the WINTER RIDING SCHOOL ▲ 190 (next to the SUMMER RIDING SCHOOL) and the stables ▲ 188.

TOWARD THE ALBERTINA. The STATE RECEPTION WING (Prunksaaltrakt), now the Austrian National Library, links the ballroom wing to the AUGUSTINIAN WING (Augustinertrakt), and forms the square of Josefsplatz. The latter wing is continued on one side by the hothouses, on the other by the Church of the Augustinians and the Albertina.

FESTSAALTRAKT. The Festsaaltrakt, which connects the Leopold Wing, the Old Palace and the New Palace, has been a convention center since 1958. It includes the reception hall (Festsaal) and the CEREMONIAL HALL (Zeremoniensaal), both former throne-rooms. The center also makes use of rooms in the Leopold Wing (the Secret Council Room and the Marble Room), the Old Palace (the Knights' and Halberdiers' Rooms, and the Radetzky apartments) and the ballroom wing. Balls are often held here ● 58.

NEUE BURG. Even more imposing than the rest of the Hofburg is the New Palace (Neue Burg), which extends right out to the Ring ● 84, ▲ 197. This neo-Renaissance building (in the style of the Ring) is built on a curve. There is a colonnade along the second-floor gallery; the first-floor statuary tells of Austrian history, with likenesses of a Marcoman (a member of the tribe that inhabited Austria in antiquity), a Roman legionnaire, a missionary (probably Irish), a Slav, a Frankish noble, a Magyar, a Crusader, a Lansquenet (a 16th-century German foot-soldier), a Pole and a Tyrolean. The Neue Burg also houses the collections of the Ephesus Museum and the Ethnography Museum, along with certain departments of the Austrian National Library.

THE IMPERIAL APARTMENTS

The Leopold Wing (Leopoldinischertrakt) where Maria Theresa lived is closed to the public, since it is the residence of the President of the Republic. On the other hand, the

THE BURNING OF THE REDOUTENSAAL
In November 1992, a fire swept through the Redoutensaal, the theater converted into a ballroom complex by Nicolas von Pacassi which was used for the imperial court's great entertainments and gala dinners. These rooms had served as a conference and congress center in more recent times; the Hunters' Ball and Redoutensaal Ball were both held here ● 58.

THE SCHWEIZERTOR
The Swiss gate leads from the main In der Burg courtyard to the

Swiss courtyard. It was built in 1522 as part of the façade of the Old Palace and survived Ferdinand I's (1503–64) alterations to the Hofburg during the Renaissance. The Habsburg eagle perches over it.

177

A ROYAL GYMNAST
The copper bath full of cold water into which Sissi ▲ *143, 144* plunged at 5 am each day, is perhaps less surprising than the toilet room with its wooden gymnastic fittings (below). Sissi ate very little, took frequent massages and practised gymnastics, walking and riding. This enabled her to retain a waistline

that was the envy of all throughout her life.

SISSI
"Tall and slender as she is, her movements are so noble and so natural that their grace is at once royal and animal. Beneath the mass of her chestnut hair, her little head might be that of a Greek goddess, were it not for the intense vitality which animates the perfection of her features, glitters in her shy, tender eyes, and in her magnetic glance with its nuances of sweetness and irony, audacity and modesty, dreaminess, gaiety and pity."

Comte de
Saint-Aulaire
(French Ambassador
to Vienna, 1882-91),
Franz-Joseph

apartments of Franz-Joseph I and Empress Elizabeth in the Chancellery wing (Reichskanzleitrakt), built in the 18th century by J. B. Fischer von Erlach ● *74, 80,* ▲ *138, 147* and Johann Lukas von Hildebrandt ● *75, 81,* ▲ *147* have been turned into a museum. This wing, overlooking the courtyard, was used as the offices of the Imperial Chancellery until 1806, when it was converted into apartments for Archduchess Maria Louisa. Her son the "Aiglon" ▲ *283* lived here, as well as at Schönbrunn, in his final years. Some of the rooms on the first floor were also occupied during the early years of Franz-Joseph's reign by his cousin Archduke Stephen, Palatine of Hungary. The Archduke lived here from 1848 to 1867: nowadays the apartments serve predominantly as reminders of the time of Franz-Joseph.

KAISERAPPARTEMENTS. These can be reached by way of the Michaelertor and the IMPERIAL STAIRCASE (Kaiserstiege), which leads from the rotunda to the first floor. This staircase looked on to the Halberdiers' Room (Trabantenstube). After the antechamber comes the suite of rooms said to be those of Archduke Stephen. The DINING ROOM (Speisezimmer) was where Franz-Joseph convened his general staff: the walls are covered with 16th-century Flemish tapestries illustrating the *Labors of Hercules*. After dinner, the officers would move into the CIRCLE ROOM (Cerclezimmer), hung with tapestries from Brussels of the life of the Roman Emperor Augustus, or else into the SMOKING ROOM (Rauchsalon), similarly decorated with tapestries and with a bust of Maximilian I. Immediately adjoining are the emperor's private apartments. In the HALBERDIERS' ROOM (Trabantenstube), the former bedroom of the "Aiglon", are a bust of Charles V and a scale model of the Old Hofburg. The AUDIENCE HALL

> "LIKE THE EMPRESS SISSI, HER IDOL, THE YOUNG GIRL USED TO JUMP WITH A MAD BRISKNESS, SPENT HOURS IN THE STABLES AND, LIKE HER MODEL, HAD RIDDEN THE EMPEROR'S THREE HUNDRED HORSES BAREBACK."

PAUL MORAND

(Audienzsaal and Audienzzimmer) is lit by a huge Bohemian glass chandelier and decorated with frescoes of the life of Francis I ● 38 by Peter Krafft. In its corners are a bust of Francis I, and another of Franz-Joseph aged twenty-three. Franz-Joseph used to give audiences here twice a week. His aide-de-camp would summon petitioners one by one from the Audienszaal, and they would then be conducted to the Emperor's smaller audience chamber (Audienzzimmer) by his chamberlain, where Franz-Joseph awaited them. He stood behind a kind of lectern; the list of audiences appointed for January 3, 1910, still lies open on its top. On the walls of the chamber are portraits of Francis I, Ferdinand I and Franz-Joseph himself, aged forty-three. Franz-Joseph presided over his Council of Ministers in the COUNCIL CHAMBER (Konferenzzimmer). A portrait of him aged twenty hangs on the wall. The door at the back of the room gives on to the EMPEROR'S WARDROBE (Kaisergarderobe), which was the responsibility of his chamberlain, Ketterl. Franz-Joseph was always to be found wearing military uniform. The EMPEROR'S BEDROOM (Schlafzimmer) is astonishing in its spartan simplicity. Above the small iron bedstead hang four portraits of his beloved wife Sissi, along with one of Archduchess Sophia, his mother, with Franz-Joseph himself aged two. On the side tables are busts of his parents. In the GRAND SALON (Grosser Salon, Kleiner Salon) are the famous portraits of Franz-Joseph and Sissi by Franz Xaver Winterhalter. The Small Salon (Kleiner Salon), which was used as a smoking room, contains an assortment of souvenirs and a painting of Maximilian. Following on from the Emperor's apartments, those of the Empress occupy space in the AMALIENBURG, the Palace of Joseph I's widow, Empress Amelia (1678–1711), where Czar Alexander I resided during the Congress of Vienna ● 38. Like her husband, Sissi was content to sleep on an iron

From top to bottom: The dining room, the red salon (or Boucher Salon), the salon and bedroom of the Empress, and the Grand Salon.

▲ The Hofburg

"The three Monarchs riding"
Czar Alexander I, Francis I, Emperor of
Austria and Frederick-William III of Prussia
(Albertina Museum ▲ 196).

MICHAELERTOR
The Michaelertor
▲ 174, 175, 181 was
built in the 18th
century in the hollow
of the concave façade
of the North Wing
(Michaelertrakt). It is
a fine example of the
Baroque style, with
columns, balconies
and statues of the
labors of Hercules.
The façade is flanked
on either side by a
monumental
fountain, created by
Hellmer and Weyr at
the close of the 19th
century, which is an
allegory of the power
of the empire on land
and sea.

bedstead, which was taken out each
morning to make more room in the
EMPRESS' SALON AND BEDROOM
(Wohn und Schlafenzimmer der
Kaiserin). In this beautiful room is
the Empress' small desk along with
her oratory, a Madonna ensconced
in a kind of Gothic niche. After the
bathroom (Badezimmer) and the
TOILET ROOM (Toilettenzimmer)
comes the red GRAND SALON (Grosser Salon), where the
imperial couple took breakfast together. Despite her
occasional breaches of protocol, Sissi never lost the
Emperor's love and respect; his apartments are full of
pictures of her. After her death, the Emperor forbade anyone
to enter the rooms where she had lived; they were later
partially reoccupied by Charles I. In the grand salon the most
interesting objects are a statue of
Napoleon's elder sister Eliza, by Canova,
and two bisque statuettes of
Franz-Joseph aged fifty-seven and Sissi at
fifty. The red, white and gold SMALL
SALON (Kleiner Salon) is dedicated to the
memory of Sissi, with busts, a portrait
and a glass case containing objects that
belonged to her. Looking out over the
AMELIA COURTYARD (Amalienhof), the
BERGL SALON (Berglzimmer), which is
closed to the public, is decorated with exotic frescoes by
Johann Bergl ▲ 164, 278.

ALEXANDER I'S APARTMENTS. After the GRAND ANTECHAMBER
(Grosser Vorzimmer), which contains a life-size statue of Sissi
and portraits of the children of Maria Theresa ▲ 144
(including Marie-Antoinette), are the apartments of Czar
Alexander I. No trace remains of his having occupied these
richly decorated quarters, only a series of portraits of Charles
I, who used these apartments as an audience chamber and
work room. After the VESTIBULE (Eingangzimmer), with its
busts of Charles I and Zita, come the Rococo RECEPTION
SALON (Empfangsalon), with fine Gobelins tapestries on a
red background after cartoons by François Boucher. These
were a present from Marie-Antoinette to Joseph I on the
occasion of his visit to Paris in 1777. The STUDY
(Arbeitszimmer), covered in hangings made in
Brussels, is where Charles I signed his abdication.
The long royal table in the DINING ROOM
(Spiesezimmer), which was always set, could
seat up to ten diners. Etiquette required that
all knives and forks be set to the right of the
plates. The SMOKING ROOM is an extension of
the Czar's apartments; it is dedicated to Rudolph
and Franz-Ferdinand, the two archdukes who died
under tragic circumstances.

CHARLES I
The last
emperor of
Austria
abdicated in
1918 ▲ 144.

SCHATZKAMMER ★

The contents of the imperial treasury
(Schatzkammer) were assembled by Ferdinand I
(1503–64), then enriched by his successors, who

THE ROOFS OF THE HOFBURG
From left to right, and from top to bottom: the
monument to Prince Eugène which stands in front of the Heldenplatz wing ▲ 207, the
Michaelertor dome ▲ 174, 175, 180, a detail of the Neue Burg, the splendid decoration on the
roof of the Austrian National Library ▲ 192, and four details of the Michaelertor dome.

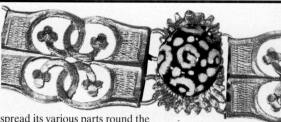

spread its various parts round the palace. It was not until the reign of Charles VI that the treasure was all brought together here.

INSIGNIA OF THE HOLY ROMAN EMPIRE. The crown of the Holy Roman Empire was the emblem of sovereignty over a major part of Europe for more than a thousand years. For a long time it was mistakenly known as the Crown of Charlemagne, though it was probably made in the 10th century for Otto II. Made of gold in the Byzantine and Carolingian style, it is topped by a cross, a hoop of gold and precious stones added during the 11th century for Conrad II. Other imperial insignia are the 12th-century golden Orb, the Gothic Scepter, the Imperial Cross (11th–13th centuries), the Carolingian gospel-book on which the emperor swore his oath, the Sword of Charlemagne (which is in fact an oriental saber), the Holy Lance and the Processional Cross. The first rooms also display the emblems of the Habsburgs as Kings of Bohemia and Hungary and Archdukes of Austria, including the crown, orb and scepter carved from a narwhal's tooth which was commissioned by Rudolph II from the goldsmiths of Prague. Mantles with long trains were used during formal imperial ceremonies; the purple one worn by Francis I at his coronation is embroidered with gold, with a collar of ermine. Note also the magnificent robes embroidered by Maria Theresa herself for her grandchildren's christenings. Most of the principal gems of the Emperors, were carried into exile by the last Habsburgs; those that remain include the Columbian Emerald (1680 carats), the Golden Rose of the Pope given by Pius VII to Francis I's wife Carolina-Augusta, and a two-headed eagle made with an amethyst, an opal and a hyacinth. The cup passed at the Last Supper, in which Joseph of Arimathea caught the blood of Christ, was the subject of a great number of chivalric fables. For many centuries it was believed that the chalice (otherwise known as the HOLY GRAIL) in the imperial treasury was indeed the true grail; this cup, fashioned from one of the largest agates in the world, in fact dates from the 4th century. Similarly, the narwhal tooth was thought to be the horn of a unicorn.

ROYAL HEIRLOOMS OF SICILY. Through numerous alliances and inheritances, the royal insignia of

THE CHAIN OF THE GOLDEN FLEECE▲ *133.* In Greek mythology, Jason sailed forth in his ship the *Argos* to seek the Golden Fleece and on his travels he overcame a race of giants, a terrible harvest of a crop of dragons' teeth sown in a field. Philip the Good, Duke of Burgundy, founded the Order of the Golden Fleece in 1429, Charles V gave it special kudos by recruiting its members from among Austria's higher nobility and men of state.

Shown here are the accoutrements of the members and heralds of the order: mantles of purple velvet, tabards embroidered with coats of arms, suits of armor, and jewelry, including the 18th-century Cross of the Oath and the goblet of Philip the Good.

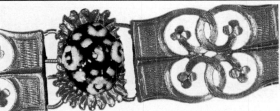

the Norman kings of Sicily were handed down to the Hohenstaufens and subsequently to the Habsburgs. The finest piece is a red silk embroidered mantle that was worn by Roger II of Sicily on the day of his coronation.

THE GOLDEN FLEECE. A small gallery of portraits commemorates the principal members of the Valois-Burgundy family. Also displayed are various altar coverings and liturgical vestments. The Treasure of the Golden Fleece came from the dowry of Marie of Burgundy, daughter of Charles the Rash, who married Maximilian I.

MUSEUM OF RELIGIOUS ART. The ecclesiastical treasury contains a number of objects which were used at services attended by the court. St Stephen's purse – a reliquary which is said to have belonged to Charlemagne and to have contained the blood of the first Christian martyr – is thought to be the oldest item here. Other curiosities include a reliquary containing a nail from the True Cross, a casket containing fragments of wood from the same source, and a small temple-reliquary containing one of St Peter's teeth.

The 8th-century Holy Lance (Langobardisch-Karolingisch, above); the Scepter of Austria (below).

BURGKAPELLE

Next to the treasury is the Palace Chapel of the Assumption (Burgkapelle) which was built in the Gothic style by Frederick III in the 15th century (1415–93). The chapel was redecorated several times in subsequent years, but in the 19th century it was decided that it should be restored to its original form. The catafalque in which the coffins of deceased Habsburgs lay in state was traditionally placed in this chapel while members of the public were allowed to pay their last respects. Today the internationally renowned Vienna Boys' Choir ● *54,* ▲ *270* often put on performances here.

The Parthian Frieze.

EPHESOS-MUSEUM

Objects excavated in 1866 by Austrian archeologists at
Ephesus in Asia Minor are displayed in the Museum of
Ephesus in the New Hofburg. (Excavations are continuing
there today.) Ephesus became a major commercial port and
financial center of Asia Minor from the 8th century BC
onward, thanks to its trade with the Orient. It was also a
religious center for the cult of Artemis, to whom a great
temple, the Artemision, was erected in the 6th century BC.

Ephesus fell successively under the rule of
Croesus, the King of Lydia who was famous for his
wealth; Cyrus, King of Persia; Alexander the
Great; Mithridates, King of Pontus; and the
Roman dictator Sylla. In 54 AD St Paul and
St John founded the first Christian communities
at Ephesus, and the Virgin Mary died there.
Later Ephesus was visited by the Emperor
Hadrian (in whose honour a temple was built),
before falling first into Byzantine and finally
into Turkish hands.

A MYSTICAL VISION. The German nun Anna
Katharina Emmerich (1774–1824) re-lived the
Passion of Christ on several occasions and was marked
with the stigmata. Her visions, recounting the life of
the Virgin and of Christ's Apostles, were transcribed by
the German writer Clemens Brentano; forty years after
the death of the "Nun of Dülmen", her visions helped
the archeologists working on the dig at Ephesus to
locate the house in which St Paul and St John are
thought to have lived.

FRAGMENTS OF THE TEMPLE OF ARTEMIS. Parts of the
Artemision, the Roman Theater, the Odeon, the
Temple of Hadrian, the stadium, the agora, the forum,
the Library of Celsus and the road of Kouretes were

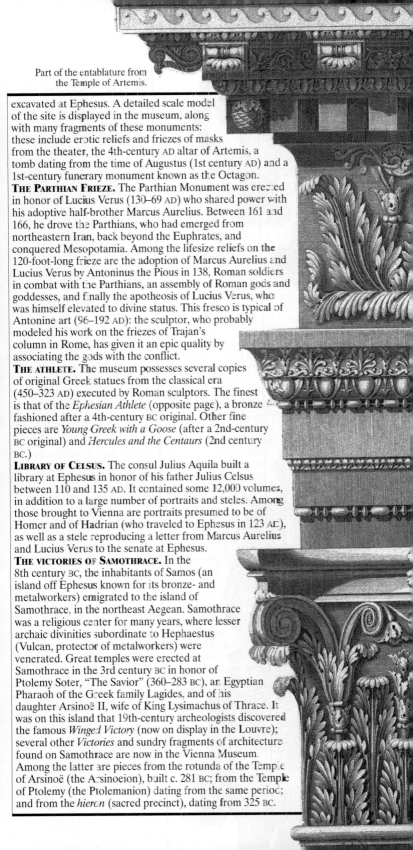

Part of the entablature from the Temple of Artemis.

excavated at Ephesus. A detailed scale model of the site is displayed in the museum, along with many fragments of these monuments: these include erotic reliefs and friezes of masks from the theater, the 4th-century AD altar of Artemis, a tomb dating from the time of Augustus (1st century AD) and a 1st-century funerary monument known as the Octagon.

THE PARTHIAN FRIEZE. The Parthian Monument was erected in honor of Lucius Verus (130–69 AD) who shared power with his adoptive half-brother Marcus Aurelius. Between 161 and 166, he drove the Parthians, who had emerged from northeastern Iran, back beyond the Euphrates, and conquered Mesopotamia. Among the lifesize reliefs on the 120-foot-long frieze are the adoption of Marcus Aurelius and Lucius Verus by Antoninus the Pious in 138, Roman soldiers in combat with the Parthians, an assembly of Roman gods and goddesses, and finally the apotheosis of Lucius Verus, who was himself elevated to divine status. This fresco is typical of Antonine art (96–192 AD): the sculptor, who probably modeled his work on the friezes of Trajan's column in Rome, has given it an epic quality by associating the gods with the conflict.

THE ATHLETE. The museum possesses several copies of original Greek statues from the classical era (450–323 AD) executed by Roman sculptors. The finest is that of the *Ephesian Athlete* (opposite page), a bronze fashioned after a 4th-century BC original. Other fine pieces are *Young Greek with a Goose* (after a 2nd-century BC original) and *Hercules and the Centaurs* (2nd century BC.)

LIBRARY OF CELSUS. The consul Julius Aquila built a library at Ephesus in honor of his father Julius Celsus between 110 and 135 AD. It contained some 12,000 volumes, in addition to a large number of portraits and steles. Among those brought to Vienna are portraits presumed to be of Homer and of Hadrian (who traveled to Ephesus in 123 AD), as well as a stele reproducing a letter from Marcus Aurelius and Lucius Verus to the senate at Ephesus.

THE VICTORIES OF SAMOTHRACE. In the 8th century BC, the inhabitants of Samos (an island off Ephesus known for its bronze- and metalworkers) emigrated to the island of Samothrace, in the northeast Aegean. Samothrace was a religious center for many years, where lesser archaic divinities subordinate to Hephaestus (Vulcan, protector of metalworkers) were venerated. Great temples were erected at Samothrace in the 3rd century BC in honor of Ptolemy Soter, "The Savior" (360–283 BC), an Egyptian Pharaoh of the Greek family Lagides, and of his daughter Arsinoë II, wife of King Lysimachus of Thrace. It was on this island that 19th-century archeologists discovered the famous *Winged Victory* (now on display in the Louvre); several other *Victories* and sundry fragments of architecture found on Samothrace are now in the Vienna Museum. Among the latter are pieces from the rotunda of the Temple of Arsinoë (the Arsinoeion), built c. 281 BC; from the Temple of Ptolemy (the Ptolemanion) dating from the same period; and from the *hieron* (sacred precinct), dating from 325 BC.

TWO PIECES OF SILVER TABLEWARE BELONGING TO MARIA THERESA
The court collection of china and silver in the Michaelertrakt includes sumptuous sets of tableware from China, France (Sèvres), Germany (Saxe), Italy (Milan) and Austria (Augarten ▲ 269).

The breastplate and armor of Ferdinand I.

THE COLLECTIONS

The son of Ferdinand I and the brother of Maximilian II, Ferdinand of the Tyrol (1529–95) ▲ 210 like all the Renaissance princes, loved the arts. Using his own considerable fortune (along with that of his wife, the daughter of the banker Welser who had loaned money to Charles V to buy his election as Holy Roman Emperor in 1519), Ferdinand built up a collection of old weapons, musical instruments and ethnographic objects which were later passed on to the great museums of Vienna.

HOFTAFEL- UND SILBERKAMMER. Among the finest items in the court collection of china and silverware are the Milan Centerpiece, a gilded 100-foot-long bronze platter dating from the early 19th century, the English service given to Emperor Franz-Joseph by Queen Victoria, three Sèvres services given by Marie-Antoinette to her brother Joseph II when he visited Paris in 1777 (she also gave the tapestries now hanging in the red salon of the imperial apartments), and an extensive gilt silver service. This service, designed for a hundred and forty guests, was made by Guillaume Biennais (1764–1834), a Paris silversmith fashionable during the first French Empire. Most of Biennais' plates are modeled on the paintings of Louis David, the official portraitist of the Revolution and the Empire, who was a passionate student of Greek and Roman antiquity.

RÜSTUNGEN- UND WAFFENSAMMLUNG. The Hofburg's collection of arms and armor (Rüstungen-und Waffensammlung) is one of the largest in the world. It was started by Ernest I, Duke of Austria (1377–1424) in the 15th century, and enlarged by Archduke Ferdinand of the Tyrol (1529–95). Its oldest weapons date back to the Barbarian invasions of the 5th century AD, while the most splendid parts of the collection were fashioned during the Renaissance – notably the ceremonial armor of Charles V, and that of his son Philip II of Spain and of Francis I of France, made in Milan during the 16th century. Note also Maximilian II's golden sword (1551), his rose-leaf ornamental accoutrements, and an extensive collection of Turkish weapons.

SAMMLUNG ALTER MUSIK-INSTRUMENTE ★. The finest pieces in the collection of old musical instruments (Sammlung alter Musik-Instrumente) come from the collections of Archduke Ferdinand of the Tyrol, which he assembled at Ambras. Others belonged to Archduke Ferdinand-Charles (1754–1806), son of Maria Theresa, who married Maria-Beatrice d'Este. The d'Este princes, a great North Italian family related to the Sforzas and the Borgias, had collected a large

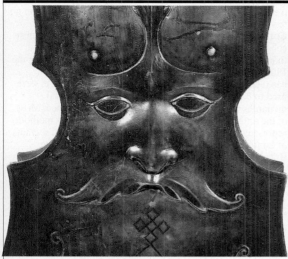

EUROPEAN CONCERT
The history of
European music is
retraced with a
display of
instruments. Note the
clavicytherium, an
ancestor of the
harpsichord (17th-
century), Maria
Theresa's tortoise-
shell violin (18th-
century) and the
trumpet of Ferdinand
of the Tyrol (16th-
century). A mandolin
(Pandurina) and
details of violas
(above).

number of works of art in their various residences, in
particular collectible musical instruments (some of these were
kept in the former property of the marquess of Obizzi, near
Padua).

MUSEUM FÜR VÖLKERKUNDE

The Museum of Ethnography (Museum für Völkerkunde)
possesses more than a hundred and fifty
thousand objects from all over the world,
collected over the centuries either by the
Habsburgs themselves or by ethnologists
working for the Austrian government.
MONTEZUMA'S DIADEM. The museum is
particularly rich in objects from the Aztec
Empire of ancient Mexico: it inherited both
the collections sent by the conquistador
Hernán Cortés to Charles V after the
taking of Tenochtitlan in 1520, and also those of the ill-fated
Emperor of Mexico, Maximilian ▲ *145*. It holds the feathered
crown of the Aztec Emperor Montezuma II (1466–1520)
▲ *207*, who was killed in the revolt of the Aztecs against the
forces of Cortés. Today, Mexico is calling for the return of this
diadem. Many other objects of Latin-American origin are
kept here, especially pieces from Brazil. Francis I's daughter,
the Archduchess Marie-Leopoldine, married Peter I of
Alcantara, Emperor of Brazil, in 1817. At that time Austria
sent a team of scholars to Rio de Janeiro, among them the
naturalist Johann Naterer (1787–1843) who provided the
Museum of Ethnography with innumerable objects acquired
from the Amazon Indians.
CAPTAIN COOK'S COLLECTIONS. The oceanic section of the
museum was started off with the collections of Captain Cook,
purchased in London in 1806 by Francis I; Africa, Australia
and Asia, the destinations of many Austrian ethnographic
expeditions, are also well represented. All these elements
complemented and enriched the collections of Ferdinand of
the Tyrol ▲ *210*. Archduke Franz-Ferdinand ▲ *145*, who

IN BLACK AND WHITE
Keyboard
instruments which
belonged to famous
musicians are
displayed. These
include Haydn's
harpsichord ● *49*,
▲ *152, 162, 164*,
Mozart's pianoforte
(*Hammerflügel*,
above) ● *48*, ▲ *162*
the piano given by the
Erhard Company to
Beethoven ● *51*,
▲ *298* in 1803, Liszt's
organ-harmonium
and the pianos of
Schubert, Brahms
● *51*, Schumann
▲ *153*, Wolf and
Mahler ● *52*.

Captain James Cook (1728–79, above right) circumnavigated the world three times between 1768 and 1779.

Self-Portrait by Vincent Van Gogh (top); *Bather* by Pierre-Auguste Renoir (above).

An early 18th-century Indian warrior, from the Museum of Ethnology.

COOK AND THE PACIFIC
Cook discovered the Society Islands, the East Coast of Australia and the Sandwich Islands, where he was murdered by natives. He brought back geographical, zoological and ethnographic information, some of which was acquired by the Vienna Museum of Ethnography.

traveled round the world in 1892–3, brought back with him no fewer than fourteen thousand Asian objects.

COLLECTION OF THE ART OF BENIN. One of the world's finest collections of the art of Benin, the kingdom that preceded today's Nigeria, is also displayed in the museum. Between the 18th and 19th centuries, a style of court art consisting of bas-reliefs and figurines evolved in Benin. These works were used to decorate the palaces of the *obas*, the powerful monarchs who reigned over the entire Gulf of Guinea. Most of the sculptures, which were cast using the lost wax method, represent the sovereign, the queen mother, warriors, servants or hunters. When the city of Benin was captured by the British Army in 1897, the *oba* went into exile and his property was sold at auction in London: Austria bought seventy-four bronzes.

NEUE GALERIE

On the second floor of the STABLE BLOCK (Stallburg), at the far end of the Ballroom, the Neue Galerie is an annex of the Museum of Art History ▲ *208*. This gallery is "new" in that it was established on the premises of the former picture gallery, created in the 17th century and later moved to the Belvedere ▲ *246* by Maria Theresa in 1776.

FRENCH IMPRESSIONISTS. This gallery contains a superb collection of European paintings, and several Impressionist masterpieces: a *Bather* by Renoir, several Monet landscapes, a Van Gogh *Self-Portrait*, portraits by Degas and Manet, a still-life by Cézanne, a Pissarro landscape and *Portrait of a Woman in Bed* by Toulouse-Lautrec. Other major French artists represented here are Millet, Corot, Géricault, Delacroix, Courbet and the sculptor Auguste Rodin. The German schools are also present, notably the Romantics (Caspar David Friedrich), the Realists (W. Leibl, H. Thoma) and the Impressionists (M. Liebermann, Lovis Corinth).

SPANISCHE REITSCHULE ★

The Spanish Riding School ▲ *190* (Spanische Reitschule) occupies the stables (Stallburg) and trains either in the winter or the summer school. It was originally based in quarters on Josefsplatz.

THE WINTERREITSCHULE. The winter manège (Winterreitschule) was built at the close of the 17th century, in the space once occupied by the apartments of Maximilian II; it was completed in 1729 and is the recognized Baroque masterpiece of its architect,

A PASSION FOR HORSES
The Habsburgs were ready to sacrifice almost anything for their horses. In the 16th century, Maximilian II gave up the new apartments built by his father, Ferdinand I, so that stables could be installed in their place. Then came the project for the winter manège (left) beside the stables (below) and still inside the palace proper.

Joseph Emanuel Fischer von Erlach ● *80,* ▲ *302.* The manège, which is painted white throughout, is surrounded by a double gallery and a high colonnade: a box crowned by a triangular pediment was included for the emperor's use, and stucco bas-reliefs of immaculate white add a further touch of refinement. The winter manège was opened in 1735 by Charles VI ● *36,* ▲ *192,* who had originally commissioned it; his monogram in relief and his portrait may be seen on the walls and in the emperor's box. Just as they do today, the riders would ride forth in impeccable order. Then they would go through the sequence of complex exercises which have since established the great renown of the Spanish Riding School.

THE SOMMERREITSCHULE. In summer, the exhibitions of the Spanish Riding School are given at the summer manège (Sommerreitschule), which is in the courtyard adjoining the winter manège.

JOSEFSPLATZ

This square is named after Joseph II (1741–90), whose equestrian statue by Franz Anton von Zauner (c. 1795–1807) may be seen in its center. The same architect, Nikolaus von Pacassi ▲ *192,* was employed to redesign all the surrounding façades between 1760 and 1770, and this is what gives the square its extraordinary unity. Before it was remodeled, it was used for tournaments and for training the horses of the Spanish Riding School.

BALLS, CONCERTS AND CAROUSELS
The winter manège (below) was not just a theater for elaborate dressage. The Lipizzaners were also used for equestrian carousels and ballets, in which dancers and riders performed to the music of orchestras amid magnificent scenery. During the Congress of Vienna ● *38,* the aristocracy of Europe participated in balls organized in the manège, as well as attending concerts there.

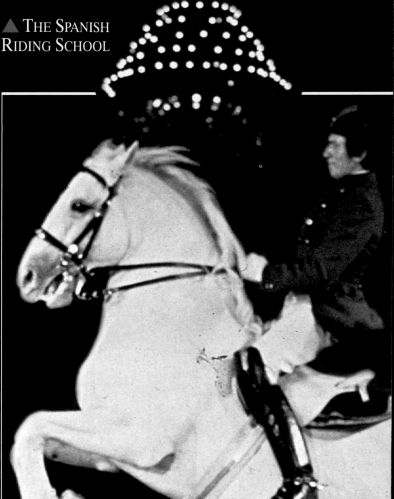

THE ART OF DRESSAGE

With the outbreak of the French Revolution in 1789, the great stables of Versailles were abandoned and the Master of the Horse, La Guérinière, left for Vienna, where he taught equestrian art at the Spanish Riding School. Like the famed Cadre Noir at Saumur, the Viennese school specializes in dressage – a highly skilled discipline entirely different from show-jumping which became popular in the 19th century. Many of the more advanced exercises in dressage may be traced to the French tradition.

In 1562, Maximilian II's brother, Archduke Charles, who had inherited estates in the north of today's Slovenia, established several major studs at Lipizza, near Trieste, to which he brought Spanish thoroughbreds (hence the name of the school) for cross-breeding with Karst horses. The "Lipizzaner" strain was created at the end of the 16th century with these studs, which thereafter supplied horses to the Spanish Riding School and the Austrian Household Cavalry. When the Italians and subsequently the Yugoslavs annexed Trieste and Slovenia after World War One, Austria decided in 1920 to found its own Lipizzaner stud at Piber, near Graz, in Styria. Today the white horses of the Spanish Riding School are bred both at Lipizza (Lipice) and at Piber.

THE WINTER MANÈGE
The public is admitted several times a day to watch the demonstrations and schooling of riders in the winter manège ▲ *188* at the Hofburg.

THE "SILVER STALLIONS"
The Lipizzaners of the Spanish Riding School have been white ever since an imperial decree proclaimed that they should be so at the beginning of the 19th century. Before that time the Habsburgs were just as likely to select piebald, bay, spotted or chestnut horses. Empress Sissi was a keen collector of horses, but her preference, unlike her husband's, was not for "silver stallions", but for dark thoroughbreds.

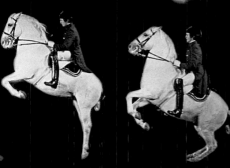

PACES
The riders have a huge repertoire of "paces", the advanced exercises which demonstrate the most elegant points of a horse. The paces are divided into low paces (pirouettes, pawing the ground, passage, changing leg on alternate steps of a canter, Spanish walk and trot) and high paces (curvets, cabrioles and croupades).

I. Stadt.
Josefsplatz

"THE THIRD MAN"
Film-lovers will recognize the Pallavinci Palace, before whose monumental gateway Carol Reed filmed one of the first scenes of *The Third Man* ● 42, ▲ 267.

The ballroom, the Austrian National Library and the Augustinian Church all look onto Josefsplatz, which adjoins Augustinerstrasse.

PALLAVICINI PALACE. This palace at no. 5 has a remarkable door framed by caryatids, the work of von Zauner in 1786 (like the later statue of Joseph II). This classical palace was built in the same period by Ferdinand von Hohenburg on the site of a former convent where Elizabeth of Austria, daughter of Maximilian II and wife of Charles IX of France, died in 1592. Today it is used a convention center.

THE VIENNA WALTZ SCHOOL. Also facing the Hofburg, on the corner of Bräunerstrasse, is the Ellmayer dancing school ● 58.

PALFFY PALACE. With its handsome Renaissance façade, the Palffy Palace overlooking Josefsplatz was the scene of Mozart's first performance of *The Marriage of Figaro* ▲ 48 in 1785. This palace stands on the site of the old imperial chancellery; today it serves as Austria House, scene of a wide variety of cultural activities.

NATIONALBIBLIOTHEK

The imperial court's library, which became the Austrian National Library (Nationalbibliothek) in 1920, was scattered all around the Hofburg before Charles VI commissioned J. B. Fischer von Erlach ● 74, 80, ▲ 138, 147, 302 and his son Josef Emanuel to design a permanent building in 1722.

PRUNKSAAL ★. The result is the magnificent hall (Prunksaal) in which the collections of the Habsburgs and Prince Eugène ● 35, ▲ 147, 247 are stored (Joseph II purchased the prince's books on his death in 1736). With marble, carved wainscoting, a painted cupola covered in frescoes of the *Apotheosis of Charles VI* by Daniel Gran, columns and statues, this room is remarkably like a Baroque church interior, complete with nave and oval transept. But the Prunksaal quickly became too small to house the growing collections, and the library had to expand into additional departments containing manuscripts, maps and a Museum of Globes in the Augustinian wing; papyri and musical scores, recordings and a film library in the Albertina; periodicals, reading rooms, portraits, engravings and more than eight hundred thousand photographs in the Neue Hofburg.

THE GUTENBERG BIBLE. The sheer wealth of the library makes it impossible to display all its treasures at one time, so temporary exhibitions are organized all year round. In total, the Austrian National Library possesses more than two and a half million printed books, among them a Gutenberg Bible.

AN ITALIAN ARCHITECT
Maria Theresa's favorite architect, Nikolaus von Pacassi (1716–90), was trained in the French classical school. A few years after Fischer von Erlach and Hildebrandt ● 75, 81, ▲ 147, he was commissioned to redesign, enlarge and complete their buildings in a calmer, more ponderous style. Pacassi was innundated with work, ranging from the Hofburg and Schönbrunn ▲ 247 to the Theresianum ▲ 243 and the Hetzendorff Palace.

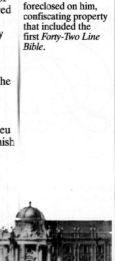

The other great treasures include a Byzantine manuscript of
512 of a medical treatise by the Greek Dioscorides, who lived
in the 1st century AD; the 8th-century Gospel Books of
St Cuthbert and those of Johannes von Troppau (written by
Duke Albert III of Austria in 1368); a 12th-century
antiphonal, or book of liturgical chants from St Peter's at
Salzburg; the Books of Hours of Charles the Rash and of
Galeazzo Sforza, Duke of Milan (both 15th century); and the
Theuerdank, a historical text written by Maximilian I
(1459–1519) printed in 1517.

GLOBENMUSEUM. The museum of maps and globes
(Globenmuseum) contains atlases by Willem Janszoon Blaeu
● *194*, and a globe made in 1541 for Charles V by the Flemish
mathematician and geographer
Mercator (1512–94). Four large
globes made by the Venetian
geographer Vincenzo

THE BLAEU ATLAS. In 1605, the Dutchman Willem Janszoon Blaeu (1571–1638) published a map of the world in Amsterdam, and followed it in 1619 with his famous atlases: *Theatrum Mundi* and *Theatrum Urbium et Monumentorum.*

Flat projections of the terrestrial globe in the *Atlas* (opposite); a heliocentric armillary sphere (below.)

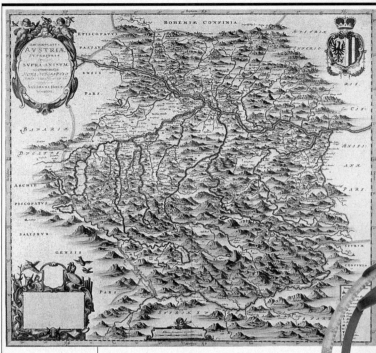

BLAEU AND VERMEER In Blaeu's time, the sea trade of the United Provinces was expanding into Northern Europe, Asia and Africa. All Europe was supplied by the

Coronelli (1650–1718) who worked at the court of Louis XIV are also displayed. Although it is a geographical map, the *Peutinger Table* is kept in the manuscript section; it is actually a superb 16th-century copy made by the German humanist Conrad Peutinger (1465–1547) of a 3rd- or 4th-century AD Roman map. Although the place names are somewhat misplaced, this map is ahead of its time in indicating reliefs, sites and mileages.

OTHER SECTIONS. The Austrian National Library also includes a restoration institute, the ESPERANTO MUSEUM and the theater archives that contain more than a million works, including photographs, maquettes and manuscripts of plays.

Low Countries. On his death, Blaeu's son Jan carried on his business. Vermeer of Delft ▲ 220, a friend of the Blaeu family, often included maps in his paintings, for which he is said to have paid a fee.

AUGUSTINERKIRCHE UND KLOSTER

Integrated as they are into the Hofburg, the church and former monastery of the Augustinians (Augustinerkirche und-Kloster) form a massive ensemble together with the Albertina and the hothouses (Palmenhaus). The Albertina, along with several sections of the Austrian National Library, occupies the monastery premises. The Gothic church is a favorite venue for aristocratic weddings, and the annual mass for Franz-Joseph is celebrated here on the anniversary of his death, November 21. Anton Bruckner

● *52* frequently played on the old organ of the Augustinerkirche, which originally came from the demolished Spanish Benedictine church (Schwarzspanier). It was here that he composed, and played for the first time in public, his *Mass in F Minor* (1872). This musical tradition is kept up to this day: a classical orchestra plays at mass every Sunday in the Augustinerkirche.

THE TOMB OF MARIA-CHRISTINA. Apart from the miraculous statue at the church entrance, the most remarkable features here are the handsome pulpit, the high altar and, above all, the monumental tomb of Maria-Christina of Saxony-Teschen (1742–98), daughter of Maria Theresa, who was the governor of the Low Countries in 1778 (her husband Albert of Saxony founded the gallery of drawings known as the Albertina ▲ *196*). This funerary monument is one of the masterpieces of the Italian sculptor Canova (1757–1822), who was chiefly inspired by Greek and Roman sculpture and was highly fashionable at the various European courts, including that of Napoleon, during the 19th century.

THE CRYPT OF THE HABSBURG HEARTS. A curiosity of the Augustinerkirche is the crypt (Habsburger Herzgruft) in which the hearts of the Habsburg family ● *29*, ▲ *143, 144, 280* have been kept in silver urns ever since the reign of Matthias II in the early 17th century. Since that date, and following an unchanging ritual, the bodies of the imperial family have been literally dismantled after death: the hearts came to the Augustinerkirche, the viscera went to the crypt at St Stephen's Cathedral and what was left over was laid to rest in the crypt of the Capuchins ▲ *142*.

ALBERTINAPLATZ

At the end of the AUGUSTINERSTRASSE, an old bastion of the Hofburg dominates Albertinaplatz. Above it stands the equestrian statue of Archduke Albert (1817–95) by Kaspar Zumbusch. Backing onto the bastion is the monumental, late 19th-century DANUBE FOUNTAIN (Donaubrunnen), the work of Mortiz von Löhr and Johann Meixner. The IMPERIAL GARDENS ▲ *207* and the GREENHOUSES are adjacent to the square.

I. Stadt. **Augustiner** Straße.

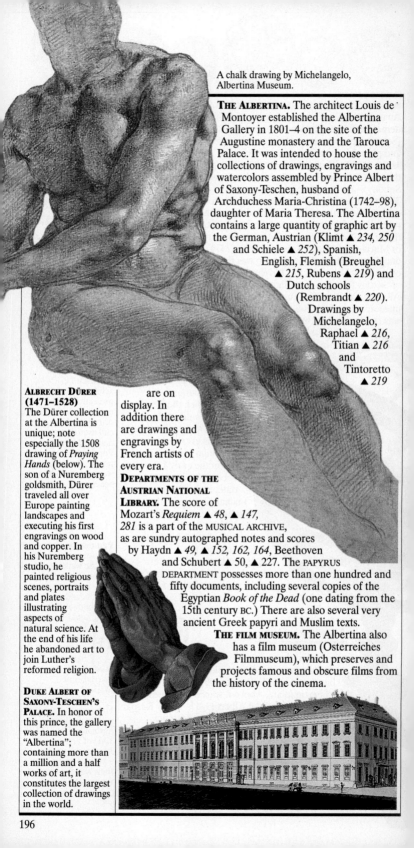

A chalk drawing by Michelangelo, Albertina Museum.

THE ALBERTINA. The architect Louis de Montoyer established the Albertina Gallery in 1801–4 on the site of the Augustine monastery and the Tarouca Palace. It was intended to house the collections of drawings, engravings and watercolors assembled by Prince Albert of Saxony-Teschen, husband of Archduchess Maria-Christina (1742–98), daughter of Maria Theresa. The Albertina contains a large quantity of graphic art by the German, Austrian (Klimt ▲ *234, 250* and Schiele ▲ *252*), Spanish, English, Flemish (Breughel ▲ *215*, Rubens ▲ *219*) and Dutch schools (Rembrandt ▲ *220*). Drawings by Michelangelo, Raphael ▲ *216*, Titian ▲ *216* and Tintoretto ▲ *219*

ALBRECHT DÜRER (1471–1528)
The Dürer collection at the Albertina is unique; note especially the 1508 drawing of *Praying Hands* (below). The son of a Nuremberg goldsmith, Dürer traveled all over Europe painting landscapes and executing his first engravings on wood and copper. In his Nuremberg studio, he painted religious scenes, portraits and plates illustrating aspects of natural science. At the end of his life he abandoned art to join Luther's reformed religion.

are on display. In addition there are drawings and engravings by French artists of every era.

DEPARTMENTS OF THE AUSTRIAN NATIONAL LIBRARY. The score of Mozart's *Requiem* ▲ *48*, ▲ *147, 281* is a part of the MUSICAL ARCHIVE, as are sundry autographed notes and scores by Haydn ▲ *49*, ▲ *152, 162, 164*, Beethoven and Schubert ▲ *50*, ▲ *227*. The PAPYRUS DEPARTMENT possesses more than one hundred and fifty documents, including several copies of the Egyptian *Book of the Dead* (one dating from the 15th century BC.) There are also several very ancient Greek papyri and Muslim texts.

THE FILM MUSEUM. The Albertina also has a film museum (Osterreiches Filmmuseum), which preserves and projects famous and obscure films from the history of the cinema.

DUKE ALBERT OF SAXONY-TESCHEN'S PALACE. In honor of this prince, the gallery was named the "Albertina"; containing more than a million and a half works of art, it constitutes the largest collection of drawings in the world.

THE RING

▲ THE RING

URBAN EXPANSION
By the mid-19th century, Vienna had spread well
beyond its walls, with palaces and new urban districts
being constructed in the suburbs.

The Ring, which is the wide boulevard
surrounding the Old City, forms a huge circle
2½ miles in diameter and 61 yards wide. One of
the most elegant thoroughfares in Europe, it
was built in the second half of the 19th century
to take the place of the original fortifications –
ramparts, towers and bastions – which protected
Vienna from the besieging Turks in 1529 and
1683. Military strategy evolved during the 18th
and 19th centuries, and armies preferred to
fight in the open, where a decision could be
reached in a single day, rather than to endure
protracted sieges. Napoleon entered Vienna
without a single blow after Austerlitz (1805) and
Wagram (1809). In December 1857, Franz-
Joseph signed
the decree
authorizing the
demolition of
the city's
fortifications.

Like Baron Haussmann, who opened up
broad streets through medieval Paris at
much the same time, Franz-Joseph
(right) favored the construction of
a wide boulevard. This would
make it easier to move
troops to quell
disturbances (in
1848 the regular
forces which
intervened against
the rebels emerged
from behind the
fortifications).

FRANZ-JOSEPH
The boulevard gave
Vienna a cleaner and
more distinguished
appearance, more
properly reflecting
the greatness of the
Habsburgs ▲*134, 143*.

INAUGURATION PARADES AROUND THE RING
The Viennese were skeptical and even hostile to the Ring during early construction, but when the new promenade was finally opened in 1865 their delight knew no bounds. The imperial army paraded in full ceremonial uniform, and the people danced to Johann Strauss the Younger's *Demolition Polka*.

THE RING
BUILDING SITES
Along the Ring, new building sites sprang up everywhere. The State Opera was opened in 1869, followed by the Academy of Applied Arts, the Academy of Fine Arts, the Votive Church, the Parliament and the City Hall. Around ten public buildings and private palaces were constructed for the Viennese aristocracy and Austria's new captains of industry.

The greatest architects in Europe were summoned to Vienna; in conformity with Franz-Joseph's somewhat conservative taste, these architects invented no new styles, but sought inspiration in the past. The Ring gives the visitor a lesson in art history, from Greek antiquity to the Baroque period, by way of Romanesque, Gothic and Renaissance styles.

View of the Schanzel, near the Danube.

Building on Franz-Josephs-Kai (right) and one on the corner of Franz-Josephs-Kai and Werdertorgasse (far right).

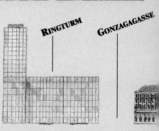

RINGTURM
The Ring tower was completed in 1955.

FRANZ-JOSEPHS-KAI

RINGTURM

GONZAGAGASSE

SCHOTTENRING

DANUBE

PLATZ/MONUMENT

FRANZ-JOSEPHS-KAI ▲ 229,
230 The quays were heavily bombed in 1945 ● 42, and few of their original buildings remain.

ROSSAUERKASERNE
The architecture of these large barracks, built in 1869, is similar to that of the Army Museum ▲ 258.

The monument to the Hoch und Deutschmeister (formerly the Regiment of the City of Vienna) on Deutschmeisterplatz, stands in front of the Rossauerkaserne.

The Fruit Market on the Schanzel, by Alois Schorn.

The temporary Stock Exchange on the site of today's Börse was the scene of "Black Thursday", May 9, 1873. The stock market plunging on that day ended a period of prosperity, and its effects were felt even in the US.

No. 24
This fine building from the historicist epoch is now the site of the *Ring Cafeteria*.

BÖRSE
The Stock Exchange at no. 16 was designed by Theophil von Hansen (1871–7). It was partly burned down in 1956.

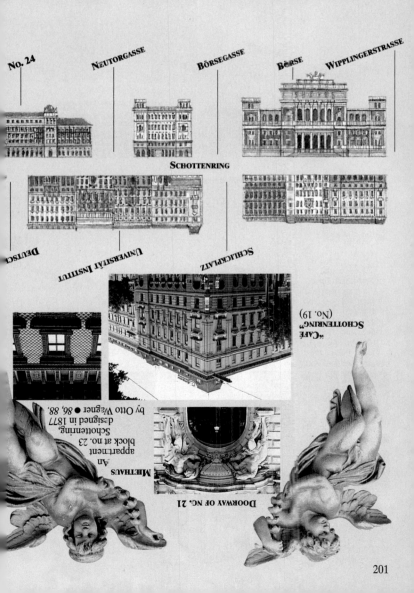

No. 24 **NEUTORGASSE** **BÖRSEGASSE** **BÖRSE** **WIPPLINGERSTRASSE**

SCHOTTENRING

DEUTSC **UNIVERSITÄT INSTITUT** **SCHLICKPLATZ**

"CAFÉ SCHOTTENRING" (No. 19)

MIETHAUS
An apartment block at no. 23 Schottenring, designed in 1877 by Otto Wagner ● 86, 88.

DOORWAY OF NO. 21

201

VOTIVKIRCHE
The neo-Gothic Votive Church was constructed by the architect Heinrich von Ferstel between 1856 and 1879.

"TO HAVE A PLAY PUT ON AT THE BURGTHEATER WAS THE GREATEST DREAM OF EVERY VIENNESE WRITER."
STEFAN ZWEIG

ZWEIG'S BIRTHPLACE
At no. 14 is the birthplace of the writer Stefan Zweig.

1. Schottengas...

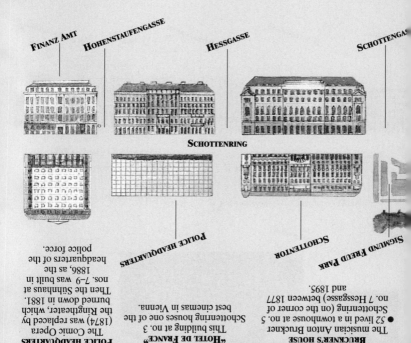

FINANZ AMT

HOHENSTAUFENGASSE

HESSGASSE

SCHOTTENGAS...

SCHOTTENRING

POLICE HEADQUARTERS

SCHOTTENTOR

SIGMUND FREUD PARK

POLICE HEADQUARTERS
The Comic Opera (1874) was replaced by the Ringtheater, which burned down in 1881. Then the Sühnhaus at nos. 7–9 was built in 1886, as the headquarters of the police force.

"PLAZA" HOTEL (11 Schottenring). Left and below.

"HOTEL DE FRANCE"
This building at no. 3 Schottenring houses one of the best cinemas in Vienna.

BRUCKNER'S HOUSE
The musician Anton Bruckner ● 52 lived in a townhouse at no. 5 Schottenring (on the corner of no. 7 Hessgasse) between 1877 and 1895.

I. Stadt. Dr. Karl Lueger-Ring.

EPHRUSSI PALACE
This palace at no. 14 Dr Karl Lueger Ring was designed by Theophil von Hansen, architect of the nearby Parliament building (1873).

LIEBENBERG MEMORIAL
J. A. von Liebenberg was mayor of Vienna during the 1683 siege. On the ruins of the 17th-century Melk Bastion (Mölkerbastei), demolished in 1872, stands the Pasqualati house ▲ 166.

THE "CAFÉ LANDTMANN"
This establishment, which has been managed by several generations of the Querfeld family, is a favorite meeting place for members of the Parliament opposite, and for people who have just attended plays at the nearby Burgtheater.

PHRUSSI PALACE   MÖLKERBASTEI   LIEBENBERG MEMORIAL   SCHREYVOGELGASSE   CAFÉ LANDTMANN   OPPOLZERGASSE

SCHOTTENRING   **DR KARL LUEGER RING**

VOTIVKIRCHE   UNIVERSITÄT   GRILLPARZERSTRASSE

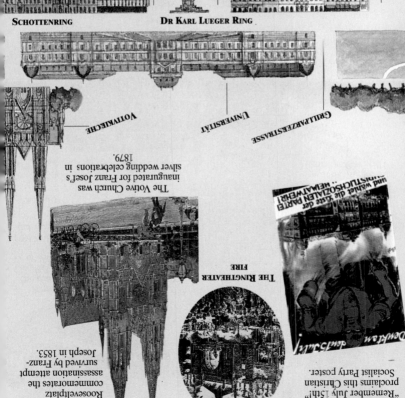

The Votive Church was inaugurated for Franz Josef's silver wedding celebrations in 1879.

VOTIVKIRCHE ● 85
The Votive Church on Rooseveltplatz commemorates the assassination attempt survived by Franz-Joseph in 1853.

THE RINGTHEATER FIRE

THE FIRE AT THE UNIVERSITY
"Remember July 15th!" proclaims this Christian Socialist Party poster.

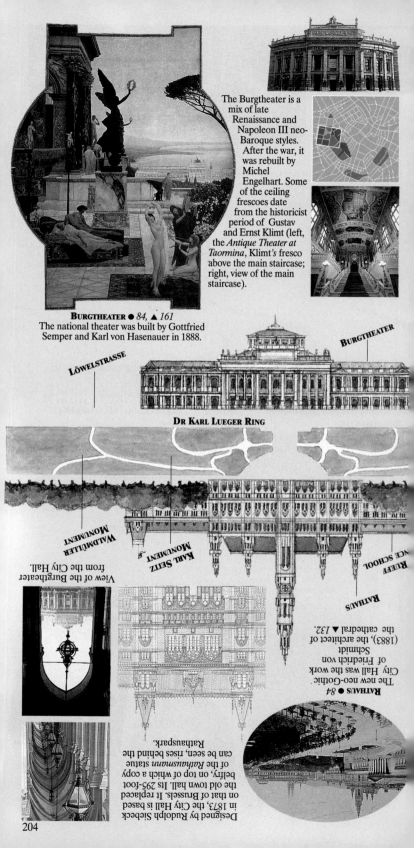

The Burgtheater is a mix of late Renaissance and Napoleon III neo-Baroque styles. After the war, it was rebuilt by Michel Engelhart. Some of the ceiling frescoes date from the historicist period of Gustav and Ernst Klimt (left, the *Antique Theater at Taormina*, Klimt's fresco above the main staircase; right, view of the main staircase).

BURGTHEATER ● *84,* ▲ *161*
The national theater was built by Gottfried Semper and Karl von Hasenauer in 1888.

LÖWELSTRASSE

BURGTHEATER

DR KARL LUEGER RING

WALDMÜLLER MONUMENT

KARL SEITZ MONUMENT

RUEFF FENCE SCHOOL

RATHAUS

View of the Burgtheater from the City Hall.

RATHAUS ● *84*
The new neo-Gothic City Hall was the work of Friedrich von Schmidt (1883), the architect of the cathedral ▲ *132.*

Designed by Rudolph Siebeck in 1873, the City Hall is based on that of Brussels. It replaced the old town hall. Its 295-foot belfry, on top of which a copy of the *Rathausmann* statue can be seen, rises behind the Rathauspark.

The Volksgarten is strewn with small buildings: the Temple of Theseus by Nobile (right, 1820), a miniature replica of the Theseion at Athens, with a statue by Müllner in front (1921); the monument to the Empress Elizabeth (1907); an octagonal café; and several pools (1866–80) with statues.

This garden, like the Burggarten, was laid out on the site of the fortifications destroyed by Napoleon in 1809. It was opened to the public as soon as it was completed in 1823.

KAISERIN ELISABETH MONUMENT

THESEUS TEMPLE

VOLKSGARTEN

DR KARL RENNER RING

STRAUSS LANNER MONUMENT

RATHAUSPARK

ATHENEBRUNNEN

PARLIAMENT

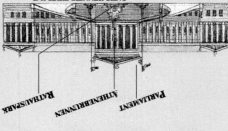

PARLIAMENT
The Parliament, built by Theophil von Hansen between 1874 and 1883, is inspired by Greek antiquity. The statues by the steps are of ancient historians. The Austrian Republic was proclaimed in front of the Parliament in 1918.

FOUNTAIN OF ATHENE (1902) ● 85
Athene sits atop this fountain. At her feet, allegorical statues represent Austria's rivers.

RATHAUS

STRAUSS LANNER MONUMENT
The musicians Strauss and Lanner ● 56, rivals during their lifetimes, were reconciled by their sculptor in 1905.

GRILLPARZER MEMORIAL Karl Kundmann, Karl von Hasenauer and Rudolf von Weyr collaborated on this monument, built in 1889.

The bas-reliefs of the Grillparzer Memorial ● 60, 62, ▲ 147 reproduce some of the playwright's best-known scenes.

"CAFÉ MEIEREI" This open-air establishment adjoining the university is open from early April to the end of September. It serves several specialties of Viennese cuisine.

Café-Meierei Volksgarten

VOLKSGARTEN   GRILLPARZER MONUMENT

DR KARL RENNER RING

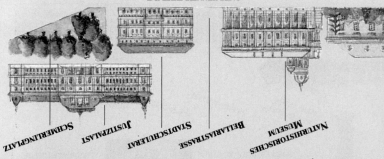

SCHMERLINGPLATZ   JUSTIZPALAST   STADTSCHULRAT   BELLARIASTRASSE   NATURHISTORISCHES MUSEUM

AUERSPERG PALACE AND THE VOLKSTHEATER
Behind the Palace of Justice are the Volkstheater and the Auersperg Palace. The latter was the headquarters of the provisional national committee, a Resistance movement founded in 1944 ● 42.

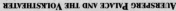

JUSTIZPALAST
The Palace of Justice (1881), in the German Renaissance style, was burned down in 1927. From 1945 to 1955, it was the seat of the Allied High Command. Below, the main staircase.

HEADDRESS OF MONTEZUMA
This can be seen at the Museum of Ethnography ▲ 187 (Museum für Völkerkunde, Heldenplatz, I) at the Neue Burg ▲ 177.

NEUE BURG
The part of the Neue Burg (1881–1913) which overlooks the Ring is known as the main building. It was to have been extended by a triumphal arch over the Ring which would have joined it to the Art History Museum. A similar building was to have faced the Neue Burg, linked to the Natural History Museum by another triumphal arch: and the ensemble was to have formed an imperial forum.

STRASSENBAHN HALTESTELLE

BURGTOR
Built by P. von Nobile (1824) to a design by L. Cagnola, the Burgtor was altered by R. Wondracek (1934), who turned it into a monument to the victims of World War One. A monument has now been added to it in memory of the Austrian Resistance.

HELDENPLATZ
The Burgtor leads to Heroes' Square, with its statues of Archduke Charles ● 38, ▲ 261 and Prince Eugène ● 35, ▲ 247, completed in 1860 and 1865, respectively.

BURGTOR　　NEUE BURG　　BURGGARTEN

BURGRING

MARIA THERESIA MONUMENT　　MESSEPALAST　　KUNSTHISTORISCHES MUSEUM　　BABENBERG STRASSE　　ESCHENBACHGASSE

MESSEPALAST. The exhibition hall occupies the former court stable block. It was started by J. B. Fischer von Erlach in 1719 and completed by his son Josef Emanuel in 1723. It was also altered between 1850 and 1854.

MARIA THERESA MONUMENT
A work by the sculptor K. von Zumbusch (1830–1915). The riders are generals and the statues of the central group are reliefs honor sixteen individuals, among them Haydn and Mozart ● 48.

KUNSTHISTORISCHES MUSEUM ● 84, ▲ 208 AND NATURHISTORISCHES MUSEUM
The Museum of Art History and the Natural History Museum were built in the Italian Renaissance style by Karl von Hasenauer (interior decoration) and Gottfried Semper (façades) between 1872 and 1891. The main entrances on Maria-Theresienplatz are flanked by allegorical figures.

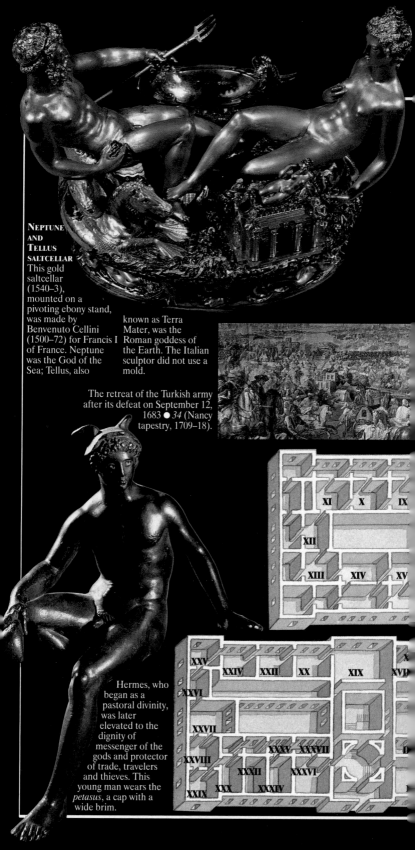

NEPTUNE AND TELLUS SALTCELLAR
This gold saltcellar (1540–3), mounted on a pivoting ebony stand, was made by Benvenuto Cellini (1500–72) for Francis I of France. Neptune was the God of the Sea; Tellus, also known as Terra Mater, was the Roman goddess of the Earth. The Italian sculptor did not use a mold.

The retreat of the Turkish army after its defeat on September 12, 1683 ● *34* (Nancy tapestry, 1709–18).

Hermes, who began as a pastoral divinity, was later elevated to the dignity of messenger of the gods and protector of trade, travelers and thieves. This young man wears the *petasus*, a cap with a wide brim.

XI   X   IX
XII
XIII   XIV   XV

XXV   XXIV   XXII   XX   XIX   X
XXVI   XVI
XXVII
XXVIII   XXXV   XXXVII   D
XXXII   XXXVI
XXIX   XXX   XXXIV

THE GENIUS CELLINI
This goldsmith's jewel, made by the sculptor for Francis I of France, is an allegory of the universe: an elephant carries the Earth while horses support Neptune. The four winds and the hours of the day also feature.

SECOND FLOOR
The coin collection (Münzkabinett) is kept on this floor.

"BEZOAR"
This 16th-century Spanish bezoar stands on a tripod in the form of three lions, decorated with emeralds from the New World. The *bezoar*, a concretion formed by indigestible matter in the bodies of certain animals, was considered to be an excellent antidote for all sorts of poisons.

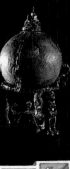

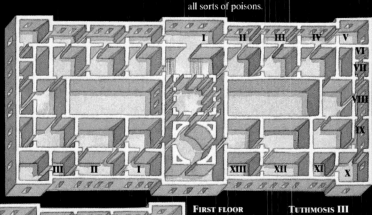

FIRST FLOOR
Devoted entirely to paintings, the first floor consists of two galleries (Gemäldegalerie): one of Italian and Spanish paintings; the other of Dutch, Flemish and German paintings.

TUTHMOSIS III
A black basalt bust of the 18th-Dynasty Pharaoh Tuthmosis (1504–1450 BC).

MEZZANINE
There are three different collections on the mezzanine floor: sculpture and decorative arts (Sammlung für Plastik und Kunstgewerbe), Greek, Etruscan and Roman antiquities (Antikensammlung) and Egyptian antiquities (Aegyptische Sammlung).

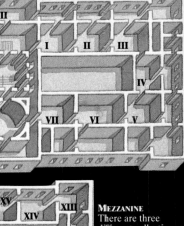

The Art History Museum of Vienna is one of the richest in Europe. The building was constructed to plans by Karl Hasenauer and Gottfried Semper (1870–91), and its collections ▲ 208 are divided into five departments, the painting section being the most extraordinary. Ferdinand I (1503–64) created a first "Cabinet Room of Arts and Wonders" at the Castle of Ambras near Innsbruck. His nephew Rudolph II assembled a large collection of paintings (notably by Brueghel) in his castle at Prague. His successor, Matthias, transferred the court of Prague to Vienna, bringing the collection with him. Leopold I inherited a number of Flemish and Italian pictures, and the Habsburgs' links with the Spanish branch of their family allowed the Austrian emperors to round off their collection very well.

Ferdinand of the Tyrol, son of Ferdinand I, himself a great collector, shown in a portrait by Francesco Terzio kept at Ambras; the Ambras collection is a part of the "Kunst". Below, *View of the Imperial Stables at the Hofburg*, by Franz Alt.

"THE CITY HAS FINE CATHEDRALS, OLD, ILL-PAVED STREETS, THE BEAUTIFUL BLUE DANUBE AND MUSEUMS FILLED WITH TREASURES (THE BRUEGHELS ALONE ARE WORTH THE TRIP)."

JOSEF VON STERNBERG

GIUSEPPE ARCIMBOLDO

The Emperors of Austria (Rudolph in particular) gave a warm welcome to this highly original Milanese painter. Arcimboldo (c. 1527–93) customarily painted faces in vegetable form. Thus in *Winter* (1573, opposite) he portrays Francis I of France as a tree trunk, using knots of wood and poisonous fungi to give him human features. The overall effect of phantasmagoria is very striking, but the details are perhaps more interesting still.

JAN VAN EYCK (c. 1390–1441)

The great master Jan van Eyck was treated like a prince all his life. He traveled all over Europe at a time when few people did so, visiting France, Spain and Portugal. Van Eyck far outstripped the fashions of his time; he freed his paintings from Gothic constraints and rediscovered the true simplicity of nature. Realism was the principal characteristic of his art. Though some of van Eyck's work was religious, he excelled at portraiture. His *Cardinal Nicolas Albergati* (1431) is one of his greatest works (right). This Polish cardinal is painted in an uncompromising manner but with no hint of caricature. The powerful physique and deeply-scored features indicate a strong personality; but the depth of understanding in the cardinal's eyes belie his physical appearance.

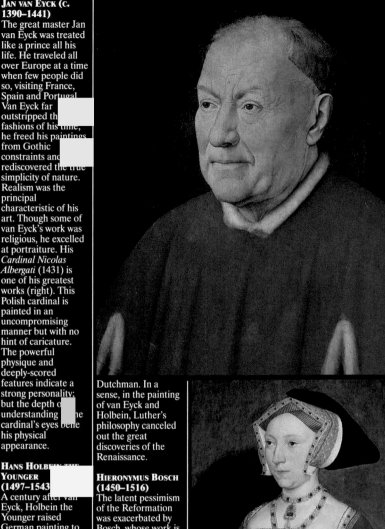

HANS HOLBEIN THE YOUNGER (1497–1543)

A century after van Eyck, Holbein the Younger raised German painting to its highest point. He settled in England in 1532, after the triumph of the Reformation, and reached the zenith of his career as official painter to the English court. He had the same objectivity and regard for detail as van Eyck, as is shown by his *Portrait of Jane Seymour* (right), and his faces have much the same gravity as those of the Dutchman. In a sense, in the painting of van Eyck and Holbein, Luther's philosophy canceled out the great discoveries of the Renaissance.

HIERONYMUS BOSCH (1450–1516)

The latent pessimism of the Reformation was exacerbated by Bosch, whose work is amply represented at Vienna. In his eyes Christ's *Bearing of the Cross* (right-hand page) becomes a masquerade of grimaces, gesticulations, ferocious faces, and shrieks. The painting in effect depicts a scene from hell. The peoples of northern Europe, despite the Renaissance, were allowing their demons to escape.

After the gaiety and convincing materialism of his *Village Wedding*, Pieter Brueghel the Elder (c. 1525–69) produced the heartbreaking landscape of *Hunters in Winter*. Elie Faure describes it as follows: "The violet and black winter is more painful, with its frozen ground crackling to the very tips of the tree-branches, than it is when snow has covered its naked carcass and muffled all its sounds – except for the voices of men who come forth, and are astonished to find themselves alone." More than half the known paintings of Brueghel the Elder are to be found in the Vienna Art History Museum.

GIORGIONE (1477–1510)

With Giorgione, Italian painting broke new ground. Not content with Giotto's literal transpositions or with Raphael's harmonious ones, Giorgione evolved a poetic, almost esoteric way of looking at the world. Every one of his paintings is an enigma. The *Three Philosophers* (right) has provoked much commentary: some critics believed the figures represented Pythagoras, Plato and Zoroaster, symbolizing the diversity of mankind. But this ingenious interpretation has recently been overturned by the results of an x-ray, which show the sages to be no more than a trio of astrologers. Strictly speaking, the works of Giorgione have no particular meaning – which makes them all the more mysterious.

RAPHAEL (1483–1520)

"Raphael does not abandon himself to his theme", wrote Taine. "He remains sober and moderate; he studiously avoids going to extremes of movement or expression. He purifies types and arranges poses with great care. It is this taste for moderation and good measure, along with his spiritual delicacy, that carries him to the summit of his art." The *Madonna of the Meadows* (above), better known as the *Madonna of the Belvedere*, is a magnificent example of the classical style. The triangular composition, harmonious gestures and sweet expressions are entirely characteristic of the classical manner. The aim of symmetry in classicism is to establish contact with the spiritual world.

TITIAN (c. 1485–1576)

The approach of Titian, the "Doge of Color" and the painter of the *Madonna of the Cherries* (c. 1512–15, top right), is entirely different; beginning with a Raphael-style composition, he gives color precedence over form. Palma the Younger said of his master Titian that he "roughed out his paintings by first brushing in blocks of color, which served as a bed or foundation for what he wished to express, and on these he could build afterward."

"LONG BEFORE THE GERMAN MUSICIANS, GIORGIONE WAS THE
HERALD OF MODERNISM. GIORGIONE CREATED THE SYMPHONY.
HE IS THE FATHER OF PAINTING."

ÉLIE FAURE

217

"RUBENS, RIVER OF FORGETFULNESS, GARDEN OF IDLENESS,
PILLOW OF FLESH WHERE ONE CANNOT LOVE, BUT WHERE LIFE
RUNS AND MOVES ABOUT WITHOUT CEASING..."

CHARLES BAUDELAIRE

PETER PAUL RUBENS (1577–1640)

The *Nude of Hélène Fourment* (1638), sometimes called *Woman in a Fur Coat*, is a portrait of Ruben's second wife. The painter never tired of painting Hélène in all kinds of costumes, and in unabashedly sensual states of undress. Here (far left) she is seen half-naked under a fur-lined coat: laughing and blushing, she stares at her reflection in the mirror, while the painter himself seems confounded by such abundance of youth. The great design of Rubens, the heir of Titian, was not to express the harmony of reason like Raphael, nor the power of intelligence like Leonardo, but simply to express the infinite resources of life. He allowed himself to be carried away by life, dedicating his entire oeuvre to it. He was thus the precursor of Fragonard and Renoir.

TINTORETTO (1518–94)

The Biblical story of *Suzannah Bathing* (1560's, above) inspired several paintings by Tintoretto: another is in the Louvre. In the version in Vienna's Art History Museum, the painter seems to align himself with Veronese, and in doing so reaches the acme of his powers: the skillful handling of perspective, the extraordinary luminosity of the nude, the transparency of the veils, all combine to give this canvas a distinctly sensual flavor. Tintoretto did not stop at this material vision, however. Beyond its simple carnality, the work offers a moral lesson. The old men on the left, in a daring top-to-bottom perspective, seem plunged in the hell of unsatisfied desire, while Suzannah, gloriously haloed, represents innocence before the Fall.

219

VERMEER OF DELFT (1632–75)

The Artist in His Studio (right) is one of the museum's masterpieces, painted by Johannes Vermeer shortly before his death. From the point of view of its subject matter only, the picture seems banal; its powerful poetry lies in its rendering. "The letter is unimportant; so are the women. Likewise the world from which letters are brought. The world, in fact, has become a painting," wrote Malraux. The light, which comes from an invisible window, is unearthly; the painter (seen from behind) is mysterious; the girl dressed for a wedding is enigmatic. To crown all, an open map suggests fascinating voyages. The spectator feels himself to be in a theater; the heavy drapes held by a simple cord to the left will shortly fall like the curtain of a stage, and the play will be ended.

REMBRANDT VAN RIJN (1606–69)

The model for *The Portrait of Titus*, or *The Reader* (top right) was Rembrandt's fourth son from his union with Saskia. He was the only one of Rembrandt's children to survive into adulthood and this may explain the special tenderness with which the artist treats this young man. Only the hands and books are bathed in light; the face is not, and it is this that lends the portrait its strangeness.

"REMBRANDT WAS HAUNTED BY HIS OWN FACE, WHICH HE AT FIRST LOADED WITH DISGUISES, NOT TO ADORN IT AS SOME HAVE THOUGHT, BUT TO MULTIPLY IT."

ANDRÉ MALRAUX

In the paintings of Rembrandt, the light does not come from without, as it does in the work of Caravaggic, but from within. In this way he bares the souls of his subjects.

DIEGO VELAZQUEZ (1599–1660)
Velazquez' technique is entirely different: far from revealing his subjects' inner souls,

he treats them as the objects of pure poetry (above, portraits of the Infanta Margarita-Theresa, the Infanta Maria Theresa, and Don Felipe-Prosper). Margarita-Theresa, a little princess with an obstinate face, then aged eight, is transformed into a blue-and-gold gem by a few fluid brushstrokes.

BURGGARTEN

The garden of the Imperial Palace (1820), the former court promenade, was opened to the public in 1919. It has a number of fine statues, among them one of Mozart (below and

detail, far right, 1896), one of Francis of Lorraine (1781) and a monument to Franz-Joseph (1904).

GOETHE MONUMENT
The statue of Goethe (1900) by Edmund Hellmer stands in the middle of Goethestrasse.

The palaces of the brewer A. Dreher (no. 4), the industrialist A. Ritter von Schoeller (no. 6) and the banker and art patron F. Schey (no. 8) line the north side of the Opernring.

MOZART MONUMENT — BURGGARTEN — GOETHE MONUMENT — SCHEY PALACE — SCHOELLER PALACE — DREHER PALACE

OPERNRING

FRANZ VON SUPPÉ'S HOUSE — ROBERT STOLZ PLATZ — SCHILLER MONUMENT — HOTEL — SCHEY HAUS

OPERNRING AND OPERNRINGHOF

The houses at nos. 7 and 23 Opernring are typical of the first period of construction of the Ring (1861–3). The Opernringhof, a large modern building facing the Opera, is by Jonas Königswater (1956). It replaces the Heinrichhof, destroyed by bombs during World War Two ● 42.

SCHILLER MONUMENT

A statue of the poet F. von Schiller, by Schilling (1876), stands in front of the Fine Arts Academy.

THE SUPPÉ HOUSE

The operetta composer Franz von Suppé died at no. 23 Opernring.

AKADEMIE DER BILDENDEN KÜNSTE

The Fine Arts Academy (1876), a neo-Renaissance building by Hansen, has a façade covered in antique statuary and, inside, a fresco of *The Fall of the Titans* by Anselm Feuerbach. There is also a gallery (Flemish, German, Spanish and Italian schools).

SECESSION ● 86, ▲ 232.

The Secession Pavilion is set back somewhat from the Fine Arts Academy.

STAATSOPER

Wrecked by bombing, the neo-Renaissance Opera by A. Siccard von Siccardsburg and E. van der Nüll (1869) was rebuilt by Erich Boltenstern in 1955.

The frescoes in the foyer by Moritz von Schwind illustrate (among other works) *Fidelio* (above) which was performed on the day of the reopening in 1955.

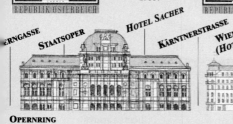

ERNGASSE — **STAATSOPER** — **HOTEL SACHER** — **KÄRNTNERSTRASSE** — **WIENER PALACE (HOTEL BRISTOL)** — **TODESCO PALACE**

OPERNRING

KÄRNTNER RING

OPERNRINGHOF — **TOURIST OFFICE** — **SIRK ECKE** — **MEINL**

MEINL ECKE
The "Meinl Corner" is the headquarters of the coffee manufacturer Julius Meinl ● 72, ▲ 136.

"CAFÉ MUSEUM"
Designed by Loos in 1899 the café had chairs by the famous chair manufacturer Thonet ▲ 158.

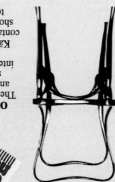

OPERNPASSAGE
The Opera Passage, an underground street at the intersection of the Ring and Kärntnerstrasse, contains a number of shops and the city tourist office.

KARLSPLATZ ▲ 240
The famous metro station designed by the architect Otto Wagner ● 86, 88 stands behind the Künstlerhaus.

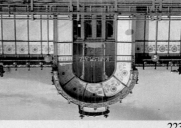

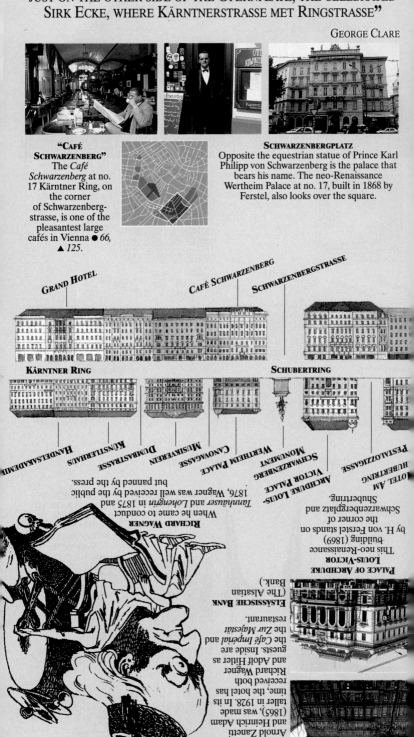

"FROM THE APARTMENT AT NO. 3 OPERNRING, SHE COULD SEE, JUST ON THE OTHER SIDE OF THE OPERNPLATZ, THE CELEBRATED SIRK ECKE, WHERE KÄRNTNERSTRASSE MET RINGSTRASSE"

GEORGE CLARE

"CAFÉ SCHWARZENBERG"
The *Café Schwarzenberg* at no. 17 Kärntner Ring, on the corner of Schwarzenberg-strasse, is one of the pleasantest large cafés in Vienna ● 66, ▲ 125.

SCHWARZENBERGPLATZ
Opposite the equestrian statue of Prince Karl Philipp von Schwarzenberg is the palace that bears his name. The neo-Renaissance Wertheim Palace at no. 17, built in 1868 by Ferstel, also looks over the square.

GRAND HOTEL

CAFÉ SCHWARZENBERG

SCHWARZENBERGSTRASSE

KÄRNTNER RING

SCHUBERTRING

HANDELSAKADEMIE

KÜNSTLERHAUS

DUMBASTRASSE

CANOVAGASSE

MUSIKVEREIN

WERTHEIM PALACE

SCHWARZENBERG MONUMENT

ARCHDUKE LOUIS-VICTOR PALACE

PESTALOZZIGASSE

HOTEL AM HUBERTRING

RICHARD WAGNER
When he came to conduct *Tannhäuser* and *Lohengrin* in 1875 and 1876, Wagner was well received by the public but panned by the press.

PALACE OF ARCHDUKE LOUIS-VICTOR
This neo-Renaissance building (1869) by H. von Ferstel stands on the corner of Schwarzenbergplatz and Schubertring.

ELSÄSSISCHE BANK
(The Alsatian Bank.) restaurant.

"HOTEL IMPERIAL"
The former Württemberg Palace, by Arnold Zanetti and Heinrich Adam (1865), was made taller in 1928. In its time, the hotel has received both Richard Wagner and Adolf Hitler as guests. Inside are the *Café Imperial* and the *Zur Majestät* restaurant.

224

LEINTENBERGER PALACE
Built for the Austrian property owner and industrialist Baron Friedrich Leintenberger in 1871, this palace at no. 16 Parkring adjoins the Henckel Palace.

THE TRAMWAY
The red and white Viennese tramway is painted in the colors of the city.

SKENE AND KINSKY PALACES
The palace built in 1870 for the textile magnate and member of parliament Alfred Skene, and that of the

banker Eugen Kinsky occupy nos. 6 to 14.

RINGSTRASSEN GALERIEN
The program for this portion of the ring is construction and restoration – hence the ensemble of hotels, shops and apartment buildings known as the Ringstrassen Galerien.

A building on the corner of the Schubertring and Fichtegasse.

FICHTEGASSE   JOHANNESGASSE

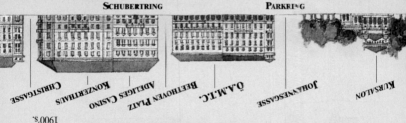

SCHUBERTRING   PARKRING

CHRISTGASSE   KONZERTHAUS   ADELIGES CASINO   BEETHOVEN PLATZ   Ö.A.M.T.C.   JOHANNESGASSE   KURSALON

WIENFLUSSPORTAL
Vienna's favorite open-air spot in the Stadtpark is known as the "Gate of the Wien River". An Art Nouveau ensemble ● 86 of kiosks, balustrades and stone stairways was built here in the early 1900's.

Ö.A.M.T.C.
The headquarters of the Austrian Automobile and Touring Club (Österreichischer Automobil Motor und Touringclub) is at no. 1 Schubertring.

"KURSALON"
This Renaissance-style tearoom may be entered via no. 33 Johannesgasse. Designed by Johann Graben (1865–7) it was a venue frequented by Eduard Strauss, brother of Johann the Younger ● 57. Today, waltzes are still danced on the terrace in fine weather.

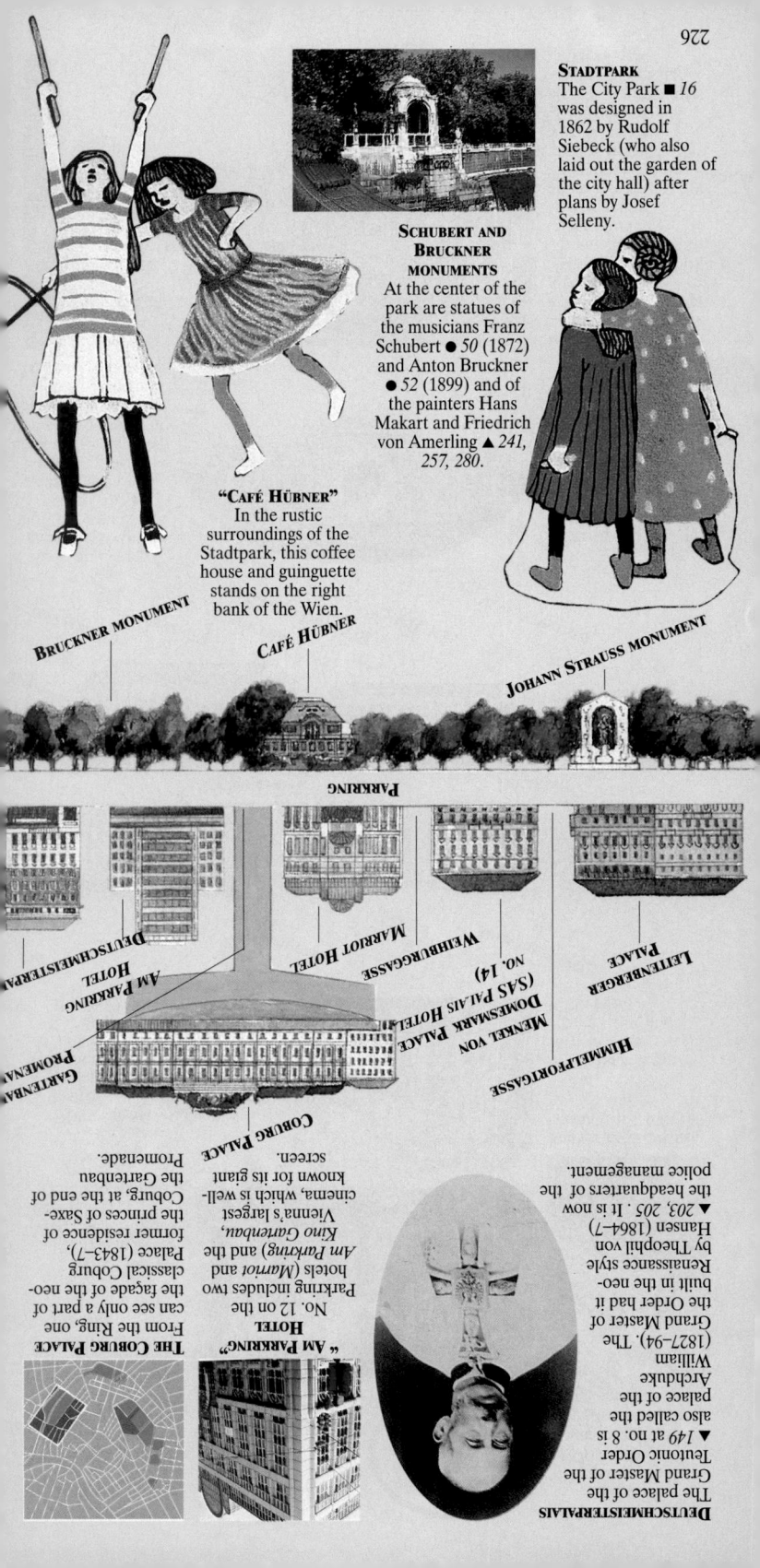

STADTPARK

The City Park ■ *16* was designed in 1862 by Rudolf Siebeck (who also laid out the garden of the city hall) after plans by Josef Selleny.

SCHUBERT AND BRUCKNER MONUMENTS

At the center of the park are statues of the musicians Franz Schubert ● *50* (1872) and Anton Bruckner ● *52* (1899) and of the painters Hans Makart and Friedrich von Amerling ▲ *241, 257, 280.*

"CAFÉ HÜBNER"

In the rustic surroundings of the Stadtpark, this coffee house and guinguette stands on the right bank of the Wien.

BRUCKNER MONUMENT

CAFÉ HÜBNER

JOHANN STRAUSS MONUMENT

PARKRING

DEUTSCHMEISTERPALAIS

AM PARKRING HOTEL

MARRIOT HOTEL

WEIHBURGGASSE

DOMESMARK PALACE (SAS PALAIS HOTEL, NO. 14)

LEITENBERGER PALACE

GARTENBAU PROMENADE

COBURG PALACE

MENKEL VON

HIMMELPFORTGASSE

THE COBURG PALACE

From the Ring, one can see only a part of the facade of the neo-classical Coburg Palace (1843–7), former residence of the princes of Saxe-Coburg, at the end of the Gartenbau Promenade.

"AM PARKRING" HOTEL

No. 12 on the Parkring includes two hotels (*Marriot* and *Am Parkring*) and the *Kino Gartenbau*, Vienna's largest cinema, which is well-known for its giant screen.

DEUTSCHMEISTERPALAIS

The palace of the Grand Master of the Teutonic Order ▲ *149* at no. 8 is also called the palace of the Archduke William (1827–94). The Grand Master of the Order had it built in the neo-Renaissance style by Theophil von Hansen (1864–7) ▲ *203, 205.* It is now the headquarters of the police management.

COLLOREDO PALACE

This private townhouse (no. 66) was lived in by the Colloredo family, whose most prominent member was the Prince-Archbishop of Salzburg who tyrannized Mozart.

DUMBA PALACE

This palace at no. 4 belonged to Nikolaus Dumba, an art patron of Greek extraction.

KARL LUEGER MONUMENT

The statue of the Mayor of Vienna (1897–1910) stands on the square named after him. Karl Lueger, who founded the Austrian Christian Socialist party, was a lawyer much loved by the common people because he installed modern public facilities managed by municipal companies in working-class areas. Above, a painting of Lueger by Wilhelm Gause.

COLLOREDO PALACE ZEDLITZGASSE DUMBA PALACE DR KARL LUEGER MONUMENT DR KARL LUEGER PLATZ CAFÉ PRÜCKL FALKERSTRASSE

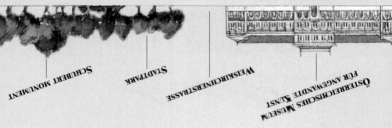

PARKRING   STUBENRING

SCHUBERT MONUMENT STADTPARK WEISKIRCHNERSTRASSE ÖSTERREICHISCHES MUSEUM FÜR ANGEWANDTE KUNST

"COMBAT AT MINERVE"

This tapestry dating from the first quarter of the 15th century is displayed at the Museum of Applied Arts (Österreichisches Museum für angewandte Kunst), at no. 5 Stubenring.

JOHANN STRAUSS MONUMENT

In 1925, Edmund Hellmer installed a procession of marble relads (far right) around the bronze statue of Strauss the younger (right) ● 57.

FRANZ SCHUBERT

A painting by Gustav Klimt (1899) ▲ 204, 250 representing Schubert ● 50 at the piano (below), which was commissioned for the Dumba Palace. This is a copy: the original was destroyed during World War Two.

227

THE CHAMBER OF COMMERCE
At nos. 8–10 Stubenring is a Jugendstil and neo-classical building by Baumann (1907) ● *86*. It is now the Vienna Chamber of Commerce (Kammer der gewerblichen Wirtschaft für Wien).

Aluminum air vent for the heating system at the Postsparkasse.

POSTSPARKASSE ● *88*
The Post Office Savings Bank (1904–12) that dominates Georg-Coch-Platz is the masterpiece of the Viennese Secession ▲ *232* architect Otto Wagner ● *86*, ▲ *237, 240, 294*. In front is the statue of the bank's founder, Georg Coch (1842–90).

"CAFÉ PRÜCKL"
This café, at no. 24, on the corner of Lueger Platz, is one of the most convivial establishments in Vienna.

POSTSPARKASSE

ROSENBURSENSTRASSE   KAMMER DER GEWERBLICHEN WIRTSCHAFT FÜR WIEN

STUBENRING

MUSEUM FÜR ANGEWANDTE KUNST   MARXERGASSE   OSKAR KOKOSCHKA PLATZ

MUSEUM FÜR ANGEWANDTE KUNST
The Museum of Applied Arts and the academy next door, both built in the Italian Renaissance style (1871) by Heinrich von Ferstel ▲ *224*, were enlarged by Ludwig Baumann in 1906–8. The museum contains collections of old furniture, ceramics, glassware, carpets and textiles. In front of the school is a statue of Oskar Kokoschka ▲ *254*, by Alfred Hrdlicka (1986).

HUNDERT-WASSERHAUS ● *94*
In Löwengasse to the east of the Ring is the irregular, gaudy, golden-domed building designed by the painter Hundertwasser (1983–5).

FRANZ-JOSEPHS-KAI AND THE DANUBE CANAL ▲ 230

This quay runs along the Danube Canal and closes the circular Ring Boulevard to the northeast. Its broad avenue is dominated by Ruprechtskirche ● 75, ▲ 154 and lined with hotels and restaurant terraces. At the edge of Schwedenplatz is the landing stage for the river boats. A monument in Morzinplatz marks the site of the former Gestapo building, where many Viennese died.

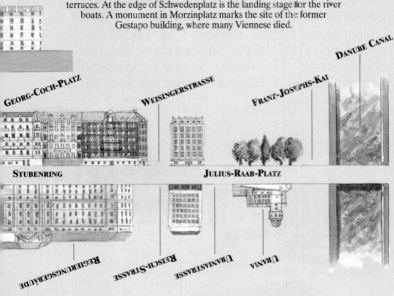

GEORG-COCH-PLATZ
WEISINGERSTRASSE
FRANZ-JOSEPHS-KAI
DANUBE CANAL
STUBENRING
JULIUS-RAAB-PLATZ
REGIERUNGSGEBÄUDE
REISCH-STRASSE
URANIASTRASSE
URANIA

URANIA
This Jugendstil building ● 86 by Max Fabiani (1909–10) stands at no. 1 Uraniastrasse, beside the Danube Canal and Julius-Raab-Platz.

The Urania building contains an observatory and a large theater: concerts are also staged here.

REGIERUNGSGEBÄUDE
Formerly the ministry of war, this building is now a civil service office. It was constructed in 1913 by Franz Neumann and served as the staff headquarters for the Habsburgs during World War One. In front is a statue of Marshal Radetzky ▲ 261 (1992).

229

The straightening of the Danube and the extension of the city (by joining Vienna proper to the Leopoldstadt, in 1850) led to a proliferation of bridges. Architects tended to give each new construction a distinctive artistic character – hence the series of bridges over the Wien, which were built in the Jugendstil manner with stone pilings, floral ornamentation and metal parapets.

SCHWEDENBRÜCKE
(Ferdinandsbrücke until 1920.)
The Ferdinandsbrücke (below) was Vienna's first solid bridge and opened on May 22, 1819. It replaced a pontoon and was built using the new technique of underwater construction.

FRANZENSBRÜCKE
(1803). Destroyed by the Viennese in 1809 while defending the city from the French, it was restored in 1899.

ASPERN BRÜCKE (rebuilt
and reopened in 1919). Aspernplatz (Julius Raab Platz since 1976) dates from the early 20th century. To its right is the "Kristallhof" (1905, destroyed in 1945); the Urania was built in 1910.

SALZTORBRÜCKE
(Stephaniebrücke until 1920.)

SCHWEDENBRÜCKE, MARIENBRÜCKE AND SALZTORBRÜCKE. In the foreground is a metro station by Otto Wagner▲ 241; on the far side of the river, the old houses of the Leopoldstadt ▲ 265.

FROM SECESSION TO MUSIKVEREINSGEBÄUDE

SECESSION ★

AN ART NOUVEAU MANIFESTO. The Secession Pavilion, built in 1898, stands in the center of the major Friedrichstrasse intersection, to the south of the Opernring, beside the ACADEMY OF FINE ARTS ▲ *222*. This large white cube topped by a gilded dome was designed by Joseph Maria Olbrich ● *87*, a pupil of Otto Wagner ● *86, 88*, ▲ *228, 237, 240* as a manifesto for the new movement launched by the Union of Young Artists. Its purpose was to stage the exhibitions of the Viennese avant-garde, which was at that time extolling the Jugendstil (Art Nouveau) ● *86*. Built on the square plan, the pavilion is not as stark as it might seem; floral friezes in bas-relief, Medusa masks and owls ornament the façade. As a whole, the pavilion is a two-tone harmony of white and gold, all the more striking since its recent renovation.

THE SECESSIONIST MOVEMENT. The Secessionist movement was started in 1897 by a group of young painters, architects and decorators trained at the nearby Academy of Fine Arts, most of whom were pupils of the architect Otto Wagner; its leader was the painter Gustav Klimt ▲ *250*. The movement was called "Secessionist" because these young artists began by "seceding" from the ARTISTS' ASSOCIATION (Künstlerhaus) ▲ *224*, which they considered too "official" and mediocre, and from the esthetic of historicism favored by Franz-Joseph ● *41*, ▲ *142, 144, 178*, which they considered thoroughly decadent. The composer Gustav Mahler ● *52, 301* was closely allied to the Secessionists. He entered their circle in 1902 following his marriage, in the Karlskirche ▲ *238*, to Alma Schindler, the daughter of a painter who for a while had shared a studio with Hans Makart ● *103*, and whose mother had remarried the Secessionist painter Carl Moll ● *104*.

THE END OF HISTORICISM. During the second half of the 19th century, Franz-Joseph sanctioned the destruction of Vienna's ramparts, which were replaced by the huge buildings along the Ring ● *84*, ▲ *198* (the Votive Church, the new University, the City Hall, the National Theater, the Parliament, and so on). All these buildings were designed in the Historicist style, with references and decorative motifs borrowed from Greek, Gothic and Renaissance art. Toward the end of the century,

SECESSION II AND SECESSION III
A poster (1898–9) by Joseph Maria Olbrich.

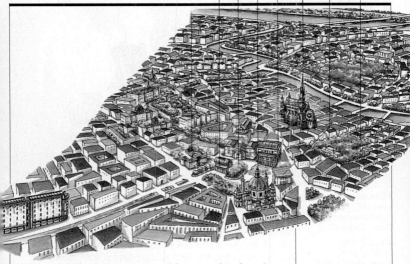

SECESSION
KÜNSTLERHAUS
KARLSPLATZ
KARLSKIRCHE
MUSIKVEREINGEBÄUDE
STEPHANSDOM
HISTORISCHES MUSEUM
DER STADT WIEN
STADTPARK

Viennese intellectuals began to call into question the values of liberal culture, and the architecture of the Ring became the symbolic target of their attacks. Although Gustav Klimt and Otto Wagner had shone as historicists (the former was responsible for the ceilings of the Burgtheater ● *204*, for example), they joined up with the group which between 1897 and 1898 created the celebrated pavilion, whose bare, geometrical outlines caused as much of a furor as the bold dictum inscribed on its pediment: "Der Zeit ihre Kunst, der Kunst ihre Freiheit" ("Every epoch has its art, and every art its freedom"). A comment about Joseph Maria Olbrich by Kirk Varnedoe, taken from *Vienna 1900*, can be applied equally well to the entire Secessionist movement: "In his reaction to the historicist stereotypes of the Ringstrasse, Olbrich deliberately cast about for something that would be indecipherable in terms of western convention, the symbolist mystery of an 'enigmatic key to the registers of emotion'."

THE GARDEN. Next to the sculpted bronze group representing the Roman general Mark Antony seated in a chariot harnessed to lions (the work of Arthur Strosser, 1854–1927), the garden is arranged in terraces to accommodate the pavilion's CAFETERIA.

🚶 Half a day

THE SECESSIONISTS
Joseph Maria Olbrich (left). In the photo below: Anton Stark, Gustav Klimt, Koloman Moser, Adolph Boehm, Maximilian Lenz (lying down), Ernst Stoehr, Wilhelm List, Emil Orlik, Maxi Kurzweil, Leopold Stolba (with cigarette), Carl Moll (lying down) and Heinrich Vogeler.

"THE HOSTILE FORCES"
A detail from the *Beethovenfries*.

EXHIBITIONS
A ticket to the *Kunstschau* of 1908 (right), one of the most famous exhibitions mounted by the Klimt group.

A piece of fabric printed with the "Secession" motif.

A MUSEUM OF MODERN ART. A large proportion of the furniture and the original decoration inside the pavilion disappeared during World War Two. Notable losses were the pieces of Secession-style furniture designed by Joseph Maria Olbrich and Josef Hoffmann, and the striking bust of Beethoven sculpted by Max Klinger (which now adorns the Gewandhaus, or concert hall, in Leipzig). The work of the Secession movement was to some extent neglected until its discovery in the 1960's. Today in the vacant spaces within the pavilion exhibitions of all kinds of contemporary art are regularly organized, and there is a bookshop which sells a wide range of exhibition catalogues, posters and postcards.

"BEETHOVENFRIES" ★ . There is a striking contrast between the Beethoven Frieze (Beethovenfries)and the frescoes of the Burgtheater ▲ *204* that Gustav Klimt had painted fifteen years earlier in 1888. In the interval, Klimt, the heir to historicism, invented a highly personal and radically innovative way of painting. For their fourteenth collective exhibition, which was scheduled for 1902, the Secessionist artists decided on the theme of the genius of Ludwig van Beethoven ● *50*, ▲ *298*. A gigantic sculpture by Max Klinger in honor of the master was displayed in the pavilion, representing him as an Olympian figure imposing order on the eagle of existence through the power of art. At the same time Gustav Klimt set about creating a monumental fresco for the building based on the composer, the Beethovenfries. The immense frieze is more than 110 feet long and extends across four walls of the pavilion; the work is executed in casein on a base of stucco encrusted with gemstones. It is considered today to be one of Klimt's masterpieces. The frieze was taken down after the 1902 exhibition, and belonged for many years to a private collector,

SECESSION

before being bought back by the Austrian government in the 1970's. After restoration, it was replaced in its original position in the renovated Secession pavilion.

A MAZE OF SYMBOLS. On the left as you enter the room, the frieze begins with the theme of *Nostalgia for Past Happiness*, symbolized by flying figures. Then comes a group representing *The Pains of the Weak*; the Weak (a kneeling couple) are seen imploring the mercy of the Strong (in the person of a knight in armor). On the small wall at the end of the room, Klimt painted *The Hostile Powers* (the giant Typheus and his daughters, the Three Gorgons) against whom the gods are shown to be striving in vain. Here also are allegories of sickness, madness, death, sloth, luxury and intemperance, accompanied by the symbol of *Grief*, a crouching woman. On the long right-hand wall, the flying figures reappear, symbolizing happiness and the aspirations of humanity. *Poetry and Music* (the latter represented by a woman playing the lyre) and all the arts lead man to supreme happiness. The fresco is then interrupted by a window embrasure, through which the statue of Beethoven can be seen. It continues on the far side of the window with a group of women and a choir of angels framing an embracing couple. These figures are meant to illustrate the *Ode to Joy*, the final movement of Beethoven's *Ninth Symphony*. Gustav Mahler ● *52*, ▲ *301*, who was a friend of Klimt's, is likely to have advised him in his choice of themes. (In addition to this frieze, the city of Vienna possesses all the artist's preliminary drawings, studies and sketches for it, which are kept at the Albertina ▲ *196*.)

THE DECO ARTS
Josef Hoffmann (1870–1956) and Koloman Moser (1868–1918) designed furniture (opposite); Otto Wagner often created original furniture for his buildings; and the other Secessionist artists designed jewelry, tableware, silver and gold objects, fabrics and posters. They also illustrated books, along with their own review, *Ver Sacrum.*

ADOLF LOOS (1870–1933)
The *Café Museum* ▲ *223*, an early building by Adolf Loos ● *86, 90*, ▲ *142, 174* was completed in 1899, one year after his break with the Secessionist movement.

FRIEDRICHSTRASSE

"CAFÉ MUSEUM". A few minutes walk from the Secession Pavilion at no. 6 Friedrichstrasse stands the *Café Museum*, built by Adolf Loos in 1889 (one year after the pavilion). Loos was a member of the Secession to start with, but decided to break with the movement in 1898 since he wanted to develop a more functional and starker architectural aesthetic than that of his colleagues Joseph Maria Olbrich and Otto Wagner. Long before the public scandal caused by his Haas Haus on Michaelerplatz ▲ *174*, the *Café Museum* so perfectly represented the architect's new doctrine of severity and simplicity that Loos' contemporaries mischievously nicknamed it "The Nihilism Café". As such it became the principal meeting place for the writers, artists and musicians of the Secessionist movement ● *67*. Today it is a student café and has lost much of the purity of the original design; the furniture has been changed and posters have been put up, covering part of the walls, which were originally kept as bare as a monastery refectory. A pioneer of functional architecture whose

THE MARKETS
Wienzeile is best known for the FOOD MARKET (Naschmarkt), which is held all week long on its central reservation (*naschen* means "to nibble" or "eat with relish"). Many of the stalls are kept by Orientals, especially Chinese and Turks, selling exotic produce; Orientals also run the small restaurants which are scattered around the market. Every Saturday a FLEA MARKET is set up in the open air at the far end of the Naschmarkt.

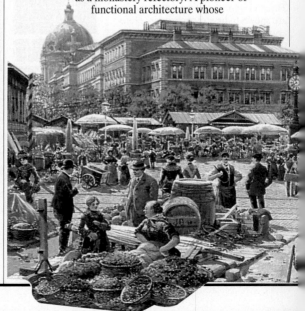

moment of glory was not to come until the 20th century, Loos built villas and shops and little else, all in his radical and distinctive style.

WIENZEILE

Wienzeile (the banks of the Wien) is an avenue running southwest from Mariahilf in the 6th District all the way to the Schönbrunn Palace ▲ *274*, passing the Secession Pavilion on the way. It is a road with several broad curves following the lines of the meandering river Wien, part of which (from Naschmarkt to the Stadtpark ▲ *226*) runs underground. Perhaps the road really should be called Secession Avenue, since several of its buildings as well as the Secession Pavilion are in the style of the movement.

BUILDINGS BY OTTO WAGNER. Two very fine residential buildings on the avenue, nos. 38 and 40, were designed by Otto Wagner ● *86, 88*. The façade of the spectacular MAJOLIKAHAUS is entirely covered in a pattern of ceramic tiles representing a huge blossoming tree with branches that spread all round it. The building next door, occupying the corner, was also built in 1898 (at the same time as the Secession Pavilion). It has a more refined décor, with a façade by Koloman Moser of gilded medallions framing women's faces, golden palm fronds and golden climbing vines. The other buildings of special interest here are the METRO STATIONS ▲ *240* designed by Otto Wagner (Kettenbrückengasse, Pilgramgasse and Margaretengürtel) and several further residential buildings in the Secession style.

"CAFÉ SPERL". The *Café Sperl* (1880), situated at no. 11 Gumpendorferstrasse, northwest of Wienzeile, remains a favorite meeting-place for Viennese intellectuals ● *66*.

JUGENDSTIL BUILDINGS
Buildings by Otto Wagner on the Linke Wienzeile (above), including the Medallion House, no. 38, and the Majolikahaus, no. 40.

MORNING COFFEE
"It was about seven in the morning when we arrived at the door of the *Café Magerl*. The first white rays of sunlight were visible, gilding the bread rolls, the poppyseed galettes and the salted baguette loaves. The first coffee, virginal, fresh-roasted and aromatic, wreathed us like a second morning. Joseph Branco sat beside me, dry, dark, southern, gay, wide awake and bursting with health. I was ashamed of my blood pallor and night-owl's fatigue."
Joseph Roth,
The Crypt of the Capuchins

ST CHARLES BORROMEO
St Charles Borromeo, Archbishop of Milan (1538–84), took care of that city's plague victims in 1576, without a thought for his own health. He also played a leading role at the Council of Trent, which launched the Counter-Reformation, and prevented the rise of Protestantism in northern Italy. For these two reasons Emperor Charles VI chose him to be the patron saint of his new church.

As in all Baroque buildings, the décor is sumptuous; valuable materials are used, notably polychrome marble.

KARLSKIRCHE

To the southeast of Karlsplatz, just before the great gardens, stands the church of St Charles Borromeo (Karlskirche). This is without doubt the most impressive Baroque building in Vienna. It was commissioned from J. B. Fischer von Erlach ● *74, 80,* ▲ *138, 147,* by Charles VI, who had made a vow to build a church dedicated to St Charles to mark his relief at the end of the plague epidemic in 1713. Fischer von Erlach directed the construction of Karlskirche from 1716 to 1723, and his son Josef Emanuel took over from 1723 to 1737 to complete the building. Facing the church is a work by the British sculptor Henry Moore, donated to the city of Vienna by the artist.

PLAGUE AND HERESY. Right from the time of Charles V and his son Philip II of Spain, the Habsburgs had taken the side of the Popes against the Protestants. The Karlskirche is not merely a votive church; it is also intended to glorify the secular power of the Holy Roman Emperors and the Catholic faith they championed. The blend of Romanesque, Greek and Byzantine styles symbolizes these two aspects of the emperor's authority. Whether this blend succeeds is still a matter of some debate: some find it too disparate, others argue that the borrowings from ancient architecture, all of them perfectly integrated, are a tribute to the wide culture of the church's architects.

GREEKS, ROMANS AND CHINESE. From the outside, Karlskirche is reminiscent of certain great Roman basilicas of the Renaissance, notably St Peter's. More original is the framing of the dome by two columns which look like minarets. These are obviously inspired by the columns of Trajan and Marcus Aurelius in Rome ▲ *185.* From close up, the roofs of the two side pavilions seem to be borrowed from Chinese pagodas.

DUAL SYMBOLISM. The monuments and sculptures that cover the Karlskirche are loaded with symbolism. The Christian faith is glorified by sculpted angels (at the entrance), by the representation of virtues such as faith, hope and charity (over the pediment and the side pavilions) and by the outsize statue of St Charles Borromeo (over the pediment). A further study of the church reveals other less obvious symbols of the power of the Habsburgs. The two columns, for example, are a reference to the legendary Pillars of Hercules in Spain, which were included in the coat of arms of Charles V. Note also the eagles and imperial crowns carved on the tops of these two columns, and the spiral bas-reliefs around them representing episodes from the life of St Charles Borromeo. Other decorative devices embody the two themes of steadfastness and courage – *Constantia et Fortitudo* – the motto of Charles VI, who

was the patron of the church.

AN OVAL NAVE. Inside the church, one discovers that the dome is not round but oval, as is the nave below it. The natural light falling from the windows around the dome blends softly with the muted artificial light rising from beneath. The fresco on the dome represents the apotheosis of St Charles Borromeo: assisted by the Virgin, he implores the Holy Trinity to rid the world of the plague. Several groups of angels and allegorical scenes, arranged in a series of concentric circles, occupy this oval space. At its center is the turret of the dome, with the Dove of the Holy Spirit painted at its top. In the fresco, note on the left the angel putting a torch to Luther's Bible. Johann Michael Rottmayr also painted the fresco above the organ loft, a celebration of music: *St Cecilia amid the Heavenly Choirs*.

THE ALTAR. The high altar represents St Charles Borromeo ascending into heaven on a cloud surrounded by angels. Its impact is overwhelming and theatrical, like that of all Baroque works, and it was probably designed by Fischer von Erlach. In addition, the church contains a number of paintings and altarpieces by other artists: *Jesus and the Roman Centurion, The Healing of the Paralytic, St Elizabeth of Hungary* by Daniel Gran, *The Resurrection of the Son of the Widow of Naim* by

THE DOME
The fresco by Johann Michael Rottmayr ▲ *139, 293* contains a range of old pinks and pale blues which harmonize with the other colors of the dome's interior.

The magnificent Karlskirche organ.

Karlsplatz (a postcard from the turn of the century).

239

Martino Altamonte and *The Assumption* by Sebastiano Ricci. The pulpit, choirstalls and confessionals are all high Baroque.

THE TREASURY. The best pieces here are the vestments of St Charles and a gold and silver reliquary bearing the imperial crown and the two-headed Habsburg eagle.

KARLSPLATZ

A number of architects and urban designers have criticized the confused appearance of Karlsplatz, which has been altered several times with no particular logic. The siting of the church at an angle in order to prolong Argentinierstrasse posed something of a problem; so did the Vienne River ▲ *225* running behind it. The church could not be moved, and yet it had somehow to be the dominant feature of the square. Many other difficulties also had to be faced, including the not inconsiderable one of diverting the river.

KARLSPLATZ STATION. Among the more recent buildings here are the splendid metro pavilions designed by Otto Wagner ● *86, 90*, ▲ *228, 237, 294*. Recently renovated, these compact structures of glass and metal were built at the end of the 19th century, when Otto Wagner was commissioned to design all Vienna's metro stations, galleries and bridges. Instead of settling for cold, functional architecture, Wagner determined to use all the Jugendstil resources and refinements he could think of; and the resulting design was a riot of curves and gilded floral motifs which gives the stations a lavish appearance. Today, the two pavilions of Karlsplatz are home to a small **WAGNER MUSEUM** and a minute café.

TECHNISCHE UNIVERSITÄT. This institution was founded in 1815 by Johann Joseph Prechtl. The university building, at no. 13 on the square, was built between 1816 and

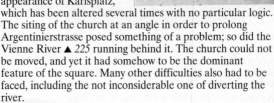

JOHANNES BRAHMS

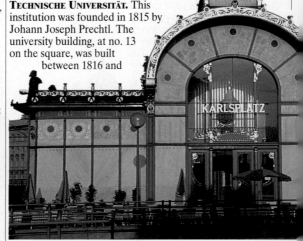

KARLSPLATZ

1818 in the neo-classical style, by Joseph Schemerl von Leytenbach. Its main façade of Ionic columns faces the Resselpark. Most of the statues in this park represent Austrian inventors: Josef Ressel himself who designed propellors for ships, Siegfried Markus (the internal combustion engine) and Joseph Madersperger (the sewing machine). In the same company is a statue of the composer Johannes Brahms by Rudolf Weyr.

HANDELSAKADEMIE. The neo-Gothic façade (1860–2) of the school of commerce is decorated with statues of great thinkers and discoverers including Adam Smith and Christopher Columbus. The sculptor of these was Ferdinand Fellner the Elder.

HISTORISCHES MUSEUM DER STADT WIEN. To the left of Karlskirche is Vienna's history museum (Historisches Museum der Stadt Wien). Opened in 1959, this institution contains a large collection of objects and documents covering the history of the city from Neolithic times to the present. In the first rooms are objects found during excavation of the Roman camp of Vindobona and relics dating from the earliest Barbarian invasions. The Middle Ages are represented, among other things, by a display of fragments of sculptures and stained glass from the Cathedral ▲ 132, along with weapons and armor from the era of the first Holy Roman Empire. With the Renaissance came the Reformation, followed by the Counter-Reformation, followed by the first Turkish siege. A collection of sculptures, engravings, paintings and maquettes recall Baroque Vienna during the time of the second siege ● 34 and the construction of the city's principal buildings. After the 18th-century Age of Enlightenment comes the brief Napoleonic interlude, followed by the Congress of Vienna ● 38. After this comes the Biedermeier epoque ● 62, illustrated by various paintings (Amerling ▲ 280, Fendi, Schindler, Waldmüller, ● 100) and a recreation of the playwright Franz Grillparzer's ● 62, ▲ 147 apartment. The museum's final rooms are devoted to the Secession period ● 86, 88, with designs and plans by Otto Wagner, furniture by Koloman Moser, paintings by Gustav Klimt ▲ 227, 250 and finally works by 20th-century artists including the Expressionists Egon Schiele ● 252 and Oskar Kokoscha ● 254 and sculptures by Fritz Wotruba ▲ 288.

AN ORANGE CUBE. For the time being, during the conversion of the imperial stables ▲ 189, 190 behind the Kunsthistorisches Museum ▲ 208 into a contemporary art gallery for the collections of the Museum of the 20th Century (Museum moderner Kunst in the Liechtenstein Palace ▲ 292), an ugly cube-shaped metal building has been installed almost directly opposite the Secession. Though temporary in nature, this hideous construction seems destined to remain in place for some years to come.

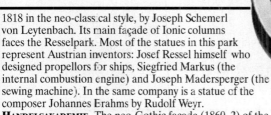

OTTO WAGNER AND THE METRO
Otto Wagner was appointed architectural adviser to the emperor in 1894, and commissioned by the Vienna municipality to design the city's public transport facilities. At that time Vienna was building one of the world's first underground train systems (after London, but before Paris). Becoming a member of the Secession movement in 1899, Otto Wagner designed about thirty stations, most of which looked like tiny palaces. Some of the prettiest are those at Karlsplatz, Schönbrunn (Hofpavilion) ▲ 286, and the Stadtpark ▲ 226.

A TEMPLE OF THE ARTS
The façade of the Künstlerhaus is adorned by statues of the great painters: Leonardo da Vinci, Michelangelo, Raphael ▲ 216, Titian ▲ 216, Dürer ▲ 196, and Velázquez ▲ 221.

A poster by A. H. Schram in 1902, for the annual Künstlerhaus exhibition.

GOLDENE SAAL ● 54
Unlike most major concert halls, the one at the Musikvereinsgebäude is not inspired by the Italian model, with orchestra rows, boxes and balconies positioned around a kind of amphitheater. Instead, the huge gilded room is rectangular in form, and can hold up to two thousand people. In 1911, the auditorium, already embellished with large numbers of caryatids and muses (right), was improved by a coffered ceiling which altered its acoustics considerably.

KÜNSTLERHAUS. The Viennese Visual Artists' Cooperative was founded in 1861; it was in reaction to this humdrum institution that the adherents of Klimt ▲ 227, 250 started their Secession movement ▲ 222, 232 in 1897. The headquarters of the association (Künstlerhaus ▲ 224) was constructed between 1865 and 1868 by August Weber, in the style of the Italian Renaissance to plans by a consortium of architects. Today it serves as a theater and is also used by the history museum for exhibitions and conferences.

MUSIKVEREINSGEBÄUDE. The Friends of Music building (Musikvereinsgebäude) is on Dumbastrasse, in front of the Künstlerhaus. The music association was founded in 1812; its Renaissance-style headquarters, designed by Theophil von Hansen (1813–91), dates from 1867–9. Just as he did later when designing the Parliament ▲ 205, Hansen made free use of Greek elements of architecture. This building is now the home of the Vienna Philharmonic Orchestra ● 54, which the world's greatest conductors have directed for the last one hundred and fifty years. The concerts organized by the Friends of Music association are internationally famous; their "Goldene Saal", one of the finest auditoriums in Vienna, is the scene of the Strauss concert, held annually to celebrate the New Year, shown on television all over the world. This auditorium with exceptional acoustics is decorated with sixteen gilded caryatids facing one

another the length of its side walls; the ceiling fresco, *Apollo and the Nine Muses*, is by August Eisenmenger. The building is next to the Palace of the Duchy of Wurtemburg, now the *Imperial Hotel* ▲ 224, on the Kärntnerring ▲ 223.

FROM THERESIANUM TO ZENTRALFRIEDHOF

STEPHANSDOM
SCHWARZENBERG
PALACE
UNTERES BELVEDERE
OBERES BELVEDERE
RIESENRAD
ARSENAL

🚗 **Half a day**

THE THERESIANUM:
A SUMMER RESIDENCE
Leopold I ● *31, 35*
▲ *138, 275*, Joseph I
and Charles VI
▲ *142, 302* spent their
summers at the
Theresianum.

The façade of the
Theresianum,
decorated with
Francis II's coat of
arms.

S̄outh of the Ring
▲ *198* and karlskirche
▲ *238* are the neighborhoods
of WIEDEN (4th
District) and FAVORITEN
(10th District), both full of
handsome buildings which stand in
their own gardens.

THE THERESIANUM

FROM THE FAVORITA TO THE THERESIANUM. The
Favorita was the Habsburgs' summer residence
until it was destroyed by the Turks ● *34* in 1683. The newly
constructed Schönbrunn ▲ *274* then took over as the summer
palace. On the ruins of the old Favorita, the Italian architect
Ludovico Burnacini constructed the Theresianum (1687–90),
a long, austere building fronting Favoritenstrasse. It was
named after Maria Theresa ● *36,* ▲ *260, 291,* who established
a college there to train young aristocrats for public-service
careers. Later it became the DIPLOMATIC SCHOOL
(Diplomatische Akademie). The headquarters
of Austrian Radio (Österreichische Rundfunk)
are now in the park of the Theresianum where
it fronts Argentinestrasse.

SCHWARZENBERGPLATZ

Schwarzenbergplatz is named after Prince Schwarzenberg, the general who commanded the allied armies against the French at the Battle of Leipzig in 1813, and whose statue – the SCHWARZENBERGDENKMAL – stands in the square.

RUSSEN DENKMAL. In the middle of the square (which the Russians rechristened "Stalinplatz") stands a memorial to the Liberation of Vienna by the Red Army (Befreiungsdenkmal der roten Armee), a replica of the ones at Budapest, Bucharest, Sofia, Warsaw and Riga. The Viennese call it the "Monument to the Unknown Looter". At the end of the Soviet occupation in 1955, Austria agreed to maintain the memorial in good condition, but the promise was not kept. Today this last vestige of the Red Army in Vienna has to be guarded round the clock by policemen, so bitter are the city's memories of the Soviet interlude; but probably the greatest injustice of the Russen Denkmal now is that it obscures part of the façade of the Schwarzenberg Palace.

THE SCHWARZENBERG PALACE. The palace, which looks out on the square from behind the equestrian statue of Prince Karl Philipp Schwarzenberg, is now a luxury hotel (*Im Palais Schwarzenberg*, no. 9). It was one of the very first aristocratic palaces to be built as a summer residence outside the city walls. In about

ZENTRALFRIEDHOF
DR. KARL
LUEGER KIRCHE

1697, Prince Mansfeld-Fondi commissioned a first building from the great Baroque architect Johann Lukas von Hildebrandt ● *75, 81,* ▲ *147*; after this the latter's rival Johann Bernhard Fischer von Erlach ● *74, 80,* ▲ *138* and his son Josef Emanuel carried out alterations in about 1720 for the Schwarzenberg princes.

DESTROYED FRESCOES

On either side of a central building with a colonnaded flight of steps and a squat tower are the two wings, each decorated with pilasters. The lavish interior was recently renovated, but the frescoes by Daniel Gran, which were destroyed by bombing during World War Two ● *42,* could not be saved.

RENNWEG

A NEO-RENAISSANCE PALACE BY OTTO WAGNER. The broad Rennweg avenue begins at Schwarzenbergplatz, and continues toward the Lower Belvedere. Opposite the Schwarzenberg Palace is the splendid mansion that Otto Wagner ● *86, 88* ▲ *228, 237, 240* built for himself in 1891. At that time the architect had not yet joined the Secession movement ▲ *232* and was drawing on the Italian Renaissance for inspiration. There is a noticeable difference between the upper and lower registers of the Wagner Palace (which was

The owner of the Schwarzenberg Palace, now a hotel, is Prince Charles von Schwarzenberg, from Bohemia. In 1989 he became general secretary to the President of the Czech Republic in Prague.

The Belvedere Palaces owe their name to the magnificent view from the Upper

Palace of Vienna and the Vienna woods ■ *18*.

THE FRENCH GARDENS
The gardens, which ascend in terraces from the Lower to the Upper Belvedere, were designed at the beginning of the 18th century by the French landscape architect Dominique Girard. They include wide lawns, immense parterres, several pools and countless statues including the curious sphinxes near the Upper Belvedere. The enigmatic smile of one of these sphinxes is shown opposite.

later bought by the Hoyos family): on the first and second floors, the façade is very somber with projecting stonework, while at the top of the building the windows are surrounded by garlands of flowers.

THE GARDENS. The GARDENS OF THE SCHWARZENBERG PALACE (Schwarzenberggarten) merge to the east with the magnificent Belvederegarten, the park surrounding the two BELVEDERE PALACES ★.

SALESIANERINENKIRCHE. The Baroque dome of the Church of the Salesian Convent (designed by Donato Felice d'Allio and built between 1717 and 1730) ▲ *303* precedes the far larger structure of the Belvedere.

GARDEKIRCHE. The Guards' Church (Gardekirche), which stands opposite the entrance to the Lower Belvedere on the far side of the Rennweg, originally belonged to the imperial hospital before becoming the Polish church. It was built by Nikolaus von Pacassi ▲ *192* in the Rococo style, shortly after the little theater at the Schönbrunn Palace ▲ *274*.

UNTERES BELVEDERE ★

The Rennweg runs past the old STABLES and thence to the entrance of the Lower Belvedere (Unteres Belvedere), former residence of Prince Eugène of Savoy.

HERCULES AND APOLLO. "He was short and ugly, with a snub nose, flaring nostrils and an upper lip so narrow that he could not close his mouth". The unprepossessing figure thus described by the Duchess of Orléans was none other than Prince Eugène, whom she met at Versailles. Perhaps it was somehow to compensate for his physical defects that the prince had himself represented as Apollo on the ceiling of his palace and devoted much of his time to the cultivation of beauty, amassing a fabulous collection of works of art. The two Belvedere Palaces, which almost outshine their contemporary, Schönbrunn ▲ *274*, were commissioned by Prince Eugène at a time when his military fame was at its height. He had succeeded in ejecting

the Turks from Hungary forever ● *34*, and now turned to his other passion, as a patron of the arts. As a young general in 1693 he had bought himself a site for his future summer palace. Twenty years later he was in a position to employ Johann Lukas von Hildebrandt, one of the two greatest architects in Europe, to turn the project into reality. Hildebrandt's rival, J. B. Fischer von Erlach ● *74, 80*, ▲ *138* was engrossed at the time in the building of Schönbrunn; the two architects had already collaborated on the plans for Prince Eugène's winter palace ▲ *147*, begun in 1697–8. The Lower Belvedere was the first of the two palaces to be completed; it stands on a site overlooking the Rennweg between the Schwarzenberg Palace and the Salesian Convent. The Upper Belvedere was built between 1721 and 1722 on a promontory dominating the park and the Lower Belvedere.

CONQUEROR OF THE TURKS. Prince Eugène of Savoy (1663–1736) was born in France; his first ambition was a career in the church, but he changed his mind and opted instead to enter the army of Louis XIV. When in 1683 the king refused to give him command of a regiment he went to Austria to serve Emperor Leopold I against the Turks. With his victory at Zenta in 1697, Eugène enabled the empire to recover Hungary and won fame throughout Europe. As commander-in-chief of the Habsburg armies from 1697 (under Leopold I and subsequently under his sons Joseph I and Charles VI), Prince Eugène won a series of victories over the Ottoman Empire. In 1703 he was appointed president of the Austrian monarchy's war council; he fought against the armies of Louis XIV during the War of the Spanish Succession and

"A MASKED BALL AT THE RUSSIAN EMBASSY"

"The theme of the ball gave the lie to history: clearly Prince Eugène did not finally eject the Turks at Peterwardein in 1716, because the Grand Turk, the master of Vienna, was still entertaining his subjects there. That evening His Highness stood in person at the top of the monumental staircase at the Stolberg Palace. Beneath a giant plasterboard crescent lit by electricity ... His Highness received his guests with his favorite sultana at his side. On his head, which bore a pumpkin-like turban reminiscent of Carpaccio, trembled a crest of diamonds next to which the plumes of the great Hungarian magnates looked as common as badger tufts. The Amphitryon saluted his guests as they came by ... the entire diplomatic corps was present, in addition to every foreigner of consequence who happened to be in Vienna."

Paul Morand,
Fin de siècle

Details of the
architecture (top) and
the gardens (above)
of the Belvedere.

completed the eviction of the Turks from Hungarian territory
between 1716 and 1717. Thanks to him, Austria embarked on
a long period of uninterrupted peace and prosperity, and
during this time he himself constructed his winter palace
▲ 147 and the two palaces of the Belvedere. So vast was his
influence on the conduct of Austrian affairs that he was
nicknamed the "Backroom Emperor".

FRANZ-FERDINAND. After the suicide of his cousin Rudolph
▲ 145 at Mayerling ◆ 323, Archduke Franz-Ferdinand
(1863–1914) became the heir to the throne. Bitter rivalry
emerged between the aging Franz-Joseph ● 41, ▲ 142, 178
and the young archduke Franz-Ferdinand, who meddled
constantly in affairs of state, rarely missing an opportunity to
criticize the policies of his uncle, whom he thought much too
timid. On one occasion he wrote to the Pope to block the
appointment of a bishop, and on another he sent a telegram
to Austria's ambassadors countermanding official
instructions. In effect he ran a kind of opposition government,
which advocated more vigorous policies. Yet there was one
point on which he was deeply vulnerable. Franz-Ferdinand
had made a mésalliance which he was obliged to turn into a
morganatic marriage, thus forfeiting for his heirs any claim to
the throne. When he was assassinated in 1914, the reaction in
Europe was one of relief that a future despot had been
eliminated; but within months the continent was embroiled in
World War One.

TREATIES AND CONFERENCES. After their acquisition by the
Austrian Republic, the two palaces
were the scene of a

number of historic events. Hitler organized diplomatic conferences in them; and in 1955 the Belvedere Treaty, which brought to an end the Allied occupation of Austria ● *33*, was signed in the Lower Belvedere by Antoine Pinay for France, John Foster Dulles for the US, Molotov for the Soviet Union, Harold Macmillan for Great Britain and Leopold Figl for Austria. The Austrian constitution was ratified there in the same year. Since the beginning of the century the Lower Belvedere has housed the Museums of Austrian Baroque and Medieval Art and the Upper Belvedere has been the Gallery of 19th- and 20th-Century Austrian Art.

THE MAIN COURTYARD. A monumental gate leads through to the main courtyard of the palace. It is crowned by allegories of Strength and Wisdom, and by the Cross of Savoy, Prince Eugène's coat of arms. From the courtyard one can see the orangery which houses the Museum of Medieval Austrian Art (Museum mittelalterlicher Österreichischer Kunst ▲ *256*) and the imposing Baroque façade of the Lower Belvedere. Designed by Hildebrandt at the beginning of the 18th century, the latter is a harmonious integration of seven buildings of varying lengths. The central building is ornamented with several pilasters, statues, and balustrades at attic level; it is flanked by two wings, which sport small pavilions at each end. This first palace, Prince Eugène's summer residence (he also had a winter one ▲ *147* within the city walls) is a majestic edifice.

BAROCKMUSEUM. Inside, the Museum of Baroque Art ● *80-1* has been organized in several different rooms, some of them really splendid: the GALLERY OF MARBLES (Marmorgalerie); the mirror gallery, or GOLDEN ROOM (Goldenkabinett), with fine gilded Rococo wainscoting; and the GALLERY OF GROTESQUES (Groteskensaal), decorated with grotesque frescoes by Jonas Drentwett which include several grimacing masks by Franz Xavier Messerschmidt.

THE GROTESQUES
When the first frescoes were uncovered at Pompeii, they were buried by earth which had to be excavated. The motifs found in the "grottoes" were referred to as "grotesques".

GRIMACING FACES
The most startling items in the Museum of Baroque Art are Franz Xavier Messerschmidt's grimacing heads. He was a highly unconventional artist (1736–83), who was greatly appreciated at the Austrian court. To avenge himself on people who mocked his strange clothes and eccentric manners the sculptor sketched them as "heads of characters", but for the most part Messerschmidt's faces are based on his own.

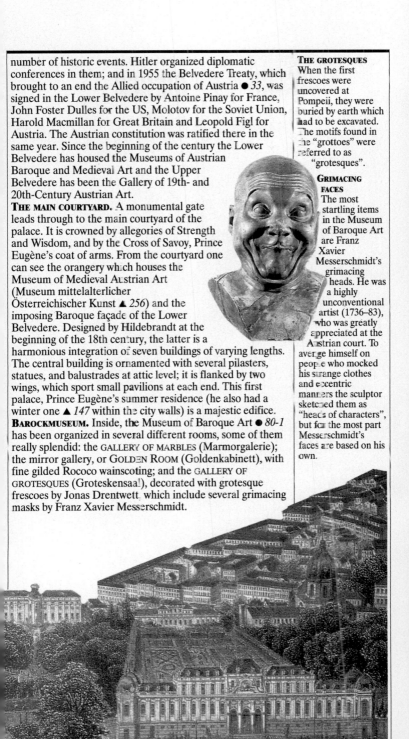

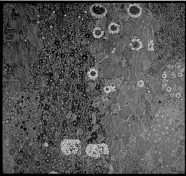
The Sunflower Garden, 1905

The year 1902, in which Gustav Klimt (1862–1918) unveiled his revolutionary *Beethovenfries* ▲ *234* at the Secession Exhibition ● *86*, ▲ *232*, was a turning point in his career. Both in his landscapes (above, *The Sunflower Garden*, 1905) and in his portraits of women (right, *Portrait of Adele Bloch-Bauer*, 1907), Klimt used a geometrical approach blending figures with their backgrounds in the same overall tones. Always stopping short of pure abstraction, he juggled with the ambiguities of form; in his paintings bodies, flowers and faces are liable to crop up at any moment in a cascade of color, as in

this astonishing portrait of a matriarch of the Viennese Jewish community. Abstraction and symbolism characterize Klimt's paintings. In the *Portrait of Adele*

Bloch-Bauer, the decorative motifs suggest psychological conflicts. The mosaics of San Vitale at Ravenna, which Klimt visited in 1903, led him to this mannered primitivism, which became the trademark of early 20th-century Viennese decorative arts. This primitivism is seen in the vignettes by the illustrator Carl-Otto Czeschka (1878–1960) which influenced Fritz Lang's *Die Niebelungen*, and in the tunic worn by Klimt himself (below). This was designed by Emilie Flöge, who sold clothes inspired by the new aesthetic in her Vienna shop.

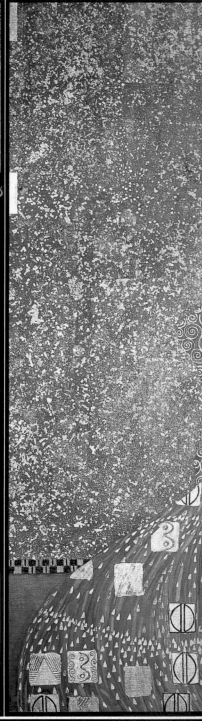

"BY PAINTING, YOU TRANSFORM YOURSELF, FAIRYLIKE, INTO A MAN OF IRREPROACHABLE MODERNITY: SOMETHING WHICH, ON AN EVERYDAY BASIS, YOU MAY NOT QUITE BE."

PETER ALTENBERG TO GUSTAV KLIMT

"AND SCHIELE AND KLIMT, THOSE PAINTERS OF KITSCH, ARE HOWEVER TODAY MORE MODERN THAN ANYONE ELSE, WHICH IS WHY, IN THE END, KLIMT AND SCHIELE SO DISGUST ME."

THE OLD MASTERS

As recently as thirty years ago, Egon Schiele (1890–1918) was virtually forgotten in art history: today, he has taken his place alongside Modigliani and Van Gogh in the ranks of the great doomed artists, those

own legend. In the event, Egon Schiele was very young when he made contact with the collectors who were to enable him to achieve what is now rightly considered to be one of the great lifeworks of the 20th century. He was by nature anguished and oversensitive: "I must see something new, and explore it" wrote. "I want taste the dark waters, see the trees shiver to pieces, and come unawares upon life swarming in the hedges." This

who suffered materially and saw nothing in their lifetimes of the acclaim which was later to crown their work. His trial on a vice charge involving a beautiful young girl, the burning of an erotic drawing before the court, and his prison sentence are the best-known landmarks in Schiele's career. His short life was full of trauma, beginning with the death of his syphilitic father and ending with the artist's own death from the same epidemic which had already killed his wife Edith, pregnant at the time with their first child. Schiele, who was wont to represent himself as St Sebastian transfixed by the arrows of his critics, contributed considerably to his

voracious curiosity impelled him to seek in everything the vital shared pulse th breaks down th barrier between man and nature. His landscapes are much more than mere expressions of his mood; they are paintings of the fate of humankind (above, *The Trees*, 1917). He uses the naked human body, with mortified flesh, bleeding sex and jutting bones, as a means to investigate the nature of love and pain. In *The Family* (opposite, 1917) he can be recognized as the figure protecting his family with the gesture of an injured bird. However, Edith and the unborn child are not those represented in the picture, which was to be one of a series for a mausoleum.

> "ONE NEED ANSWER TO NO ONE FOR A WORK OF ART; BUT FOR A
> HOUSE ONE MUST ANSWER TO ALL THE WORLD. ... THE WORK OF
> ART IS REVOLUTIONARY, THE HOUSE IS CONSERVATIVE."
>
> ADOLF LOOS

Oskar Kokoschka (1886–1980) and Richard Gerstl (1883–1908) were both influenced by the works of Holder, Munch and Van Gogh, exhibited in Vienna between 1904 and 1906. Gerstl abandoned his ornamental arabesques to seek cruder harmonies through heavy brushwork and dislocated forms. There is no social message in this solitary artist's work, whose only interest was philosophy. Gerstl's only friends were musicians of the Vienna School ● 52, whose uncompromising aesthetic somehow legitimized his own. He was one of Arnold Schönberg's best friends, and indeed Schönberg's wife left him for Gerstl, who committed suicide shortly afterwards after destroying part of his work. His *Laughing Man* (above) is a self-portrait from 1907. Encouraged by his friend Adolf Loos ▲ *174*, Kokoschka was also seduced by expressionism. He abandoned the stark graphics of his first years in Berlin and Vienna, in favor of an increasingly violent style. In his portraits from 1908 to 1915 the only thing that counts is the subject. His aim was to capture the essence of his models (opposite, *Portrait of Carl Moll* ● *104*, 1914).

One of the gateways of the Upper Belvedere.

"Garp explained to her that the Upper Belvedere contained only the nineteenth - and twentieth-century paintings, but Jenny said that the nineteenth and twentieth centuries were enough for her.

3., Prinz Eugen-Straße

Garp explained that she could at least walk … to the Lower Belvedere and see the Baroque collection, but Jenny shook her head; she had taken … art history courses … she'd had enough education, she said."
John Irving,
The World According to Garp

The museum also possesses the lead originals for sculptures by Georg Raphael Donner which adorn the Neuer Markt fountain ▲ *141*, as well as some Baroque paintings (many of them projects for frescoes) by Johann Michael Rottmayr ● *139*, *159*, *293* and Anton Franz Maulbertsch ▲ *167*.
MUSEUM MITTELALTERLICHER KUNST. The Museum of Medieval Art is housed in the former ORANGERY. It possesses some spectacular altarpieces, particularly from the 15th century.

OBERES BELVEDERE ★

Like the Lower Belvedere, the Upper Belvedere (Oberes Belvedere) is made up of seven different buildings skillfully united. The difference lies in its much greater elegance; the result is more Baroque, with an Oriental touch which lends it great charm.
A MASTERPIECE OF IRONWORK. The public entrance to the palace is by way of its south gate, which is flanked by two stone lions, or else by climbing up through the terraced gardens which open out in front of the Lower Belvedere. The gate is one of the great achievements of Baroque wrought iron.
A FAIRYTALE PALACE. The south façade of the Upper Belvedere is best viewed from the Landstrasser Gürtel. Its statues, Rococo decorations and elegant domed roofs are mirrored in an immense pool of water. During the 18th

century the Viennese began to take an interest in Orientalism and inevitably they fell under the spell of the Upper Belvedere Palace, which is more like something out of *The Thousand and One Nights* than the residence of a European prince. The illusion was all the more convincing when Prince Eugène organized lavish masked balls and firework displays. From many points of view this palace bears the imprint of the Orient; the long roofs of the main buildings are similar to the ceremonial tents of the Turkish viziers who came to lay siege to Vienna in 1683, while the pavilions on the wings have domes reminiscent of the mosques of Istanbul. Furthermore the façade's abundant decoration resembles a magnificent piece of Arab gold work.

THE VESTIBULE. The interior is just as sumptuous as the exterior, with monumental Atlas figures ● *82*, ▲ *157* supporting the low vaults of the entrance vestibule.

THE AUSTRIAN 19TH- AND 20TH-CENTURY GALLERY. Since 1953, the Upper Belvedere has been the home of the extraordinarily rich Gallery of 19th- and 20th-Century Austrian Art (Österreichische Galerie des 19. und 20. Jahrhunderts). Here also is the glorious Baroque MARBLE ROOM (Grosser Marmorsaal), all in pink marble, with a fresco of the *Apotheosis of Prince Eugène* by Carlo Carlone on its ceiling. The Austrian Gallery possesses nearly all the paintings of Gustav Klimt ▲ *250* and Egon Schiele ▲ *252*, a large number of canvases by Oskar Kokoschka ▲ *254*, and works by Carl Moll and the Norwegian painter Edvard Munch. From the 19th century, there is a highly representative collection of paintings by Hans Makart ● *103*, Friedrich von Amerling ▲ *241, 280*, Ferdinand Georg Waldmüller ● *100* and Rudolf von Alt ● *103*, among others.

SCHWEIZERGARTEN

MUSEUM DES 20. JAHRHUNDERTS. Vienna has two museums dedicated to modern art: the Liechtenstein Palace ▲ *292* and the Museum of the 20th Century (Museum des 20. Jahrhunderts). Exhibitions of contemporary art are regularly staged in the latter.

View of Vienna from the Upper Belvedere.

MARMORGALERIE
The Marble Room at the Baroque Art Museum is covered in stucco ornaments and decorated with a magnificent ceiling fresco by Martino Altomonte (1657–1745): *The Triumph of Prince Eugène, Conqueror of the Turks*. This Neapolitan painter was also known as Martin Hohenberg. In 1684, he became court painter to John Sobieski, King of Poland ● *34*, and lived in Austria from 1702 onward.

In the Swiss garden (Schweizergarten) behind the pavilion is a park containing sculptures from all over the world.

MUSEUM OF THE 20TH CENTURY
The museum occupies a modern structure which was displayed at the 1958 Universal Exhibition in Brussels.

MUSEUM OF MILITARY HISTORY ★
After the 1848 Revolution ▲ 40, Franz-Joseph ▲ 144, 178 decided to build an arsenal and barracks near Vienna. The arsenal was designed in a Byzantine-Moorish style by Theophil von Hansen, architect of the Stock Exchange ▲ 201 and the Parliament ▲ 205.

HEERESGESCHICHTLICHES MUSEUM

ARSENAL. The imperial and royal artillery arsenal was built like a massive fortress between 1848 and 1856. It consists of no fewer than thirty-one buildings, one of which is the Museum of Military History (Heeresgeschichtliches Museum). All the collections accumulated by the Habsburgs since the 11th century were kept on these huge premises. Shortly after the opening of the museum in 1869 the collection of arms and armor was moved to the Hofburg ▲ 175; even so the museum's exhibits are more than sufficient to trace in detail the history of the imperial armed forces up to World War One.

MILITARY LEADERS. Taking the museum in more or less chronological order, begin on the first floor, which can be reached by way of the vaulted neo-Gothic vestibule. Backing onto each column here is the marble statue of one of the principal sovereigns or military commanders of the empire. A staircase leads up to the second floor, which begins with THE HALL OF FAME. The frescoes in this room and in the ones adjoining it are all by Karl von Blaas (1815–94), whose particular brand of realism suited the taste of Franz-Joseph. They all depict battles, especially the celebrated battle of Zenta (1697) against the Turks, and those of the campaigns against Napoleon ● 38.

THE THIRTY YEARS' WAR. The next rooms are devoted to the 17th century, a time when the science of warfare was developing apace all over Europe. The Thirty Years' War (1618–48) pitted the Catholic Habsburgs against the Protestant princes of Germany, and, together with the war against the Turks, had a profound impact on military practice. The Low Countries under William of Orange, and Sweden under Gustavus Adolphus, began to use smaller, better-trained, more mobile armies equipped with overwhelming firepower. The infantry (harquebusiers, musketeers and pikemen)

played a crucial rôle, while the advent of brass and iron cannons suddenly made artillery much lighter and more easily maneuverable, turning it into an independent military force. As to cavalry, the traditional cuirassier divisions were bolstered by light dragoons. But while Gustavus Adolphus created a peasant army devoted to the cause of Protestantism, the Habsburgs tended to hire mercenaries. The most famous of these was the Czech Albrecht Valdstjin (1583–1634), known as Wallenstein in German, who placed his private army at Ferdinand II's disposal. Another great mercenary figure was the Siennese Octavio Piccolomini (1600–56) who fought the Swedes, notably at the Battle of Lutzen in 1632. In these first rooms of the museum, there are numerous objects, weapons and paintings that evoke this ruinous conflict which was finally brought to an end by the Treaty of Westphalia in 1648.

THE WAR AGAINST THE TURKS. The empire was weakened by the Thirty Years' War and looked an easy target for the Turks, who had already annexed the Balkans. During the reign of Mehmet IV (1648–87) the Ottoman Empire launched an offensive which reached its climax with the siege of Vienna in 1683 ● *34*. The museum displays a number of trophies taken from

The Reception Room (left), the Staircase (center) and the Chamber of Generals (right) in the Museum of Military History.

THE ASSASSINATION OF WALLENSTEIN
The German princes eventually dislodged Wallenstein, once Ferdinand II's paramount general. He negotiated with the enemy and was assassinated after he threatened to march on Prague.

PICCOLOMINI
Piccolomini played a major rôle in Wallenstein's assassination. During the Thirty Years' War he commanded the cavalry against the Swedes and the German Reformists at Nördlingen and defeated Richelieu's troops at Thionville (1640). Ferdinand III made him a prince of the empire in

259

"FIELD MARSHAL LAUDON ON HORSEBACK ON THE BATTLEFIELD OF KUNERSDORF"
This great general defeated Frederick II at Kunersdorf, on August 12, 1759. The painting is by Sigmund l'Allemand (1878).

MONTECUCCOLI
After the Thirty Years' War, Raimundo Montecuccoli (1609–80) fought the Turks as an Austrian marshal at Saint Gotthard (1664). He took part in the campaigns against the armies of Louis XIV from 1672. Montecuccoli wrote several books on military strategy.

the Turks, in addition to a *View of the Siege of Vienna*, showing the relief of the town by John Sobieski. Among other things, you can see the mortar that sparked the explosion of the powder magazine in Belgrade during the Turkish occupation of 1717, and the tent of the Grand Vizier Dahmat Ali, in which Prince Eugène dictated the news of his victory in a message to Charles VI. Prince Eugène also fought for Charles VI in the War of the Spanish Succession; this ended in 1715 to the advantage of Louis XIV, who put his grandson Philip V on the throne of Spain.

"MATER CASTRORUM" ● *36*, ▲ *158, 291*.
The reign of Maria Theresa (the "Mother of Encampments") was overshadowed by her rivalry with Frederick II of Prussia. From the day of her father's death, she fought Frederick for the right to the throne (the War of the Austrian Succession), later challenging the Prussian armies at Kolin (1757) during the Seven Years'

Turkish muskets from the
18th century (below left).

War (1756–63). At that time the
imperial forces were commanded by
Marshal von Daun (1705–66), one of
the first soldiers to receive the Order of
Maria Theresa. The museum has portraits
and mementoes of other generals who served
during the Seven Years' War, notably Lacy
(1725–1801) and Laudon (1717–90).

STATUE OF THE ARCHDUKE CHARLES. The
equestrian statue in the middle of the room
assigned to Archduke Charles is a replica of the
one in Heldenplatz ▲ 207. There are also portraits
of the prince with his family and at the battle of
Aspern ● 38. Francis II's brother, Archduke Charles
von Habsburg (1771–1847), Duke of Teschen, led the
imperial armies throughout the Revolutionary Wars.
In 1792 he fought Dumouriez at Jemappes, at Amberg
and at Wurzburg against Jourdan and Moreau
(1796–7), and against Bonaparte during the Second
Coalition's war with France (1799–1801). Appointed
President of the Imperial War Council in 1801, he
opposed an immediate declaration of war on Bonaparte.
After Austerlitz (1805) he reorganized the Austrian army
and fought Napoleon tenaciously at Eckmahl,
Aspern-Essling and Wagram. After 1809, he retired to write
books on military theory.

THE RADETZKY ROOM. During the 1848 revolution ● 38, the
new chancellor Felix von Schwarzenberg (1800–52) and his
brother-in-law Windischgrätz put down the insurrections in
Vienna ● 40 and Prague, while Marshal Radetzky
(1766–1858) fought the nationalist movement in Italy. This
room contains mementoes of the marshal and a painting of
the battle of Novara (1849). There are also pictures of the
defeats at Solferino (1859), against the French and the
Piedmontese, and at Sadowa (1866), against the Prussians.
After this period of waning influence in Europe, the
Austro-Hungarian dual monarchy entered a period of peace
which was only interrupted by the occupation of
Bosnia-Herzegovina in 1878. Then in 1914 a Serbian
nationalist assassinated Archduke Franz-Ferdinand at
Sarajevo ▲ 145.

THE AUSTRIAN NAVY. In the rooms devoted to the navy, the
most interesting items are the model of the frigate *Novara*,
which sailed round the world between 1857 and 1859, and
records of the expedition to the North Pole between 1872
and 1874, which resulted in the discovery of Franz-Josefs-
Land.

The colors of Prince
Eugène of Savoy's
Regiment of
Dragoons, and a
commemorative
medal of Joseph II
(above). A battalion
banner of an imperial
infantry regiment
(below).

Austria was at war
with France from
1792 on, not
surprisingly, given
that the guillotined
Marie-Antoinette was
Joseph II's sister.
Under the Directoire
regime in France
(1795–9) Bonaparte
led a brilliant
campaign against
Austria's forces in
Italy; Austria then
formed a coalition
with the other
monarchies of
Europe, which
Bonaparte defeated
at Austerlitz (1805)
and Wagram (1809)
● 32, before being
himself defeated and
sent into exile on
Elba.

The Battle of Novara,
March 23, 1849.

MUSIKER

The bust of Brahms ● *51* (below).

SANKT-MARXER-FRIEDHOF

THE MOZART CEMETERY. Southeast of the Museum of Military History is the tiny cemetery of St Mark, where Mozart ● *48* was buried on December 6, 1791. The snow and sleet prevented his friends and family from passing through the city gates, so the hearse went unaccompanied to the cemetery, which was then in the open countryside. The sexton threw Mozart's body into a common grave, and when the composer's widow arrived later nobody was able to find it for her. The cemetery itself is in the staunchest Biedermeier style ● *62*.

ZENTRALFRIEDHOF ★

At the end of the Rennweg, which is extended by Simmeringer Hauptstrasse, is the central cemetery (Zentralfriedhof), the largest graveyard in Austria (590 acres). Opened in 1874, it is said to contain the remains of more than a million people.

TOMBS OF THE FAMOUS. The central avenue between the gate and the church leads to the crypt of the presidents of the Austrian Republic and other luminaries. The best-known are those of musicians, though painters and sculptors are also here, notably Franz Alt ● *102*, Friedrich von Amerling ▲ *241, 257, 280* and Makart. In the Jewish sector are the tombs of the writers Karl Kraus and Arthur Schnitzler.

The tombs of Joseph Strauss, Johann Strauss, Franz Schubert and Beethoven (above). A memorial to Mozart (below right).

TOMBS OF THE FAMOUS
In the musicians' precinct of the central cemetery are the tombs of Gluck, Beethoven, Schubert, Brahms, Wolf and Schönberg, the Strausses and Lanner ● *48, 50, 52, 56, 58*. Haydn's tomb is in the Esterházy capital of Eisenstadt ▲ *162*. Mahler ▲ *232* is buried in the Grinzing cemetery, while Bruckner's tomb is in the crypt of St Florian's basilica.

A FORGOTTEN IMPERIAL CASTLE. The central cemetery continues on the far side of Simmeringer Hauptstrasse. Here are the CREMATORIUM, an extremely handsome piece of architecture by Clemens Holzmeister (1922) and the remains of the castle of Neugebäude. The latter was built in the 16th century by Maximilian II (1527–76), who made it his summer residence (he also acquired the old castle of Katterburg ● *30* at the same time). Following its conversion into a powder magazine, Neugebäude was stripped of whole sections of its columns and decorations, which were then used to build Schönbrunn's Roman ruins and the colonnade of the Gloriette ▲ *275, 284*.

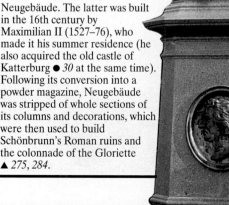

FROM THE PRATER
TO THE DANUBE

REISENRAD DONAUPARK DONAUTURM JUBILÄUMSKIRCHE VOLKSPRATER UNO-CITY

🦌 Half a day

A COMIC PLAYWRIGHT
An actor who became
a theater director in
Vienna, Johann
Nestroy (1801–62)
has remained popular
for his comedies of
manners ● *60*, which
are much cherished
by the Austrian
public. Nestroy's forte
was biting satire of
Viennese society
during the
Biedermeier era ● *62*,
which he lampooned
in dozens of farces,
comedies and
vaudevilles. His
best-known pieces are
*Der böse Geist
Lumpazivagabundus*
(1833), *Einen Jux will
er sich machen* (1842),
Der Unbedeutende
(1846) and *Judith und
Holofernes* (1849).

THE STRAUSS HOUSE
Johann Strauss the
Younger ● *57* wrote
about two hundred
waltzes and was
known as the "Waltz
King". A critic wrote
about him in 1833, "One
might call Strauss the
Younger the very
incarnation of the
waltz".

PRATERSTRASSE

Praterstrasse, to the north of the inner
city, links the Danube Canal and Schwedenplatz
to the Praterstern intersection, which is near the park and the
fairground. The excursion boat *Johann Strauss*, moored at
FRANZ-JOSEFS-KAI ▲ *200, 229*, hosts exhibitions of Viennese
waltzes ● *56* nearly every night.

"THE BLUE DANUBE". Praterstrasse, which crosses
Leopoldstadt, has several interesting buildings, notably THE
GREEN HUNTER (no. 28) in which Joseph Lanner ● *56*, the
rival of the two Strausses, played his waltz music. Near
NESTROYPLATZ was the former site of the Carl Theater, where
the celebrated writer Johann Nestroy (1801–62) was director
between 1845 and 1860. Farther on, opposite the neo-
Byzantine CHURCH OF ST JOHN NEPOMUK (1846) is
the house of Johann Strauss the Younger (no. 54). It
was in this building that Strauss composed his most
famous waltz, *The Blue Danube*, in 1867. On the
same side of the road, at no. 70, the DOGES' PALACE
(Dogenhof), a pastiche of a Venetian palazzo in a
Byzantine neo-Gothic style. This was probably built
in the 19th century, at the same time as the area
known as the "Venice of Vienna" in the Prater, where
people traveled along the canals in gondolas. This
site is now where the Ferris wheel ▲ *266* and the
merry-go-rounds of the fairground are located.

PRATERSTERN. Praterstrasse comes to an end at the
Praterstern crossroads, where the seven broad avenues that
cross Leopoldstadt converge. To the north of the crossroads
stands the forbidding Vienna North railway station, while to
the east the famous Ferris wheel rises above the treetops of
the Prater Gardens. In the middle of the square is the
TEGETTHOFF MONUMENT, to the admiral who took part in the
sea battle of Heligoland against the Danes in 1864 and
decisively defeated the Italians at the battle of Lissa in 1866.
In 1867, Tegetthoff was assigned to bring the remains of
Maximilian ▲ *145* home from Mexico.

LEOPOLDSTADT. An extensive working class area at the
northern end of the inner city, Leopoldstadt (2nd District)

The *Johann-Strauss.*

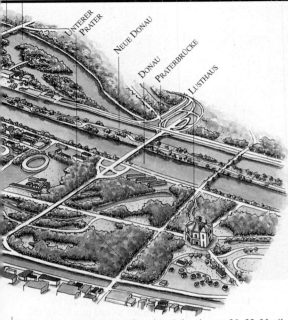

REICHSBRÜCKE
ALTE DONAU
UNTERER PRATER
NEUE DONAU
DONAU
PRATERBRÜCKE
LUSTHAUS

lies between the Danube Canal and the river ■ *20, 22*. Until World War Two, a number of Jewish shopkeepers and craftsmen lived and worked here. After the Anschluss ● *42* the National Socialists deported the Jews of Leopoldstadt and destroyed all their synagogues ▲ *156, 169*.

THE SCHÖNBERG HOUSE. The OBERE DONAUSTRASSE quay, alongside the Danube Canal, was the birthplace of Arnold Schönberg, father of dodecaphonics.

THE PRATER

A visit to the Prater has been a favorite excursion for the Viennese ever since it was opened to the public in 1766 by Joseph II. As well as abundant green spaces in which to walk and jog, it also boasts a huge amusement park dominated by the Ferris wheel, numerous open-air cafés and restaurants (which tend to be very busy on weekends) and many sports facilities.

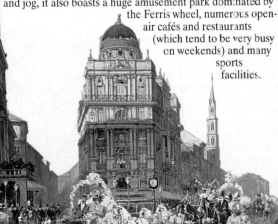

THE CONGRESS AT PLAY
During the Congress of Vienna ● *38*, kings and emperors with their suites of generals and diplomats converged from all over Europe on Vienna, where receptions and balls were held night and day. At the Prater, which for the duration became the most elegant promenade in Europe, a new dance – the waltz ● *56* – was all the rage.

ARNOLD SCHÖNBERG (1874–1951) ● *52*
Schönberg was influenced by Brahms ● *51*, Wagner and Mahler, as his *Transfigured Night* (1899) clearly shows; later his writing developed in the direction of atonality. Schönberg's *Treatise on Harmony* was published in 1911; his melodrama *Pierrot Lunaire* (1912), which employed the technique of speech-song (*Sprechgesang*), was a worldwide sensation. In 1933 Schönberg went into exile in the US, where he taught music.

PRATERSTRASSE
Joseph II was begged to open the Prater to the public, but replied that if he did so he would be "reduced to pacing the Crypt of the Capuchins, when I wish to be among my equals."

OUTLANDISH EXPLOITS
In 1898, Marie Kindl hung by her teeth from a cable hanging from one of the cabins on the Ferris wheel. In 1914 a Frenchwoman, Solange d'Atalide, rode a horse on the roof of one of its cabins. Between the wars, the Maningo Brothers did various acrobatics on the wheel for Pathé News; and in 1986 ecologists unfurled a banner at the top of it condemning nuclear power.

"VENICE IN VIENNA"
During the straightening of the Danube, small canals were dug and people used gondolas on them, hence the name of "Venice in Vienna".

FACTS AND FIGURES ABOUT THE WHEEL
The big wheel is held up by huge steel girders, and is 212 feet high; the diameter of the wheel alone is 200 feet. It includes 120 spokes made of steel cabling, weighs 474 tons, and spins at a rate of 2 feet 5 inches per second. Since World War Two it has had only 30 cabins, 15 of which bear an even number. For the wheel's 90th anniversary in 1987, cabin No. 30 was given special luxury fittings.

These swampy acres between the Danube Canal and the river were turned into a game reserve in the 16th century by Maximilian II (1527–70), shortly after he had purchased the domain of Schönbrunn ▲ *274* for the same purpose. The Prater is nearly 3,200 acres in extent: its name probably derives from the Spanish word *prado* (plain). Many of the Habsburgs, notably Charles V, Ferdinand I and Charles VI spoke Spanish as fluently as German.
THE FUN FAIR. As soon as the Prater was opened to the public, icecream and coffee sellers as well as merry-go-round operators were granted the right to ply their trades there. By the end of 1766 there were more than a hundred structures – most of them tents – which sold wine, beer, coffee and pastries. In the following century the free-spending habits of the Prater crowds attracted more and more stall-keepers to the area. They tended to concentrate in the VOLKSPRATER (the People's Prater) or the WURSTELPRATER. This area is named after Wurstel, a tragicomic, resolutely unlucky character who symbolizes the Prater; a Viennese Don Quixote figure, he is persecuted by a crocodile but manages to win out after many struggles. The Wurstelprater was liked not only by ordinary Viennese for its merry-go-rounds and taverns but also by the upper classes for its dance hall-restaurants, where the "War of the Waltzes" between Strauss and Lanner ● *56* was waged.

British film director Carol Reed filmed a scene from *The Third Man* (1949) in the Ferris wheel: the confrontation between Holly Martins (Joseph Cotten) and Harry Lime (Orson Welles). In 1986 the wheel was again used as a film set, this time for the fifteenth film in the James Bond series, starring Timothy Dalton.

RIESENRAD. At the turn of the 19th and 20th centuries, when the canals of the "little Venice" area were being filled in, leaving only the Dogenhof on Praterstrasse, the Prater fun fair was endowed with the Ferris wheel, or Riesenrad; this remains its single greatest attraction. Walter Basset, a military engineer working for Britain's Royal Navy, had the idea of constructing the wheel in imitation of those already in existence at Paris, Blackpool, London and Chicago. Its inauguration in 1897 coincided with the Universal Exhibition, which was opened a few weeks before Franz-Joseph's jubilee ▲ 271. The Ferris wheel narrowly escaped destruction in the first years of the 20th century, when its owner's heirs put it up for sale as scrap metal. At the outbreak of World War One it was requisitioned as an observation post, thus escaping demolition. It was less fortunate in World War Two ● 42, when it was blown to smithereens along with the rest of the Volksprater. Later it was rebuilt and modernized, and by May 1947 was back in operation, at the heart of a fairground in the throes of complete reconstruction.

ORSON WELLES IN "THE THIRD MAN"
● 42, ▲ 192
Reed's film, which took the Grand Prix at the Cannes Film Festival in 1949, was hugely successful and contributed significantly to the fame of the Prater's Ferris wheel.

GRAND HÔTEL VIENNE

LUSTHAUS
At the end of the main avenue is the Pleasure House (Lusthaus), now a café-restaurant. This former imperial hunting lodge was built by Isidorio Canevale ▲ *271* in 1784. For the first anniversary of the battle of Leipzig (1813) against Napoleon I, the Emperor of Austria and his allies organized a great banquet at the Lusthaus, while eighteen thousand of their troops picnicked in the surrounding park.

THE PLANETARIUM AND THE PRATERMUSEUM. Next to the Ferris wheel is the Planetarium, founded in 1927 by Zeiss, the manufacturer of optical instruments. It also contains a museum (the Pratermuseum) which retraces the entire history of the Prater. A curious house in the form of a ball stands just beside the Planetarium: this is known as the KUGELMUGEL. It is the home of a highly original character, Edwin Libburger, who proclaims it the "Smallest Republic in the World". Nearer the big wheel one can take the little train known as the LILLIPUTBAHN, which crosses part of the Prater from the fun fair to the STADIUM (Stadion).

MANNESMANN TOWER. Also between the main avenue (Hauptallee) of the Prater and the Ausstellungstrasse are the EXHIBITION GROUNDS (Messelände), with the 490-foot-tall Mannesmann Tower soaring overhead. The spring and autumn international

exhibitions are held here and in the Exhibition Palace (Messepalast) ▲ *207* each year.

SPORTING FACILITIES. Southeast of the exhibition grounds is a complex of sporting facilities, including a stadium, a swimming pool, a tennis court, a golf course and the Freudenau racecourse.

TABORSTRASSE

HAUPTALLEE
The main riding avenue (Hauptallee) crosses the Prater from end to end, from the Lower (Unterer) Prater to Freudenau. Running parallel to the Danube, this thoroughfare is now reserved for pedestrians. The aristocracy used to promenade here in carriages or on horseback.

Taborstrasse begins at the Danube Canal and Schwedenplatz and runs across Leopoldstadt.

BARMHERZIGE-BRÜDER-KIRCHE. On the right at the beginning of Taborstrasse is the monastery-hospice of the Brothers of Charity, with its huge church (Barmherzige-Brüder-Kirche) built in the 17th century. Before he became Music Master of the Esterházy Chapel ● *49*, ▲ *162*, Joseph Haydn ● *48* was intermittently employed as organist of this church between 1755 and 1758.

KARMELITERPLATZ. Taborstrasse

then passes through KARMELITERPLATZ, site of the 17th-century Josefskirche, the former Carmelite Church, which boasts a magnificent Baroque façade. On the same square is the House of the Stag (Hirschenhaus), where the Strauss family used to live ● 56.

A choir boy in the Augarten Palace.

AUGARTEN

To the north of the inner city, the 130-acre Augarten Park (above) extends to the edges of Leopoldstadt (2nd District ▲ 264) and Brigittenau (20th District ▲ 296). The park was laid out in the reign of Ferdinand II (1578–1637) and redesigned in 1712 by the French gardener Jean Trehet, who was working on the gardens of the new Schönbrunn castle at the time. Like the Prater, the Augarten was opened to the public by Joseph II in 1775.

MOZART AND BEETHOVEN. The park was formerly the site of the Alte Favorita, Leopold I's (1640–1705) palace which was destroyed during the siege of 1683 ● 34. An orangery was built on the ruins, where musicians such as Mozart ● 48, ▲ 147, 281 and Beethoven ● 51 gave concerts before members of the imperial courts of Joseph II ● 36, 291, 292 and Francis I ● 38, ▲ 182.

PORZELLANMANUFAKTUR AUGARTEN ★. This former orangery now serves as the Augarten china factory (Porzellanmanufaktur Augarten) ● 72, whose "beehive" monogram is famous all over the world. Founded in 1717 by a Dutchman, Du Paquier, the factory first operated from premises on Porzellangasse (Porcelain Street) in Vienna, before its move to Augarten. Its products were particularly fashionable during the Baroque era ● 80, 82 when it produced not only tableware but also vases and trinkets which harmonized with the Rococo décor of Viennese palaces. After a period of stiff competition from the factories of Meissen in Saxony and Sèvres in France, Augarten was given a new lease on life when Maria Theresa ● 36, ▲ 158, 280, 291 made it a state factory in 1744. At that time it was a training ground for decorators, whose ideas provided the factory with a constant source of renewal for its designs. The "Old Vienna" pattern, with its flowers and painted figures, became world-famous. After this Augarten began to draw inspiration from the French vogue for shepherds and shepherdesses, along with classical mythology and Rococo foliage and arabesques. At the close of the 18th

A choir boy in the Augarten Palace.

THE PORCELAIN FACTORY
In the 13th century Marco Polo brought the first pieces of porcelain back from China. Amsterdam merchants continued for many years to import Chinese porcelain for sale all over Europe; it was not until the end of the 17th century that Europeans discovered the secret of hard porcelain manufacture. At the beginning of the 18th century a number of factories were opened, notably that of Meissen in Saxony in 1710 and Augarten in 1717. At the close of the 18th century, Augarten was especially known for its mythological groups. Until 1744, each piece was stamped with a shield with blue stripes; after that date, Augarten ware bore the two-headed eagle of the Habsburgs ▲ 143, 144, 176, 280.

AUGARTEN CHOIRBOYS
● *54*
This institution gives musical training and general instruction to a hundred and fifty children, who are divided into four choirs. The singers are boarded in the main palace; those whose voices have broken and who are no longer members of the choir lodge in the pavilion of Joseph II.

FLAKTURM
The mass of concrete which constitutes the anti-aircraft defense tower (Flakturm) is something of an eyesore in the Augarten. Six towers of this type were built in Vienna during World War Two and have since proved impossible to destroy. The city authorities have tried and failed to camouflage the Flakturms and are now transforming them into belvederes, exhibition rooms and (most recently) restaurants.

THE RAMPARTS AND THE SCHLAG BRÜCKE
To prevent the Danube from flooding, the Viennese embarked on a huge program to straighten its bed at the close of the 18th century. The branch of the river which ran directly below the ramparts became the Danube Canal, navigable for just over 10 miles.
As to the Danube proper, its bed was dredged straight for 12½ miles at the end of the 19th century, the banks being buttressed with stone and concrete. In 1975, the Neue Donau (New Danube) parallel branch was rearranged in the same fashion.

century, when all Europe was in raptures over the excavations at Herculaneum and Pompeii, Augarten tableware was covered in grotesques and antique figures inspired by Raphael. It also produced quantities of figurines, which were avidly collected all over Europe. The advent of Napoleon I and his period of residence at Schönbrunn ● *38* launched the Empire style, and later, after the Congress of Vienna, came the Biedermeier era ● *62*. Biedermeier was particularly influential at Augarten; the factory hired a miniaturist painter, Daffinger, who launched what became known as the "idyll" pattern. The Viennese apartments of the time were filled with decorative porcelain, whether plates made to be hung on walls or pipes, snuffboxes, figurines, tea cups and teapots, all made not for use but for display in glass cabinets. With the fall of the Habsburg empire in 1918 ● *33*, the factory experienced a period of difficulty, but before long it was back on its feet inventing new designs that reflected contemporary tastes.

THE AUGARTEN PALACES. Also in the Augarten is a Baroque Palace (AUGARTENPALAST) which was built at the end of the 17th century in the style of Fischer von Erlach ● *74, 80*, ▲ *138, 147*. Bought in 1780 by Joseph II, it was subsequently neglected by the emperor, who preferred the little pavilion (JOSEPHSSTÖCKL) nearby. This structure was built by the Italian architect Isidorio Canevale ▲ *268* in 1781. These palaces were used by Pope Pius VI in 1782 and by Emperor Charles I ● *33*, ▲ *144, 180* during his

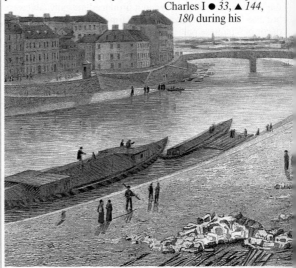

childhood. Today the Vienna Boys' Choir (Wiener Sängerknaben) ● *54* occupies the Augarten Palaces.

BRIGITTAKAPELLE. The chapel of St Bridget, a Renaissance building that dates from between 1645 and 1681, stands surrounded by more recent structures in Adalbert-Stifter-Strasse on the north side of the Augarten. Designed by Filiberto Lucchesi, it was probably a votive church, constructed during a period of concern over the threat of Swedish invasion during the Thirty Years' War ▲ *259*.

MEXIKOPLATZ. It was in Mexikoplatz and the surrounding district between the NORTH STATION (Nordbahnhof) and the Danube that political refugees from eastern Europe found a temporary asylum before continuing their emigration to other countries.

THE JUBILÄUMSKIRCHE
In 1898, the Viennese decided to celebrate Franz-Joseph's fiftieth anniversary as emperor ● *41*, ▲ *142, 144, 178* in proper style. Banquets and balls were given all over town, and the municipality began constructing the Jubilee Church (Jubiläumskirche) on Mexikoplatz. This neo-Romanesque building was not completed until 1913, by which time Franz-Joseph had only three more years to live.

THE DANUBE

Contrary to the normal perception, the Danube (Donau) ■ *20, 22* does not flow past the walls of Vienna. Instead it forms a broad inland delta here, with backwaters filled with islands and islets.

REICHSBRÜCKE. The first part of the huge imperial bridge (Reichsbrücke) leads from Mexikoplatz across the Danube. The river carries a wide variety of boat traffic, including canal boats, barges and bateaux-mouches which head downstream to Budapest in Hungary or else unload at the huge river port of Vienna. This complex includes a grain port at Albern, a general cargo port at Freudenau, and the oil port of Lobau.

DONAUINSEL. Next, the bridge spans the Danube island (Donauinsel) 13 miles long, known as "Spaghetti Island," between the Danube and the New Danube. Because it is so long and thin it is known as "Spaghetti

DONAUTURM
The Danube Park is best known for the 820-foot Danube Tower (Donauturm), which has become its emblem. Two revolving restaurants in the building, one at 520 feet, the other at 560 feet, offer panoramic views of the entire Vienna region, the valley of the Danube, the Marchfeld plain and the hills of the Vienna Woods ■ *18,* ● *68, 100.*

Island". This strip of land boasts 26 miles of beaches and is mostly devoted to water sports (sailing, canoeing and swimming), as well as soccer, cycling and rollerskating. There are also fishing zones and an animal reserve, along with specially equipped areas in which handicapped people can practice various forms of exercise. The water sports are limited to the New Danube, which is closed to merchant shipping. Having crossed the Danube, the artificial Danube Island and the New Danube, the Reichsbrücke continues across the larger Danube Island and the Old

Danube before connecting with the Donaustadt (22nd District) on the left bank of the river.

U.N. CITY. Built between 1973 and 1976, the United Nations complex consists of several parabolic tower blocks on the middle of the island between the Old and New Danubes. Opened in 1987, the AUSTRIA CENTER VIENNA, which is next to the U.N. complex, contains fourteen auditoriums with capacities ranging from fifty to four thousand people. In addition to conferences and seminars, exhibitions, galas, plays and concerts are organized here; the center also has its own radio station, restaurants, banks, travel agencies and post office.

DONAUPARK. Laid out to the northwest of the U.N. complex to mark the occasion of the international flower show of 1964, the Donaupark is the second largest green area in Vienna after the Prater. A small train carries visitors around the gardens and the artificial lake, the IRISSEE, where there is a THEATER that can seat four thousand spectators.

ALTE DONAU. To the southeast of the U.N. complex, the Danube Island is indented by the Kaiserwasser Bay; from here two channels lead through to the Old Danube (Alte Donau) and its islands (GROSS UND KLEIN GÄNSEHÄUFEL), a favorite area for walkers. The Old Danube has remained in its original winding bed, but in effect it is a backwater, closed at both ends and lost in greenery – a perfect place for sailing, canoeing or picnicking.

THE UNITED NATIONS BUILDINGS
The U.N. rents this complex from the Austrian government. It contains the headquarters of the Atomic Energy Agency and the United Nations Industrial Development Organization.

FROM SCHÖNBRUNN TO THE STEINHOF

KIRCHE AM STEINHOF

MARIA THERESIEN KASERNE

SCHÖNBRUNN FAÇADE

Two obelisks crowned with eagles frame the entrance to the main courtyard. These are not two-headed Habsburg eagles ● 29, ▲ 143, 144, 195, 280, but Napoleonic ones, placed here by Bonaparte in the course of his two visits to Vienna ● 38, after Austerlitz (1805) and Wagram (1809). Bonaparte's father-in-law, Francis I ▲ 182, retained the eagles, even after the fall of the French empire in 1815.

PURE SPRINGWATER

The water of the "beautiful spring" was exceptionally pure. Franz-Joseph ● 41, ▲ 178 offered it to his guests at lunch and dinner when he entertained at the palace.

SCHÖNBRUNN PALACE★

At the far end of the Wienzeile ▲ 237, southwest of Vienna, are the palace and gardens of the Schönbrunn Palace, the former summer residence of the Habsburgs. The first building here was the castle of Katterburg, which was destroyed by the Turks in 1529 ● 34; the ruined site was bought in 1589 by Maximilian II who wanted to set up a hunting preserve in the vicinity, with fishponds, a poultry farm and a garden of rare plants. The rebuilt castle of Katterburg thus became a hunting lodge and a working farm. It was enlarged by Rudolph II, but once again demolished in 1605 by the Hungarian forces of Stefan Bockai.

THE SPRING. Matthias II, Rudolph II's brother, succeeded him in 1612, and occasionally resided at the castle after its reconstruction. One day, when he was out hunting, he came on a beautiful spring in the woods (Schöner Brunnen) after which the site was eventually named. But the imperial family's obsession with "Schönbrunn" only began in earnest with Eleonora Gonzaga, the wife of Ferdinand II (1619–37). This Italian princess enlarged the castle and laid out new gardens, residing there during the summer months and organizing lavish entertainments.

SCHÖNBRUNN AND VERSAILLES. After the final victory over the Turks in 1683 ● 34, the Habsburg empire entered a period of peace and prosperity. Leopold I and the princes attached to the imperial court took advantage of this to build a number of fine palaces in Vienna ● 80, 82, ▲ 246. Since Schönbrunn had been destroyed in 1683, Leopold I determined to replace it with an edifice worthy of the Habsburgs' newly recovered power. For this task he commissioned J. B. Fischer von Erlach

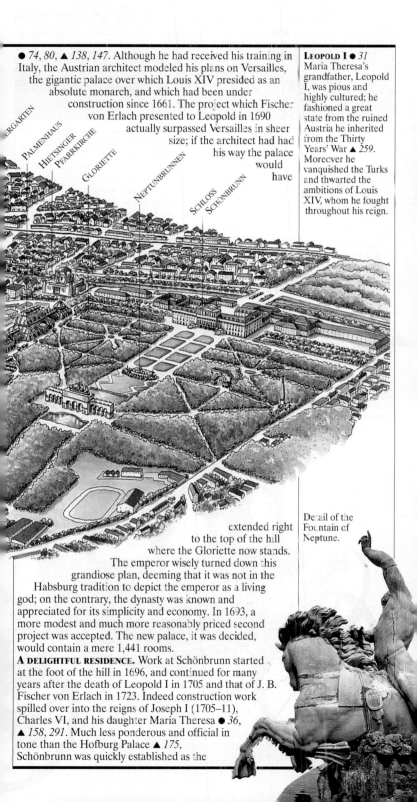

● 74, 80, ▲ 138, 147. Although he had received his training in Italy, the Austrian architect modeled his plans on Versailles, the gigantic palace over which Louis XIV presided as an absolute monarch, and which had been under construction since 1661. The project which Fischer von Erlach presented to Leopold in 1690 actually surpassed Versailles in sheer size; if the architect had had his way the palace would have

TIERGARTEN
PALMENHAUS
HIETSINGER PFARRKIRCHE
GLORIETTE
NEPTUNBRUNNEN
SCHLOSS SCHÖNBRUNN

LEOPOLD I ● 31
Maria Theresa's grandfather, Leopold I, was pious and highly cultured; he fashioned a great state from the ruined Austria he inherited from the Thirty Years' War ▲ 259. Morecver he vanquished the Turks and thwarted the ambitions of Louis XIV, whom he fought throughout his reign.

extended right to the top of the hill where the Gloriette now stands. The emperor wisely turned down this grandiose plan, deeming that it was not in the Habsburg tradition to depict the emperor as a living god; on the contrary, the dynasty was known and appreciated for its simplicity and economy. In 1693, a more modest and much more reasonably priced second project was accepted. The new palace, it was decided, would contain a mere 1,441 rooms.

A DELIGHTFUL RESIDENCE. Work at Schönbrunn started at the foot of the hill in 1696, and continued for many years after the death of Leopold I in 1705 and that of J. B. Fischer von Erlach in 1723. Indeed construction work spilled over into the reigns of Joseph I (1705–11), Charles VI, and his daughter Maria Theresa ● 36, ▲ 158, 291. Much less ponderous and official in tone than the Hofburg Palace ▲ 175, Schönbrunn was quickly established as the

Detail of the Fountain of Neptune.

The courtyard of the castle.

IMPERIAL COACHES
Considered to be the finest of its kind in the world, Charles VI's coach ● 36, ▲ 302 (below) was used for his coronation in 1714. This Rococo ceremonial carriage

Habsburgs' favorite residence. The rather casual atmosphere at Schönbrunn was in marked contrast to the rigid etiquette of Versailles, principally because the court did not lodge there. Maria Theresa wanted it to be a cosy domestic place where she could sit with her embroidery or her watercolors, in the company of her daughters. She had Schönbrunn redecorated by Nikolaus von Pacassi ▲ 192 to make it more comfortable: this was achieved by reducing the size of the private apartments to a more intimate scale, and by mitigating the somewhat pompous Baroque style of the building with touches of Rococo. In the 19th century, Schönbrunn was still in the open countryside; today it is included in Hietzing (the 13th District ▲ 286).

EHRENHOF

The visitor enters the Schönbrunn Palace by way of the huge courtyard (Ehrenhof; 66,000 feet) and the main gateway (Haupttor).

NAPOLEON'S EAGLES. Two obelisks topped by Napoleonic eagles frame the gateway. These were placed here by the French emperor during his two visits to Vienna, Austerlitz in 1805 and after Wagram in 1809. In the courtyard are two fountains erected by Maria Theresa, which represent the principal rivers and kingdoms within the

takes the form of a gilded crown, with doors covered in paintings by artists of the school of Rubens ▲ 219. Pulled by eight horses, it was used for seven coronations, including that of Charles I in the middle of World War One. Rudolph's ▲ 145, ◆ 322, berlin is shown at right.

empire. This area has witnessed several significant historical events, notably the parade of Napoleon I's Grand Army, the arrival of the Russian, British and Austrian sovereigns for the Congress of Vienna ● 38, the takeover by Hitler's troops, and the meeting between Presidents Kennedy and Krushchev in 1961. Schönbrunn served as the Soviet Army headquarters in 1945, and that of the British Army from 1945 to 1948 ● *43*.

"Maria Theresa Yellow". The yellow paint which covers the exterior of Schönbrunn later became standard for all imperial buildings. It is thought that Schönbrunn's walls were originally pink, with gray pilasters. A new coat of paint applied to the palace recently seems less orange in tone than its predecessors.

The façade. The main body of the palace spreads along the broad esplanade. Its façade ▲ *284-5* is embellished with pilasters and covered with yellow ocher paint ("Maria Theresa Yellow"). Maria Theresa came out on the balcony here to salute Count Kinsky, who had ridden from the battlefield to bring her news of the Austrian victory over the Prussians ● *36*.

The outbuildings. In addition to the palace itself, the courtyard is hemmed in by a number of outbuildings, notably the Carriage Museum (Karossensammlung) in the former winter manège. Sixty carriages of various kinds are exhibited here, among them the Berlin of Napoleon I, the phaeton of "Aiglon" and the barouche used by Sissi ▲ *119, 143, 144, 178* when she traveled incognito to Geneva in 1898. The red hearse displayed here was used for the funerals of archdukes, and the black one for sovereigns. At Maria Theresa's request, Pacassi ▲ *189, 192, 276* built the small Baroque Schloss-theater in 1747. Mozart and Haydn both performed here ● *49*. Today, the theater is used for the productions of the Vienna Chamber Opera (*Wiener Kammeroper*) ● *54*.

Sculptures in the park ▲ *284*.

The main building

Of Schönbrunn's 1,441 rooms, only forty-two on the first floor are open to the public – the remainder are rented out. These are entered via the courtyard as in the Hofburg ▲ *175*. Every room contains a large faience stove.

Bergläume. The apartments and salons of the first floor are preceded by the Bergl Salons (Berglräume) or "Indian Rooms", which are entirely decorated with exotic frescoes ▲ *180*. The ceiling of the adjoining Chapel (Schlosskapelle), constructed c. 1700, has a fine fresco by Daniel Gran ▲ *146, 304*.

The Grosse Galerie. The Great Gallery (Grosse Galerie) leads to the principal Staircase and the balcony overlooking the esplanade. Some 140 feet in length, decorated with white and gold paneling and crystal chandeliers, the Grosse Galerie is still used today for official banquets. In 1955, the closing reception following the signature of the treaty to end the Allied occupation of Vienna was held here. In 1945, a bomb fell straight through the ceiling fresco by Gregorio Guglielmi ▲ *279* which represents the territories of the empire paying homage to Maria Theresa and Francis I, but by an

The small theater
Joseph II and his sister Marie-Antoinette (the future Queen of France) are shown dancing in the ballet *The Triumph of Love* (1764) by Gluck ● *48*. The Habsburgs loved and practiced all the arts: especially dance, music, theater and painting. Mozart conducted *The Theater Director* at the small theater; his *Don Giovanni* was also performed here.

Detail of a fresco in the Berglräume ▲ *277*, by
Johann Bergl (1718–89).

incredible stroke of luck failed to explode.

KARUSSELLZIMMER AND LANTERNZIMMER. On either side of
the Grosse Galerie are the CAROUSEL ROOM (which owes its
name to a painting of the Spanish Riding School ▲ *190* by
Meytens ● *98*; it also boasts a large portrait
of Charles VI ● *36*), and the LANTERN ROOM,
which served as an antechamber.

KLEINE GALERIE. An extension of the
Grosse Galerie overlooking the park,
the Small Gallery (Kleine Galerie) is
also painted white and gold, with a fresco by
Guglielmi ▲ *277, 279* (*The Union of the House
of Habsburg-Lorraine with the Holy Roman
Empire*). Decorated by Pacassi ▲ *189, 191, 276*, the
Kleine Galerie was formerly used for children's
parties and small banquets, and music would sometimes be
played here. On either side of the room are the Chinese
Cabinets, one round and one oval. The former (Chinesischen
Rundkabinett), which was Maria Theresa's secret study, is
linked via a bare staircase with the floor above, where
Chancellor von Kaunitz lodged.

THE ROSA SALONS. Originally the apartments of Joseph I,
these rooms are named after Joseph Rosa, who decorated
them with frescoes of Swiss and Italian landscapes prefiguring
Romantic art. The MAIN ROSA SALON
contains a fresco of the ruins of
Habsburg, the cradle of the imperial
family.

THE RIGHT WING

**THE APARTMENTS OF FRANZ-JOSEPH AND
SISSI.** The imperial couple occupied
fifteen rooms in the right wing of the
palace. These are
reached by a
monumental
staircase above
which is a ceiling
fresco by Sebastiano
Ricci entitled *Allegory
of the Princely Virtues*
(1702); in it an angel
symbolizing the "love of virtue"
takes the hand of the future
Joseph I and shows him the
path he must follow. A first
room, adjoining the
staircase, was used as a
GUARD ROOM; next is the ANTECHAMBER
(Wartezimmer), with a Biedermeier
● *62* billiard table, where
petitioners waited to be
announced. The AUDIENCE
CHAMBER is also known as the
"Walnut Salon" (Nusszimmer),
because its walls are covered in
walnut wainscoting whose
brown tones harmonize with the

> **"WE MUST HAVE THEATRICAL ENTERTAINMENTS! WITHOUT THEM LIFE IN SUCH A HUGE PALACE IS IMPOSSIBLE..."**
> MARIA THERESA

From top to bottom: The Mirror Gallery; the official Dining Room; Princess Sophia's salon; and the Garten Perronsaal Salon (19th-century engravings from the Museum of the City of Vienna ▲ *241*).

"I want to go to Schönbrunn!" said Herr von Trotta, and he drove to Schönbrunn. The persistent drizzle hid the palace and the Steinhof asylum alike. Herr von Trotta headed up the avenue, that same avenue which he had taken so long ago on his way to the secret audience, during the affair involving his son.**"**
Joseph Roth,
The Radetsky March

A EUROPEAN PAINTER
The Baroque painter Gregorio Guglielmi (1714–73) was a truly European artist. Born in Rome, he worked at the studio of the great traveler Sebastiano Conca. From 1753 onward, Guglielmi followed the example of his master, first to Dresden, then to Vienna in 1755 before returning to Turin in 1765. He died at St Petersburg. During his time in Vienna he painted the ceilings of the great and small galleries, along with that of the Academy of Sciences ▲ *151*, at the request of Maria Theresa.

A FAMILY LIFE
Family life was vitally important to the Habsburgs and set firmly apart from their duties as monarchs. This was the case throughout the long reign of Maria Theresa, who with her husband and their sixteen children projected the image of a united family with simple tastes and pleasures including embroidery, painting and botany. Maria Theresa and her children at the Feast of St Nicolas (right); Joseph II at the bedside of his wife, newly delivered of yet another baby (opposite).

MARIA THERESA AND JOSEPH II
The personalities of Maria Theresa and her son Joseph II ● 36, ▲ 291 left a deep imprint on Austria. The latter (below) ruled jointly with his

mother (right) in mourning after the death of Francis I, from 1765 to 1780. (Both portraits are by Heinrich Friedrich Fueger, 1751–1818.)

FRANCIS I
Francis I of Lorraine, the husband of Maria Theresa, who became Francis I, Holy Roman Emperor, by election in 1745, must be distinguished from his grandson Francis II, who became Francis I, hereditary Emperor of Austria in 1806 ● 38, ▲ 182.

red damask furniture. Among other things, this salon contains busts of Franz-Joseph wearing the chain of the Order of the Golden Fleece ▲ 133, 183, and of his father Archduke Franz-Karl. Next is Franz-Joseph's STUDY, which overlooks the courtyard; the walls and chairs are covered with brown ribbed fabric. This room and the one adjacent to it contain several portraits and statuettes of Franz-Joseph, Sissi and Archduke Rudolph ▲ 145.

A BEDROOM. The ROOM IN WHICH FRANZ-JOSEPH DIED – a simple, comfortable chamber – is decorated in the same brown fabric. A painting on the wall depicts the deathbed scene on November 21, 1916. After visiting the two small cabinets, the visitor is led through to the DRESSING ROOM, which is hung with pink brocade. With its twin beds of dark wood and its prie-dieu, the BEDROOM shared by Franz-Joseph and Sissi is as austere as a monk's cell. On the walls hang two paintings of the *Madonna and Child*, one by Carlo Dolci, the other by Guido Reni.

EMPRESS ELIZABETH'S SALON. The walls of this room are covered in light gray brocade, and the furniture in flowered red silk. Several pastel portraits by Jean-Etienne Liotard of Maria Theresa's children decorate this room, which looks out onto the imperial private garden. Note also the paintings by Hackert (*The Grape Harvest, The Grain Harvest*). Marie-Antoinette's salon, with its white and gold paneling and chairs covered in red damask, is one of the largest rooms in the imperial apartments. It is dominated by a huge portrait of Francis I in the costume of a Knight of the Order of the Golden Fleece ▲ 241 by Friedrich von Amerling (1803–87) ▲ 241, the official court painter.

THE CHILDREN'S BEDROOM. The chairs in this room, which is also paneled in white and gold, are covered in pale blue damask. There are several portraits of Maria Theresa here, along with a wardrobe which was used as a desk by her daughter Marie-Antoinette; at one point this was removed by Sissi and installed at her villa *Achilleion* on the Greek island of Corfu.

FRÜHSTÜCKZIMMER. The breakfast room, on the corner of the right wing of the palace, has a splendid view over the park. Its walls are studded with twenty-six medallions containing placemats embroidered by Maria Theresa and her daughters.

THE YELLOW SALON. This room takes its name from its chairs, which are covered in yellow damask. On the walls hang portraits of Maria Theresa's children by Liotard. The clock on the commode, made by the Parisian clockmaker Ridel, was a gift from Napoleon III to Franz-Joseph. Decorated in 1854, the BALCONY ROOM is the last of the apartments in the right wing. Once again the walls here are covered with white and gold paneling and with portraits of Maria Theresa's children. **SPIEGELSAAL.** The Yellow Salon communicates with the small MIRROR GALLERY, to which Maria Theresa's newly appointed ministers came to swear their oath of loyalty to the sovereign. Wolfgang Amadeus Mozart ● *48*, ▲ *147* gave one of his first recitals in this room.

The Porcelain Salon.

MOZART AT SCHÖNBRUNN
Mozart first came to Vienna in 1762, arriving from Salzburg with his father and his elder sister Nannerl. At the age of six, he gave his first concert in the small Mirror Gallery before a delighted Maria Theresa. When he slipped on the polished parquet, he was caught by the youthful Marie-Antoinette, and promptly declared that he wanted to marry her. And when he had finished playing he clambered onto the Empress' knees to give her a kiss, without the slightest regard for etiquette.

Vieux-Lacque-Zimmer
In the 18th century, art from the Far East was fashionable in Europe; rooms were filled with Chinese prints, porcelain and exotic screens, which matched home-produced Rococo ornaments.

The Gloriette
The view from Maria Theresa's bedroom, where Napoleon I later slept ● *38* when he was using Schönbrunn as his headquarters.

"Garp relaxed, when he wasn't writing, by going to the zoo; it was part of the great grounds and gardens surrounding the Schönbrunn Palace."
John Irving,
The World According to Garp

THE LEFT WING

Zeremoniensaal. After the Carousel Room and the Horse Room (stag-hunting scenes and portraits of horses along the walls), the tour continues into the left wing of the palace by way of the Hall of Ceremonies (Zeremoniensaal), also known as the Battle Room because of its gilded stucco ornaments of interlacing banners and halberds. This spacious room was used for christenings, weddings and other ceremonies within the imperial family. On the walls are scenes of the wedding of Joseph II by Martin von Meytens ● *98* and a full-length portrait of Maria Theresa ● *36.*

Blauen Chinesischen Salon. The walls of the Blue Chinese Salon, in which Charles I signed his abdication on November 11, 1918 ● *33*, are covered in wallpaper patterned with Chinese prints on a blue background. Lacquer wardrobes and Japanese porcelain vases complete this décor.

Vieux-Laque-Zimmer. Another room that shows a taste for chinoiserie is the Old Lacquer Salon, in which the Rococo style may be seen at its best: here, framed by complex designs in gilt molding, are long lacquer panels representing Japanese landscapes and flowers and birds engraved in fine gold. The room also has a rich stucco ceiling and a superb marquetry floor.

Maria Theresa's bedroom. This chamber overlooking the park follows the Vieux-Laque-Zimmer; Napoleon I slept here, and his son the "Aiglon" was in this room when he breathed his last. The walls are lined with 18th-century Brussels tapestries showing scenes of military life.

The Porcelain Room. This salon, Maria Theresa's former study, occupies the corner of the left wing. It looks out onto the Crown Prince's Garden (Kronprinzgarten), a private area cut off from the main park since the latter was opened to the public in 1779. The Porcelain Room is decorated with wooden moldings painted blue in imitation of porcelain, in the shapes of flowers, fruit and Chinese parasols. On the walls are two hundred and thirteen framed blue-wash drawings, done by Francis of Lorraine and his daughters. Fixed to the middle of the passe-partout mounting are four medallions in bas-relief featuring portraits of Francis I, the archduchesses Elizabeth and Christina, and Duke Albert of Saxe-Teschen.

Millionenzimmer. The Million Room, which was used for smaller audiences, is covered in rosewood paneling, into which are set two hundred and sixty Indian and Persian

miniatures. These cost a million florins in the 18th century, hence the name of the room. If one looks at them closely, it becomes clear that these miniatures were cut up and reassembled to fit into their cartouches.

GOBELINSALON. The tapestries in the Tapestry Salon (Gobelinsalon) actually come from Brussels, rather than Gobelins. They show scenes from the lives of Antwerp fishermen; each of the six Rococo chairs here is covered in a tapestry representing two of the seasons. The tour continues through a small room which serves as a memorial to the "Aiglon". His portrait as a child, his death mask, and (under a bell glass), the stuffed corpse of the pet lark which shared his solitude, are all exhibited here.

THE RED SALON. This former reading room covered in scarlet damask is hung with several family portraits: Joseph II in coronation robes, his brother Leopold II, and Franz-Joseph I aged eighteen and again at sixty-four, wearing the insignia of the Golden Fleece ▲ *133, 183*. The Red Salon communicates with a corner room which is decorated with frescoes and tapestries of rose garlands, and looks out onto the courtyard.

THE APARTMENTS OF FRANZ-JOSEPH'S PARENTS. The living quarters of Sophia of Bavaria and her husband Archduke Franz-Karl belong to the left wing, overlooking the main courtyard. In the Archduchess' BEDROOM, the walls and bed are covered in red velvet (it took 550 pounds of silver just to embroider the baldachin). Franz-Joseph was born in this room. Adjoining are the STUDY and SALON of

THE "AIGLON" (1811–32). When Napoleon departed for St Helena, his son, the King of Rome, and his mother, Archduchess Maria Louisa, retired to Vienna. The boy was lodged at Schönbrunn by his grandfather Francis I, who made him Duke of Reichstadt to pre-empt a French title. Abandoned by his mother, who became Duchess of Parma, the "Aiglon" died of consumption at the age of twenty-one, a much-loved member of the imperial family. He never saw his father again after Waterloo.

Archduke Franz-Karl. The salon and study contain a gallery of portraits that includes Maria Theresa, Francis of Lorraine, and each of their sixteen children. The chandelier is made of Bohemian crystal.

SCHÖNBRUNN PARK

ANTIQUE STATUARY
The garden statues are by Johann Christian Meyer, who also sculpted the groups at the Fountain of Neptune ▲ 275 and the Fountain of the Naiads in the diagonal avenues.

While J. B. Fischer von Erlach was building the palace at the end of the 17th century, the gardens around it – which had been laid out first by Maximilian II and then by Eleonora Gonzaga – were reorganized, with geometrical paths and beds by Jean Trehet, c. 1691. Later, between 1750 and 1780, Joseph Hätzl and Adrian von Stockhoven made major changes, introducing a note of fantasy into the carefully aligned parterres and shrubberies.

From the foot of the palace, a broad, straight avenue opens up a perspective culminating at the FOUNTAIN OF NEPTUNE (Neptunbrunnen), by C. Bayer. **THE GLORIETTE AND THE LITTLE GLORIETTE.** This perspective is completed by the Gloriette, a monument perched at the top of the slope on the site of J. B. Fischer von Erlach's first, rejected project for Schönbrunn Palace. The Gloriette is a neo-classical triumphal arch built by Ferdinand von Hohenberg in 1775 to commemorate the Austrian victory at Kolin (1757) against the armies of Frederick II of Prussia (the sculpted trophies are by J. B. Hagenauer, and the décor and stuccoes by Benedikt Henrici). East of the hill stands the Little Gloriette, where Maria Theresa

ROMAN RUINS
The remains of Schloss Neugebäude were used to build these imitation ruins.

sometimes took her breakfast; it is now used as a public tearoom.

TYROLEAN CHALETS. West of the hill are the GARDENS and chalets built at the request of Archduke John in 1800.

RÖMISCHE RUINE. At the foot of the slope are two monuments built by Ferdinand von Hohenberg: the OBELISK, on which are carved scenes from the history of the Habsburg family ● *29,* ▲ *143, 144, 195* and the Roman ruins (Römische Ruine). Around forty statues by Johann Christian Meyer representing heroes of Greek mythology and Roman history are dotted here and there throughout the gardens.

SCHÖNER BRUNNEN. Hidden in the woods on the left-hand side of the park (looking out from the palace) is the spring after which Schönbrunn was named. This spring, whose pure water was served at the imperial table, is housed in an artificial grotto with a statue of the nymph Egeria holding an overflowing urn.

THE FAÇADE
This is arranged around two flights of steps that lead to the balcony of the second-floor piano nobile, and two wings extended by two large pavilions.

BOTANISCHER GARTEN. Francis I ● *36,* who was passionately interested in natural sciences, financed expeditions to remote countries with a view to enriching Schönbrunn's collection of rare plants and animals. Even in Maximilian II's time, when the 16th-century Schloss Katterburg stood on this site, a number of unusual plants and trees grew here, but it was during the 18th-century reign of Francis that the Botanischer Garten at Schönbrunn was seriously developed. During the same period a menagerie was installed on the west side of the park in 1752.

TIERGARTEN. The imperial family used to visit the octagonal pavilion to observe their lions, tigers and leopards (this pavilion is now a café-restaurant). The descendants of Francis I added a set of zoological gardens (Tiergarten) to the menagerie, one of the first of its kind in Europe, which today is home to around seven hundred and fifty animals.

THE PALM HOUSE
The tropical greenhouse (Palmenhaus, 1883) made of glass and metal is a replica of the one at Kew Gardens in London.

TECHNISCHES MUSEUM FÜR INDUSTRIE UND GEWERBE

North of Schönbrunn, on the other side of Vienna ▲ *225* and in the extension of the AUER-WELSBACH PARK, is the Technical Museum of Industry and Craft. Part of the first

▲ FROM SCHÖNBRUNN TO THE STEINHOF

THE AUSTRIAN ICARUS
Between 1891 and 1896, Otto Lilienthal (1848–96) invented a series of gliders and took more than two thousand flights of between 100 and 200 yards. Finally he was killed trying out his latest flying machine, a biplane; he left behind him a treatise *Bird Flight as the Basis of the Flying Art*.

floor here is devoted to methods of land and sea transport. Among other items are Siegfried Markus' petrol-driven automobile (1888), the ship's propeller invented by Josef Ressel (1827) and in the RAILWAY MUSEUM, an *Ajax* locomotive (1841), a horse-drawn tram (1846) and Sissi's salon-coach (1873). The second floor is devoted to aviation and precision mechanics: highlights are a clock by P. Imserrus from the 16th century, an 18th-century calculating machine by Braun, a 19th-century typewriter by Mitterhofer, and a 19th-century sewing machine by Madersberger. There are also exhibits from the textile, chemical and agricultural industries. On the third floor are various inventions from the history of the postal service (including the first postcard), and from musical instrument manufacture, computer science, photography (notably Voigtländer's camera), and public works. There is also a fascinating automaton made by Friedrich von Knaus (1760) which is capable of writing.

HIETZING

An airplane built by Wilhelm Kress, Siegfried Markus' first motorized automobile, and Peter Mitterhofer's typewriter from 1864.

HIETZINGER FRIEDHOF. South of the TIROLER GARTEN at Schönbrunn is the little cemetery of Hietzing (Hietzinger Friedhof). A number of famous people are buried here, including the writer Franz Grillparzer ● *62*, ▲ *147*, *206*, the painter Gustav Klimt ▲ *227*, *250*, the composer

THE IMPERIAL METRO STATION
The Hietzing metro station (Hofpavillon), which serves Schönbrunn Palace, looks more like a temple than a railway station. It was built by Otto Wagner ● *86*, *88*, *90*, ▲ *228*, *240*, *294* in 1898, and exclusively used at the time by members of the court. Its neo-Baroque building includes an octagonal hall topped by an elegant dome. Like all Wagner's constructions, it is decorated with great refinement.

WIENER STADTBAHN: HALTESTELLE HIETZING

Alban Berg ● *53* and Chancellor Engelbert Dollfuss ▲ *159, 170*. Room was also made here for the remains of Jean-Baptiste Hanet, known as Cléry, who together with François Hue was Louis XVI's valet while he was in prison in the Temple until his execution in 1793. Cléry later published a diary of this historic period.

Adolf Loos'
Hornerhaus.

VILLA PRIMAVESI-SKYWA AND FÜRSTENHOF. Toward the end of the 19th century a series of lavish residences were built in the vicinity of Schönbrunn by members of the elite among Jugendstil ● *86*, ▲ *139* and Secession ● *86, 88*, ▲ *232* architects. Thereafter Hietzing joined Döbling ▲ *294* and Währing ▲ *293* as one of Vienna's aristocratic suburbs. To the west of the Schönbrunn gardens on Gloriettegasse stands the VILLA PRIMAVESI-SKYWA, built by Josef Hoffman in 1915 ● *86, 90*, ▲ *142, 174*, while on Trauttmannsdoffgasse is the FÜRSTENHOF building, which has a wonderfully elegant façade in relief. It was built by H. Dvorak in 1905.

HOUSES BY ADOLF LOOS. Nearby is the SCHEU HOUSE, on Larochegasse, which was designed by Adolf Loos ▲ *142, 174* in 1912, a year after his controversial building at no. 3 Michaelerplatz ▲ *174*, and in the same unadorned style. Another building by Loos here, the HORNERHAUS (1913) on Nothartgasse, has a unique convex roof; further still to the west, the VILLA VOJCSIK ● *87* on Linzerstrasse was designed by Otto Schönthal in 1901; this is a magnificent piece of Jugendstil architecture, with a highly refined façade (note the doorway in particular).

VILLAS BY OTTO WAGNER. Nearly on Huttelberg-strasse

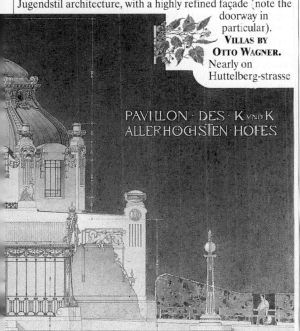

PAVILLON · DES · K UND K ALLERHOCHSTEN · HOFES

▲ From Schönbrunn to the Steinhof

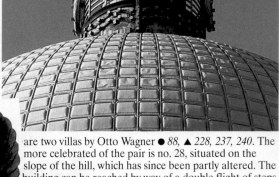

Kirche am Steinhof
● *87*
St Leopold's Church is crowned by a broad dome covered in copper plaques, with a turret similar to those of Peterskirche ● *75*, ▲ *139* and Karlskirche ● *74*, ▲ *238*.

are two villas by Otto Wagner ● *88*, ▲ *228, 237, 240*. The more celebrated of the pair is no. 28, situated on the slope of the hill, which has since been partly altered. The building can be reached by way of a double flight of steps which end at a classic portico framed by statues and frescoes.

Kirche am Steinhof ★

Just north of Schönbrunn, and west of the Ring, stands one of Otto Wagner's finest achievements: St Leopold's Church (Kirche am Steinhof). This magnificent edifice was built in 1902, shortly before Wagner's Post Office Savings Bank ● *88*, ▲ *228*, and is a worthy neighbor to the imperial architecture all around it. The Kirche am Steinhof is part of the huge am Steinhof psychiatric hospital complex commissioned here in the early 1900's by the province of Lower Austria, which also includes a spacious garden for inmates and a number of pavilions. The complex was built on the side of a hill, the top of which is occupied by Otto Wagner's church, a Secession-style ● *86, 88*, ▲ *232* building with a number of 18th-century Baroque features. Constructed in concrete, the Kirche am Steinhof is covered with a skin of thin marble, attached by studs that lend great elegance to its overall appearance. The main façade is flanked by twin belltowers, on the tops of which are statues of various saints by Richard Luksch. The PORTAL OF ST LEOPOLD, with four columns surmounted by angels, is truly remarkable; on the inside the nave, transept, choir and dome are, like the exterior, covered in plaques of white marble and flooded with light from huge windows. Wagner did not stop with the building itself; he also designed its fittings (pews and lamps) and its high altar and baldachin (the altar's

The gilded bronze angels (above) atop the four columns are by Othmar Schimkowitz. The stained glass (right) is by Koloman Moser ▲ *235*.

Kirche zur Heiligsten Dreifaltigkeit ★
The Church of the Holy Trinity on St George's Hill on the edge of the Wienerwald ■ *18*, ● *100* was designed in 1974–6 by Fritz Wotruba (1907–75).

FROM JOSEFSTADT
TO KLOSTERNEUBURG

KAHLENBERGKIRCHE GRINZING LEOPOLDSKIRCHE NUSSDORF

🚗 Half a day

"When he drew his map of repressed Desire, meaning the unconscious, just as in earlier times … men had charted the lineaments of Sensitivity, Sigmund Freud brought into the world a sort of puppet resembling modern man – ambivalent, dreamy, neurotic. I repeat that the face of this creature … had more than anything the features of a Viennese."

Michel Guérin, *Le Deuil et la Mélancolie* (in *Vienne*)

JOSEFSTADT

ALSERKIRCHE. The Church of the Holy Trinity (Alserkirche), an impressive Baroque edifice dating from the end of the 17th century, stands on Alserstrasse. Ludwig van Beethoven ● 51, ▲ 298 was buried here on March 29, 1827. More than thirty thousand people accompanied the genius to a grave in the old Währing cemetery (the coffin was disinterred and moved to the Central Cemetery ▲ 262 in 1888). This church and the adjoining chapel

are plastered with ex-votos to St Anthony, patron saint of lost causes.

PIARISTENKIRCHE. The architect Johann Lukas von Hildebrandt's ● 75, 81 best-known buildings are his palaces. This is all the more reason to visit JODOK-FINK-PLATZ in the heart of Josefstadt (8th District) to see one of his other buildings, the Piarist Church of Mary the Faithful (Piaristenkirche Maria Treu). The Church belonged to the congregation of Piarists, whose calling was to educate poor children. The handsome Baroque façade topped with a fine pediment has

THE GENERAL HOSPITAL
Arthur Schnitzler began his career as a doctor at the General Hospital (above) in 1885. Sigmund Freud qualified as a doctor in 1881. He quickly abandoned his researches into physiology to study nervous diseases. This led him to invent the science of psychoanalysis.

SIGMUND FREUD AND HIS DAUGHTER ANNA (1913)

NARRENTURM
Isidor Canevale (1730–83), the architect of the
Lusthaus ▲ 268, also built the Madmen's Tower
(the Narrenturm, below), the General Hospital and
the Josephinum ▲ 292.

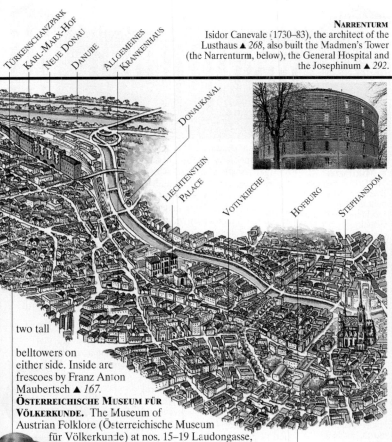

two tall
belltowers on
either side. Inside are
frescoes by Franz Anton
Maulbertsch ▲ 167.
**ÖSTERREICHISCHE MUSEUM FÜR
VÖLKERKUNDE.** The Museum of
Austrian Folklore (Österreichische Museum
für Völkerkunde) at nos. 15–19 Laudongasse,
houses an interesting collection of furniture, costumes
● 64 , tools and cribs.

ALSERGRUND

The Alsergrund (9th District) was praised in the
novels of Heimito von Doderer (1896–1966),
one of Austria's greatest but least-celebrated
writers.
FREUD-HAUS. Sigmund Freud (1856–1939)
practiced psychoanalysis in a comfortable
house at no. 19 Berggasse, Alsergrund, between
1891 and 1938. In 1938 he fled from the Nazi
régime and installed himself in London. An office
identical to the one that he used has been
reconstructed here, with the same collection of
antique statuettes. Only the famous divan here
is a replica: the original is at the Freud Museum
in London.
ALLGEMEINES KRANKENHAUS. Like Maria
Theresa (1717–80), Joseph II (1740–90) ● 36
helped create the basis for modern medicine in
Vienna by attracting respected specialists,
encouraging medical research and building
hospitals close to the city. In
1781 a military hospital was
founded so that surgeons and
doctors with practical
experience acquired on army

The Josephinum.

THE TWO PALACES BY MARTINELLI
The Italian architect Domenico Martinelli built the two Liechtenstein Palaces virtually simultaneously: the

Summer Palace (above) between 1691 and 1704, and the Winter Palace between 1694 and 1706. Like Hildebrandt, Martinelli (1650–1718) began in Rome as a pupil of Carlo Fontana. From there he traveled to Northern Europe, in particular to Prague and Vienna.

"ANATOMIA PLASTICA"
Joseph II had the idea for this collection of wax figures after visiting the anatomical museum in Bologna in 1769, and then seeing another collection of wax figurines in Florence. While in Florence he commissioned the artist who had done the figurines, Paolo Mascagni, to do a thousand like them for the Josephinum. The Viennese collection (*Anatomia Plastica*) is now world-famous and belongs to the medical history museum in the Josephinum.

campaigns could treat the sick of Vienna. They were also able to study medicine and surgery at the Military Academy, founded shortly afterward, which was known as the Josephinum. In 1784, the small military hospital was transferred to the premises of the present General Hospital (Allgemeines Krankenhaus); thereafter the hospital steadily added new facilities surrounded with courtyard-gardens, particularly the amazing MADMEN'S TOWER (Narrenturm), in a style close to the Utopian architecture of the Frenchmen Étienne-Louis Boullée and Claude-Nicolas Ledoux. Built on five floors, this monster cylinder has more than one hundred and forty cells, in which those diagnosed as lunatics were incarcerated until 1866. Today it is the MUSEUM OF PATHOLOGY AND ANATOMY (Pathologisch-anatomische Bundesmuseum), containing a startling collection of around 35,000 figurines and deformed limbs.

JOSEPHINUM ★. Like the General Hospital, the Josephinum (the former military academy of surgery and medicine) was founded by Joseph II. The emperor asked Carlo Canevale to model it on the Hôtel-Dieu hospital in Paris which he had seen during his official trip to France in 1777. The resulting structure, the Josephinum, is a conventional-looking building from the end of the Baroque age (1783–5), with an impressive library and above all a collection of wax figures for the study of anatomy. In addition to these flayed wax torsos, there are a number of mementoes of great Viennese physicians, notably some letters written by Sigmund Freud.

MUSEUM MODERNER KUNST. North of the Josephinum, in the heart of the Alsergrund, is the Liechtenstein Palace, which today houses the Museum of Modern Art (Museum moderner Kunst). This majestic Baroque palace ● 80, 82 set in its own gardens is one of the two residences built in Vienna by the princes of Liechtenstein at the close of the 17th century. Inside, the ceiling of the MAIN RECEPTION ROOM (Festsaal) is covered with frescoes by Andrea Pozzo ● 77, ▲ 149, 152, 167 (*The Apotheosis of Hercules*). Other Baroque artists

IOSEPHUS II. AUGUSTUS HIC PRIMUS

worked on the palace's décor, notably Giovanni Giulani and Johann Michael Rottmayr ▲ *139, 159* on the sculptures, and Antonio Belucci and Santino Bussi on the paintings. Most of the contemporary art movements (Jugendstil, Secession ● *86*, Expressionism, Cubism, Surrealism, Abstract Art, New Figurative Art, Pop Art and so on) are represented in the

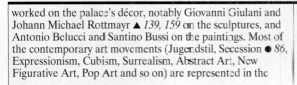

collections of the museum. Temporary exhibitions are also staged from time to time, offering a glimpse of the current international avant-garde.

SERVITENKIRCHE. Southeast of the Liechtenstein Palace is the Servite Church (Servitenkirche), designed by Carlo Canevale between 1651 and 1677. With an oval nave, this sanctuary is one of the first of its kind built in Vienna. The interior is by Giovanni Battista Barberini.

WÄHRING

STRUDELHOFSTEIGE (SCHUBERTPARK). The balustrades and huge lamps of the zigzag Strudelhof Steps (Strudelhofstiege), which have several different ramps and landings, make this one of the outstanding Jugendstil creations in Vienna. The steps link Liechtensteinstrasse to Währingerstrasse. As it proceeds away from the Ring, Währingerstrasse cuts across Nussdorferstrasse, which continues as far as Heiligenstadt and the Döblinger Gürtelstrasse, which in turn crosses Oberdöbling and

SCHUBERT'S BIRTHPLACE
Just west of the Liechtenstein Palace, in Nussdorferstrasse, a small museum devoted to Franz Schubert (1797–1828) ● *50* has been set up in the house of his birth (Schuberts Geburtshaus, no. 54), at the sign of the *Red Crayfish* (*Haus zum roten Krebs*). Schubert lived here during his earliest childhood, before moving to another house nearby, at no. 3 Saulengasse. He died aged thirty-one in a house on

Kettenbrückegasse, not far from the Naschmarkt ▲ *236*.

JOSEPH II
A bust of the institution's founder, Joseph II, sits behind one of the wax figures at the Josephinum.

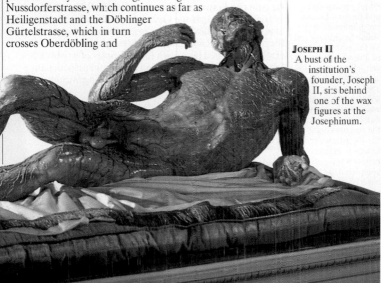

"DER TÜRKENSCHANZPARK"
"DER TÜRKENSCHANZPARK"
A painting by Johann Varrone, 1898.

"NETTOAUSGABEN DER GEMEINDE WIEN"
Distribution of Vienna's municipality budget, 1926.

❝My grandmother's apartment – I mean my grandmother Adele Schapira – took up the entire top floor of a very large house: no. 7 Türkenschanzplatz, in the 18th District of Vienna. The architect who constructed this building at the turn of the century copied the Ringstrasse style. Once the façade proper was completed, he covered it all over with countless caryatids, urns, garlands and figurines ...❞

George Clare,
Last Waltz in Vienna

Unterdöbling. This avenue runs parallel to the Danube Canal ■ *20, 22,* ▲ *271* and heads past THE UNIVERSITY COMPLEX (Universitätszentrum).

WÄHRINGER FRIEDHOF. Before being transferred to the Central Cemetery ▲ *262,* the body of Franz Schubert was buried in the former Währing Cemetery (Währinger Friedhof), which is now known as the Schubertpark, on Währingerstrasse. Beethoven was also buried here and later removed ▲ *290.*

JOHANNES-VON-NEPOMUK-KIRCHE. Still in the vicinity of the General Hospital and the Liechtenstein Palace is the pretty little church of St John of Nepomuk on Währingergürtel, which was built by Otto Wagner ● *86, 88,* ▲ *228, 237, 240* between 1895 and 1898.

VOLKSOPER. Nearby is the People's Opera (Volksoper), constructed in 1898 to mark Franz-Joseph's fiftieth jubilee. This impressive building really looks more like a circus than a theater. Ever since its opening it has been a shrine for composers and lovers of the operetta ● *60,* ▲ *299;* Mozart's *The Magic Flute* ● *48,* ▲ *147, 281* is usually performed here rather than in the State Opera on the Ring ▲ *223.*

GEYMÜLLER-SCHLÖSSEL. Northwest of the Währing, at Pötzleinsdorf, stands the Geymüller-Schlössel manor house, at no. 102 Pötzleinsdorfer Strasse, built in the 19th century by the banker J. H. Geymüller. The SOBECK COLLECTION of clocks is exhibited here, with fine examples of wristwatches, fob watches, chimney clocks and grandfather clocks dating from the 17th to the 19th centuries. The magnificent Biedermeier décor ● *62* of this house alone makes it worth the visit.

DÖBLING

TÜRKENSCHANZ. Bridging Währing (18th District) and Döbling (19th District) is the Türkenschanz Park, where part of Suleyman the Magnificent's army was encamped during the 1529 siege ● *34.* A 40-acre park was created on this high ground at the close of the 19th century, and the area quickly became a favorite resort of the Viennese; it was very popular with

the celebrated writer Arthur Schnitzler
▲ 290.

VILLA GESSNER AND VILLA MOLLER. A
major residential area with many handsome
buildings lies around the park and the
OBSERVATORY (Sternwarte). Buildings here
include the Secession-style ● 86, ▲ 232 Villa
Gessner (built in 1907 by Hubert and F.
Gessner on Sternwartestrasse) and the Villa
Moller on Starkfriedgasse (built by Adolf Loos
▲ 142, 174 in 1927–8) in the
Pötsleinsdorf suburb.

KARL-MARX-HOF. To the north of the
University complex is the remarkable
half-mile-long Karl-Marx-Hof municipal
housing project ● 92, which opens onto
Heiligenstädterstrasse. The red and ocher
central part of this ensemble is particularly
striking, with six tall towers crowned by
masts, and a series of statues and arcades
linking courtyards and gardens. Karl-
Marx-Hof contains no fewer than
1,300 apartments and stands in the
broad green area between the hills of
Döbling and Heiligenstadt to the west,
and the Heiligenstadt railway station to
the east. It was one of the 398 workers'
projects – known as ' red strongholds" –
which were built around Vienna between
1919 and 1934. This period was marked by
the confrontation between Christian
Socialists and Social Democrats in Austria; both of these
groups were also the sworn enemies of the Communist
contingent, Otto Bauer's Austro-Marxists, who were heavily
influenced by Marxist ideology. Administered by a Social
Democratic municipal council, Red Vienna was a veritable
state within a state. The municipal government tried to turn
Vienna into a showcase of the Socialist society of the future
that it wanted to promote, with a huge program of public

Posters for the
Social Democratic,
Christian Socialist
and Communist
parties from 1920,
1927 and 1919.

**FEAR OF JEWS
AND BOLSHEVIKS**
"No sooner did
our emperor's
eyes close for the
last time than we
shivered into a
hundred pieces. The
Balkans will be more
powerful than we.
Every nation will
organize its own
dirty little state and
the Jews
themselves will
proclaim a king in
Palestine. Vienna
already reeks of the
sweat of Democrats
and I can no longer
bear to be in
Ringstrasse. The
workers have red
flags and don't want
to work any more.
The priests are
already following the
people, the sermons
in the churches are
preached in Czech."
Joseph Roth,
The Radetsky March

The Socialist
municipality
promoted a campaign
for hygiene in the
schools during the
1920's.

"RED VIENNA"
Led by Karl Seitz (1869–1950, below), the mayor elected in 1923, "Red Vienna's" municipal team (H. Breitner, F. Siegel and A. Weber) laid special emphasis on public housing. Nearly all the housing built between 1923 and 1933 was within the framework of the *Höfe* complexes, projects designed for workers with collective facilities. Among the largest of

these were Sandleiten (1,587 units) in 1924, Rabenhof (1,109 units) in 1925, Karl-Seitz-Hof (1,173 units) in 1926, Karl-Marx-Hof (1,325 units) in 1927, George-

Washington-Hof (1,084 units) in 1927, Mithlingerhof (1,136 units) in 1929, and Engelsplatz (1,467 units) in 1930.

works and residential projects: between 1919 and 1934 over 64,000 new public housing units were built in the city. This housing was limited to a few districts on the north and south sides of Vienna because right up until 1918 the various classes had been divided up quarter by quarter into aristocratic, bourgeois and working-class areas. Today more than five thousand people live in Karl-Marx-Hof, which is arranged around several large inner courtyards and garden areas, the latter taking up more than eighty percent of the space allotted.

KARL-MARX-HOF UNDER FIRE. During the civil war which broke out in Vienna in February 1934 ● *33* and only lasted for a few days, Karl-Marx-Hof was the scene of a violent confrontation when it was taken over by a handful of rebels and was bombarded by the army acting on the orders of Chancellor Dollfuss. The buildings were partially destroyed and their defenders forced to surrender; subsequently an authoritarian government was installed which banned parties and unions and opened the way for the Anschluss ● *42*, which was accomplished a few years later.

BRIGITTENAU

Between the Danube and the Danube Canal ● *20, 22,* ▲ *122, 272* north of Leopoldstadt, lies Brigettenau (20th District), a working-class area strewn with railway installations and mainline stations.

OTTO-HAAS-HOF. The city council of Red Vienna constructed several workers' housing projects, comprising a total of 273 lodgings, on this site. The buildings were known collectively as the Otto-Haus-Hof. The ensemble was built in 1924 by a team of architects that included Adolf Loos ● *86, 91,* ▲ *142, 174, 236*. Loos championed the idea of building small detached houses for the project, but without much

The façade of Karl-Marx-Hof (right).

FOR GREATER COMFORT
Built by the architect Karl Ehn between 1927 and 1930, the workers' housing project of Karl-Marx-Hof sought to give the working classes more comfortable lodgings. Hence this monster complex contains not only ten different kinds of apartments (with running water, city gas and electricity) but also various other social facilities: a swimming pool, laundries, children's playgrounds, a post office, a dispensary, a chemist, a library and shops.

success; altogether, such houses (*Seidlungen*) made up only nine percent of the new housing when it was completed. Huge apartment blocks were more in line with the prevailing collectivist dogmas.

WINARSKYHOF. Another major project of 534 housing units is the Winarskyhof, which includes a series of attractive courtyards in addition to creches, shops and swimming pools. The façade of Winarskyhof is lightened by Expressionist moldings.

REUMANNHOF ● 93. The bust of Jakob Reumann, Vienna's first "red" mayor, stands in front of the public housing complex that bears his name. The Reumannhof was built between 1924 and 1926 by Hubert Gessner, architect of the Karl-Marx-Hof.

ENGELSPLATZ. Adjoining the bridge over the Danube which leads to Floridsdorf is Engelsplatz. It is overlooked by a massive residential complex of 1,467 apartments that were built in the 1930's, toward the end of the Red Vienna experiment. Constructed around a series of courtyards, Engelsplatz is flanked by several monumental-looking towers.

FLORIDSDORF

This former village (now the 21st District) on the left bank of the Danube is today a working-class area that is sandwiched between the New Danube, the Old Danube and a busy freeway junction.

KARL-SEITZ-HOF ● 92. One of the biggest projects (*Höfe*) to be constructed in the Red Vienna years, the Karl-Seitz-Hof (1,173 apartments) was built in 1926 by Hubert Gessner, one year before the Karl-Marx-Hof and after the Reumannhof. The complex has a spectacular appearance because its arc-shaped central block is crowned by a tall tower, which gives access to a wide inner street. On the left-hand side of the crescent is a clocktower. Offices, creches, shops, laundries and even a theater are features of this remarkable residence.

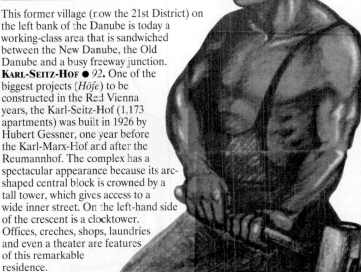

"MY MUSICAL WORKS ARE THE PRODUCT OF GENIUS AND WRETCHEDNESS, AND THOSE WHICH GIVE THE PUBLIC MOST PLEASURE ARE THOSE WHICH HAVE GIVEN ME THE GREATEST PAIN."
LUDWIG VAN BEETHOVEN

HEILIGENSTADT

This attractive village lying on the hillsides of Kahlenburg and Leopoldsberg north of Vienna is less famous for its expanse of vineyards ■ *26*, ● *68* than for the time Ludwig van Beethoven ● *51* spent there at the end of his life.

"I DON'T COMPOSE FOR THE GALLERY!" Like many other Romantics, Beethoven sought inspiration in the beauty and solitude of the Vienna woods ■ *18*, ● *100* or in bouts of seasonal work in the fields. During his visit to Heiligenstadt in 1807–8, he composed his *Sixth Symphony*, known as the *Pastoral,* in which he attempted to translate the rhythms of the universe and the sensation of an all-pervading divinity into music.

Beethoven's Testament.

"THE HEILIGENSTADT TESTAMENT". To music-lovers Heiligenstadt above all recalls Beethoven's first wretched period there in 1802. During his stay, the musician, who for six years had done everything possible to conceal the fact that he was incurably deaf, finally admitted it in his *Heiligenstadt Testament*, a document addressed to his brothers Kaspar and Johann. He also described his sense of desperation and wrote that he was tempted to commit suicide: "These ordeals brought me to the brink of despair; I came close to killing myself. Art, and art alone, stayed my hand."

HEILIGENSTÄDTER-TESTAMENT-HAUS. The *Testament* was written in the modest house at no. 6 Probusgasse (above), as was Beethoven's *Second Symphony*. Moreover, the *Third Symphony*, known as *Eroica,* was in all likelihood conceived while the composer was staying here. Part of the Testament-Haus has now been turned into a museum, where a collection of objects and engravings relating to Beethoven's time in the village is exhibited.

THE EMBLEM OF HEILIGENSTADT
St George and the dragon.

"As he gradually lost contact with the outside world, he focused more clearly on the one within him. As he grew more familiar with the management of his inner realm, he imposed, with ever greater awareness, his demands on the outer. He asked his protectors to cease paying him for his work, and instead to take care that he should never have to worry about the world, and thus be able to work for himself alone."
Richard Wagner, *Beethoven*

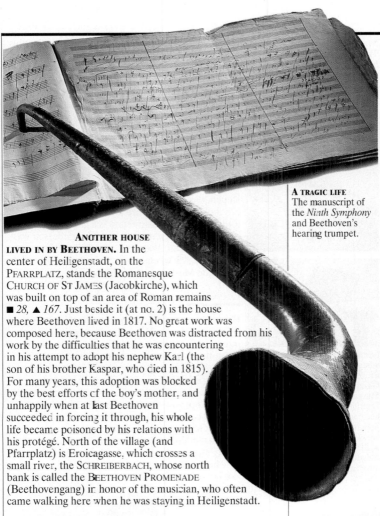

**ANOTHER HOUSE
LIVED IN BY BEETHOVEN.** In the
center of Heiligenstadt, on the
PFARRPLATZ, stands the Romanesque
CHURCH OF ST JAMES (Jacobkirche), which
was built on top of an area of Roman remains
■ *28,* ▲ *167.* Just beside it (at no. 2) is the house
where Beethoven lived in 1817. No great work was
composed here, because Beethoven was distracted from his
work by the difficulties that he was encountering
in his attempt to adopt his nephew Karl (the
son of his brother Kaspar, who died in 1815).
For many years, this adoption was blocked
by the best efforts of the boy's mother, and
unhappily when at last Beethoven
succeeded in forcing it through, his whole
life became poisoned by his relations with
his protégé. North of the village (and
Pfarrplatz) is Eroicagasse, which crosses a
small river, the SCHREIBERBACH, whose north
bank is called the BEETHOVEN PROMENADE
(Beethovengang) in honor of the musician, who often
came walking here when he was staying in Heiligenstadt.

NUSSDORF

In the hills to the north of Heiligenstadt is Nussdorf, which
overlooks the Danube. Surrounded by vines ■ *26,* Nussdorf is
famous for its guingettes, or *Heurigen* ● *68.*
THE LEHÁR-SCHIKANEDER-SCHLÖSSEL. At no. 18
Hackhohergasse is Franz Lehár's castle (Lehár-Schikaneder-
Schlössel) in which the celebrated operetta composer ● *60*
lived until his death (there is a small MUSEUM here). A native
of Hungary, Lehár (1870–1948) continued in the great
tradition of operetta founded in the 19th century by Jacques
Offenbach, a French composer of German extraction, and
Johann Strauss ● *56.* Lehár had a number of triumphs,
notably *The Merry Widow* (1905), *The Count of Luxembourg*
(1908) and *The Land of Smiles* (1929). The Baroque building
in which he lived belonged at one time to Emmanuel
Schikaneder, director of the Theater An der Wien ● *62.*
Schikaneder commissioned *The Magic Flute* from Mozart
● *48,* ▲ *147, 281* and himself wrote the libretto for the opera.

"What could this
ecstatic dreamer see,
as he passed wide-
eyed through the
swarming streets of
Vienna staring fixedly
before him, inspired
only by the world of
harmonies, the one
world that remained
alive within him?"
Richard Wagner,
Beethoven

NEW WHITE WINE
The arrival of the *Heurigen* ■ *26*, ● *68* is welcomed with music in the guinguettes; it has made the reputation of Grinzing, a small village on the upper slopes of Döbling, north of Vienna

(above). Other villages once famous for their wine, like Gumpendorf at Margareten (6th District), have become heavily populated residential areas. Karlskirche ▲ *238* and the Belvedere ▲ *246* were also surrounded by vines at one time.

He resided at Nussdorf between 1802 to 1812 and during this period met Beethoven, whom he encouraged to write operas. **BEETHOVEN AGAIN.** At no. 26 Kahlenbergerstrasse stands the 18th-century house where Beethoven lived in 1824, the year he finished his last, the *Ninth* (Choral) *Symphony*. Finally, on the southeast side of Heiligenstadt, on Grinzingerstrasse after Michaelskirche, is no. 64, another 18th-century building that was occupied by Beethoven and the family of the poet Franz Grillparzer in 1808 ● *62*, ▲ *147, 206*. The Grillparzer family finally was forced to decamp after a series of quarrels with the composer.

NUSSDORFER WEHR. The entrance to the Danube Canal (Donaukanal) ▲ *230* is barred by a stupendous lock (Nussdorfer Wehr) which is overlooked by two bronze lions on tall pedestals by Rudolph Weyr. This structure is a graceful combination of stone, glass and steel girders; it was designed by Otto Wagner ▲ *228, 237, 240* between 1884 and 1898, when he was a member of the Secession Movement ● *86, 88*, ▲ *232*.

GRINZING

HONORARY CITIZENS. Nowadays the guingettes (*Heurigen*) of Grinzing are increasingly being turned into tourist restaurants, and in summer the streets of the village are often packed with people milling about while looking for souvenirs. Even worse, speculators have taken advantage of Grinzing's fame to buy up a series of potential building sites. An international campaign is now underway to prevent such development which, if allowed to continue unchecked, would certainly lead to the destruction of the vineyards and of Grinzing's rustic character. In practice, this campaign works as a kind of club of "honorary citizens" of Grinzing. Every member of the club buys, for a nominal price, a single vine which he or she is thereafter expected to protect. Among these honorary vineyard owners are many stars and celebrities.

GRINZINGER FRIEDHOF. Music-lovers will wish to make the pilgrimage to the Grinzing cemetery (Grinzinger Friedhof) where GUSTAV MAHLER (*Gruppe 6, Reine 7*) ● *52*, ▲ *235* is buried.

KAHLENBERG

From Grinzing, two winding roads (Coblenzgasse and Höhenstrasse) lead up the 1,588-foot Bald Mountain (Kahlenberg). This was the hill down which the troops commanded by John Sobieski, King of Poland, marched on their way to crush the Turks, on September 12, 1683 ● *31, 34*, and thus ended the second siege of Vienna, which had lasted since July 14 that year.

KAHLENBERGKIRCHE. Much frequented by the local Polish community, the Church of St Joseph (Kahlenbergkirche) commemorates the lifting of the siege of Vienna; inside, see the SOBIESKI CHAPEL and the replica of the *Black Virgin of Czestochowa*.

THE VIEW FROM THE KAHLENBERG. The Kahlenberg offers a magnificent view of Vienna and the Danube Valley ■ *20, 22*, ▲ *271*. In 1809, during the French invasion of Austria, the Viennese climbed here to watch the maneuvers and battles taking place farther down the Danube at Essling-Aspern and Wagram ● *38*.

LEOPOLDSBERG

Höhenstrasse connects the Kahlenberg to the 1,394-foot Mount Leopold (Leopoldsberg), which overlooks the Danube Valley from farther east. The view across the region from the top of the Leopoldsberg is remarkable.
LEOPOLDSKIRCHE. Leopold I built a church here dedicated to his namesake, St Leopold, in the 17th century. This was destroyed during the second siege of Vienna by the Turks ● *31, 34*, then rebuilt in the Baroque style at the beginning of the 18th century.

THE LEOPOLDSBERG AND THE KAHLENBERG
At the gates of Vienna, the huge forest teeming with game made famous by Johann Strauss has remained astonishingly untouched, despite the bites taken out of it by spreading urbanization.

Leopoldsberg
Kahlenberg

"Contemplate the landscape from the top of the Kahlenberg, and you will understand what I write and what I am."
Franz Grillparzer

THE LEOPOLDSBERG
This belvedere owes its name to margrave Leopold III von Babenberg ● *28*, ▲ *138*, founder of the abbey of Klosterneuburg, who was canonized in the 15th century. After its destruction during the 1529 siege, the Babenberg castle at the summit of the hill was a ruin for many years.

At the foot of the Leopoldsberg stands Klosterneuburg, the largest of the abbeys along the Danube.

KLOSTERNEUBURG ★

The abbey of Klosterneuburg (Stift Klosterneuburg) was founded in the early 12th century by Margrave Leopold III of Babenberg, whose fortress stood close by on the top of the Leopoldsberg. This was the capital of the Eastern March (Ostmark), the future Austria. In 1156, when Henry II Jasomirgott of Babenberg was made Duke of Austria by the Holy Roman Emperor Frederick I Barbarossa (1122–90), he transferred his capital from Klosterneuburg to Vienna ● *28*.

MARGRAVE AND SAINT. The extremely pious Margrave Leopold III refused to be drawn into the quarrels between the Holy Roman Emperors and the Popes (the dispute over investitures lasted between 1059 and 1122), or into the rebellion of the German princes against the imperial power. This policy allowed him to marry Agnes, daughter of Emperor Henry II, to live in peace on his estates, and to dedicate his life to the Catholic religion. He was canonized in the 15th century and is buried in the chapel.

AUGUSTINE ABBEY, AUSTRIAN ESCORIAL. The first abbey, which belonged to the Augustine Order, was built in the Romanesque style in imitation of the Cistercian abbeys that members of the Orders of Cluny and Citeaux had built across Europe. Several centuries later Charles VI hatched a series of projects designed to give new luster to Klosterneuburg, which had been damaged by fire in 1730. Taking as his model the Escorial Palace just outside Madrid (built between 1563 and 1584), Charles determined to construct a monastery-palace that would symbolize the grandeur both of the Austrian monarchy and of the Holy Roman Empire, as well as housing a majestic family burial vault close to the Habsburg capital of Vienna.

FROM FISCHER VON ERLACH TO D'ALLIO. Charles VI gave the project to Josef Emanuel Fischer von Erlach, son of Johann Bernhard ● *74, 80*. Unfortunately the architect was involved in a plethora of other huge contracts at the time, notably the National Library ▲ *192, 196*, the Winter Manège of the Spanish Riding School ▲ *188, 190* and the Chancellery Wing of the Hofburg ▲ *175*, as well as the completion of Karlskirche ● *74*, ▲ *240* and the Schönbrunn Palace ▲ *274*. He therefore limited himself to a sketch for a grandiose project to build

THE LEGEND OF THE LOST VEIL
Leopold III decided to build his abbey on the site where he had found a precious veil lost by his wife, Agnes of Franconia. A wooden panel (above) painted by Rueland Frueauf (1470–1547), from the altar of the abbey church.

LEOPOLD III (1070–1136)
Margrave Leopold III von Babenberg ▲ *138* is the patron saint of Lower Austria.

a palace with four courtyards and nine domes. The Milanese architect Donato Felice d'Allio (1690–1780) was then called in to turn this into reality. Two difficulties immediately arose: the Habsburgs' chronic shortage of cash, and the death of Charles VI in 1740. As a result the works were limited to adding a Baroque building to the original Romanesque and Gothic abbey, with only one courtyard and two copper domes topped by the imperial crown and the archducal cap. Work was halted in 1755, then resumed in the 19th century, at which time the architect Josef Kornhausel added a wing to the Baroque building to close off the courtyard.

THE ABBEY CHURCH. From the esplanade with its LANTERN COLUMN (Lichtsäule) the visitor passes into the Abbey Church with its two belfries. Originally Romanesque, this Church was heavily modified over the course of centuries, especially in the 19th, when neo-Gothic additions were made. The CHOIRSTALLS, the ORATORY OF THE IMPERIAL COURT, the PULPIT and the ORGAN (on which Anton Bruckner ● 52, ▲ 195 often played) are highlights of the interior.

THE GOTHIC CLOISTER AND THE FREISINGERKAPELLE. Behind the Abbey Church is the Gothic cloister and the Freising Chapel (Freisingerkapelle); the latter contains an effigy of Berthold von Wehingen, Bishop of Friesing in the 14th century.

LEOPOLDSKAPELLE. The Chapel of St Leopold (Leopoldskapelle) contains one of the greatest marvels of medieval goldwork, the ALTARPIECE OF NIKOLAUS OF VERDUN (1181). It shows scenes from the Bible, and is made up of fifty-one plaques of gilded metal worked by the technique of champlevé enamel, whereby small sockets are drilled in the metal and the liquid enamel is poured over and then fired. In the chapel is a silver reliquary containing the relics of St Leopold Babenberg. The 14th- and 15th-century stained-glass windows here are magnificent.

LEOPOLDSHOF. Dominated by an ancient fortified tower, the courtyard of Leopold (Leopoldshof) is surrounded by Gothic and Renaissance buildings. In its center is the 17th-century St LEOPOLD'S FOUNTAIN.

THE MARBLE ROOM. Among the Baroque buildings constructed under Charles VI are the imperial apartments

THE LANTERN COLUMN
This 15th-century memorial (below) stands in the middle of the esplanade.

St Leopold's Fountain (left).

THE ABBEY CHURCH
The Baroque interior contains fine frescoes from the late 17th and early 18th centuries, commissioned by Charles VI from such artists as Johann Michael Rottmayr ▲ 139, 160, 293, J. G. Schmidt and G. Fanti.

NIKOLAUS OF VERDUN
A pupil of the Flemish monk Godefroid de Claire, Nikolaus of Verdun perfected the art of champlevé enamel in the 12th century. This technique, inherited from Byzantine and Carolingian art, evolved in the workshops of Maastricht, Verdun and Liège along the River Meuse, and in Cologne, Coblenz and Aix-la-Chapelle along the Rhine.

THE VERDUN ALTARPIECE
The altarpiece of Klosterneuburg (1181) is made up of illustrated enamel plaques from the Shrine of the Three Kings at Cologne Cathedral – one of the only pieces of medieval goldwork fashioned in solid gold – and from the Tournai reliquary (1205).

REMINDERS OF THE TURKS ● *34*
As in Vienna itself, plaques here commemorate the presence of the Turkish armies, recalling a battle, or the site of a redoubt.

Franz Kafka, a native of Prague (1883–1924) was for part of his life a subject of the emperor of Austria. An obscure bureaucrat, Kafka spent his leisure time writing about a world of mental anguish that failed to interest the public until after his death.

and the museum, both of which overlook the courtyard (Kaiserhof). The upper floors are reached by a monumental Baroque staircase (1723), never completed, which leads to the MARBLE ROOM with its frescoes by Daniel Gran (*The Glory of the House of Austria*, 1749). In the imperial apartments, note the TAPESTRY ROOM, which is decorated with 18th-century Brussels tapestries.

THE VIRGIN OF KLOSTERNEUBURG. The MUSEUM on the third floor contains several masterpieces, in particular a 14th-century marble Virgin of great sweetness and grace. The early 15th-century altarpiece of Albert II, the 15th-century Babenberg family tree, the Italian Renaissance statues, and the *Mercury* by Georg Raphael Donner ▲ *170, 171*, who sculpted the Neuer Markt Fountain ▲ *141*, are also well worth seeing.

TAUSENDEIMERFASS. Within the abbey precinct are the GOTHIC CHAPEL OF ST SEBASTIAN, the CELLARHOUSE and the COOPER'S SHOP, containing the "thousand-bucket-barrel" (Tausendeimerfass) made in 1704. It can hold almost 15,000 US gallons of wine. On St Leopold's Day, November 15, an annual fête is held here, with barrel-rolling competitions; a reminder that the Klosterneuburg vineyard area is one of the largest in Austria.

KIERLING

THE DEATH OF KAFKA. The Kierling sanatorium was where Franz Kafka (1883–1924) died from tuberculosis. A small museum here contains mementoes of this great Bohemian writer.

PRACTICAL
INFORMATION

◆ PRACTICAL DETAILS

MIKLITSCH

The best times to visit Vienna are May to June and September to October, when the weather is mild and often sunny. A range of cultural events are scheduled during these months, including the summer music festival (Wiener Festwochen) in May and June, and a series of concerts by the Vienna Philharmonic in September. December and January are the best winter months, when Vienna is often snowbound; at this time the city has a fairyland quality, enhanced by the winter markets.

AN INDISPENSABLE PIECE OF EQUIPMENT

When the streets are full of snow and salt in wintertime, every Viennese carries a bag containing an extra pair of shoes to change into when he goes inside.

DOCUMENTS

A national identity card less than ten years old, or a valid passport, is needed in order to enter Austria, but no visa is required. Nationals of some European countries may use a passport which has expired in the previous five years.

HEALTH

No vaccinations are required, but travelers are advised to take out some form of health insurance before leaving home.

CUSTOMS

◆ Visitors over 17 years of age may bring in the following articles tax free: 200 cigarettes or 50 cigars or half a pound of tobacco, 2.25 liters of wine and 1 liter of spirits.
◆ The total value of any tax-free gifts or souvenirs may not exceed the sum of 400 ATS.

TAX-FREE SHOPPING

There is an official procedure for reclaiming Austrian sales tax (VAT), charged at 13% on purchases over 1,000 ATS per shop.

TOUR OPERATORS

Tour operators frequently offer weekend breaks at the end of the year, including Christmas, New Year's Day and the ball season, as well as four-day weekend package tours. Opera and museum tickets may often be included in prices. There are also special "train and car" prices that cover a weekend or a full week. One-week cruises on the Danube between Passau and Budapest, stopping at Vienna, are also available.

THE "FASCHING"

The Fasching takes place every year between December 21 and Shrove Tuesday (generally in mid-February, just before Lent). The season opens with the Emperor's Ball in the salons of the Hofburg, and closes on Shrove Tuesday. The Viennese put on disguises, and form merry processions in the streets, parading round the Ring in carriages.

HOLIDAYS

New Year's Day, Epiphany (January 6), Easter Monday, May 1, Ascension Day, the first Monday after Pentecost, Corpus Christi, Assumption Day (August 15), National Day (October 26), All Saints Day, Immaculate Conception (December 8), Christmas Day, St Stephen's Day (December 26).

OFFICIAL ORGANIZATIONS

◆ AUSTRIAN EMBASSY AND CONSULAR SECTION
18 Belgrave Mews West London SW1X 8HU
Tel. 071 235 3731-4,
◆ AUSTRIAN EMBASSY (Botschaft)
3524 International Court N.W., Washington DC 20008
Tel. (202) 895 67 00
◆ CONSULATE:
Tel. (202) 895 67 67
◆ AUSTRIAN NATIONAL TOURIST OFFICE
30 St George St London W1R 0AL
Tel. 071 629 0461;
500 Fifth Avenue Suite 2009–2022 New York, NY 10110
Tel. (212) 944 6880;
11601 Wilshire Blvd. Suite 2480, Los Angeles, CA 90025
Tel. (310) 477 3332;
North Michigan Ave Suite 1950, Chicago, IL 60611
Tel. (312) 644 8029

CALENDAR OF EVENTS AND FESTIVALS

	J	F	M	A	M	J	J	A	S	O	N	D
SPANISH RIDING SCHOOL												
EXHIBITIONS				•	•	•	•		•	•		
TRAINING SESSIONS	•	•	•	•				•	•	•		
VIENNA BOYS' CHOIR												
MASSES	•	•	•	•	•	•			•	•	•	•
CONCERTS					•	•			•			
BALLS												
EMPEROR'S BALL												•
BALL SEASON	•	•										•
NEW YEAR'S EVE CONCERT	•											
WALTZ AND OPERETTA				•	•	•	•	•	•			
CONCERTS												
MOZART CONCERTS							•	•	•	–		
FESTIVAL OF MEDIEVAL MUSIC		•										
HAYDN FESTIVAL			•									
CHURCH MUSIC FESTIVAL			•									
SPRING FESTIVAL				•								
VIENNA FESTIVAL					•	•						
MARCH MARATHON			•									
PRATER FLOWER DISPLAY						•						
SUMMER MUSIC FESTIVAL						•	•	•	•			
VIENNALE FILM FESTIVAL										•		
KITE FESTIVAL										•		
SCHUBERT FESTIVAL											•	
ANTIQUE FAIR											•	
OBJETS D'ART FAIR											•	
WIEN MODERN (MUSIC)											•	
INTERNATIONAL DANCE WEEK		•						•	•			
ROCK FESTIVAL						•						

CLIMATE

Vienna's climate is moderate and continental. The winters are long (October to April) and cold (23° F to 41° F). The transition seasons in spring and autumn are short and sometimes rainy.

Months	Max.	Min.	Sun
JANUARY	1°C	-4°C	10 d.
FEBRUARY	3°C	-3°C	12 d.
MARCH	8°C	1°C	16 d.
APRIL	15°C	6°C	20 d.
MAY	19°C	10°C	22 d.
JUNE	23°C	14°C	25 d.
JULY	25°C	15°C	26 d.
AUGUST	24°C	15°C	24 d.
SEPTEMBER	20°C	11°C	21 d.
OCTOBER	14°C	7°C	16 d.
NOVEMBER	7°C	3°C	9 d.
DECEMBER	3°C	-1°C	9 d.

Max. : average maximum temperature
Min. : average minimum temperature
Sun : total days of sunshine

MODEST BUDGET FOR ONE WEEK (SEVEN DAYS)

TWO ADULTS, CHARTER FLIGHT, ** HOTEL.
Allow about £160 (UK)/$500–600 (US) for flight, and about £20/$30 per day per person for accommodation.

FAMILY BUDGET FOR ONE WEEK (SEVEN DAYS)

TWO ADULTS AND TWO CHILDREN, TRAVELING BY TRAIN AND STAYING AT A PRIVATE HOUSE
From the UK: Train fares from London, £234 adult return, £198 child aged 12 to 14, £119 child between 4 and 11. From the US: Charter flights $500–600 per person, reductions for children.
In Vienna, bed and breakfast accommodation averages £25/$35 per night per person, with a 30% reduction for children under 12.

LUXURY BUDGET FOR ONE WEEK (SEVEN DAYS)

TWO ADULTS, SCHEDULED FLIGHT, **** HOTEL.
Scheduled flight around £400 for two from London, $700–900 from New York. Allow up to £65/$90 per day per person for a high class hotel with typically Viennese atmosphere, furnishing and cuisine. Total cost for an exceptional week for two about £1,300/$3,060. (Champagne is not included.)

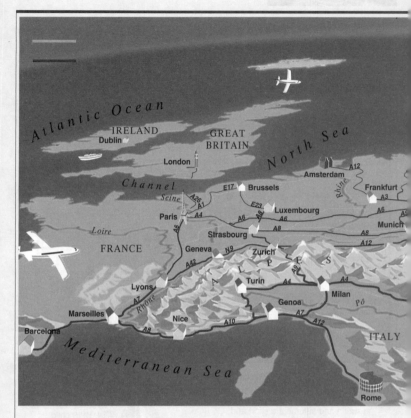

BY AIR

FROM LONDON
◆ Austrian Airlines
Tel. 071 439 1851
Reservations/fares
Tel. 071 439 0741
◆ British Airways
Tel. 081 759 5511
Reservations and
travel information
Tel. 081 897 4000
(from Greater
London)
Tel. 0345 222111
(from elsewhere in
UK and Ireland)
◆ Lauda Air
Tel. 071 630 5549
Reservations,
Tel. 071 630 5924

FROM THE US
◆ Direct flights New
York to Vienna with
Austrian Airlines and
Delta.
One-stop flights
Austrian Airlines
(Chicago to Vienna),
Lauda Air (Los

Angeles and Miami to
Vienna), TWA (New
York to Vienna).
◆ Flights from US
cities to Europe with
onward connections
to Austria with
American Airlines (to
Frankfurt, Munich,
Zurich), Continental
(to Frankfurt or
Munich), Delta (to
Amsterdam,
Frankfurt, Hamburg,
Munich or Zurich),
KLM (to Amsterdam),
Lufthansa (to
Dusseldorf, Frankfurt
or Munich), Northwest
(to Frankfurt or
Munich), Swissair (to
Geneva or Zurich),
TWA (to Amsterdam,
Frankfurt or Munich),
United (to Frankfurt,
Geneva, Hamburg or
Munich). Consult your
local travel agent for
the most convenient
flight.

◆ Schwechat
international airport is
12 miles from Vienna.

BY TRAIN
◆ British Rail
International
Information:
Tel. 071 834 2345
Recorded
information:
Tel. 0891 888731
Reservations:
Tel. 071 828 0892/
071 630 8133
Baggage:
Tel. 071 928 5151
◆ The most direct
route is from London
Victoria to Ramsgate,
then ferry to Ostend,
and train via Aachen,
Cologne, Frankfurt,
Passau and Linz.
◆ Adult fares are
£234 return;
children's fares
depend on ages:
4–11 years, £119
return; 12–13 years,
£181 return; 14

years, £198 return;
15 years, £223
return.
◆ Students and young
people under the age
of 26 can apply for
the International
Student Rail Card,
allowing unrestricted
train travel in
numerous European
countries.
◆ Other young
persons tickets
(BIGE) are also
available.

For further
information contact
British Rail
International or a
travel agent.
◆ Passenger routes
through the Channel
Tunnel are due to
become operational
in May 1994.
Travelers should
check availability and
costs before travel.

TRAVELING ◆ TO VIENNA

AIRPORT	STOPS	HOURS	JOURNEY TIME	PRICE
SHUTTLE	City Air Terminal	Apr.-Oct., 6–2.30 am, daily	20 mins	60 ATS
SHUTTLE	Südbahnhof Station, 6.40 am–10.30 pm, daily then Westbahnhof		20 mins	60 ATS
TRAIN	Wien-Mitte Station, Wien-Nord Station	5.30 am–10.05 pm, daily	30 mins	30 ATS
TAXI			20 mins	300–350 ATS

TRANSPORT TABLE		
FLIGHTS FROM THE UK		
Airline	**Departure point**	**Frequency**
AUSTRIAN AIRLINES	London Heathrow	3 flights daily
BRITISH AIRWAYS	London Heathrow	3 flights daily
BRITISH AIRWAYS	London Gatwick	3 flights daily
LAUDA AIR	London Gatwick	1 flight Mon., Wed., Thu., Sun.
		2 flights Fri.
FLIGHTS FROM THE US AND CANADA		
Airline	**Departure point**	**Frequency**
AIR CANADA	Toronto	5 flights weekly
AUSTRIAN AIRLINES	New York Kennedy	Direct flights Mon., Wed., Fri., Sat., Sun.
AUSTRIAN AIRLINES	Chicago O'Hare	One-stop flights Mon., Thur., Sat., Sun.
DELTA	New York Kennedy	Direct flight Tue., One-stop Sat.
LAUDA AIR	Los Angeles	One-stop flight Tue., Sat.
	Miami	One-stop flight Tue., Thur. Sat.
TWA	New York Kennedy	One-stop flights daily

BY CAR

take a ferry to Boulogne or Calais in France, or to take the Channel Tunnel when this opens in 1994.

◆ Freeways are toll-free throughout Austria and Germany, but charges are levied in France.

◆ Driving throughout the Continent is on the right-hand side of the road. International driving insurance is required for all drivers, but a national driving licence is adequate.

◆ The price of gasoline in Austria: Super Plus/98 Oktan (unleaded) begins at 9.60 ATS; diesel at 7.20 ATS.

◆ Austria is well-equipped with tourist information offices. There are several along the freeways leading into Vienna.

◆ Travelers from the UK can take the jetfoil from Dover to Ostend, the ferry from Dover to Zeebrugge, or the longer (7 hours) ferry service between Harwich and Hook of Holland.

◆ From Belgium or Holland well-marked highways and freeways join the international freeway network; drivers can plan their routes in advance in order to take in attractions and rest-stops along the way – the city of Cologne, in Germany, for instance, or Salzburg to the southwest of Vienna in Austria.

◆ Those wishing to tour more extensively in Europe en route to Vienna may prefer to

DISTANCES (MILES) VIENNA – OTHER EUROPEAN CITIES	
Amsterdam	575
Athens	792
Barcelona	326
Brussels	575
Budapest	155
Lisbon	1,383
London	777
Lyon	731
Madrid	1,118
Marseilles	621
Milan	388
Munich	233
Nice	744
Paris	782
Prague	155
Rome	699
Warsaw	326

TOURIST INFORMATION OFFICES AND HOTEL RESERVATIONS		
TYPE	**ADDRESS**	**OPENING HOURS**
Offizielle Tourist Information	Obere Augartenstrasse 2nd, Tel: 402 11 140	Information by phone or mail only (official headquarters) Daily 9am–7pm
Tourist-Information (Vienna)	Kärntner Strasse 38 , 1st, Tel: 513 88 92	Apr.–Oct. 8am–10pm, Nov. 9am–7pm, Dec –Mar. 10am–6pm
Freeway A1 (Freeway to the West)	Lay-by at Vienna-Auhof	
Freeway A2 (Freeway to the South)	Triesterstrasse	Mid-Mar.–June, Oct. 9am–7pm; July–Sept. 8am–10pm
Freeway A4 (Freeway to the East), Simmeringer Haide Exit	Landwehrstrasse 6	End Mar.–Sept. 8am–6pm
Northern Access	Floridsdorfer-brücke/Donauinsel	End Mar.–Sept. 8am–6pm
Westbahnhof Station	Europaplatz 1, 15th	Mon.–Fri. 6:15am–11pm
Südbahnhof Station	Wiedner Gürtel 1b, 10th	Mon.–Fri. 6:30am–10pm
DDSG (Danube Navigation Company) Information Desk	Reichsbrücke	Apr.–Oct. 7am–6pm
Airport Tourist Information	Arrival Hall	Daily Oct.–May. 8:30am–10pm, June–Sept. 8:30am–11pm
Jugend-Info Wien (Vienna Youth Information)	Dr. Karl Renner/Bellaria Passage, 1st, Tel: 526 46 37	Mon.–Fri. noon–7pm, Sat. and school vacations 10am–7pm
Österreich-Information (Information concerning the other Austrian provinces)	Margaretenstrasse 1, 4th, Tel: 58 72 000	Mon.–Fri. 10am–5pm, Thur. 10am–6pm
Niederösterreich-Information (Information about the area around Vienna)	Heidenschuss 2, 1st, Tel: 533 31 14 28	Mon.–Fri. 8:30am–5:30pm, Sat. 9am–noon

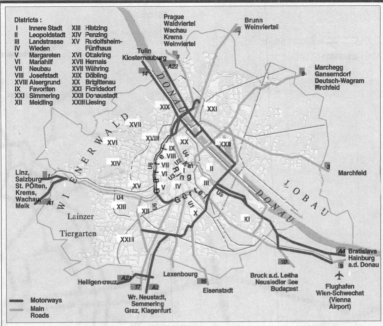

Districts:
I Innere Stadt
II Leopoldstadt
III Landstrasse
IV Wieden
V Margareten
VI Mariahilf
VII Neubau
VIII Josefstadt
XVIII Alsergrund
IX Favoriten
XXI Simmering
XII Meidling

XIII Hietzing
XIV Penzing
XV Rudolfsheim-Fünfhaus
XVI Ottakring
XVII Hernals
XVII Währing
XIX Döbling
XX Brigittenau
XXI Floridsdorf
XXII Donaustadt
XXIII Liesing

— Motorways
— Main Roads

ORIENTATION

Vienna is divided into twenty-three districts (Bezirke), spiralling outward from the 1st District (Innere Stadt), the historic center girdled by the Ring. When writing addresses in Vienna, the district in which the building stands is indicated by the second and third figures in the postal code: thus 1st District = 1(01)0, 15th District = 1(15)0, 20th District = 1(20)0.

BY CAR

Vienna is not a particularly congested city, except during rush hour between 7:30am and 8am, and in the evening around 5pm. It is nonetheless sensible to avoid driving in the 1st District because of its tiresome traffic blocks and one-way system. The rules for driving are no different to those prevailing elsewhere on the Continent (priority to vehicles approaching from the right). Speed limits are 30mph in built-up areas, 60mph on main roads, and 80mph on freeways.

CAR RENTAL

Drivers must be age twenty-one at least, and must have held a national driving license for at least one year. International driving licenses are not necessary. Car rental agencies are located in all airports and stations, and in the city center. The following major agencies are located in the 1st District:
AVIS: Opernring 1, Tel. 587 62 41
HERTZ: Kärntner Ring 14, Tel. 512 86 77 4200

DRIVERS AND PEDESTRIANS

Viennese pedestrians are studiously respectful of traffic regulations and will wait patiently for the light to change to green before crossing the street.

PARKING

Only those who live or work in the 1st District of Vienna are allowed to park outside special parking lots. Parking is permitted in other districts for a maximum period of ninety minutes, in places where the road is marked with blue lines. Parking coupons have to be purchased in advance (different colored discs correspond to the length of time paid for: for example, ninety minutes costs 60 ATS). There are plenty of public parking lots in the city center, but these are all too often filled to capacity. However, the smallness of Vienna's center and its excellent public transport system ◆ 314 mean that it is perfectly possible to have an enjoyable day out in Vienna without needing to use a car.

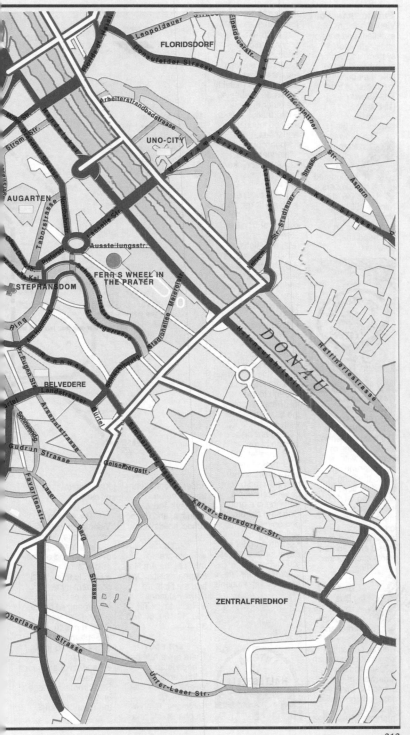

◆ LOCAL TRANSPORT

PUBLIC TRANSPORT
Vienna has an excellent and cheap public transport system, and visitors are advised not to take their cars into the center of town.
THE SUBWAY (U-BAHN)
The subway symbol is a blue U.
The subway system includes five lines designated by numbers U1 to U6 (the U5 line is still in the planning stage). Part of U6 is an overhead line, between

Westbahnhof and Heiligenstadt.
THE TRAMWAY (STRASSENBAHN)
The tram is Vienna's fastest means of transport, with a network running round the Ring in both directions and branching off it. The tram lines bear numbers 1 to 71 or letters B to O. Lines 1 and 2 and part of lines J and D do the whole circuit of the Ring.

BUS
Bus routes cover both the center and the periphery of Vienna, crossing the tram routes, between 5.30am and midnight. A network of night buses (30 minutes past midnight to 4am) runs at hourly intervals. These are

marked N (for Nachtbus) and the fare is 25 ATS; they only operate on Fridays and Saturdays between the main Ring intersections (notably Schwedenplatz) and the outer districts.
◆ Information kiosks may be found in the Karlsplatz, Stephansplatz, Praterstern and Phildelphiabrücke metro stations.

TICKETS
◆ Single ticket: 20 ATS
◆ Book of 5 tickets: 75 ATS (Metro stations, Tabak-Trafik stores)
◆ Cards and passes valid for buses, trams and metros in Zone 1 are:
• 24-hour card (45 ATS)
• 72-hour card (115 ATS)
• Weekly card (Wochenkarte) valid for holder only (125 ATS). This last, which lasts from Monday through to the following Sunday, is the best value for visitors.
• There are also section cards, valid for 8 days, at 235 ATS; these have several strips and may be used by one or several people traveling in a group. One strip per day per person may be validated.
• Children under six travel for free all year round. Foreign students under fifteen and Austrian students

under nineteen can travel free on Sundays and holidays, and during school holidays.

TAXIS
◆ There are taxi ranks at the Am Hof, Stephansplatz, Opera and the Hofburg railway stations.
◆ Radio-taxis: Tel. 31 300, 40 100, 60 160, 81 400

ON FOOT
There are a number of pedestrian zones in the center of Vienna (Innere Stadt, 1st District): Kohlmarkt, Graben, Stephansplatz and

Kärntnerstrasse are all car-free.

BY BICYCLE
Vienna has extensive cycle tracks, which are well marked all over town and on the outskirts.
◆ Bicycle tours, with commentary in English or German, are organized on the 1st and 3rd Monday of each month, May to September: 165 ATS + 60 ATS for cycle rental.
◆ Rendezvous: under the Radverleih Salztorbrücke bridge, on the right bank of the Danube Canal.

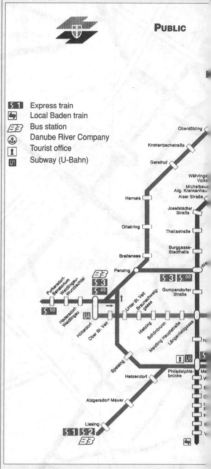

PUBLIC

S1	Express train
	Local Baden train
EE	Bus station
◎	Danube River Company
ⅰ	Tourist office
U1	Subway (U-Bahn)

314

TRANSPORT SYSTEM

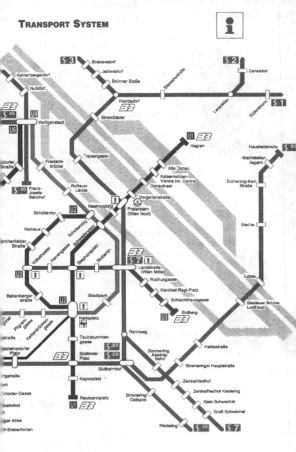

i

BY 1920'S TRAM

The original tramway, constructed in 1929, offers a two-hour circuit round the city's principal monuments as far as Schönbrunn: every weekend from May to October, Saturdays at 1:30pm, Sundays and public holidays 10am and 1:30pm. Departures from Karlsplatz, in front of the Otto Wagner Pavilion.
Prices are 150 ATS for adults, 50 ATS for children (tickets for sale at the Public Transportation Information Office, Karlsplatz).

BY BUS

Comprehensive tours of the city and short excursions outside it are offered by the various bus companies.
♦ Vienna Sightseeing Tours, Stelzhammergasse 4, 3rd District Tel. 712 46 830 (comprehensive tour, 320 ATS adults, 100 ATS children).
♦ Cityrama Sightseeing, Börsegasse 1, 1st District Tel. 534 13 or 12 (comprehensive tour, 320 ATS adults, 100 ATS children, 3 hours).
♦ Vienna Line, Johannesgasse 14, 1st District Tel. 512 8091 (comprehensive tour for 320 ATS).
♦ Vienna Line Junior (for children, June–September, 520 ATS, 4 hours).
♦ Alternative Stradtrundfahrten City Tours, Kolingasse 6, 9th District Tel. 34 33 84 (3-hour "Dreams and Reality" circuit: visit focused on the 1830–1930 period, Jugendstil and Red Vienna, 250 ATS).

CYCLING IN VIENNA

To find out more about cycling conditions in Vienna, read the brochure on *Exploring Vienna by Bicycle*, available at the City Tourist Office ♦ 342.

BY BOAT

The Danube Navigation Company (DDSG) organizes a variety of excursions and cruises on the river (with dinner and dancing on some vessels) every day from April through October. Embark from the Schwedenplatz landing stage, and tour the city from Schwedenbrücke to the Kunsthaus. The round trip of 21 miles lasts for 3 hours and costs 220 ATS (a 60 percent reduction is available for children between age 6 and 15, if accompanied). Further information from DDSG-Donaureissen, Handelskai 265, 2nd District, Tel. 217 50-0.

BY HORSE-DRAWN CARRIAGE

The hackney carriage is a charming way for a small group of between four and six people to explore Vienna during the warmer weather in spring and summer. Carriage ranks are located at Stephansplatz, Am Graben, Am Hof and the Hofburg. The fee is between 400 and 800 ATS per carriage, depending on the route chosen.

315

CURRENCY

THE AUSTRIAN CURRENCY

The Austrian monetary unit is the schilling (ATS) which subdivides into 100 groschen (G). Coins in circulation are 10 G, 50 G and 1, 5, 10 and 20 ATS. Banknotes come in bills of 20, 50, 100, 500, 1,000 and 5,000 ATS. 12 ATS = $1 US. 18 ATS = £1 UK.

TRAVELER'S CHECKS

Traveler's checks in US dollars can be changed into Austrian schillings in banks. Such traveler's checks are also accepted in some shops.

In the event of loss or theft of your ID or passport, inform the police (Tel. 133) as soon as possible.
◆ UK Consulate in Vienna: 3 Jaurèsgasse 10, 1st District, Tel. 713 15 75
◆ US Consulate in Vienna: 1 Gartenbaupromenade, Parkring 12a, (Marriot Hotel), 1st District, Tel. 31 55 11

PAYMENTS AND WITHDRAWALS

◆ All credit cards (Visa–Blue Card, Diner's Club, American Express, Eurocard, Mastercard) are accepted in most hotels, restaurants and shops.
◆ The International Blue Card enables you to withdraw up to $400 per week from automatic cash distributors.
◆ Withdrawals of up to $500 weekly in local currency can be made by a check accompanied by a Blue Card.
◆ Eurocheques are widely accepted when accompanied by a Eurocheque card.

EXCHANGE BUREAUX

◆ Money can be exchanged daily at the Westbahnhof railway station between 7am and 10pm, the Südbahnhof between 6.30am and 10pm; at the City Air Terminal (Hilton) between 9am and 12.30pm and between 2pm and 6pm; and at the Kärntnerstrasse tourist office between 9am and 7pm.
◆ The Exchange offices at the Wien-Mitte Station are open Monday to Friday between 7.30am and 7pm.

BANKS

◆ Banks and Savings Banks in Vienna are open Mon. Tues. Wed. and Fri. 8am–12.30pm and 1.30pm–3pm, and Thur. 8am–12.30pm and 1.30pm–5.30pm
◆ Austrian Banks: Bank Austria, Am Hof 2, 1st District, Tel. 711 910 Creditanstalt Bank-verein, Schotteng 6–8, 1st District Tel. 531 310
◆ Foreign Banks: American Express Bank, Kärntnerstrasse 21–3, 1st District Tel. 517 67 Diner's Club Austria, Rainergasse, 4th District Tel. 501 350 Chase Manhattan Bank, Parkring 12a, 1st District Tel. 515 890

AUTOMATIC CASH DISPENSERS (BANKOMAT)

◆ Cash dispensers at bank entrances function 24 hours a day. Most are linked to the Visa network (commission: 20 ATS per transaction). Information from Visa-Service

Kreditkarten AG, Wipplingerstrasse 4, 1st District, Tel. 534 870
◆ In the city center, automatic dispensers can be found to change all major currencies into Austrian schillings at Kärntnerstrasse 7, Kärntnerstrasse 32, Kärntnerstrasse 51, Michaelerplatz, Looshaus, Stephansplatz 2, Operngasse 8, Franz-Josefs-Kai 21, Landstrasser Hauptstrasse 1.

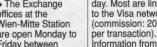

ACCOMMODATION

It is always advisable to reserve in advance, especially during holiday periods in Vienna. A deposit may be requested, or a credit card number taken on the day the reservation is made.

RESERVATIONS FROM THE UK

◆ Austria On Line
10 Wardour Street,
5th floor,
London W1V 4BQ
Tel. 071 434 7390

FROM THE US

There are numerous hotel reservations organizations in the U.S.; travel agents or the Austrian National Tourist Office can advise on individual requirements.
◆ Best Western International Inc.
Tel. (602) 957 4200
cr (800) 528 1234
Fax (602) 780 6099
◆ Vienna Central Reservation/Duyff International
Tel. (314) 434 2222
or (800) 237 5469
Fax (314) 434 6484

ARRIVING IN VIENNA AT SHORT NOTICE

◆ The tourist office can provide lists of hotels by telephone, at the following numbers: 513 88 92 or 513 40 15. Reservations can only be made on the spot (◆ 310). The tourist offices at the Westbahnhof and Südbahnhof can also reserve hotel rooms.
◆ Mitwohnzentrale, Laudongasse 7, 8th District
Tel. 402 60 61, Monday to Friday 10am to 6pm. This office can procure bedrooms and private apartments for short stays of at least 3 days. Prices from 150 ATS per day, apartments from 500 ATS.

◆ There are two youth hostel associations:
The Österreichischer Jugendherbergsverb and, Schottenring 28, 1st District
Tel. 533 53 53;
and the Österreichisches Jugendherbergswerk, Helferstorferstrasse 4, 1st District
Tel. 533 18 33
◆ Rooms in private homes:
Reisebüro Hippesroither, Neustiftgasse 66, 7th District
Tel. 93 92 19
Österreichisches Verkehrsbüro, Friedrichstrasse 7, 4th District
Tel. 58 800 153

CLASSIFICATION OF ACCOMMODATION

◆ Hotels vary from 1 to 5 stars.
◆ Pensions are simpler and smaller than hotels, often family-run with a charming atmosphere. They offer very good value (1 to 4 stars).
◆ University lodgings are transformed into hotels during student vacations: reserve well in advance.
◆ Youth hostels
◆ Rooms in private houses and apartments
◆ There are five camping grounds in the vicinity of Vienna. Prices: about 70 ATS per person per day plus 60 to 80 ATS per pitch.

EATING OUT

TYPICAL VIENNESE DISHES

◆ *Leberknödel Suppe*: soup containing liver meatballs.
◆ *Frittatten Suppe*: broth with shredded pancake.
◆ *Wiener Schnitzel*: fried scallop of veal or pork, accompanied by potatoes and green salad.
◆ *Backhendel*: fried chicken.
◆ *Gebackene Champignons*: fried mushrooms in a coating of breadcrumbs.
◆ *Tafelspitz*: a dish based on boiled beef.
◆ *Durcheinander Knoedel*: meatballs made with a mixture of bread, bacon and flour.
◆ *Gulasch*: a Hungarian dish of beef stew generously spiced with paprika.
◆ *Palatschinken*: pancakes with toppings cream, chocolate, jam, or hazelnuts.
◆ *Strudel*: irresistible rolled puff pastry cakes (Strudel means "whirl"), with a range of different fillings: of apples (Apfelstrudel), plums, cherries, blueberries or cream cheese (Topfenstrudel).

COMMON FOODSTUFFS

Apfel: apple
Birne: pear
Erbsen: peas
Erdapfel: potatoes
Frisolen: French beans
Gemüse: vegetables
Käse: cheese
Kirschen: cherries
Marillen: apricots
Obst: fruit
Paradise: tomatoes

PLACES TO GET A QUICK SNACK

◆ At a *Würstelstand*, one of the stalls on the sidewalks serving a choice of sausages with French fries.
◆ At a *Beisel*, a traditional cheap bistro.(150 ATS).
◆ In a *Keller* (cellar), where people go to drink wine and beer, and food is also served.
◆ At the *Heurigen*, taverns where new white wine is the customary drink, taken pure or with sparkling water (Gespritzt). A range of Viennese specialties are also available (particularly charcuterie and cold cuts) to the gentle accompaniment of traditional music.
◆ In the *Kaffehäuser* (cafés or tearooms) one can buy Viennese coffee and pastries. The bill is inclusive of 10.5 percent to 15 percent service charge, but it is customary to leave a tip of 10 percent on top of this.

◆ LIVING IN VIENNA

A chemist (Apotheke) is indicated by a globe like this with the letter A in red.

POST OFFICES AND MAIL

◆ Post Offices are open Mon. to Friday (8am–noon and 2–6pm). Some are open on Sat. (8–10am).
◆ Postal Information: 83 21 01 Central Post Office (open 24 hours), Fleischmarkt 19, 1st District.

◆ Stamps are sold in all Post Offices and tobacconists (*Tabak-Trafiks*).
◆ Cost of an airmail letter to the UK: 7 ATS; to the US and Canada: 14.50 ATS Postcard (airmail) to the UK: 6 ATS; to the US and Canada: 8.50 ATS

NEWSPAPERS

◆ The weekly publication *Falter* (on sale in *Tabak-Trafiks*, look for the round red and white sign) lists details of all Viennese events (price: 20 ATS).
◆ *Wien Magazin* is a monthly publication aimed at visitors to Vienna and written in four languages (price: 28 ATS).
◆ The popular daily newspapers are: *Der Standard*, *Die Presse*, *Kronen Zeitung Kurier*, (prices: from 8 to 12 ATS).

IN THE STREET

Visitors to Vienna will be greatly helped by the large number of Tourist Office publications (◆ 310) and also by the helpfulness of the Viennese themselves. The publications are printed in all major languages in the form of magazines; they are reviewed to ensure that the information on Viennese life and entertainment that they carry is right up to date.

FINDING YOUR WAY
Free maps are supplied to all visitors; even so, if you get lost, you can always rely on the kindness of ordinary Viennese, many of whom speak excellent English.

HOSPITALS
KRANKENHÄUSER
Währinger Gürtel 18–20 (children), 9th District Tel. 40 400
Spitalgasse 23, 9th District Tel. 40 400.

TELEPHONE

◆ The code for the US and Canada from Vienna is 00 1.
◆ To call Austria from the US and Canada, dial 011-43-1.
◆ The code for the UK from Vienna is 00 44.
◆ To call Austria from the UK dial 010 4 31.

◆ The code for Vienna from abroad is 1; from within Austria the code is 02 22.
◆ The number of figures in Viennese telephone numbers varies. The only constant is that a zero at the end of the number means the call will be answered at a switchboard.
◆ Phone booths accept both 1.5 ATS (150 Groschen) and 10 ATS coins, or phone cards (Telefon-Wertkarte), which may be purchased in *Tabak-Trafiks* or Post Offices for 100 ATS or 50 ATS.

USEFUL TELEPHONE NUMBERS

◆ Ambulance: 144
◆ Hospital emergencies: 144
◆ Doctor: 141
◆ Emergency chemists: 1550
◆ Police: 133
◆ Fire department: 122
◆ Directory enquiries (Austria): 16
◆ International directory enquiries: 08
◆ Telegrams: 190
◆ Flight information: 711 100
◆ Train information: 1717
◆ Lost property: 313 44 9211
◆ Vehicle breakdown service (two asscociations): ÖAMTC: 120 ARBÖ: 123

THE COST OF A PHONE CALL (AT&T TARIFFS)

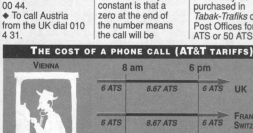

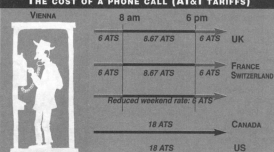

VIENNA	8 am		6 pm	
	6 ATS	8.67 ATS	6 ATS	UK
	6 ATS	8.67 ATS	6 ATS	FRANCE SWITZERLAND
	Reduced weekend rate: 6 ATS			
		18 ATS		CANADA
		18 ATS		US

PRICES

1 COFFEE: 30 ATS

1 HALF-LITER OF BEER: FROM 25 ATS

1 BOTTLE OF WINE: FROM 140 ATS

1 DISH OF THE DAY: FROM 80 ATS

1 MUSEUM ADMISSION: 20–90 ATS

1 THEATER TICKET: 150–700 ATS

1 ADMISSION TO THE PRATER: 28 ATS

ACCOMMODATION FOR ONE PERSON: 600 ATS

INTERNATIONAL CLOTHING SIZES

US	UK	AUSTRIA
MEN'S JACKETS/SUITS & OVERCOATS		
36	36	46
38	38	48
40	40	50
42	42	52
44	44	54
46	46	56
MEN'S SHIRTS		
12	12	30–1
12½	12½	32
13	13	33
13½	13½	34–5
14	14	36
14½	14½	37
15	15	38
15½	15½	39–40
16	16	41
16½	16½	42
17	17	43
17½	17½	44–5
LADIES' COATS & JACKETS		
6	8/30	38
9	10/32	40
10	12/34	42
12	14/36	44
14	16/38	46
16	18/40	48

US	UK	AUSTRIA
ADULTS' SHOES		
5½	4	37
6	4½	38
6½	5	38
7	5½	39
7½	6	39
8	6½	40
8½	7	41
9	7½	41
9½	8	43
8½	8½	41
10–	9	43
10½	9½	44
11	10	44
11½	10½	45
12	11	46
CHILDREN'S SHOES		
0	0	15
1	1	17
2	2	18
3	3	19
4	4	20
5	5	22
6	6	23
7	7	24
8	8	25
8½	8½	26
9	9	27
10	10	28
11	11	29
12	12	30
13	13	32
LADIES' SUITS/DRESSES		
6	8	36
8	10	38
10	12	40
12	14	42
14	16	44
16	18	46
18	20	48
20	22	50
22	24	52

ITEMS TO TAKE HOME WITH YOU

◆ Lodens
◆ Augarten porcelain
◆ Petit-point embroidery
◆ Art Nouveau fabrics
◆ Painted wooden toys
◆ Antiques (old books, paintings, coins, medals)
◆ Spirits: apricot-, apple-, pear-, or plum-flavored Schnapps
● Mozart Kugeln: chocolates filled with marzipan and nougat

OPENING HOURS

SHOPS
◆ Shops open Monday to Friday between 9am and 5pm and Saturday between 9am and 12.30am. However, on the first Saturday of the month practically all shops except food shops are open 8am–5pm.
◆ The principal shopping streets in Vienna are: the pedestrian precinct of Kärntnerstrasse-Graben-Kohlmarkt, Mariahilferstrasse, Landstrasser Hauptstrasse and the pedestrian precincts of Favoritenstrasse and Meidlinger Hauptstrasse.

MARKETS
◆ For fruit, vegetables and other comestibles go to: Rochusmarkt, at the junction of Landstrasse Hauptstrasse and Salmgasse in the 3rd District; and to Naschmarkt, Linke Wienzeile, in the 6th District.
◆ For flea markets go to: Wienzeile in the 6th District, near the Kettenbrückengasse Metro Station; an Art and Antiques Market (Kunst und Antik Markt) is held on the banks of the Danube (in the 1st District) every weekend in the summer months, May to September.

RESTAURANTS
Lunch is usually served between noon and 2pm and dinner from 6pm. As a rule Viennese restaurants will not take orders after 10pm. Nevertheless, around Seitenstettengasse, the bars and restaurants stay open till about 1am.

TIME
Austria is one hour ahead of Greenwich Mean Time (GMT).

The Danube Valley at Donauschleife.

Sailboats on the Neusiedlersee.

THE CASTLES OF MARCHFELD

The plain of Marchfeld occupies an area of about 300 square miles to the northeast of Vienna. Its name, Maraha, derives from the Illyrian word "marus", meaning "marsh", and from the Germanic "Ahwa", meaning "river". Along the middle of the plain's bed runs the "March", which is the frontier between Austria and Slovakia.

ORTH AN DER DONAU
The citadel of Orth contains a regional museum and an angling museum. Its chapel, known as the Fishermen's Chapel, dates from 1529; a special mass is celebrated here on the Feast of St Peter and St Paul.

SACHSENGANG
The oldest fortifications in the Danube area are to be found in the dense forests of Sachsengang. In 1809, Napoleon's forces came up against bitter resistance in this area.

OBERSIEBENBRUNN
This castle has four 17th-century wings; it was altered in the 19th century by the architect Johann Lukas von Hildebrandt, who gave it its present Baroque appearance.

NIEDERWEIDEN
Niederweiden Castle was built by J. B. Fischer von Erlach and enlarged by Hildebrandt in the French and Italian Palladian styles. A central dome dominates its two wings. Fischer von Erlach placed an oval hall between these wings.

ECKARTSAU
This hunting lodge converted into a Baroque castle saw the final weeks of the Austro-Hungarian monarchy. Emperor Charles lived here before going into exile in 1918.

MARCHEGG
The 17th-century castle of Marchegg, altered in the 18th century, now contains the Hunting Museum of Lower Austria.

THE BURGENLAND AND LAKE NEUSIEDL

A 116-mile round trip excursion to the southeast of Vienna.

LAXENBURG
(12½ miles from Vienna)
At the foot of the Wienerwald hills stands the Blue Castle, a house built in the time of Maria Theresa near Laxenburg. Francis I later added a lake with artificial islands, bridges and a splendid rocky grotto. Another adjunct was the Emperor's Pavilion in the park, an imitation medieval castle known as Franzensburg.

EISENSTADT
(23 miles from Vienna)
Visit the Bergkirche in the capital of Burgenland. Haydn is buried here.

RUST AM NEUSIEDLERSEE
(35 miles from Vienna)
A small town famous for its storks' nests.

JOIS
(56 miles from Vienna)
A beautiful view across Lake Neusiedl.

NEUSIEDLERSEE
This 124-square mile lake, sometimes called the "Sea of Vienna", extends right up to the Hungarian frontier. On its far bank the steppe (Puszta) begins. The surrounding region, which is the least populated in Austria, contains a large number of smaller lakes, many of them wildlife preserves; the Lange Lacke, protected by the World Wildlife Fund, is home to a large population of herons, teals and egrets, in addition to pike, carp, and perch.

NEUSIEDL AM SEE
This is a popular resort for the Viennese, many of whom come here for weekends. In summer, there is sailing, windsurfing and fishing (mostly from boats); in winter, ice skating and wind sledging.

Skating on the Neusiedlersee.

The Wachau near Loiben. *Krems, the wine-making capital of the Danube Valley.*

AN EXCURSION UP THE DANUBE VALLEY

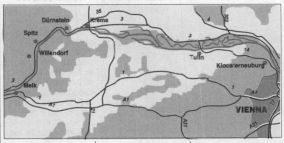

This round trip of about 125 miles explores the Wachau, the area of the Danube Valley area between Krems and Melk, which abounds in magnificent landscapes, castles and monasteries.

KLOSTERNEUBURG

This celebrated Augustinian monastery, about 8 miles from Vienna, was destroyed by fire and later rebuilt. Here lie the relics of the patron saint of Lower Austria, Leopold III. The abbey of the Augustinian canons is open to the public from May 1 to November 15, Tel. 22 43 6210 212. Admission: 40 ATS.

TULLN

(24 miles from Vienna)

The basilica in this Roman river port, the Pfarrkirche Sankt Stephan, is splendid.

KREMS

(45 miles from Vienna)

One of the principal market towns of the Danube Valley, Krems is also famous for its Gothic, Renaissance and Baroque houses. The Benedictine monastery of Gottweig, beyond the river linking Stein to Mautern, was founded in 1083. Rebuilt in the 18th century by the architect Johann Lukas von Hildebrandt, it now resembles a palace.

DÜRNSTEIN

(50 miles from Vienna)

This village lies in the shadow of the 12th-century castle where Richard the Lionheart was held captive. The sky-blue Baroque tower overlooking the former Augustinian convent is now one of the prettiest parish churches in Austria. Open April 1–Oct. 31. Tel. 2711 219.

SPITZ

(57 miles from Vienna)

A group of 16th-, 17th- and 18th-century houses surrounds the late Gothic church of St Moritz.

WILLENDORF

(60 miles from Vienna)

This is the site where the celebrated statuette "Venus" was discovered. About 4 inches in height and dating from the 3rd century BC, it is now exhibited at the Naturhistorisches Museum in Vienna.

MELK

(67 miles from Vienna)

Melk, on the banks of the Danube, is dominated by its famous Benedictine monastery (Stift Melk). The buildings as they appear today were built between 1702 and 1709 by Jacob Prandtauer.

The 80,000-volume library and the marble hall here are well worth the journey. Open April 3–November 7, Tel. 2752 2312-52, admission 45 ATS.

EXCURSIONS BY RIVER BOAT, TRAIN OR BUS, ORGANIZED BY THE DDSG

◆ Vienna – Linz – Passau – Wachau: cabins are available on the vessel (800 ATS), and bicycles may be taken on board.

◆ The first cruise of the season through the Wachau between Melk and Krems (238 ATS per passenger) takes place in April.

◆ One-day excursions are available to Bratislava (200 ATS per person; you also need a valid passport to enter Slovakia).

INFORMATION

DDSG-Donaureisen Handelskai 265, 2nd District Tel. 217 500.

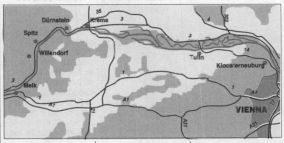

ES WIRD EIN WEIN SEIN

VND WIR WERDN NIMMER SEIN

A view of Mayerling, a quiet village in the Vienna woods.

Emperor Franz-Joseph.

Empress Elisabeth.

MÖDLING AND GUMPOLDSKIRCHEN

Mödling, a small town of about 20,000 people south of Vienna, is a pleasant resort today. In 1818 and 1819 Ludwig von Beethoven stayed here at no. 79 Haupstrasse while he was working on his *Missa Solemnis*. Just outside Mödling stands the fortress of Liechtenstein. About 12 miles south of Vienna, the village of Gumpoldskirchen is renowned for its splendid wines (Rotgipfler, Zierfandler and Rheinriesling); there are a number of welcoming *Heurigen* here where the wines may be sampled. Walkers will enjoy the recently created "Beethoven Trail", which starts from Gumpoldskirchen and winds its way through the Vienna woods.

BADEN

Baden is a spa dating back to Roman times; it lies 16 miles south of Vienna, at an altitude of between 700 and 800 feet. It owes its existence to the hot sulphur springs discovered here by the Romans. The baths were popular in the Middle Ages and during the Renaissance, but it was not until the early 19th century that Baden became known internationally. In 1803, Emperor Francis made Baden fashionable and people flocked to try the waters. The springs yield up to 1,717,300 US gallons of hot water daily, at an average temperature of 96.8˚F.
EMPEROR FRANZ-JOSEPH MUSEUM
Tel. 2252 41100
Open April–Sept. 30
Admission 20 ATS.

THE WIENERWALD

From the beginning of the 14th century, musicians, poets and painters have come to live in the vicinity of Vienna. The romantic landscape of hills, vineyards and pine forests that attracted them extends as far as the Kurpark at Baden; the Kurpark is the departure point for 37 miles of beautifully maintained hiking trails. One outstanding example is the Rocks Trail, which goes past the Ferdinand-Raimund and Rudolfshof observation points as well as the Mitterberg and the Helental. Maps of these trails, general tourist maps and various detailed brochures are available at the departure point in Baden's main square (Hauptplatz) where there is a tourist office (Hauptplatz 2).
MAYERLING
22 miles southwest of Vienna is the peaceful little town of Mayerling, which would probably have remained completely obscure had Archduke Rudolph and his mistress, Maria Vetsera, not committed suicide there in 1889. A Carmelite convent now stands on the site of the hunting lodge where Rudolp is said to have killed himself. A room and a chapel in the convent are maintained as a memorial to the Archduke. They are open all year round, from 9am to 5pm in winter and from 10.30am to 6pm in summer.

The Carmelite convent at Mayerling, built on the site of the hunting pavilion.

The convent gardens.

THE DRAMA AT MAYERLING

Archduke Rudolph, an eccentric and fragile personality, was married to Archduchess Stephanie of Belgium, and fell in love with a young girl, Maria Vetsera. At a reception given by the German Ambassador to Vienna on January 27, 1889, Maria Vetsera publicly refused to acknowledge Stephanie, Rudolph's wife, who was representing the absent Empress. The following day Franz-Joseph had a heated interview with his son, after which Rudolph went off to kill himself and his mistress. Maria Vetsera was buried close to the scene of her death, in the village cemetery at Heiligenkreuz. Today there is a tomb slab there bearing the inscription *Wie eine Blume sprosst der Mensch auf und wird gebrochen* ("Human beings, like flowers, bloom and are crushed").

Rudolph's body was taken back to the Hofburg. The Emperor had the hunting lodge rapidly demolished and replaced it with a neo-Gothic chapel, which is open to visitors. The official version of the story put out by the court in 1889 proclaimed the archduke's death a suicide, but the people continued to believe that he had been assassinated. Though suicide is the more probable explanation, the reasons for it still seem mysterious: were they political, financial, or merely lunatic? In 1982, Empress Zita von Habsburg shed fresh light on the affair when she told the Vienna daily *Kronen Zeitung* of her belief in a political plot culminating in the assassination of Rudolph at Mayerling. On December 22, 1992, the same paper revealed that the coffin of Maria Vetsera had been stolen four years previously. Following police investigations, a Linz businessman confessed his guilt; since the death of his own wife he had become obsessed with the Mayerling affair. He led the police to the stolen coffin, which was handed over to the medical Institute of Vienna.

HINTERBRÜHL

The Brühl Valley, through which the River Mödling flows, was a popular venue for excursions during the Biedermeier era. Today, thousands of visitors, especially children, come each year to see the *Seegrotte* at *Hinterbrühl*, which contains the largest underground lake in Europe. Hitler used this cave as an aircraft factory during World War Two. The *Seegrotte* is open all year round, Tel. 2236 26364, admission 46 ATS. At the edge of the village is the picturesque Hölrichsmüle mill. This is where Franz Schubert met Rosi, the miller's daughter-in-law, who inspired his song-cycle *Die Schöne Mullerin* (*The Beautiful Miller's Wife*), in 1823. Today the mill is an inn, which serves *Millirahmstrüdel*, delicious savories made with cream cheese, which are a particular speciality of the Wienerwald.

HEILIGENKREUZ

The Cistercian abbey of Heiligenkreuz between Hinterbrühl and Mayerling, was founded in 1133 by Margrave Leopold III von Babenberg. His grandson, Leopold V, Duke of Austria, endowed it with a fragment of the Holy Cross given to him by the King of Jerusalem during the 12th century (hence the name of "Holy Cross"). The abbey, which is open to the public, is still occupied by a community of about sixty monks.

A sausage shop on the Graben.

Inside "Café Demel".

INFLUENCES OF THE OLD EMPIRE

Among the great culinary specialties of Vienna, Hungary contributed its *Gulasch*, a type of stew made from morsels of beef simmered with onions, garlic, paprika and cumin. Soups such as *Gulaschsuppe* (with potatoes), and *Palatschinken*, which are pancakes filled with jam or nuts, are also both Hungarian in origin. Czechoslovakia provided delicious Prague hams and sauerkraut soup. Roast goose with meatballs and red cabbage is an import from Poland, along with stuffed cabbage. *Cevapcici*, a dish of spicy grilled meatballs, and *Chachlyk*, lamb brochettes with onion and green and red peppers, both originated in Serbia.

SOME AUSTRIAN SPECIALTIES

Traditional dishes include *Wienerschnitzel*, a fried breaded escalope of veal; *Wienerbackhendl*, deboned and breaded fried chicken; and *Tafelspitz*, boiled beef. Meatballs (*Knödel*) accompany soups and meat dishes. Other Viennese specialties are *Strudel* ("whirls"), rolls of puff pastry stuffed with apples and dried raisins and spiced with cinnamon. There are also *Strudel* stuffed with cherries, strawberries and nuts.

RECIPE FOR *SACHERTORTE*
(from the Sacher Hotel's cookbook)
Ingredients: 5 oz dark chocolate, ½ cup butter, ½ cup granulated sugar, ½ cup confectioners' sugar, 6 eggs, 1 cup flour, apricot jam, vanilla. Melt the chocolate. Add the softened butter, the confectioners' sugar and the vanilla and mix well. Add the egg yolks and beat. Mix in the chocolate. Whip the eggwhites until stiff and add to the mixture, along with the granulated sugar. Knead with a wooden spoon. Add the flour; then place in a mold and bake at 340°F for 15 minutes with the oven door ajar, then for a further 1 hour with the door shut. Turn out of the mold and allow to cool for 20 minutes. Coat with warm apricot jam. **Ingredients for icing:** ⅔ cup confectioners' sugar, ¼ pint water, 6 oz chocolate. Heat the sugar and water (5–6 mins), add the melted chocolate and stir with a wooden spoon until the mixture is moderately thick. Layer the cake with the mixture (¼ inch) and allow to cool.

THE HISTORY OF A FAMOUS CAKE

In 1832 Franz Sacher, a junior chef at Prince Metternich's court, invented the recipe for *Sachertorte*, as is proved in a letter written in 1888 by his son Eduard. In that year, Sacher's famous pastry was exported "to Paris, London and Berlin, and even across the Atlantic". Today every pastryshop in Vienna makes *Sachertorte*, but the exact recipe has always been a closely guarded secret. For this reason a 25-year legal battle over the exclusive right to the name *Original Sachertorte* was conducted between the Sacher company and the patisserie *Demel*. In 1965, the court found in favor of *Sacher*, which henceforth had the sole right to call its recipe "original". Only true connoisseurs of pastries can tell the difference!

BAKERS AND CONFECTIONERS

The bakers of Vienna invented the croissant (*Kipfel*) during the Turkish siege of 1683, borrowing its shape from the emblem on the Ottoman banners. Since then, pastries – "Viennoiseries" – have been a Viennese specialty.
LUDWIGBROT,

SIMMERINGER
Hauptstrasse 25, 1st District
Tel. 74 11 520
ALTMANN U. KÜHNE
Graben 30, 1st District
Tel. 553 09 27
Purchases come in highly original wrappers: boxes shaped like suitcases, commodes or hatboxes.

PATISSERIES AND TEAROOMS

Demel
Kohlmarkt 14
Sacher
Philharmoniker-strasse 4
Gerstner
Kärntnerstrasse 15
Lehmann Louis
Graben 12
Heiner
Kärntnerstrasse 21, and Wollzeile 9
(All are situated in the 1st District.)

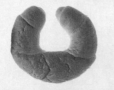

At the "Café Sperl".

The new vintage ("Heurigen") is ready!

VIENNESE CAFÉS

The word *café* in Vienna designates both the beverage and the place where it is drunk (see the different kinds of coffee in the "Useful words and phrases", page 336). By 1873, the year of the Universal Exhibition, coffee had already become a Viennese institution: in 1885, there were more than 500 *cafés* in Vienna. Today there are roughly 400 traditional cafés, 400 café-restaurants, 600 espresso bars and 200 coffeehouses. "To be at the café is to be at a home from home", wrote Peter Altenberg, the Viennese poet and café habitué. For the price of a single coffee, you can spend the afternoon talking, reading the newspapers which are supplied free of charge, and observing the other clients. Some people have mail addressed to "their café", receive phone calls there, and in general use it to entertain their friends. To the Viennese, the café is simultaneously a place to relax, an office, and a drawing room.

CAFÉ CENTRAL
Intersection of Herrengasse and Strauchgasse, 1st District
Tel. 533 37 63 26

A rendezvous for artists, writers and philosophers: habitués were the poet Altenberg, the literary critic Karl Kraus and Leon Trotsky.
CAFÉ HAWELKA
Dorotheergasse 6, 1st District
Tel. 512 82 30
A contemporary ambience.
CAFÉ LANDTMANN
Dr Karl Lueger Ring 4, 1st District
Tel. 523 06 21
The most luxurious café in Vienna.
CAFÉ MUSEUM
Friedrichstrasse 6, 1st District
Tel. 56 52 02
Politicians, students, painters and sculptors from the Academy of Fine Arts patronize this café.
CAFÉ IN DER SECESSION
The décor is a mixture of traditional furniture and Italian ceramic.
CAFÉ DIGLAS
Wollzeile 10, 1st District
Tel. 512 84 01
CAFÉ GRIENSTEIDL
Michaelerplatz 2, 1st District
Tel. 535 26 92
One of the city's oldest cafés, recently renovated.

SPECIALIZED CAFÉS

Some cafés carry on the tradition of the café-concert.
CAFÉ SCHWARZENBERG
Kärntner Ring 17, 1st District
Tel. 512 73 93
CAFÉ IMPERIAL
Kärntner Ring 16, 1st District
Tel. 501 10 389
CAFÉ PRÜCKL
Stubenring 24, 1st District
Tel. 512 38 93
CAFÉ BRÄUNERHOF
Stallburggasse 2, 1st District
Tel. 512 38 93
The following are literary cafés, where regular meetings and other literary events take place.
CAFÉ SPERL
Gumpendorferstrasse 11, 6th District
Tel. 56 41 58
CAFÉ SCHOTTENRING
Schottenring 30, 1st District
Tel. 34 34 21
CAFÉ DOMMAYER
Dommayergasse 1, 13th District
Tel. 877 54 65
ALTE BACKSTUBE
Lange Gasse 34, 8th District
Tel. 43 11 01

BARS

The "Bermuda Triangle" quarter around Ruprechtskirche emerged as a popular drinking area in the 1970's.
ROTE ENGEL
Rabensteig, 1st District
Open Mon.–Wed. in winter, 5pm–2am, and Thurs., Fri., Sat. till 4am. *Live music from 9:30pm, billiards room. Cheese sandwiches and wine.*
KRAH-KRAH
Rabensteig 8, 1st District
Tel. 533 19 38
Open daily 11am–2am. Live music Sun. 11:30pm. *Choice of 40 beer brands, sandwiches.*
KAKTUS
Seitenstettengasse, 1st District
Tel. 533 19 38
Open daily 6pm–2am. *Cabaret ambience.*
JAZZ LAND
Franz-Josefs-Kai 29, 1st District
Tel. 533 25 75
Open Tues. to Sat. 7pm–1am: music from 9pm onward.

THE "HEURIGEN"

The same word (*Heurigen*) is used for these establishments and the new wine which is drunk in them. Some *Heurigen* are on the vineyards themselves, and as a rule they are highly convivial places: one sits by the barrels at long pine tables, listening to the *Schrammelmusik* of violins, guitars, clarinets and accordions. The entrances to most of the *Heurigen* are marked by a pole festooned with flowers or pine boughs, signifying that they have the right to sell wine which is either mature or in the process of maturing. The *Heurigen* are not, however, restaurants in the full meaning of the term, since they only serve cold buffet food.

◆ Music, dance, theater

The splendid Goldene Saal (Golden Room) at the Musikverein.

Vienna's principal playhouse, the Burgtheater.

THE "FASCHING"

The *Fasching*, or carnival season, runs from 31 December to Ash Wednesday.

TRADITIONAL BALLS
The season opens with the *Kaiserball*, or Emperor's Ball, which is held at the Hofburg on New Year's Eve, December 31. The other balls are organized later by the professions (the Florists' Ball, the Philharmonic Orchestra Ball, the Doctors', Jurists', Café Owners', Hunters', and Conjurors' Balls) and held at a variety of grand venues. The first Thursday in February is the traditional date for the Opera Ball, the main event at which debutantes are presented, although every ball has some sort of debutante presentation. Out of about 600 couples put forward as candidates, only 200 will be selected to dance on the specially constructed floor. A total of some 300 balls take place at Vienna during the *Fasching*.

MASKED BALLS
As well as the traditional balls, a series of *Gschnas*, or masked balls, is held at the *Metropol*. This establishment, much favored by the youth of Vienna, specializes in rock and roll, jazz and pop music.

METROPOL HERNALSER STADTTHEATER
Geblergasse 50, 17th District
Tel. 43 35 43
Shrove Tuesday marks the close of the season. On this day the Viennese go into the streets in elaborate disguises, and a parade of floats is held on the Ring.
The Viennese have been theater addicts ever since the 18th century. Performances commonly begin at 7pm or 7:30pm.

FEDERAL THEATERS (BUNDESTHEATER)

BURGTHEATER
Dr Karl Lueger Ring 2, 1st District
Tel. 514 44 22 18
One of the city's most beautiful playhouses, founded in 1776 by Joseph II, the Burgtheater specializes in works by the great playwrights Goethe, Schiller, Schnitzler, Hoffmannsthal, Raimund, and Nestroy.

AKADEMIETHEATER
Liszstrasse 1, 3rd District
Tel. 514 44 29 59
Modern, avant-garde drama is performed.

PRIVATE THEATERS

VOLKSTHEATER
Neustiftgasse 1, 6th District
Tel. 93 27 76
Built at the close of the 19th century, this theater was originally intended for light comedy. Today its productions are mostly contemporary and avant-garde.

MESSEPALAST
Messeplatz 1, 7th District. Tel. 526 05 60

THE THEATERS

ODEON
Taborstrasse 10, 2nd District
Tel. 214 55 62

KAMMERSPIELE
Rotenturmstrasse 20, 1st District
Tel. 533 28 33
Humorous, satirical productions.

VIENNA'S ENGLISH THEATER
Josefsgasse 12, 8th District
Tel. 402 12 60
Productions in English.

RAIMUNDTHEATER
Wallgasse 18–20, 6th District
Tel. 599 77 27
Operettas and musical comedies.

BALLET AND DANCE
Every year, week-long summer and winter dance festivals are held in Vienna. These feature all styles, in the most complete repertoire in Europe.

INTERNATIONAL TANZWOCHEN
B.P 155, 9th District, tel 93 55 58

TANZTHEATER
Burggasse 38, 7th District Tel. 96 39 34

THEATERGRUPPE 80
Gumpendorferstrasse 67, 6th District
Tel. 585 222

TICKETS AND RESERVATIONS

CENTRAL TICKET OFFICE FOR THE FOUR FEDERAL THEATERS
(Staatsoper, Volksoper, Burgtheater and Akademietheater)

ÖSTERREICHISCHER BUNDESTHEATERVERBAND BUNDESTHEATERKASSEN
Hanuschgasse 3, Goethegasse 1, 1st District
Tel. 514 44 2960 or 2959

TICKET-EXPRESS
Waltergasse 14, 4th District
Tel. 505 23 24

VIENNA TICKET SERVICE
B.P. 160, 4th District
Tel. 587 98 43

ÖSTERREICH VERKEHRSBÜRO
Opernpassage Top 1, 1st District
Tel. 587 67 65

FLAMM
Kärntner Ring 3, 1st District
Tel. 512 42 25

MME SILVIA MÜHRINGER
Wiedner Haupstrasse 18, 4th District
Tel. 587 78 90

The Vienna Boys' Choir: one of the four 24-member choirs, in sailor uniforms.

A street accordionist, playing the traditional Viennese "Schrammelmusik".

FESTIVALS

Music in Vienna goes back to the *Minnesänger* (troubadours) of the Middle Ages. This tradition is continued in today's festivals, of which the Wiener Festwochen is the oldest and most prestigious.

SPRING FESTIVAL, WIENER FRÜHLINGFESTIVAL
Every year, in the Goldene Saal at the Musikverein.

VIENNA FESTIVAL, WIENER FESTWOCHEN
Lehargasse 11, 6th District
Tel. 586 16 76
Founded in 1951, the Vienna Festival stages literally hundreds of musical and theatrical productions over a period of four weeks in May and June.

KLANGBOGEN SUMMER FESTIVAL
Laudongasse 29, 8th District
Tel. 40 08 410
Nearly 150 concerts are held in Vienna's best auditoriums. From Bach to Viennese light operas and "Schrammelmusik".

VIENNA CLASSICAL MUSIC FESTIVAL, FESTIVAL WIENER KLASSIK
Preindlgasse 1, 13th District
Tel. 877 52 08
Palaces and churches serve as a backdrop to this festival, which specializes in the works of the great composers who lived in Vienna (Mozart, Haydn, and Beethoven).

WIEN MODERN
Since 1988, this festival directed by Claudio
Abbado has concentrated on the work of contemporary composers such as Zimmerman and Boulez, among others. It is held between October and November, at the Konzerthaus.

WIENER SCHUBERTIADE
This festival presents the complete works of Schubert, numbering about a thousand pieces. It was started in 1982, and is held at the Musikverein in November.

CABARETS

Between the two World Wars, the Viennese had a choice of 25 cabarets. Today this form of entertainment is making a comeback, with about ten authentic cabarets operating year-round.

KULISSE
Rosensteingasse 39, 17th District
Tel. 45 38 70
A former suburban theater, converted to cabaret in 1980.

SPEKTAKEL
Hamburgerstrasse 14,
5th District
Tel. 587 06 53

THEATER KABARETT SIMPL
Wollzeile 36, 1st District
Tel. 512 47 42
The only remaining site of the great inter-war era of Viennese cabaret.

RADIO

ORF-FUNKAUS
Argentinierstrasse 30a, 4th District
HQ of Austrian Radio, with a substantial auditorium.
RADIO WIEN ON 89.9 MHz
BLUE DANUBE RADIO ON 103.8 MHz

ORCHESTRAS AND AUDITORIUMS

MUSIKVEREINSGEBÄUDE
Bösendorferstrasse 12, 1st District
Tel. 505 81 90
Created by the Friends of Music (Gesellschaft der Musikfreunde) in 1867, this building is the HQ of the Philharmonic Orchestra. the Wiener Philharmoniker. This orchestra, which celebrated its 150th anniversary in 1992, undertakes ten different programs each year, a total of 60 concerts.

KONZERTHAUS
Lothringerstrasse 20, 3rd District
Tel. 712 46 86

LEARNING TO WALTZ

ELMAYER DANCE SCHOOL
Braunerstrasse 13, 1st District
Tel. 505 24 04

KURSALON CAFÉ
Stadtpark, Johannesgasse 33, 1st District
Tel. 713 21 810

This center, founded in 1913, is bigger but less refined than the Musikverein. It is the home of the Vienna Symphony Orchestra, the city's second orchestra, which was founded in 1919.

STAATSOPER (OPERA)
Opernring 2, 1st District
Tel. 514 44 26 50
Symphonies, concertos, chamber music and song-cycles are performed here, as well as full-scale opera. The opera house was opened in 1869 by Emperor Franz-Joseph (who found it "singularly ugly"). Despite this early verdict, the building has become a symbol of Austria.

VOLKSOPER (COMIC OPERA)
Währinger Strasse 78, 9th District
Tel. 514 44 33 18
An opera house built in 1898, which specializes in performances of light opera (Jacques Offenbach, Johann
Strauss, and Franz Lehár).

THEATER AN DER WIEN
Linke Wienzeile 6, 6th District
Tel. 588 30 265
Operettas, ballets, musicals and popular comedies by Raimund and Nestroy are staged here.

SCHLOSSTHEATER
Im Schönbrunner, 13th District,
Tel. 876 42 73 18
Productions of operas by Mozart are often staged here.

WIENER KAMMEROPER
Fleischmarkt 24, 1st District
Tel. 513 60 72
Operas and comic operas are staged here, transferring to the Schlosstheater in summer.

HOFMUSIKKAPELLE
Hofburg, 1st District
The Vienna Boys' Choir (Wiener Sängerknaben) has been singing at Sunday Mass in the imperial chapel for more than 500 years.

◆ MUSEUMS AND ART GALLERIES

The Hofburg, from Michaelerplatz.

The Secession
Pavilion.

The
Hundertwasserhaus.

PRINCIPAL MUSEUMS AND GALLERIES

KUNSTHISTORISCHES MUSEUM (1)
Maria-Theresien-Platz, Burgring 5, 1st District
Tel. 521 77
Closed Mondays.
Open alternate Tuesdays and Fridays 6–9 pm.
The largest museum in Vienna. Archeology, decorative arts and paintings (Flemish, Dutch, German, Italian, Spanish, French, English) from the 15th to the 18th centuries.

GRAPHISCHE SAMMLUNG ALBERTINA (2)
Augustinerstrasse 1, 1st District
Tel. 532 83
Open daily.
A superb collection of drawings and engravings: 50,000 masters' drawings and 1,200,000 original engravings.

MUSEUM FÜR MODERNE KUNST (MUSEUM OF MODERN ART) (3)
Liechtenstein Palace, Fürstengasse 1, 9th District
Tel. 34 12 59
Closed Tuesdays.
A fascinating range of works by artists such as Kupka, Kokoschka, Klimt and Schiele, and from the Jugendstil epoch.

SCHLOSS SCHÖNBRUNN (7)
Schönbrunner Schloss Strasse, 13th District
Tel. 811 13

Imperial apartments, French-style park and zoo (Tiergarten).

SECESSION PAVILION (8)
Friedrichstrasse 12, 1st District
Tel. 587 53 07
Closed Mondays.
Vienna's first Jugendstil building, constructed by Joseph Maria Olbrich, a pupil of Otto Wagner; frieze by Gustav Klimt in homage to Beethoven's Ninth Symphony, temporary exhibitions.

THE HOFBURG (IMPERIAL PALACE) (4)
See especially: The Kaiserappartements (apartments of Emperor Franz-Joseph and Empress Elisabeth), the Hofburgkapelle, the Schatzkammer (Treasury) and the Spanish Riding School (Spanische Reitschule).

BELVEDERE (6)
Two different palaces: the Lower Belvedere (Unteres Belvedere), containing the Museum of Baroque Art and the Museum of Medieval Art; and the Upper Belvedere (Oberes Belvedere), containing the collections of the Gallery of 19th- and 20th-Century Austrian Art.

ÖSTERREICHISCHE GALERIE DES 19. UND

20. JAHRHUNDERTS (6)
Prinz-Eugen Strasse 27, 3rd District
Tel. 78 41 580
Closed Tuesdays.
The best-known paintings of Schiele, Kokoschka and Klimt.

AKADEMIE DER BILDENDEN KÜNSTE GEMÄLDEGALERIE (ACADEMY OF FINE ARTS GALLERY) (8)
Schillerplatz 3, 1st District
Tel. 588 16 225
Closed Mondays.
Works by 17th-century Dutch and Flemish painters including Rubens, as well as a superb altarpiece of the Last Judgement by Hieronymus Bosch, and Venetian views by Francesco Guardi.

NATURHISTORISCHES MUSEUM (MUSEUM OF NATURAL HISTORY) (1)
Maria-Theresien-Platz, Burgring 7, 1st District
Tel. 521 770
Closed Tuesdays.
The collections cover history, paleontology, mineralogy, anthropology, botany, zoology.

ADMISSION
Vienna has more than fifty municipal, national and private museums. With a few rare exceptions, the municipal museums are closed on Mondays and the national museums on Tuesdays.
Admission fees for each museum (there is no longer a pass which allows entry to several of them at a time) vary between 20 ATS and 90 ATS. The most important institutions are concentrated in the 1st and 3rd Districts. The Schönbrunn Palace is somewhat isolated in the 13th District, the other museums being scattered around the rest of the town. If one counts all the monuments, churches, musicians' houses and other sites, there is a total of well over one hundred major tourist attractions in Vienna.

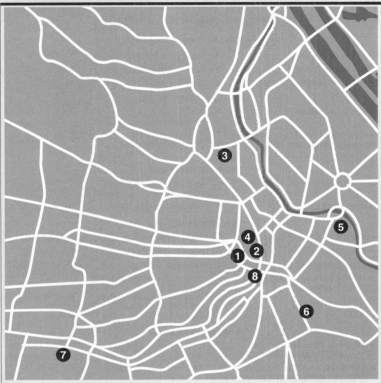

TWELVE MUSICIANS' HOUSES

MOZART:
FIGAROHAUS
Domgasse 5, 1st District
Tel. 513 62 94

HAYDN MUSEUM
Haydngasse 19, 6th
District
Tel. 596 13 07
*Joseph Haydn lived
and died in this house.
One of the rooms is
dedicated to Johannes
Brahms.*

SCHUBERT:
GEBURTSHAUS
(BIRTHPLACE)
Nussdorfer Strasse 54,
9th District
Tel. 34 59 924

STERBEZIMMER
(PLACE OF DEATH)
Kettenbrückengasse 6,
4th District
Tel. 57 39 072

JOHANN STRAUSS
WOHNUNG
Praterstrasse 54,
2nd District
Tel. 24 01 21
*Johann Strauss the
Younger lived in this
house.*

BEETHOVEN HOUSES:
PASQUALATIHAUS
Mölker Bastei 8, 1st
District
Tel. 535 89 05

TESTAMENT HAUS
(HEILIGENSTADT)
Probusgasse 6, 19th
District,
Tel. 37 54 08

EROICA HAUS
Döblinger Hauptstrasse
92, 19th District
Tel. 369 14 24

VILLA LEHAR
SCHIKANEDER
Hackhoferstrasse 18,
19th District
Tel. 37 18 213

GLUCK
Wiedner Hauptstrasse
32, 4th District

JOHANNES BRAHMS
Karlsgasse 4,
4th District
*The house where he
died.*

RICHARD STRAUSS
Jacquingasse 8–10, 3rd
District
*The villa built between
1922 and 1926 for the*

SIX MAJOR ARCHITECTURAL WORKS

German musician.
HILDEBRANDT HOUSE
Singerstrasse 3, 1st
District
*This building, which
dates from the 14th and
15th centuries, was
given extra elevation in
1721 in the style of the
celebrated architect
Johann Lukas von
Hildebrandt.*
LOOSHAUS
Michaelerplatz 3, 1st
District
*Adolf Loos constructed
this building for
apartments and shops
in 1910–11. Today, it
houses a bank and is a
prime example of early
20th-century functional
architecture.*
ANKERHAUS
Graben 10, 1st District
*A department store
designed by Otto
Wagner.*
MAJOLIKAHAUS
Linke Wienzeile 40, 6th
District
*Another building by
Otto Wagner, named
the Majolika House
because of its exterior
of colored tiles.*

FRENCH EMBASSY
Schwarzenbergplatz 12,
4th District
*This building is a
significant example of
the French Art Nouveau
style. It was
constructed between
1906 and 1909 by
Georges-Paul
Chédanne.*
HUNDERTWASSERHAUS (5)
At the corner of
Kögelgasse and
Löwengasse, 3rd
District
*A residential building,
designed by the painter
Hundertwasser and
built between 1983 and
1985. It includes fifty
apartments, all different
in style, inhabited by
artists.*
HAAS HAUS
Stephansplatz 12,
1st District
*Built by Hans Hollein in
1988–90, the
glass-and-steel walls of
this ultra-modern
building reflect the
Stephansdom. It has
been vigorously
condemned by many
Viennese.*

OTHER CULTURAL ATTRACTIONS

ANTIQUITY, ARCHEOLOGY

◆ Ephesos Museum	Neue Burg, Heldenplatz, 1st	Tel. 521 770
◆ Römische Ruinen	Markt, Hoher Markt 3, 1st	Tel. 535 56 06
◆ Römische Baureste Am Hof	Am Hof 9, 1st	Tel. 505 87 47

15TH–18TH CENTURY ART

◆ Neidhart-Fresken	Tuchlauben 19, (15th-century frescoes)	Tel. 535 90 65
◆ Österreichisches Barockmuseum (Museum of Austrian Baroque Art)	Rennweg 6a,3rd in the Lower Belvedere.	

19TH–CENTURY ART

◆ Neue Galerie of the Hofburg	Hofburg, Josefsplatz, 1st (19th-century European paintings)	
◆ Hermesvilla	Lainzer Tiegarten, 13th	Tel. 804 13 24

20TH–CENTURY ART

◆ Ernst Fuchs Privatmuseum	Hüttelbergstrasse 26, 14th,	Tel. 94 85 75
◆ Kunsthaus Wien	Hüttelbergstrasse 26, 14th,	Tel. 94 85 75
◆ Kunstforum Wien	Karlsplatz, 1st	
◆ Metro stations designed by Otto Wagner	Stadtbahn-Haltestelle Karlsplatz Karlsplatz, 1st Stadtbahn Hofpavilion Hietzing Schönbrunner Schloss Strasse, 13th	Tel. 877 15 71

RELIGIOUS ART

◆ Dom und Diözesanmuseum (Museum of Religious Art)	Stephansplatz 6, 1st	Tel. 515 52 560
◆ Sammlung Religiöse Volkskunst (Collection of Popular Religious Art)	Johannesgasse 8, 1st	Tel. 512 13 37
◆ Museum mittelalterlicher österr. Kunst (Museum of Austrian Medieval Art)	Rennweg 6a, 3rd Lower Belvedere Palace	
◆ Virgilkapelle (Chapel of Blessed Virgin)	Stephansplatz, 1st	Tel. 513 58 42
◆ Kaisergruft (Imperial Crypt)	Neuer Markt, 1st	Tel. 512 6853 12
◆ Herzgruft der Habsburger in der Augustinerkirche	Augustinerstrasse 3, 1st	Tel. 533 70 99
◆ Schatzkammer des Deutschen Ordens (Treasury of the Teutonic Order)	Singerstrasse 7, 1st	Tel. 512 10 656
◆ Stephansdom	Stephansplatz, 1st	Tel. 515 52 526
◆ Kirche Am Steinhof	Baumgartner Höhe 1, 14th	
◆ Kirche zur Heiligsten Dreifaltigkeit (Trinity Church or Wotruba Church)	Mauer, corner of Georgsgasse and Rysergasse, 23rd	Tel. 88 16 185
◆ Glockenmuseum (Clock Museum)	Troststrasse 38, 10th	Tel. 604 34 60
◆ Ankeruhr (Anchor Clock)	Hoher Markt 10–11, 1st	
◆ Zentralfriedhof (Central Cemetery)	Simmeringer Hauptstrasse 234, XIe	Tel. 76 55 44
◆ Friedhof St Marx (St Mark's Cemetery)	Leberstrasse 6–8, 3rd	
◆ Bestattungsmuseum (Funerary Museum)	Goldeggasse 19, 4th	Tel. 501 95 227

DECORATIVE ARTS AND APPLIED ARTS

◆ Österreichisches Museum für angewandte Kunst (Austrian Museum of Applied Arts)	Stubenring 5, 1st	Tel. 711 360
◆ Hoftafel und Silberkammer (Porcelain and Silver Collection of the Hofburg Court)	Michaelerplatz, 1st	Tel. 587 55 54 51
◆ Bundesmobiliensammlung (Antique Furniture Collection),	Mariahilferstrasse 88, 7th	Tel. 893 42 40

OTHER CULTURAL ATTRACTIONS

◆ Uhrenmuseum der Stadt Wien (Museum of Clocks and Watches)	Schulhof 2, 1st	Tel. 533 22 65
◆ Geymüller Schlössl	Khevenhüllerstrasse 2, 18th	Tel. 47 31 39
◆ Museum der Gold und Silberschmiede (Museum of Gold- and Silverwork)	Zieglerstrasse 22, 7th	Tel. 93 33 88
◆ Modesammlung (Fashion section of the Vienna History Museum)	Hetzendorfer Strasse 79, 12th	Tel. 802 16 57

HISTORY OF AUSTRIA AND HISTORY OF VIENNA

◆ Historisches Museum der Stadt Wien	Karlsplatz, 4th	Tel. 505 87 47
◆ Heeresgeschichtliches Museum (Museum of Military History)	Arsenal, Building 18, 3rd	Tel. 78 23 03
◆ Sammlung von Waffen und Rüstungen (Arms and Armor Museum in the Hofburg)	Neue Burg (New Palace), Hofburg, 1st	
◆ Museum des österreichischen Freiheitskampfes (Museum of the Austrian Resistance)	Altes Rathaus, 1st Wipplingerstrasse 8, 1st	Tel. 534 36 332
◆ Jüdisches Museum der Stadt Wien (City of Vienna Jewish Museum)	Eskeles Palace, Dorotheergasse 11, 1st,	Tel. 535 04 31

LITERATURE

◆ Goethe Museum	Augustinerstrasse 1, 1st	
◆ Adalbert Stifter Museum	Mölker Bastei 8, 1st	Tel. 637 06 65
◆ Heimito von Doderer Gedenkstätte	Währinger Strasse 43, 9th	

ETHNOGRAPHY

◆ Museum für Völkerkunde (Ethnography Museum)	Neue Burg, Heldenplatz, 1st	Tel. 521 770
◆ Museum für Volkskunde (Museum of Austrian Folklore)	Laudongasse 15–19, 8th	Tel. 43 89 05

SCIENCE

◆ Globenmuseum der österreichische Nationalbibliothek (National Library Globe Museum)	Josefsplatz 1, 1st	Tel. 534 10 397
◆ Josephinum (Museum des Institutes für Geschichte der Medizin)	Währinger Strasse 25/1, 9th	Tel. 403 21 54
◆ Pathologisch Anatomisches Bundesmuseum (Museum of Pathology)	Altes Allgemeines Krankenhaus Alser Strasse 4, Spitalgasse 2, 9th	Tel. 43 86 72
◆ Niederösterreichisches Landesmuseum (Museum of Lower Austria)	Herrengasse 9, 1st	Tel. 531 10 35 05
◆ Sigmund Freud Museum	Berggasse 19, 9th	Tel. 319 15 96
◆ Weinbaumuseum (Viticulture Museum)	Döblinger Hauptstrasse 96, 29th	Tel. 37 69 39
◆ Gartenbaumuseum (Horticulture Museum)	Parc d'Oberlaa, west entrance, 10th	Tel. 68 11 70

TRANSPORTATION

◆ Wiener Strassenbahnmuseum	Erdbergstrasse 109, 3rd	Tel. 712 12 01
◆ Fiakermuseum (Carriage Museum)	Veronikagasse 12, 17th	Tel. 43 26 070
◆ Eisenbahnmuseum (Railway Museum)	Mariahilferstrasse 212, 14th	
◆ Wagenburg (Historic Automobile Collection)	Schönbrunn 13th	Tel. 82 32 44

LEISURE

◆ Pratermuseum (Prater Museum)	Prater, Hauptallee, IIe	Tel. 24 94 32 74
◆ Österreichisches Theatermuseum	Lobkowitzplatz 2, 1st	Tel. 512 88 000
◆ Filmmuseum (Cinema Museum)	Augustinerstrasse 1 (Albertina), 1st	Tel. 533 70 540

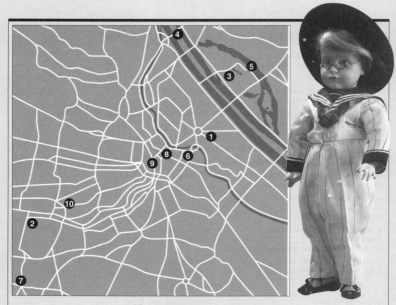

MUSEUMS, INDOOR ACTIVITIES

MUSEUMS

PUPPEN- UND SPIELZEUG-MUSEUM (TOY AND DOLL MUSEUM)
Schulhof 4, 1st District
Tel. 535 68 60
This museum, which was opened in 1991, contains a fascinating collection of 600 dolls and other 19th-century toys.

ZIRKUS UND CLOWNMUSEUM (CLOWN AND CIRCUS MUSEUM)
Karmelitergasse 9, 2nd District
Tel. 211 06 127
A magnificent collection of objects connected with clowns and circuses.

WAGENBURG (IMPERIAL VEHICLES)
Schloss Schönbrunn, 13th District
Tel. 82 32 44
An exhibition of 60 antique motor cars, sleds and sedan chairs, vehicles dating from 1690 to 1917. The prize exhibit is the richly gilded and ornamented imperial carriage.

HAUS DES MEERES (TERRARIUM AND AQUARIUM)
Esterházypark, 6th District
Tel. 587 14 17
An aquarium containing a selection of 3,000 fish (notably sharks) and reptiles. Feeding time is 3pm daily, Sunday 10am for reptiles.

NATURHISTORISCHES MUSEUM (NATURAL HISTORY MUSEUM)
Maria-Theresien-Platz, 1st District
Tel. 521 770
One room is specially adapted for children, with games and information and reproductions of dinosaur skeletons.

PLANETARIUM (PRATER)
Hauptallee, 2nd District
Tel. 24 94 32

URANIA STERNWARTE (URANIA OBSERVATORY) (6)
Uraniastrasse 1, 1st District
Tel. 24 94 32

ENTERTAINMENT

CINEMA IMAX (10)
Mariahilferstrasse, 15th District
Tel. 894 0101
Open daily
9.30am–8.30pm.
The length of the films shown is around 40 minutes. Laser shows, short films in 3D, documentaries (such as "Secrets of the Antarctic") are viewed on a screen 478 square yards in size.

IMPERIAL-KINO (8)
Rotgasse 9, 1st District
Tel. 533 32 23
Programs of Walt Disney cartoons.

WIENER URANIA PUPPENTHEATER (PUPPET THEATER)
Uraniastrasse 1, 1st District.
The theater is open between October and May. Performances are given every day at 3pm or 4.30pm.

PUPPENTHEATER LILARUM
Philipsgasse 8, 14th District
Tel. 89 42 103
Small theater for children, open October to March.

MÄRCHENBÜHNE "DER APFELBAUM"
Burggasse 28–32, 7th District
Fairy tales.

RONCALLI'S CIRCUS
Rathausplatz, 1st District
Daily performances from August to October at 8pm in front of the City Hall on Rathausplatz.

VIENNA BOYS' CHOIR
Every Sunday, the Vienna Boys' Choir performs in the Imperial Chapel.
Sung Masses: 50 to 220 ATS.

SPANISH RIDING SCHOOL
Exhibitions take place from April to June in the Summer Manège and from September to October in the Winter Manège. Visitors may watch training sessions and exhibitions. Seats are 200–700 ATS; standing room is 160 ATS. Training sessions are 70 ATS (adults), 20 ATS (children).
The Lippizzaner horses are a blend of Andalusian and thoroughbred Arab stock. Born with black coats, which turn white at the age of eight, they are trained to dance to polka, gavotte, quadrille and waltz music.

CHILDCARE
BABYSITTER DES ÖSTERREICHISCHEN AKADEMISCHEN
Mühlgasse 20,
Tel. 57 35 24; 80 to 100 ATS per hour.
BABYSITTERZENTRALE
Herbstrasse 6–10,
Tel. 95 11 35

Puppen & Spielzeug MUSEUM

> **"HE SPENT THE EVENING WITH HIS YOUNG WIFE AT RONACHER'S, A VARIETY ESTABLISHMENT. TO THOSE WHO MADE COMMENTS … HE REPLIED: 'WHY NOT? INTERMEDIARY ARTISTS INTEREST ME STRANGELY. MOREOVER ARE THERE NOT FAIRGROUND STALLS AT THE PRATER?'"**
> PETER ALTENBERG

The aptly named "Liliputbahn" miniature railroad, which crosses part of the Prater.

Windsurfing on the Danube.

A toyshop window.

OPEN-AIR ACTIVITIES

THE PRATER (1)

The largest park in the center of Vienna was a hunting preserve until Joseph II opened it to the public in 1776. Today it is a broad green expanse edged with woodland, which includes the Wurstelprater, a kind of permanent fairground.

THE FERRIS WHEEL (RIESENRAD) Panoramic views of the city from heights of 200 feet, operating daily 11am–6pm. Open from Easter to the end of October, from morning through to midnight.

OTHER ATTRACTIONS A range of sports, including bowling, horseriding, tennis, football. In the Grüner Prater (Green Prater) there is walking, canoeing on the Heustadlwasser, and cycling on the Hauptallee. Children will enjoy the *Lilliputbahn* miniature railroad.

DONAUPARK (3)

This 300-acre park connects the Old and the New Danube. The Donauturm, 825 feet high, offers the highest viewpoint in Vienna. There is boating on the Old Danube (Alte Donau): kayaks, dinghies and sailboats are for hire. Alternatively, try cycling along the various trails.

ALTE DONAU (4)

This branch of the Danube, fed by underwater springs, serves as a pleasure-boat marina. Its banks, which abut the working-class 21st and 22nd Districts, have been fully adapted with a range of leisure facilities. The city's first open-air swimming bath, the Gänsehäufel, was opened here before World War One, in 1907.

DONAUINSEL (5)

In 1981, the New Danube Canal (Neue Donau) was dug next to the Danube as a drainage facility. This created the Donauinsel, a long, narrow island (nicknamed "Spaghetti Island" because of its shape) offering 26 miles of beaches for watersports and other leisure activities, with boats, bicycles, sailboards, jetskis and rollerskates for rent. For picnicking and sunbathing there are abundant green areas and sheltered inlets; special zones have been set aside for naturists.

ZOOS

LAINZER TIERGARTEN (7) A natural reserve for animals including wild boar and deer, open from Palm Sunday until November 1, Wednesday to Sunday, and holidays.

TIERGARTEN SCHÖNBRUNN The zoo at Schönbrunn (2) is the world's oldest, founded in 1752. Children can pet the rabbits, sheep and alpacas here. Open daily. The main entrance is at Hietzinger Tor.

WIENERWALD

A crescent of wooded hills covering several hundred square miles, the Wienerwald skirts the city's west side from north to south. Ten hiking trails are clearly marked at the termini of the various city transportation systems. Maps of these trails may be obtained at the City Hall (Rathaus) information office, Monday to Friday, 8am–6pm.

LOBAU

The Lobau is a low-lying marshy region, with many wild and secluded bathing spots. There is a cycling track along the dike called the *Hubertusdamm*, which leads from the 91A Roter Hiasl bus stop, or *Panozzalacke*. There is also cross-country skiing in winter.

NEUSIEDLERSEE

There are plenty of activities for young and old alike, including sailing and skating.

BICYCLE RENTAL

Vienna Bike, Wasagasse 28, 9th District Tel. 319 12 58 Rentals and organized circuit, every Monday at 4pm from May to September.

OTHER RENTAL ADDRESSES: Radverleih Salztorbrücke, 1st District, or Radverleih Hochschaubelin, 2nd District.

CHRISTMAS MARKETS

Every year during the period of Advent, Christmas markets are held on the Freyung and the Rathausplatz. Against a backdrop of Christmas trees and wreaths, vendors sell hand-painted Christmas ornaments, homemade candles, wooden toys, cribs, and decorated sweetmeats. Groups of singers performing Christmas carols and storytellers recounting fairy tales add to the seasonal atmosphere.

FATHER CHRISTMAS MARKET Rathausplatz, 1st District

CHRISTMAS MARKET 7 Spittelberggasse

NASCHMARKT

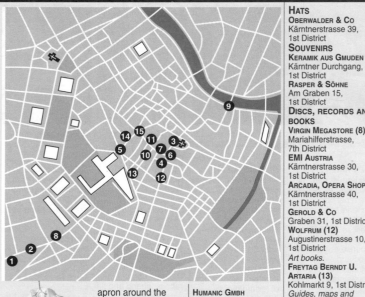

HATS
OBERWALDER & CO
Kärntnerstrasse 39,
1st District

SOUVENIRS
KERAMIK AUS GMUDEN
Kärntner Durchgang,
1st District
RASPER & SÖHNE
Am Graben 15,
1st District

DISCS, RECORDS AND BOOKS
VIRGIN MEGASTORE (8)
Mariahilferstrasse,
7th District
EMI AUSTRIA
Kärntnerstrasse 30,
1st District
ARCADIA, OPERA SHOP
Kärntnerstrasse 40,
1st District
GEROLD & CO
Graben 31, 1st District
WOLFRUM (12)
Augustinerstrasse 10,
1st District
Art books.
FREYTAG BERNDT U. ARTARIA (13)
Kohlmarkt 9, 1st District
Guides, maps and street plans.

DEPARTMENT STORES

The Viennese have taken to shopping centers just like everyone else, but they still retain their fondness for smaller, more refined stores. A new complex of stores was built on Stephansplatz during the 1980's.

TRADITIONAL STORES
GERNGROSS (1)
On the intersection of Kirchengasse and Mariahilferstrasse, 7th District
HERZMANSKY (2)
Mariahilferstrasse 26–30, 7th District

SHOPPING CENTERS
HAAS HAUS (3)
Stephansplatz 12, 1st District
"LA GALLERIA"
Landstrasser Hauptstrasse 101, 3rd District
LUGNER-CITY
Gablenzgasse 5–13, 15th District

The shops in Vienna are open Monday to Friday 9am–6pm, Saturdays 9am–12.30pm. On the first Saturday of the month the shops open until 5pm only. The more elegant and expensive establishments may be found in the center of town, between the Hofburg, the Graben and Kärntnerstrasse.

BOUTIQUES

CLOTHES
The traditional Austrian women's costume, or *Dirndl*, a full-skirted dress with a tight bodice and an apron around the waist, has attracted the attention of international fashion designers. For men, the gray-blue or green *Loden* wool fabric makes excellent overcoats and jackets (*Valker*).
RESI HAMMERER (4)
Kärntnerstrasse 29–31, 1st District
LODEN PLANKL (5)
Michaelerplatz 6, 1st District
LANZ
Kärntnerstrasse 10, 1st District
TOSTMANN & CO K
Schottengasse 3a, 1st District
The best-stocked shop in Vienna for traditional dress; sells and rents traditional Austrian costumes.
KLEIN ABER FEIN STRICKMODE AUSTRIAN HANDWORK
Herrengasse 6, im Hochhaus beim Michaelerplatz, 1st District

SHOES
BALLY GMBH
Kärntnerstrasse 9,
1st District
HUMANIC GMBH
Kärntnerstrasse 51,
1st District
BELLEZA
Kärntnerstrasse 45,
1st District
SCHEER
Bräunerstrasse 4,
1st District
ZAK
Kärntnerstrasse 51,
1st District

LINGERIE
WOLFORD WIEN
Modecenterstrasse 22,
Haus A1, 3rd District
Wolford has now branched out from its original stocking line and now offers a complete range of women's lingerie.
PALMER'S
Several addresses in Vienna.

JEWELERS
JUWELIER HABAN (6)
Kärntnerstrasse 2,
1st District
RUDOLPH HÜBNER
Am Graben 28,
1st District
KOCHERT
Neuer Markt 15,
1st District
GALERIE V & V
Bauernmarkt 19, 1st District

A luxury store on the Graben, one of Vienna's most attractive shopping streets.

FOR THE HOME

CHINA AND GLASS
GALERIE LOBMEYR (11)
Kärntnerstrasse 26, 1st District
Hungarian glass and china.

WIENER PORZELLANMANUFAKTUR AUGARTEN (7)
Stock im Eisen Platz 3–4, 1st District
The Augarten porcelain factory.

LINEN
ZUR SCHWABISCHEN JUNGFRAU
Graben 26, 1st District
Domestic linen.

JUNGMANN & NEFFE
Albertinaplatz 3, 1st District
Recently restored fabric shop.

BACKAUSEN
Kärntnerstrasse 33, 1st District
Furnishing fabrics.

SILVER
JAROSONSKI AND VAUGOIN
Zieglergasse 24, 7th District

FLOWERS (BLUMEN)
MATERN
Herrengasse 10, 1st District
RUHMANN
Singerstrasse, 1st District
SADTLER
Opernring 13, 1st District
HIRING EVENING CLOTHES, DRESSES, DISGUISES AND COSTUMES
LAMBERT J. HOFER
Margaretenstrasse 25, 4th District
HAIR STYLIST
RUDOLPH SCHIFF
Kärntnerstrasse 8, 1st District

ART GALLERIES

Most of the galleries are to be found in the 1st District in the area around Blutgasse and Bäckerstrasse. There are a number of them, and many specialize in contemporary art.

GALERIE HILGE
Dorotheergasse 5, 1st District
Tel. 512 5315
Figurative and abstract art.

GALERIE NÄCHST ST STEPHAN
Grünangergasse 1, 1st District
Tel. 512 12 66
A major showcase gallery for avant-garde, conceptualist and minimalist artists.

GALERIE AMBIENTE
Lugeck 1, 1st District
Tel. 513 11 30
The foremost Jugendstil gallery.

GALERIE KRINZINGER
Seilerstätte 16, 1st District
Features many artists from the 1960's, along with representatives of the new Austrian art.

GALERIE GRITA INSAM
Köllnerhofgasse 6, 1st District
Video art.

GALERIE PETER PAKESCH
Ungargasse 27, 3rd District
Exhibiting work by younger artists.

ART AND ANTIQUES

The antique dealers of Vienna tend to be concentrated in the area around the Dorotheum.

FLEA MARKETS
Markets are held daily in some quarters of Vienna. The most famous of these is the Naschmarkt, which is open every Monday and Saturday between 7am and 6pm.

KUNST UND ANTIKMARKT (9)
Donaukanal Promenade, Schwedenplatz und Schottenring Metro Station.
Oper weekends.

NASCHMARKT
Flomarkt, 6th District
The biggest flea market in Vienna.

AUCTION ROOMS
DOROTHEUM (10)
Dorotheergasse 17, 1st District
Tel. 515 600
One of the world's largest auction houses, founded in 1707 by Josepa I. The Dorotheum was originally planned as a pawnshop; today it occupies several floors which are permanently stacked with old furniture, paintings, jewelry, china, clothes and knick-knacks.

FURNITURE
Around Josefsplatz, Augustinerstrasse, Spiegelgasse, Plankengasse and Dorotheergasse, one can find authentic Rococo, Biedermeier and Jugendstil pieces, including furniture by the great designers Michael Thonet and Josef Hoffmann.

GALERIE SLAVIK
Himmelpfortgasse 17, 1st District
Tel. 513 48 12
A range of antiques together with contemporary designs.

MAK-DESIGN SHOP
Weiskirchnerstrasse 3, 1st District
Creations by designers from the Academy of Applied Arts.

THONET WOHNEN
Kohlmarkt 6, 1st District
Copies of Thonet's famous bistro chair design.

◆ Useful words and phrases

◆ URBAN VOCABULARY ◆

Bezirk: district
Strasse: street
Gasse: small street
Einbahnstrasse: one-way street
Anfang: beginning
Ende: end
Hof: court
Ring: the ring, the boulevard around the city
Gürtel: ring road
Garten: garden
Rathaus: City Hall
Haus: house
Platz: square
Fussgänger: pedestrians
Zone: pedestrian precinct
Palais, Palast: palace
Museum: museum
Kirche: church
Kloster: monastery
U-Bahn: subway
Strassenbahn: tramway
Zug: train
Städteschnellzug: express train
Schnellbahn: fast suburban train
Bahnhof: station
Verengte Fahrbahn: shortcut
Umleitung: diversion
Vorsicht !: Beware!
Kurzparkzone: regulated parking zone
Insel: island
Kai: quay
Ufer: bank
Brücke: bridge
Donauinsel: island in the Danube
See: lake
Wald: forest
Autobahn: freeway
Steinschlag: landslide

◆ BUSINESS, COMMERCE ◆

Offen: open
Geschlossen: closed
Kaffeehaus: café (place)
Bäckerei: bakery
Konditorei: patisserie (food and place)
Confiserie: confectioner
Zückerbäcker: confectioner (candies for children)
Heuriger: guinguette, tavern
Gasthaus: inn
Beisl: restaurant
Installateur: plumber
Coiffeur, Friseur: hairdresser
Tabak-Trafik: tobacconist (sells stamps, phone cards)
Juweliere: jeweler
Wechselstube: exchange
Markt: market
Kaufhäuser: department stores
Trachtenmode: Austrian fashions
Tankstelle: gas station
Fernsprecher: telephone
Briefmarken: stamps
Krankenhaus: hospital
Apotheke: pharmacy

◆ EXCURSIONS ◆

Right: rechts
Left: links
Guide: fremdenführer
Object of interest: Sehenswürdigkeit
Visit: besichtigung
Viewpoint: aussicht
Tickets: karten
Concert: konzert
Open-air concert: gartenkonzert
Atonal music: atonale musik
Religious music: kirchenmusik
Chamber music: kammermusik
Cinema: kinotheater (place)
Theater: theater
Play: theaterstück
Going to the theater: das theater besuchen
Theater ticket office: theaterkartenbüro
Skating rink: eisbahn
Embassy: botschaft

◆ FOOD ◆

To eat: essen
To drink: trinken
Cold: kalt
Hot: heiss
Salt: salz
Sugar: zucker
Breakfast: frühstück
Lunch: mittagessen
Snack: jause
Dinner: abendessen
Pork: schweinefleisch
Beef: rindfleisch
Stewed beef: tafelspitz
Veal: kalbfleisch
Fish: fisch
Sausage: wurst
Potatoes: kartoffeln
Rice: reis
Bread: brot
Roll: semmel
Cake: kuchen
Turnover: strudel
Young wine: heuriger
White wine: weisswein
Red wine: rotwein
Beer: bier
Fruit juice: fruchtsaft
Mineral water: mineralwasser
Coffee: kafee
Waiter: Herr Ober
Menu: speisekarte
The bill please: aahlen, bitte!

◆ COFFEE ◆

Kleiner/Grosser Schwarzer: small/large black coffee
Melange: half coffee, half milk,
Melange mit Schlag: large cup of coffee with whipped cream and milk
Kapuziner: coffee with milk and cream
Schale Gold: weak coffee

Kleiner/Grosser Brauner: small/large coffee with cream
Verkehrt: almost white with milk
Einspänner: black coffee in a glass with whipped cream (Schlagobers, or Schlag)
Doppelschlag: more whipped cream than coffee
Türkischer: Turkish coffee
Fiaker: coffee with rum
Franziskaner: coffee with milk, cream and grated chocolate
Mazagran: cold coffee with ice cubes and a drop of rum, served with a straw
Eiskaffee: vanilla ice cream laced with cold black coffee, whipped cream and wafers
Teeschale licht: large cup of tea with milk

◆ MONEY ◆

Credit card: Kreditkarte
Travelers' checks: reiseschecke
Bicycle rental: fahrradverleih
Car rental: autovermietung
To buy: kaufen
To rent: mieten
Black and white film: schwarzweissfilm
Color film: farbfilm
Cheap: billig
Expensive: teuer

◆ ACCOMMODATION ◆

Lodgings: eine Pension
Hotel: ein Hotel
Single bedroom: einzel
Double bedroom: Doppelzimmer
What is the price for one night?: was kostet eine übernachtung?
Youth hostels: Jugendherberge
Toilets: toiletten

◆ CONVERSATION ◆

Mrs: Frau
Miss: Fräulein
Mr: Herr
good day: Grüss Gott (Thank God – typically Austrian)
good morning, hello: Guten Tag, Guten Morgen (in the morning)
good evening: Guten Abend
goodbye: Auf Wiedersehen
hi: Servus (used between friends in Vienna)
goodbye: Baba (another very familiar Viennese expression)
thanks: Danke schön
please: Bitte
excuse me: Verzeihung
I don't understand: Ich verstehe nicht
Do you speak English?:
Sprechen Sie Englisch?
yes: ja
no: nein
I would like: Ich möchte

◆ THE DAYS OF THE WEEK ◆

Monday: Montag
Tuesday: Dienstag
Wednesday: Mittwoch
Thursday: Donnerstag
Friday: Freitag
Saturday: Samstag
Sunday: Sonntag
Week: woche
Weekend: wochenende
Public holiday: feiertag, festtag

◆ THE MONTHS ◆

January: Januar
February: Februar
March: März
April: April
May: Mai
June: Juni
July: Juli
August: August
September: September
October: Oktober
November: November
Decembre: Dezember

◆ NUMBERS ◆

1: eins
2: zwei
3: drei
4: vier
5: fünf
6: sechs
7: sieben
8: acht
9: neun
10: zehn
20: zwanzig
21: einundzwanzig
30: dreissig
40: vierzig
50: fünfzig
60: sechzig
70: siebzig
80: achtzig
90: neunzig
100: hundert
1 000: tausend
1000 000: million
first: erste, erstere
second: zweiter
third: dritter, e, es
fourth: vierter
fifth: fünfte(r)

Useful addresses

⚡ Panorama
C City center
◧ Isolated
◍ Luxury restaurant
◑ Typical restaurant
○ Budget restaurant
🏨 Luxury hotel
🏠 Typical hotel
⌂ Budget hotel
P Parking
🚐 Supervised garage
□ Television
☺ Quiet
≋ Swimming pool
▭ Credit cards
☀ Reduction for children
✗ Pets not allowed
♫ Music
📯 Live band

◆ CHOOSING A HOTEL

	PRICE	VIEW	QUIET	TYPICAL HOTEL	RESTAURANT	BAR	SPECIAL PRICES FOR CHILDREN	SWIMMING POOL	PARKING	NO. OF ROOMS
1st DISTRICT										
HOTEL AMBASSADOR	+++++	•	•		•	•			•	106
HOTEL BRISTOL	+++++	•	•		•	•	•		•	146
HOTEL DE FRANCE	+++++	•	•		•	•			•	214
HOTEL IMPÉRIAL	+++++				•	•				145
HOTEL SACHER	+++++	•	•		•	•			•	118
HOTEL VIENNA PLAZA	+++++	•	•		•	•	•		•	223
HOTEL BAJAZZO	++++		•					•	•	12
CAPRICORNO	++++		•						•	46
HOTEL DOMINO	++++		•					•		6
HOTEL EUROPA	++++	•	•		•	•			•	102
HOTEL GRABEN	++++	•	•		•			•	•	46
K + K PALAIS HOTEL	++++		•		•	•	•	•	•	66
HOTEL KAISERIN ELISABETH	++++	•	•			•		•	•	63
HOTEL KÖNIG VON UNGARN	++++		•		•	•		•		33
HOTEL MARC AUREL	++++		•			•			•	18
HOTEL OPERNRING	++++	•	•						•	35
HOTEL RATHAUSPARK	++++	•	•	•		•		•	•	117
HOTEL ROYAL	++++	•	•		•			•	•	81
HOTEL AM SCHUBERTRING	++++		•			•	•		•	39
HOTEL AM STEPHANSPLATZ	++++	•	•	•	•			•	•	62
HOTEL TIGRA			•			•		•	•	75
HOTEL AUSTRIA	++++		•					•		46
HOTEL KÄRNTNERHOF	+++	•	•					•		43
HOTEL POST	+++		•		•			•		107
HOTEL WANDL	+++	•	•	•		•	•		•	138
HOTEL ZUR WIENER STAATSOPER	+++		•					•		22
MERCURE WIEN CITY									•	
HOTEL PENSION CITY			•					•		
PENSION AVIANO	++++	•	•	•			•	•	•	17
PENSION ARENBERG	++++	•	•							22
PENSION CHRISTINA	++++	•	•				•	•		33
PENSION DOMIZIL	++++		•			•		•	•	21
PENSION NEUER MARKT	++++	•	•	•	•	•		•	•	37
PENSION PERTSCHY	++++	•	•				•	•		43
RIEMERGASSE APPARTEMENT–PENSION	++++	•	•					•		14
PENSION ELITE	+++			•		•		•	•	27

	PRICE	VIEW	QUIET	TYPICAL HOTEL	RESTAURANT	BAR	SPECIAL PRICES FOR CHILDREN	SWIMMING POOL	PARKING	NO. OF ROOMS
PENSION GEISSLER	♦♦♦		●		●				●	23
PENSION LERNER	♦♦♦								●	7
PENSION NOSSEK	♦♦♦	●		●				●		26
PENSION RESIDENZ	♦♦♦	●	●	●				●		13
PENSION SUZANNE	♦♦♦	●							●	19
PENSION ACLON	♦♦	●		●				●		22
3rd DISTRICT										
SCHWARZENBERG	♦♦♦♦♦				●	●				38
HOTEL VIENNA HILTON	♦♦♦♦♦	●		●	●	●	●		●	600
HOTEL INTER CONTINENTAL	♦♦♦♦	●	●				●		●	492
PULLMAN HOTEL BELVÉDÈRE	♦♦♦♦	●		●	●	●			●	211
6th DISTRICT										
HOTEL BEETHOVEN	♦♦♦♦	●	●						●	36
HOTEL SCHNEIDER	♦♦♦♦	●	●					●		71
PENSION ESTERHÀZY	♦									15
7th DISTRICT										
K + K HOTEL MARIA THERESIA	♦♦♦♦	●		●	●	●	●	●	●	123
HOTEL TANGRA	♦♦	●						●		28
PENSION REIMER	♦♦							●		14
8th DISTRICT										
HOTEL JOSEFSHOF	♦♦♦♦	●		●		●		●	●	43
PENSION ALSERGRUND	♦♦									58
PENSION AUERSPERG	♦♦									75
PENSION CARINA	♦♦									21
PENSION COLUMBIA	♦♦									8
PENSION KOPER	♦♦							●		16
PENSION LEHRERHEIM DES LEHRERHAUSVEREINES	♦♦		●					●	●	40
PENSION WILD	♦							●	●	14
PENSION EDELWEISS			●	●			●	●	●	
9th DISTRICT										
HOTEL ATLANTA	♦♦♦♦		●	●	●				●	57
HOTEL REGINA	♦♦♦♦	●	●		●	●		●	●	124
HOTEL AM SCHOTTENPOINT	♦♦♦	●				●			●	17
PENSION BLECKMANN	♦♦♦		●					●	●	14
PENSION VERA	♦♦	●								14
17th DISTRICT										
PENSION AM LERCHENFELD	♦♦									15

◆ Choosing a restaurant

	LUXURY	BUDGET	TYPICAL	PANORAMA	TERRACE	AFTER MIDNIGHT	ORCHESTRA	PARKING
1st DISTRICT								
BIERHOF			●		●	●		
BIERLEUTGEB			●					
BISTROT DE FRANCE	●			●				
BREZELG'WÖLB			●	●	●			
CAFÉ LANDTMANN			●	●	●			
DEMELS	●			●				
DIGLAS			●		●			
DO & CO	●							
DO & CO IM HAAS HAUS	●			●				
FIGLMÜLLER			●					
GÖTTWEIGER STIFTSKELLER			●					
GRIENSTEIDL			●	●				
GULASCHMUSEUM			●		●			
KÖNIGSBACHER			●	●	●			
KORNAT	●							
KORSO	●				●		●	
KRAH-KRAH		●			●	●		
KUPFERDACHL			●		●			
LE SIÈCLE IM SAS HOTEL	●							
LUSTIG ESSEN					●			
MILJÖÖ			●			●		
MONGOLIAN BARBECUE			●					
NOODLES & CO	●			●	●	●	●	
OFENLOCH			●		●			
OPERA			●			●		
OSWALD UND KALB			●					
PAULUSSTUBEN			●	●	●			
PFUDL			●	●				
PÜRSTNER			●		●			
ROSA ELEFANT			●		●	●		
ROSENBERGER MARKT		●						
S'MÜLLERBEISL			●		●			
SIRK ROTISSERIE	●			●				●
SOWIESO			●		●	●		
STADTBEISL			●	●	●			
TRATTORIA SAN CARLO			●	●				
TRZESNIEWSKI			●					
WALFISCHECK		●			●			
WARSTEINER			●		●	●		
WERNER'S			●		●			
WRENKH	●				●			
ZU DEN DREI HACKEN			●		●			
ZU DEN DREI HUSAREN	●							
ZUM BASILISKEN			●		●			
ZUM BETTELSTUDENT		●			●	●		

	LUXURY	BUDGET	TYPICAL	PANORAMA	TERRACE	AFTER MIDNIGHT	ORCHESTRA	PARKING
ZUM KÖNIG VON UNGARN				•	•			
ZUM LEUPOLD			•	•	•			
ZUM SCHWARZEN KAMEEL			•					
ZUM SUPPENTOPF			•					
ZUM WEISSEN RAUCHFANGKEHRER			•					
ZUR MAJESTÄT	•							
ZWÖLF APOSTELKELLER			•					•
2nd DISTRICT								
ALTES JÄGERHAUS			•	•	•			
LUSTHAUS			•	•	•			•
SCHWEIZERHAUS			•	•	•			•
VINCENT	•							•
3rd DISTRICT								
IM KUNSTHAUS			•	•				
PALAIS SCHWARZENBERG	•				•			
ROTISSERIE PRINZ EUGEN	•							•
STEIRERECK	•							•
VIER JAHRESZEITEN	•							
4th DISTRICT								
ZU DEN DREI BUCHTELN			•					
5th DISTRICT								
ALTES FASSL			•		•			
MOTTO			•		•	•		
SCHLOSSGASSE 21			•		•	•		
6th DISTRICT								
HAUSWIRTH	•				•			
LUDWIG VAN			•	•				
7th DISTRICT								
ECK			•					
PLUTZER BRÄU					•	•		
ZU EBENER ERDE & ERSTEN STOCK		•	•		•	•		
ZUR STADT KREMS			•		•			
8th DISTRICT								
MARIA TREU		•	•				•	
LE TUNNEL								
9th DISTRICT								
REGINA			•	•	•			
13th DISTRICT								
VILLA HANS MOSER	•							
15th DISTRICT								
ALTWIENERHOF	•				•			
VIKERL'S LOKAL			•					
19th DISTRICT								
FISCHERBRÄU			•		•			
22nd DISTRICT								
STRANDCAFÉ			•	•				

FROM THE UK AND THE US

TRANSPORT

AIRLINES
See p. 308 for further
information, addresses
and frequency of flights.

TRAVEL AGENTS IN THE US
AIMS – AMERICAN
INSTITUTE OF MUSICAL
STUDIES
6621 Snider Plaza
Dallas, TX 75205
Tel. (214) 363 2683
*Music studies, concert
performances.*
AMBASSADOR TRAVEL
1409 Duncan Avenue
Pittsburgh, PA 15237
Tel. (412) 366 7200
Wine and song tours.
DEBUTANTE HOLIDAYS
ABROAD INC.
210 Heightbrook
Avenue
Pelham Manor, NY
10803
Tel. (914) 738 2398
*Tours include:
Debutante Ball "the
Rosenkavalier", Vienna
Boys' Choir.*
GRAND EUROPEAN
TOURS
4000 Kruse Way Place
2–245
Lake Oswego, OR
97035
Tel. (503) 635 9627
*"Best of Europe" and
"Great European" coach
and rail tours.*
GRAND CIRCLE TRAVEL
347 Congress Street
Boston, MA 02210
Tel. (617) 350 7500
*Senior citizens' "Alpine
Village Sampler" tour
and Danube River
cruises.*
HOPE COLLEGE
Fried Int'l Center
112 E. 12th Street
P. O. Box 9000
Holland, MI 49422-9000
Tel. (616) 394 7605
*Undergraduate summer
school classes.*
IDYLL LTD
P. O. Box 405
Media, PA 19063
Tel. (215) 565 5242
Fax (215) 565 5142
*Independent tours
Apr. –Oct.*
INTERHOSTEL
UNIVERSITY OF NEW
HAMPSHIRE
6 Garrison Avenue
Durham, NH
03824–3529
Tel.(603) 862 1147

*Educational tours for
the over 50's.*
PETER MCLEAN LTD
650 Poydras Street,
#2404
New Orleans, LA 71030
Tel. (504) 581 1278
*Undergraduate study
tours.*
SAGA INTERNATIONAL
HOLIDAYS LTD
222 Berkeley Street
Boston, MA 02116
Tel. (617) 262 2262
Tours for senior citizens.
TRAVCON INC.
65 Lasalle Road, #300
West Hartford, CT
06107
Tel. (203) 232 9939
*First-class city tours
and Christmas specials.*

UK AUSTRIAN TRAVEL SPECIALIST

AUSTRIAN HOLIDAYS
10 Wardour Street, 5th
floor,
London W1V 4BQ
Tel. 071 434 7399
Contact Austrian
National Tourist Office
(see p. 306) for details
of other tour operators.

◆

AIRPORT

PRACTICAL INFORMATION

**INFORMATION-
FLUGHAFEN WIEN**
Flughafen Schwechat
Open daily
8.30am–11pm
*Desk indicated
with an "i" for
information*

TRANSPORT

SCHWECHAT AIRPORT
Tel. 711 10
Open daily 6am–12am

AIRLINES
AUSTRIAN AIRLINES
Flughafen Schwechat
Tel. 711 10-2231
or 711 10-2232
Open daily 6am–8.30pm
LAUDA AIR
P. O. Box 51
Flughafen Schwechat
Tel. 711 10-2081, 2082,
2083, 2084
Open Mon.–Fri.
8.30am–5.30pm

◆

1ST DISTRICT INNER CITY

PRACTICAL INFORMATION

**INFORMATIONS-
ZENTRUM DER STADT
WIEN**
Friedrich Schmidt Halle
Rathaus
Tel. 403 89 89
Open Mon.–Fri
8am–6pm

JUGEND INFO WIEN
Dr. Karl Renner Ring
Bellaria Passage
Tel. 526 46 37
Open Mon.–Fri.
noon–7pm
Open Sat. and public
holidays, 10am–7pm
*Information for young
people and students.*

TOURIST OFFICE
Kärntnerstrasse 38
Tel. 513 88 92

Open daily 9am–7pm
*All major languages
spoken. Free maps and
brochures, tour
reservations, exchange.
For hotel reservations
call 211 14 -66.*

POLIZEI (POLICE)
Stephansplatz U-Bahn
Station
Tel. 313 47-2023
Open 24 hours

**POSTAMT (POST
OFFICE)**
Barbaragasse 2
Tel. 512 76 81-0
Open 24 hours

EXCHANGE

WECHSELSTUBE
Kärntnerstrasse 51
Open 24 hours
*Automatic cash
exchange machine in
front of the Opera.*

WECHSELSTUBE
Stephansplatz 2
Open daily 8am–6pm
*In front of the
Cathedral.*

TRANSPORT

BY RIVER BOAT
DDSG-DONAUREISEN
Schwedenbrücke
Station
Tel. 217 50-451
Open daily
*Specializes in Danube
cruises.*

AIRLINES
AUSTRIAN AIRLINES
Kärntner Ring 18
Tel. 717 99 or 505 57 57
Open Mon.–Fri.
9am–5pm
LAUDA AIR
Opernring 6
Tel. 514 770
Open Mon.–Fri.
8.30am–5.30pm

CYCLE HIRE
COOPERATIVE FAHRRAD
Unter der Salztorbrücke
Tel. 532 82 34 Open
Apr.–Oct. 9am–8pm

CAR HIRE
AVIS
Opernring 1
Tel. 587 62 41
Open Mon.–Fri. 9am–
5pm
Also at the airport.
HERTZ
Kärntner Ring 17
Tel. 512 86 77
Open Mon.–Fri.
8.30am–5pm

CULTURAL ATTRACTIONS

ADALBERT STIFTER MUSEUM
Mölker Bastei 8
Tel. 637 06 65
◆ 329

AKADEMIE DER BILDENDEN KÜNSTE
Schillerplatz 3
Tel. 588 16 225
Open Tue. and
Thur.–Fri. 10am–2pm
Open Wed. 10am–1pm
and 3pm–6pm
Open Sat., Sun. and
public holidays
9am–1pm ▲ 159

ALBERTINA
Augustinerstrasse 1
Tel. 534 83
Open Mon.–Tue. and
Thur. 10am–4pm
Open Wed. 10am–6pm
Open Fri. 10am–2pm
Open Sat.–Sun.
10am–1pm
Closed Sun. July–Aug.
▲ 196

ALTES RATHAUS
Wipplingerstrasse 8
Tel. 53436–779/332
Open Mon. and
Wed.–Thur. 9am–5pm
*The former City Hall
contains the archives of
the Austrian Resistance
from World War Two
(stairway 3).* ● 84

BÖRSE
Börseplatz
Open Mon.–Fri.
9am–5pm
Closed Sat.–Sun. and
public holidays.
*19th-century
Renaissance-style
Stock Exchange.* ▲ 201

BURGKAPELLE
Hofburg Im
Schweizerhof
Open Tue. and Thur.
2.30pm and 3pm, Jan.
15–June and Sept.
15–Dec. 15.
Masses on Sundays and
all Christian feast days
9.15am, Jan.–June,
Sept.–Dec.
*Chapel of the Imperial
Palace.* ▲ 183

BURGTHEATER
Dr. Karl Lueger Ring 2
Tel. 514 44 2613
Open July–Aug 1pm,
2pm, 3pm
Open Tue. and Thur.
4pm and Sun. 3pm,
Oct.–Apr.

Visits by appointment,
May–June and Sept.
▲ 204

DOM- UND DIÖZESANMUSEUM
Stephansplatz 6,
passage
Tel. 512 52 560
Open Tue.–Wed.,
Fri.–Sat. 10am–4pm
Open Thur. 10am–6pm
Open Sun. and public
holidays 10am–1pm
*Museum of the
Cathedral and diocese.
Beside the Cathedral,
on its south side.*

EPHESOS MUSEUM
Neue Burg 1
Heldenplatz
Tel. 521 770
Open 10am–4pm
Closed Tue.
*The Museum is housed
in the more recent
buildings of the Palace,
facing Heldenplatz.*
▲ 184

FILMMUSEUM
Augustinerstrasse 1
(Albertina)
Tel. 533 70 540
Open Mon.–Sat.
evenings, Oct.–May.
*A museum-cum-cinema
with substantial film
archives in German and
other languages. Film
festivals in summer.*
◆ 331

HERMESVILLA
Lainzer Tiergarten
Tel. 804 13 24
● 119

HERZGRUFT DER HABSBURGER
Augustinerstrasse 3
In the Augustinerkirche
Tel. 533 70 99
Open Mon.–Tues. and
Thur. 8am–9.30am
Open Wed.
8am–8.45am
Open Fri. 8am–8.45am
and 10am–noon
*In the church of the
Augustines.* ▲ 195

HISTORISCHES MUSEUM DER STADT WIEN
Karlsplatz
Tel. 505 87 47
Open Tue.–Sun.
9am–4.30pm
▲ 241

HOFBURG – KAISERAPPARTEMENTS
Michaelerplatz
Tel. 587 55 54515

Open Mon.–Sat.
8.30am–noon and
12.30pm–4pm
Open Sun. and public
holidays
8.30am–12.30 pm
▲ 178

JÜDISCHES MUSEUM DER STADT WIEN
Eskeles Palace
Dorotheergasse 11
Tel. 535 04 31
Open 10am–6pm
Closed Sat.
*Beside the synagogue
in the old Jewish
quarter in central
Vienna.*

KAISERGRUFT
Neuer Markt
Tel. 512 63 5312
Open daily 9.30am–4pm

KUNSTHISTORISCHES MUSEUM
Maria-Theresien-Platz
Burgring 5
Tel. 521 770
Open Tue., Thur.–Sun.
10am–6pm
Open Tue., Thur.–Fri.
6–9pm for some
exhibitions. ▲ 208

LEHAR SCHIKANEDER SCHLÖSSL
Hackhofergasse 18
Tel. 371 82 13
▲ 299

MARIA AM GESTADE
Passauerplatz
*Church of St Mary's on
the Bank.* ▲ 172

MICHAELERKIRCHE
Michaelerplatz
*Vienna's most beautiful
square, facing one of
the entrances to the
Hofburg (on the
Kohlmarkt side).*
▲ 174

MINORITENKIRCHE
Minoritenplatz
▲ 161

MOZART ERINNERUNGSRÄUME
Domgasse 5
Tel. 513 62 94
Open 9am–12.15pm and
1pm–4.30.
Closed Mon.
*A museum in the
"Figarohaus" tracing the
composer's life and
times.* ▲ 150

MUSEUM FÜR VÖLKERKUNDE
Neue Burg, Heldenplatz
Tel. 521 770

Open daily 10am–4pm.
*The Austrian National
Collection of Ethnic Art
is in a wing of the
Imperial Palace.
Highlights include
Mexican, West African
and Polynesian art.*
▲ 187

NATIONALBIBLIOTHEK
Josefsplatz 1 Prunksaal
Tel. 534 10 397
*Closed for the duration
of the restoration work
on the Hofburg,
damaged by fire in
1992.* ▲ 192

NATURHISTORISCHES MUSEUM
Maria-Theresien-Platz
Burgring 7, 1st floor
Tel. 521 770
Open 9am–6pm
Closed 3pm in winter,
closed Tue.
*Opposite the
Kunsthistorisches
Museum.*
▲ 128

NEIDHART-FRESKEN
Tuchlauben 19
Tel. 535 90 65
Open 9am–12.15pm and
1pm–4.30pm
Closed Mon.

ÖSTERREICHISCHES MUSEUM FÜR ANGEWANDTE KUNST
Stubenring 5
Tel. 711360
Open 11am–6pm
Night opening Thur. 9pm
Closed Tue.
*Permanent and
temporary modern art
exhibitions.* ▲ 228

12 Demel
13 Café Bar in der Weiner Secession
14 Café Landtmann
15 Café -Hotel Europa
16 Zum Schwarzen Kameel
17 Diglas
18 Mongolian Barbecue
19 Zu den Drei Husaren
20 Roter Engle
21 Café Central
22 Pfudl
23 Wrenkh
24 Korso
25 Zum Basilisken

PARLAMENT
Dr. Karl Renner Ring 3
Tel. 401 10 2211
Open Mon.–Fri. 11am and 3pm
Open Mon.–Fri. July–Aug. 9am, 10am, 11am, 1pm, 2pm and 3pm
▲ 205

PESTSÄULE
Graben
Monument to the end of the last plague, which spread right up to the gates of Vienna. ▲ 138

PETERSKIRCHE
Petersplatz
Currently under renovation; the dome is painted with frescoes by J. M. Rottmayr. ▲ 139

PUPPEN- UND SPIELZEUGMUSEUM
Schulhof 4
Tel. 5356860
Open daily exc. Wed. 10am–6pm ▲ 168

RATHAUS
Friedrich Schmidt Platz
Tel. 40 389 89
Open Mon.–Fri. 1pm
City Hall, in the middle of its own park area, overlooks a bustling square. Exhibitions in summer and lots of events for children in advent, leading up to Christmas. ▲ 205

RÖMISCHE BAURESTE AM HOF
Am Hof 9
Tel. 505 87 47 46
Open Sat., Sun. and public holidays 11am–1pm

RÖMISCHE RUINEN
Hoher Markt 3
Tel. 535 56 06
Open 9am–12.15pm and 1pm–4.30pm
Closed Mon.
Another of Vienna's numerous Roman ruins.

RUPRECHTSKIRCHE
Rupertsplatz
The oldest Romanesque church in Vienna, fortunately undamaged by Allied bombing raids during World War Two ▲ 154

SCHATZKAMMER DES DEUTSCHEN ORDENS
Singerstrasse 7
Tel. 512 10 656
Open 10am–6pm
Closed Tue.
Displays of coins and relics of the medieval Teutonic knights. ▲ 149

SCHOTTENKIRCHE
Freyung
Backing on to the "Scottish Monastery," in front of the Ferstel Palace. ▲ 163

SCHOTTENSTIFT
Freyung
A former monastery on the Freyung. ▲ 164

SCHULHOF
Am Hof
▲ 168

SECESSION PAVILION
Friedrichstrasse 12
Tel. 587 53 07
Open Tue.–Fri. 10am–6pm
Open Sat., Sun., and public holidays 10am–4pm
Named after the movement that broke with 19th-century Austrian classicism. Famous frieze by Gustav Klimt in the basement, exhibitions of modern art on the ground floor. ▲ 232

SPANISCHER REITSCHULE
Josefsplatz
In the Hofburg.
Tel. 533 90 31 or 533 90 32
Fax 535 01 86
Open Tue.–Sat. am, March–June.
The Spanish Riding School, with its celebrated Lipizzaner horses. ▲ 190

STAATSOPER
Opernring 2
Tel. 514 44 2613
Guided tours daily 10am, 11am, 1pm, 2pm and 3pm, July–Aug.
Open for visits by appointment Sept–June
Austria's National Opera. ▲ 223

STEPHANSDOM
Stephansplatz
Tel. 515 52 563 or 515 52 526
Guided tours Mon.–Sat. 10.30am and 3pm, Sun. 3pm and 7pm, June–Sept.
CATACOMBS
Open daily 10am, 11am, 11.30am, 2pm, 2.30pm, 3.30pm, 4pm and 4.30pm
SOUTH TOWER
Open 9am–5.30pm Mar.–Oct., 9am–4.30pm Nov.–Feb.
NORTH TOWER
Open 9am–5.30pm
St. Stephen's Cathedral stands in the heart of Vienna's pedestrianized city center. ▲ 132

SYNAGOGUE
Seitenstettengasse
The main synagogue in the old Jewish quarter. Jewish museum inside.
▲ 156

UHRENMUSEUM DER STADT WIEN
Schulhof 2
Tel. 533 22 65
Open daily exc. Mon. 9am–4.30pm
Closed Mon.
Clock and watchmaking are an old Viennese tradition.

URANIA STERNWARTE
Uraniastrasse 1
Tel. 24 94 32
Open Wed., Fri.–Sat. 8pm Apr.–Sept.
Closed Aug.
A former observatory in the middle of the city – still used in clear weather. The other part of the building contains the oldest cinema in Vienna. ▲ 229

VIRGILKAPELLE
Stephansplatz
Tel. 513 58 42
Open 9am–12.15pm and 1 pm–4.30pm
Closed Mon.
The chapel contains a fine selection of ceramics. ▲ 136

VOLKSGARTEN
Volksgarten
Public Gardens just behind the Hofburg in the center of Vienna, one of the world's finest landscaped parks.
▲ 205

SHOWS

BURGTHEATER
Dr. Karl Lueger Ring 2
Tel. 514 44 22-18

ENSEMBLE-THEATER
Petersplatz 1
Tel. 535 32 00

HOFMUSIKSKAPELLE-SÄNGERKNABEN
Hofburg

KAMMERSPIELE
Rotenturmstrasse 20

FESTIVAL WIENER KLASSIK
Preindlgasse 1
Tel. 877 52 08

METROPOL, HERNALSER STADTTHEATER
Geblergasse 50
Tel. 433 543

MUSIKHOCHSCHULE
Johannesgasse 8

PALFFY PALACE
Josefsplatz 6
Tel. 512 56 81-0

STAATSOPER
Opernring 2
Tel. 514 44 26-50

SCHLOSSTHEATER IM SCHÖNBRUNNER
Schönbrunn Palace
Tel. 876 42 73-18

WIENER KAMMEROPER
Fleischmarkt 24
Tel. 513 60 72

KARTENBÜRO FLAMM
Kärntner Ring 3
Tel. 512 42 25

TICKET SALES
KULISSE
Rosensteingasse 39
Tel. 45 38 70
ÖSTERREICHISCHER BUNDESTHEATER VERBAND/
BUNDESTHEATER-KASSEN
Hanuschgasse 3
Goethegasse 1
Tel. 514 44 29-59 or 514 44 29-60
Fax 513 15 13
Open Mon.–Sat. 7am–7pm

Ticket outlet behind the opera for the four national theaters (Burgtheater, Akademietheater, Staatsoper and Volksoper). Sale of opera tickets a week in advance only. Tickets can be reserved by phone or fax (payment by credit card).
OEKISTA
Reichratstrasse 13 or Karlsgasse 3, 4th District or Türkenstrasse 4, 9th District
Tel. 408 78 21
Open Mon.–Fri. 9am–5pm
Travel agency for students. With an international student card (ISTC) you can buy any unsold tickets at the opera for 50 ATS. Only carriers of national student cards can obtain the ISTC.
REISEBÜRO INTROPA
Kärntnerstrasse 38
Tel. 515 14-0
Open Mon.–Fri. 9am–5pm
Beside the Tourist Office; sells tickets to various shows, notably the Spanish Riding School.

RESTAURANTS

BIERHOF
Eing. Haarhof
Tel. 533 44 28
Open Mon.–Sat. 11am–2pm
Closed Sun., public holidays
One of the best restaurants in Vienna. Its cooking is based on beer. You can eat outdoors in a small, quiet courtyard.
150–350 ATS
◑ 🄲 ♫

BIERLEUTGEB
Bäckerstrasse 12
Tel. 512 26 37
Open Mon.–Sun. 5pm–2am
A basement restaurant, with a bar on the ground floor, in the old university quarter.
150–300 ATS
◑ 🄲 ♫

BISTRO DE FRANCE
Schottenring 3
Tel. 34 35 40 3370
Open Mon.–Sun.

11am–11.30pm
In the Hotel de France. International and Austrian specialties, and vegetarian dishes.
200–500 ATS
◍ 🄲 ⛷ ☐

BREZELG'WÖLB
Ledererhof 9
Tel. 533 88 11
Open Mon.–Sun. 11.30am–1pm
Cellar premises in a small courtyard, set back from Am Hof. Classical music.
150–300 ATS
◑ 🄲 ⛷ ♫

CAFÉ LANDTMANN
Dr. Karl Lueger Ring 4
Tel. 532 06 21
Open Mon.–Sun. 8am–midnight
A somewhat expensive Viennese institution, opposite the City Hall and Theater. Terrace. World-famous home-made desserts.
150–400 ATS
◑ 🄲 ⛷ ☐

DEMEL'S
Kohlmarkt 11
Tel. 535 17 17
Open Mon.–Sun. 11am–8pm
A small oyster bistro opposite the celebrated Demel patisserie.
350–600 ATS
◍ 🄲 ⛷

DIGLAS
Wollzeile 10
Tel. 512 84 01
Open Mon.–Sat. 7am–11.30pm
Restaurant and tearoom.
150–300 ATS
◑ 🄲 ☐

DO & CO
Akademiestrasse 3
Tel. 512 64 74
Open Mon.–Fri. 9.30am–6.30pm, Sat. 9am–2.30pm
Closed Sun., public holidays.
Businessmen's restaurant.
400–750 ATS
◍ 🄲 ☐

DO & CO IM HAAS HAUS
Stephansplatz 12, 7th floor
Tel. 535 39 690
Open Mon.–Sat. noon–midnight
Closed Sun. and public

holidays
In the modern building on St Stephen's Square, with the most beautiful terrace in central Vienna in summer.
400–800 ATS
◍ 🄲 ⛷ ☐

FIGLMÜLLER
Wollzeile 5
Tel. 512 61 77
Open 11am–10pm
In a tiny alley. Wiener Schnitzel is a specialty.
200–300 ATS
◑ 🄲

GÖTTWEIGER STIFTSKELLER
Spiegelgasse 9
Tel. 512 78 17
Open Mon.–Thur. 8am–10pm
Open Fri. 8am–9pm
Closed Sat., Sun. and public holidays
Open Sat. 9am–2pm in December
Viennese bistro, frequented by regulars.
120–250 ATS
◑ 🄲

GRIENSTEIDL
Michaelerplatz 2
Tel. 535 26 92 or 93
Open daily 8am–midnight
Opposite the entrance to the Hofburg.
Breakfast till 11am.
150–300 ATS
◑ 🄲 ⛷ ☐

GULASCHMUSEUM
Schulerstrasse 20
Tel. 512 10 17 or 512 10 18
Open daily 9am–midnight
Over a hundred varieties of goulash.
100–200 ATS
◑ 🄲

KÖNIGSBACHER
Walfischgasse 5
Tel. 513 12 10 or 513 10 49
Open Mon.–Fri. 10am–midnight
Open Sat. 10am–4pm
Closed Sun. and public holidays
Typical Viennese bistro with a terrace for use in summer.
100–200 ATS.
◑ 🄲 ⛷

KORNAT
Marc Aurel Strasse 8
Tel. 535 65 18
Open Mon.–Sat. 11am–3pm and 6pm–1am
Closed Sun. and public holidays
Dalmatian restaurant. Fish specialties.
300–500 ATS
◍ 🄲

KORSO
Mahlerstrasse 2
Tel. 515 16 540
Open noon–3pm and 7pm–1am
Open Sat 7pm–1am
Closed July–Aug. at noon
One of the best restaurants in Vienna, opposite the Opera.
800–2,500 ATS
◍ 🄲 ⛷ ☐ ⌂

KRAH-KRAH
Rabensteig 8
Tel. 533 81 93
Open 11am–2am
In the "Bermuda Triangle".
80–450 ATS
🄲 🄲 ♫

KUPFERDACHL
Schottengasse 7
Tel. 533 93 81
Open Mon.–Fri. noon–3pm and

6pm–midnight
Open Sat. 6pm–midnight
Beside Zum Leopold.
200–450 ATS
◑ C ☐

LE SIÈCLE IM SAS HOTEL
Weihburggasse 32
Tel. 515 17-1960
Open Mon.–Sat. noon-3pm
Open Sun. 11am–3pm
The restaurant of the SAS Palace Hotel, popular with businessmen.
800–1,500 ATS
◍ C ☐

LUSTIG ESSEN
Salvatorgasse 6
Tel. 533 30 37
Open Mon.–Sat. 11.30am–midnight
Closed Sun. and public holidays
Small lunchtime restaurant.
50–150 ATS
C

MILJÖÖ
Dorotheergasse 19
Tel. 513 19 44
Open daily 11am–2am
There is a French-style atmosphere in this renovated basement.
200–400 ATS
◑ C ☐ ♫

MONGOLIAN BARBECUE
Fleischmarkt 4, 1st floor
Tel. 535 31 76
Open Mon.–Sun. noon–3pm and 5.30pm–12.30am
Next door to the Rosa Elefant.
150–300 ATS
◑ C

NOODLES & CO
Karlsplatz 5
Tel. 505 38 39
Open Sun.–Fri. 11am–3pm and 6pm–4am
Open Sat. 11am–4am
In the Künstlerhaus.

Italian specialties. Piano is played from 10pm. Terrace in summer.
300–600 ATS
◍ ⊡ C ☀ ☐ 🎺

OFENLOCH
Kurrentgasse 8
Tel. 533 88 44
Open daily 10am–midnight
Terrace in summer.
350–600 ATS
◑ C ☐

OPERA
Augustinerstrasse 12
Tel. 512 71 59
Open Mon.–Sun. 10am–2am
Viennese and international cuisine, situated behind the Opera.
200–300 ATS
◑ C ☐

OSWALD UND KALB
Bäckerstrasse 14
Tel. 512 13 71 or 512 69 92
Open daily 6pm–1am
Small restaurant, a former haunt of Viennese intellectuals.
150–300 ATS
◑ C

PAULUSSTUBEN
Walfischgasse 7
Tel. 512 81 36
Open Mon.–Sun. 11am–1am
A traditional Viennese lunch establishment near the Moulin Rouge, part "Heuriger", part bistro.
100–250 ATS
◑ C ☀ ☐

PFUDL
Bäckerstrasse 22
Tel. 512 67 05
Open daily 9am–midnight
Small restaurant close to the old university. A Viennese institution.
180–300 ATS
◑ C ☀

PÜRSTNER
Riemergasse 10
Tel. 512 63 57
Open daily 10am–midnight
Traditional cooking, tables are set out on the pavement in summer.
150–350 ATS
◑ ⊡ C ☐

ROSA ELEFANT
Fleischmarkt 4

Tel. 63 75 30
Open daily 4pm–2am
Near the "Bermuda Triangle". Cool terrace in summer.
150–300 ATS
◑ C ☐ ♫

ROSENBERGER MARKT
Maysedergasse 2
Tel. 512 34 58
Open Mon.–Sun. 11am–11pm
Cafeteria on three floors, near the Opera.
150–300 ATS
○ C

S'MÜLLERBEISL
Seilerstätte 15
Tel. 512 42 65
Open Mon.–Sun. 11am–3pm and 5.30pm–11pm
One of the last "Beisls" in Vienna.
80–200 ATS
◑ C ☐

SIRK ROTISSERIE
Kärntner Ring 1
Tel. 515 16 552
Open daily 7am–10am, noon–3pm and 6pm–1am
Open 7pm–11pm July–Aug.
On the second floor of the Hotel Bristol. A café is on the first floor.
400–1,000 ATS
◍ C ☀ ☐ P

LA SORBETTERIA DI RANIERI
Kärntnerstrasse 28
Tel. 512 31 34
Open Sun.–Wed. 8am–2am
Open Fri.–Sat. 8am–6am
Small, modern Italian restaurant. Tables are set outside on the street, which is closed to traffic.
200–350 ATS
◍ C ☀ ♫

SOWIESO
Grashofgasse 1
Tel. 512 12 36 or 512 63 88
Open daily noon–4am
In a cul-de-sac in the center of town. Outdoor seating is available in summer.
150–250 ATS
◑ C ☐

STADTBEISL
Naglergasse 21
Tel. 533 33 23
Open daily 9am–midnight

Typical Viennese "Lokal", which has been here since the early 17th century. Cooking based on traditional Viennese recipes.
300–500 ATS
◑ C ☀

TRATTORIA SAN CARLO
Mahlerstrasse 3
Tel. 513 89 84

Open daily noon–3pm and 6.30pm–11.30 pm
Good Italian restaurant, round the corner from the Opera.
250–500 ATS
◑ C ☀ ☐

TRZESNIEWSKI
Dorotheergasse 1
Tel. 512 32 91
Open Mon.–Fri. 9am–7.30pm
Open Sat. 9am–1am or 9am–6pm
Closed Sun., public holidays
A favorite haunt of fanatical shoppers.
75–150 ATS
◑ C

WALFISCHECK
Walfischgasse 8
Tel. 512 69 80
Open Mon.–Fri. 7am–9pm
Open Sat. 10am–10pm
Closed Sun. and public holidays
Fish specialties.
100–250 ATS
○ C ☐

WARSTEINER
Grashofgasse 4
Tel. 513 82 18
Open daily 11am–1am
Named after the beer brand; opposite the Sowieso.
200–400 ATS
◑ ⊡ C ☐ ♫

WERNER'S
Schönlaterngasse 13
Tel. 513 97 98
or 513 97 99
Open Mon.–Sat.
6pm–2am
Closed Sun. and public
holidays
Good value for money.
200–400 ATS
◐ ▣·· ◳ ▭ ♫

WRENKH
Bauernmarkt 10
Tel. 533 15 26
Open Mon.–Sat.
11am–2pm and
6pm–midnight
Closed Sun. and public
holidays.
Vegetarian specialties.
250–450 ATS
◍ ▣·· ◳

ZU DEN DREI HACKEN
Singerstrasse 28
Tel. 512 58 95
Open Mon.–Fri.
9am–midnight
Open Sat. 10am–3pm
Closed Sun. and public
holidays
*Typical central Vienna
restaurant: Schubert is
said to have dined here.
Terrace in summer.*
150–300 ATS
◐ ◳ ▭

**ZU DEN DREI
HUSAREN**
Weihburggasse 4
Tel. 512 10 92
Open Mon.–Sun.
noon–3pm and
6pm–2am
*One of the best
restaurants in Vienna.*
500–1,000 ATS.
◍ ◳ ▭

ZUM BASILISKEN
Schönlaterngasse 3/5
Tel. 513 31 23
Open Mon.–Thur
11am–2am
Open Fri.–Sun.
11am–4am
*In the old part of town.
Terrace.*
200–400 ATS
◐ ▣·· ◳ ▭

ZUM BETTELSTUDENT
Johannesgasse 12
Tel. 513 20 44
Open daily 10am–2am
*Viennese and
international cooking in
a quiet, central street.*
150–300 ATS
◐ ▣·· ◳ ▭

**ZUM KÖNIG VON
UNGARN**
Schulerstrasse 10

Tel. 512 53 19
Open noon–3pm and
6pm–midnight
Closed Sat.
*Famous restaurant in
the hotel of the same
name.*
400–800 ATS
◳ ⤳ ▭

ZUM LEUPOLD
Schottengasse 7
Tel. 533 93 81
Open Sun.–Fri.
9am–midnight
Open Sat. 5pm–midnight
*One of the best-value
restaurants in Vienna.*
250–500 ATS
◐ ◳ ⤳ ▭

**ZUM SCHWARZEN
KAMEEL**
Bognergasse 5
Tel. 533 89 67
Open Mon.–Fri.
9am–7pm
Open Sat. 9am–2.30pm
Closed Sun. and public
holidays
*Seated dining in the
restaurant section;
standing in the bistro.
Hot toasted hors
d'œuvres a specialty.*
100–500 ATS
◐ ◳

ZUM SUPPENTOPF
Wipplingerstrasse 21
Tel. 533 24 35
Open Mon.–Fri.
7am–7.30pm
Closed Sat.–Sun. and
public holidays
Ideal for snacks.
150–300 ATS
◐ ◳ ▭

**ZUM WEISSEN
RAUCHFANGKEHRER**
Weihburggasse 4
Tel. 512 34 71
Open daily noon–1am
*Traditional cooking in
one of the city's oldest
"Beisls".*
200–350 ATS
◐ ◳ ▭

ZÜR MAJESTÄT
Kärntner Ring 16
Tel. 501 10 356
Open daily noon–3pm
and 7–11pm
*Luxury restaurant in the
Hotel Imperial. One of
Vienna's outstanding
chefs.*
1,000–3,000 ATS
◍ ◳ ▭ ℗

**ZWÖLF
APOSTELKELLER**
Sonnenfelsgasse 3
Tel. 512 67 77
Open daily
4.30pm–midnight
*A "Heuriger" within the
walls of Vienna, with
huge cellars.*
150–250 ATS
◐ ◳

HOTELS

HOTEL AMBASSADOR
Neuer Markt 5
Tel. 514 66
Fax 513 29 99
*Hotel dating from the
19th century. Bedrooms
furnished in the
Biedermeier style.*
*****
2,800–4,000 ATS
⌂ ◳ ⤳ ▭ ☖ ℗

HOTEL AUSTRIA
Wolfengasse 3
Tel. 515 23
Fax 515 23–506
*Situated in a quiet cul-
de-sac.*
***
1,200–1,500 ATS
⟊ ◳ ▭ ☖

HOTEL BAJAZZO
Esslinggasse 7
Tel. 533 89 03
Fax 535 39 97
*Modern hotel in a quiet
part of town.*
****
1,480–1,900 ATS
⌂ ⟊ ▣·· ◳ ▭ ☖
℗
◐ ◳ ▭

HOTEL BRISTOL
Kärntner Ring 1
Tel. 515 160
Fax 515 16 55-0
*One of Vienna's best
(and most expensive)
hotels. Opened in 1892.*
*****
4,320–4,400 ATS
⌂ ◳ ⤳ ▭ ⚘ ☖
℗

CAPRICORNO
Schwedenplatz 3–4
Tel. 533 31 040
Fax 533 76 71-4
*Just off the Ring.
Cavernous bedrooms;
irreproachable service.*
****
1,500–2,100 ATS
⌂ ◳ ▭ ☖ ⛟

HOTEL DOMINO
Gölsdorfgasse 4
Tel. 535 06 75
Fax 535 06 75-78
*Central, overlooking a
large square.*
****
1,280–1,780 ATS
⌂ ⟊ ◳ ▭ ☖

HOTEL EUROPA
Neuer Markt 3
Tel. 51 59 40
Fax 513 81 38
*An elegant hotel in a
central location.*
****
2,150–2,600 ATS
⌂ ◳ ⤳ ▭ ☖ ℗

HOTEL DE FRANCE
Schottenring 3
Tel. 34 35 40
Fax 31 59 69
*On the Ring and close
to the city center.*
*****
2,400–3,600 ATS
⌂ ◳ ⤳ ▭ ☖ ℗

HOTEL GRABEN
Dorotheergasse 3
Tel. 512 15 31
Fax 512 15 31-20
*At the edge of a
pedestrian precinct,*

close to the antique dealers' quarter of town. Italian and Austrian restaurants in the hotel.
****
1,500–2,000 ATS

HOTEL IMPERIAL
Kärntner Ring 16
Tel. 501 100
Fax 501 10 410
Statesmen and stars stay here.
*****
4,600–5,000 ATS

K + K PALAIS HOTEL
Rudolfsplatz 11
Tel. 533 13 53
Fax 533 13 53 196
Calm, central, recently renovated hotel.
****
1,500–1,980 ATS

HOTEL KAISERIN ELISABETH
Weihburggasse 3
Tel. 515 26
Fax 51226-7
Very Viennese, very luxurious, very good value.
****
1,650–2,150 ATS

HOTEL KÄRNTNERHOF
Grashofgasse 4
Tel. 512 19 23
In a cul-de-sac near Heiligenkreuzhof. Some apartments available.
***
1,300–1,600 ATS

HOTEL KÖNIG VON UNGARN
Schulerstrasse 10
Tel. 51 58 40
Fax 51 58 48
One of Vienna's most charming hotels: an old building, a winter

garden. Reasonable prices for luxury accommodation.
****
1,800–2,000 ATS

HOTEL MARC AUREL
Marc Aurel Strasse 8
Tel. 533 52 260 or 533 36 40-0
Fax 5330078
Modern, centrally located hotel.
****
1,200–1,400 ATS

HOTEL OPERNRING
Opernring 11
Tel. 587 55 18
Fax 587 55 18-29
Almost directly opposite the Opera.
****
1,400–2,400 ATS

HOTEL PENSION CITY
Bauernmarkt 10
Tel. 533 95 21
Fax 535 52 16
Close to the center.
850–1,050 ATS

HOTEL POST
Fleischmarkt 24
Tel. 51 58 30
Fax 513 83 80-8
In a quarter undergoing heavy renovation, this is one of the cheapest establishments in the center of town.
***
650–750 ATS

HOTEL RATHAUSPARK
Rathausstrasse 17
Tel. 404 12
Fax 404 12-761
Between the University and the City Hall.
****
1,400–1,750 ATS

HOTEL ROYAL
Singerstrasse 3
Tel. 515 68
Fax 513 96 98
In the heart of the city.
****
1,450–2,300 ATS

HOTEL SACHER
Philharmonikerstrasse 4
Tel. 514 56 or 52 55 75
Fax 514 57-810
The best-known hotel in Vienna, opened in the 19th century by the Sacher brothers. Bedrooms renovated recently. Reliable quality and service.
*****
3,200–4,600 ATS

HOTEL AM SCHUBERTRING
Schubertring 11
Tel. 71 70 20
Fax 713 99 66
Modern architecture blended with Jugendstil. Also apartments for rent.
****
1,400–2,250 ATS

AM STEPHANSPLATZ
Stephansplatz 9
Tel. 53 40 50
Fax 53 40 57-11
In the center of Vienna, facing the Cathedral. Also houses the Café Dom.
****
1,550–2,060 ATS

HOTEL TIGRA
Tiefer Graben 14
Tel. 533 96 41
Fax 533 96 45
Two buildings side by side, one modern, one traditional. Apartments available.
****
1,300–1,800 ATS

HOTEL VIENNA PLAZA
Schottenring 11
Tel. 313 900
Fax 313 90-160
Built in 1989, this is the most luxurious hotel in town, patronized by stars and big businessmen. The interiors have a Jugendstil appearance.
*****
3,900–4,400 ATS

HOTEL WANDL
Pandersplatz 9
Tel. 534 550
Fax 534 55 77
In a quiet street just off the Graben. Apartments for up to five available.
***
1,350–1,600 ATS

MERCURE WIEN CITY
Fleischmarkt 1a and 2
Tel. 534 60-0
Fax 534 60 23-2
In the old heart of Vienna. Apartments available.
1,990–2,900 ATS

HOTEL ZUR WIENER STATTSOPER
Krugerstrasse 11
Tel. 513 12 74
Fax 513 12 74–15
Close to the Opera;

quiet, though central.
***
1,100–1,200 ATS

PENSION ARENBERG
Stubenring 2
Tel. 512 52 91
Fax 513 93 56
This hotel on the edge of the Ring is part of the Best Western chain.
****
1,650–1,800 ATS

PENSION AVIANO
Marco d'Aviano Gasse 1
Tel. 512 83 30
Fax 512 81 65
A well-run pension with small rooms and a typical Viennese atmosphere.
****
900–1,100 ATS

PENSION CHRISTINA
Hafnersteig 7
Tel. 533 29 61

Fax 533 29 61-11
Part of a four-star hotel chain set back from the street in a quiet area.
****
1,000–1,200 ATS
🏨 🛏 🄲 ⚥ 🏠

PENSION DOMIZIL
Schulerstrasse 14
Tel. 513 31 99
Fax 512 34 84
All comforts.
****
1,300–1,500 ATS
🛏 🄲 🏠 🚗

PENSION ELITE
Wipplingerstrasse 32
Tel. 533 25 180 or 533 51 13-0
Fax 535 57 53
In the center of town, founded in 1911.
***
1,200–1,450 ATS
🏨 🄲 🅿

PENSION GEISSLER
Postgasse 14
Tel. 533 28 03
Fax 533 26 35
***
650–1,050 ATS
🏠 🄲 🏠 🅿

PENSION LERNER
Wipplingerstrasse 23
Tel. 533 52 19 or 34 35 69
***
840–900 ATS
🏠 🄲 🅿

PENSION NEUER MARKT
Seilergasse 9
Tel. 512 23 16
Fax 513 91 05
On the same square of the same name.
****
1,000–1,300 ATS
🏨 🄲 🔅 🏠 🅿

PENSION NOSSEK
Graben 17
Tel. 533 70 41
Fax 535 36 46
Bedrooms with views of the Graben.
***
950–1,250 ATS
🏨 🄲 🔅

PENSION PERTSCHY
Habsburgergasse 5
Tel. 534 49
Fax 534 49-49
Part of a Viennese hotel chain. In a quiet street just off the Graben. Private elevator.
****
1,000–1,300 ATS
🏨 🄲 ⚥ 🏠

PENSION RESIDENZ
Ebendorferstrasse 10
Tel. 43 47 86-0
Fax 434 78 65-0
Just behind the old university. Very pleasant area, particularly good for walking.
***
1,000–1,150 ATS
🏨 🄲 🔅 🏠

RIEMERGASSE (APPARTEMENT-PENSION)
Riemergasse 8
Tel. 512 72 200
Fax 513 77 78
Behind the Cathedral, in a recently restored precinct. Apartments available. Prices according to the number of people accommodated.
****
1,100–1,200 ATS
🏨 🄲 🏠

PENSION SUZANNE
Walfischgasse 4
Tel. 513 25 07
Close to the Opera.
***
900–1,000 ATS
🏠 🄲 🔅 🅿

CAFÉS

ALT-WIEN
Bäckerstrasse 9
Tel. 512 52 22
Open daily 10am–2am
In a small street, close to the University. Home-made tarts.
50–100 ATS
🄲 🔅

BAWAG CAFÉ
Tuchlauben 5
Tel. 534 53 2606
Open Mon.–Sat. 8am–8pm
Open Sun. 9am–8pm
Good for coffee and cakes.
25–50 ATS
🄲 🔅

BRÄUNERHOF
Stallburggasse 2
Tel. 512 38 93
Open Mon.–Fri. 7.30am–7.30pm
Open Sat. 7.30am–6pm
Open Sun. 8am–6pm
You can sit for hours over a cup of coffee, while reading a newspaper and listening to the cellist (at weekends).
50–100 ATS
🄲 🍵

BURGGARTEN-MEIEREI
Burggarten Palmenhaus
Tel. 533 10 33
Open daily 11am–9pm
Quiet spot in the garden behind the Hofburg. Terrace in summer, palm house in winter.
50–100 ATS
🄲 🔅

CAFÉ BAR IN DER WIENER SECESSION
Friedrichstrasse 12
Tel. 56 93 86
Modern cuisine.
🍴 🄲 🔅

CAFÉ CENTRAL
Herrengasse 14
Tel. 533 37 6326
Open Mon.–Sat. 8am–6pm
Closed Sun. and public holidays
In the Ferstel Palace, close to the Hofburg.
▲ 160
50–150 ATS
🄲 🔅

DIGLAS
Wollzeile 10
Tel. 512 84 01
Open Mon.–Sat. 7am–11.30pm
Open Sun., public holidays 10am–11.30pm
Plain cuisine.
50–100 ATS
🄲 🗔

CAFÉ HOTEL EUROPA
Kärntnerstrasse 18
Tel. 515 940
Open daily 8am–11.30pm
Glassed-in terrace looking out on to the street.
75–150 ATS
🄲 🔅 🗔

CAFÉ DE L'EUROPE
Graben 31
Tel. 533 10 52
Open Mon.–Sun. 6.30am–midnight
Outdoor tables in summer.
60–120 ATS
🄲 🔅

GRIENSTEIDL
Michaelerplatz 2
Tel. 535 26 92
Open 8am–midnight
Terrace café on the forecourt of the Hofburg.
80–150 ATS
🄲 🔅 🗔

CAFÉ HAWELKA
Dorotheergasse 6
Tel. 512 82 30

Open Wed.–Mon. 8am–2am
Open Sun., public holidays 4pm–2am
Artists' meeting place.
50–100 ATS
🄲

KURSALON
Johannesgasse 33
In the Stadtpark
Tel. 713 21 81
Open daily 2pm–11pm
In a former ballroom, in the center of Vienna's municipal gardens. Terrace, operettas in summer (till the end Oct.)
100–200 ATS
🍴 🄲 🔅 🗔

CAFÉ LANDTMANN
Dr. Karl Lueger Ring 4
Tel. 532 06 21
Open daily 8am–midnight
Between the mayoral offices and the City Theater.
150–350 ATS
◑ 🄲 🔅 🗔

CAFÉ MUSEUM
Friedrichstrasse 6
Tel. 565 202
Open daily 7am–11pm
Original furnishings by Adolf Loos.
50–120 ATS
🍴 🄲

CAFÉ SACHER
Philharmonikerstrasse 4
Tel. 51 45 78 46
Open daily 6.30am–11.30pm
In the Sacher Hotel, facing the Opera.
50–120 ATS
🄲 🔅 🗔

TIROLERHOF
Tegetthofstrasse 8
Tel. 512 78 33
Open Mon.–Sat. 7am–9pm
Open Sun., public holidays 9.30am–8pm
In a quiet, central position.
75–150 ATS
🄲

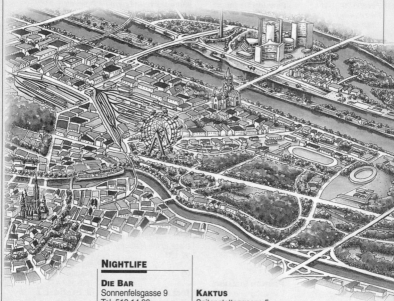

NIGHTLIFE

DIE BAR
Sonnenfelsgasse 9
Tel. 513 14 99
🇨 ♫

DUESENBERG
Stubenring 4
Tel. 513 84 96
A huge bar, very few chairs, music.
🖼 ♫

ECHO
Passauer Platz 2
Tel. 533 89 84
🇨 ♫

EDEN BAR
Liliengasse 2
Tel. 512 74 50
🇨 ▭

HOPFERL
Naglergasse 13
Tel. 533 26 41
Connected with the Bierhof via underground passages.
🇨 🔆 ♫

VOLKSGARTEN CAFÉ
Burgring 1
Tel. 63 05 18
Open Mon.–Thur.
8pm–2am, Fri.–Sat.
8pm–4am, Sun., public
holidays 5pm–2am
At the entrance to the gardens, near the Ring. A dancing school in the evenings,
80–150 ATS
🖼 🇨 🔆 🅿 ♫

VOLKSGARTEN-MEIEREI
In the Volksgarten
Tel. 533 21 05
Open Apr. 1–Sept. 31
8am–9pm, Sept.–Dec.
9am–6pm
Terrace at the center of the gardens.
75–120 ATS
🖼 🇨 🔆

KAKTUS
Seitenstettengasse 5
Tel. 533 19 38
A younger crowd tend to frequent this club, situated in the "Bermuda Triangle".
🇨 ♫

KOLAR BEISL
Kleeblattgasse 5
Tel. 533 52 25
In a small alley in the old part of the 1st District. Bar, low vaulted ceiling.
🖼 🇨

LE SPLENDID
Jasomirgottstrasse 3
Tel. 533 34 30
Big discotheque in front of the Cathedral. Dance music, best on Sat. evenings.
Admission: 80 ATS
🇨

LUKAS
Schönlaterngasse 2
Tel. 513 50 90
Student bar, open very late.
🇨 ♫

MONTEVIDEO
Annagasse 3a
Tel. 513 85 74
Central Vienna's leading nightclub. Very fashionable. Dance and soul music. Best nights: Thur. (Admission: 100 ATS) and Sat.
🇨

MOULIN ROUGE
Walfischgasse 1
Tel. 512 21 30
Traditional show with striptease during the week, fashionable discotheque at weekends. Prices are very expensive, though. Admission: 150 ATS
🇨

NEW YORK NEW YORK
Annagasse 8
Tel. 513 86 51
Small bar with terrace opposite the Montevideo discotheque.
🇨 ▭ ♫

NEW YORKER
Biberstrasse 9
Tel. 513 75 29
Popular bar.
🖼 🇨

OSKAR
Concordiaplatz 2
Tel. 638 355
Open 4.30pm–2am
Very large bar, food served after midnight.
🖼 🇨

P 1
Rotgasse 9
Tel. 535 99 95
Emphatically male clientele.
🇨 ♫

PETER'S CAFÉ HARTAUER
Riemergasse 9
Tel. 512 89 81
Open 8am–2am
One of Vienna's more venerable bars.
🖺 🇨

REISS BAR
Marco d'Aviano Gasse 1
Tel. 512 71 98
Singles bar.
🇨 ♫

ROTER ENGEL
Rabensteig 5
Tel. 535 41 05
In the "Bermuda Triangle"; downstairs bar, upstairs billiard room. Live music Thur. to Sat., from 10pm.
🇨 🍺

SANTO SPIRITO
Kumpfgasse 7
Tel. 512 99 98
Classical music.
🇨 ♫

STEINZEIT
Fischerstiege 9
Tel. 533 97 60
Hard rock.
🖺 🇨 ♫

TRAM BAR
Krugerstrasse 6
Tel. 5125145
A bar designed to resemble the interior of a tram.
🇨 ☀ ▯

VOLKSGARTEN
Burgring 1
Tel. 630 518

Open 8am–2am
Discotheque with garden and fountains.
Admission: 60 ATS
🇨 ♫

WEIN COMPTOIR
Bäckerstrasse 6
Tel. 512 17 60
Specialist wine bar.
🇨 ♫

WUNDER-BAR
Schönlaterngasse 8
Tel. 512 79 89
A small mezzanine bar with a few tables.
🇨 ♫

FOOD SHOPS

DEMEL (PATISSERIE)
Kohlmarkt 14
Tel. 533 17 17 or 533 55 16
Open daily 11am–10pm
Terrace with view across Michaelerplatz.
100–250 ATS
🇨 ☀

◆

**2ND DISTRICT
LEOPOLDSTADT**

PRACTICAL INFORMATION

REISEBÜRO IM BAHNHOF WIEN MITTE
Landstrasser

Hauptstrasse
Tel. 5800-31070
Open daily 8am–6.30pm
Travel agency inside the station.

TRANSPORT

STATION
BAHNHOF WIEN MITTE
Landstrasser
Hauptstrasse
Tel. 5800-31070
Open daily
6am–midnight

CYCLE RENTALS
NEUE WIENER HOCHSCHAUBAHN
Prater Weg 113
Tel. 260 165
Open daily 9am–6pm in summer

CAR RENTALS
AUTOHANSA
Franzensbrückenstrasse 20
Tel. 214 16 94
Open Mon.–Fri.
9am–5pm

CULTURAL ATTRACTIONS

AUGARTEN
Augarten
Small, quiet park.

JOHANN STRAUSS-WOHNUNG
Praterstrasse 54
Tel. 240 121
Open daily exc. Mon.
9am–12.15 pm,
1pm–4.30pm

PLANETARIUM
Prater hauptallee
Tel. 249432
The Vienna Planetarium is near the Ferris wheel.

PRATER
Prater
▲ 265

RIESENRAD (FERRIS WHEEL)
Prater
Tel. 262 130
Open Apr.–Sept.
9am–11pm
Open Feb., Mar., Oct.
10am–10pm
Nov., Dec., Jan.
11am–6pm

SHOWS

ODEON
Taborstrasse 10
Tel. 214 55 62

VINDOBONA
Wallensteinplatz 6
Tel. 33 42 31

RESTAURANTS

ALTES JÄGERHAUS
Freudenau 255
Tel. 218 95 77
Open Wed.–Sun.
9am–11pm
Closed Mon., Tue.
At the Prater, on the way to the racecourse.
250–400 ATS
🌓 🖺 ☀ 🅿

LUSTHAUS
Freudenau 254, at the end of the Praterhauptallee
Tel. 218 95 65
Open Mon.–Sat.
11am–11pm
Open Sun.
11 30am–7pm
In the Prater woods, a few minutes by car from the Freudenau racecourse.
150–400 ATS
🌓 🖺 ☀ 🅿

SCHWEIZERHAUS
Prater 116
Tel. 218 01 52
Open daily 10am–11pm
Closed Nov.–March
Over 2000 seats in

summer. Near the
fairground.
150–300 ATS
◐ ☐·· ⤋ ☐

VINCENT
Grosse Pfarrgasse 7
Tel. 214 15 16
Open Mon.–Sat.
11.30am–2pm,
6pm–2am
Closed Sun. and public
holidays
300–700 ATS
Ⓜ ☐··

3RD DISTRICT LANDSTRASSE

TRANSPORT

BUS
VIENNA AIRPORT BUS
SERVICE
City Air Terminal
Hilton Hotel
Tel. 5800–35 404 or
5800–35 405
Operates daily
5am–11.30pm
*Shuttle bus service from
the city center to the
airport and back. Every
30 min, 5am–8.30am;
every 20 min
8.30am–8pm; every 30
min 8.30pm–11.30pm.
Shuttle to and from
Westbahnhof and
Südbahnhof hourly
5.40am–11.50pm.*

CAR HIRE
BUDGET RENT A CAR
Am Stadtpark
Hilton Hotel
Tel. 756 565

Open Mon.–Fri.
8.30am–5.30pm

CULTURAL ATTRACTIONS

FRIEDHOF ST MARX
Leberstrasse 6–8
Open Apr.–Oct.
7am–5pm
Open May–Sept.
7am–6pm
Open July-Aug.
7am–7pm
Open Nov.–Mar.
7am–nightfall
Mozart's tomb.

HEERESGESCHICHT-LICHES MUSEUM
Arsenalstrasse
Tel. 78 23 03
*The Military History
Museum is in the former
arsenal and royal
artillery building.*

KUNSTHAUS WIEN
Untere
Weissgerberstrasse 13
Tel. 712 04 91
Open daily 9am–7pm

MUSEUM DES 20. JAHRHUNDERTS
Schweizergarten
*The Museum of the
20th Century is devoted
to contemporary art, as
is that in the
Lichtenstein Palace.*

MUSEUM MITTELALTERLICHER ÖSTERREICHISCHER KUNST
Lower Belvedere
*Noteworthy 15th-
century altarpieces.*

ÖSTERREICHISCHE GALERIE DES 19. UND 20. JAHRHUNDERTS
Prinz-Eugen Strasse 27
Im Belvedere
Tel. 784 15 80
Open daily. exc. Mon.
10am–5pm
In the Upper Belvedere,

the former summer
residence of the
Habsburgs.

SHOWS

AKADEMIETHEATER
Lizstrasse 1
Tel. 514 44 29 59

KONZERTHAUS
Lothringerstrasse 20
Tel. 712 46 86

RASUMOFSKY PALACE
Rasumofskygasse 23

RESTAURANTS

GOTTFRIED
Marxergasse 3
Tel. 713 82 56
Open Sun.–Fri.
noon–3pm,
6pm–midnight
Open Sat. 6pm–midnight
*Luxurious. New
Austrian cuisine.*
750–2,000 ATS
☐·· ☐

IM KUNSTHAUS
Weissgerberlände 14
Tel. 712 04 97
Open daily
10am–midnight
*In the
Hundertwasserhaus.
Terrace in summer.*
150–350 ATS
◐ ☐·· ⤋ ☐ ♫

PALAIS SCHWARZENBERG
Schwarzenbergplatz 9
Tel. 784 51 56 00
Open daily
noon–2.30pm,
6pm–11pm
*First-class cuisine and
gardens with a view of
the park.*
800–2,500 ATS
Ⓜ Ⓒ ☐ ☐

ROTISSERIE PRINZ EUGEN
Am Stadtpark
Tel. 717 00 353
Open Mon.–Fri. noon–
2pm, 7–11pm , Open
Sat., Sun. 7pm–11pm
*Austrian and
international cuisine in
the Hilton Hotel.*
600–1,200 ATS
Ⓜ ☐·· ☐ ☐

STEIRERECK
Rasumofskygasse 2
Tel. 713 31 68
Open Mon.–Fri.
noon–3pm and
7pm–midnight
Closed Sat.-Sun. and
public holidays

*A pioneer of new
Austrian cuisine.
Excellent menu and
winelist.*
800–2,000 ATS
Ⓜ ☐·· ☐

VIER JAHRESZEITEN
Johannesgasse 28
Tel. 711 22 143
Open daily noon–3pm,
7pm–midnight
Closed Sat. lunch, Sun.
evening
*The restaurant of the
Intercontinental Hotel.
Pianist in the evenings.*
700–1,500 ATS
Ⓜ Ⓒ ☐ ☐ ►

HOTELS

INTERCONTINENTAL HOTEL
Johannesgasse 28
Tel. 711 220
Fax 713 44 89
*Between the
Stadtpark and the
Kursalon.*
****
2,730–3,900 ATS
🏛 ☐·· Ⓒ ⤋ ☐ ⅄
⌂ ☐ ♫

PULLMAN HOTEL BELVEDERE
Am Heumarkt 35–37
Tel. 716 160
Fax 716 16 844
Conveniently central.
****
1,640–1,850 ATS
🏛 ☐·· ☐ ⅄ ⌂ 🚗

PALAIS SCHWARZENBERG
Schwarzenbergplatz 9
Tel. 784 515
Fax 784 714
Luxurious and stylish.
*****
4,000–5,200 ATS

HOTEL VIENNA HILTON
Am Stadtpark
Tel. 717000
Fax 713 06 91
A classic hotel.
*****
3,600–4,000 ATS

4TH DISTRICT WIEDEN

USEFUL ADDRESSES

FAHRRADBÜRO
Krankenberggasse 11
Tel. 505 84 35
Open Feb.–Dec.
2pm–6pm
Information for cyclists.

ÖSTERREICH URLAUBSINFORMATION
Margaretenstrasse 1
Tel. 587 20 00
Open Mon.–Fri.
9am–5.30pm
Information about Austria, but no hotel reservations.

ZIMMERNACHWEIS IN SÜDBAHNHOF
Wiedner Gürtel
Tel. 835 168
Open daily
6.30am–10pm in summer, 6.30am–9pm in winter.
Hotel reservation service.

CULTURAL ATTRACTIONS

KARLSKIRCHE
Karlsplatz
Fischer von Erlach's masterwork. Frescoes by J. M. Rottmayr.

SCHUBERT STERBEZIMMER
Kandtenbrückengasse 6
Tel. 573 90 72
Open daily exc. Mon.
9am–12.15pm,
1pm–4.30pm
Franz Schubert died in this house.

SHOWS

BÖSENDORFER SAAL
Graf-Starhemberg-Gasse 14
Tel. 656 651

MME SILVIA MÜHRINGER
Wiedner Hauptstrasse 18
Tel. 587 78 90

ORF-FUNKHAUS
Argentinierstrasse 30a

TICKET SALES
VIENNA TICKET SERVICE
B.P. 160
Tel. 587 98 43

RESTAURANTS

ZU DEN DREI BUCHTELN
Margaretenstrasse 11
Tel. 587 13 10
6pm–midnight
Closed Sat., Sun., public holidays
The entrance is difficult to find. French cuisine. Very popular and very good.
200–350 ATS
❶ ❑··

5TH DISTRICT MARGARETEN

SHOWS

SPEKTAKEL
Hamburgerstrasse 14
Tel. 587 06 53

THEATER KABARETT SIMPL
Wollzeile 36
Tel. 512 47 42

RESTAURANTS

ALTES FASSL
Zieghelfgasse 37
Tel. 554 298
Open Tue.–Sat.
6pm–1am
Open Sun. noon–3pm,
6pm–1am. Closed Mon., public holidays
An extensive menu and pleasant surroundings.
200–400 ATS
❶ ❑·· ❑

MOTTO
Schönbrunner Strasse 30 / Rüdigergasse 2
Tel. 587 06 72
Open daily 8pm–4am
(terrace 6pm–11pm)
Good late-night restaurant, with music and neon restrooms.
250–450 ATS
❶ ❑··

SCHLOSSGASSE 21
Schlossgasse 21
Tel. 550 767
Open daily noon–2am
Garden in summer. Extensive wine list and good menu with nouvele cuisine.
150–350 ATS
❶ ❑·· ♫

6TH DISTRICT MARIAHILF

CULTURAL ATTRACTIONS

HAYDN MUSEUM
Haydngasse 19
Tel. 596 13 07
Open daily exc Mon.
9am–12.15pm,
1–4.30pm

SHOWS

KARETT UND KOMÖDIE AM NASCHMARKT
Linke Wienzeile 4
Tel. 587 22 75

KONSERVATORIUM
Mariahilferstrasse 51

RAIMUNDTHEATER
Wallgasse 13–20
Tel. 599 77 27

THEATER AM DER WIEN
Linke Wienzeile 6
Tel. 588 30 265

THEATERGRUPPE 80
Gumpendorferstrasse 67
Tel. 565 222

WIENER FESTWOCHEN
Lehargasse 11
Tel. 586 16 76

RESTAURANTS

HAUSWIRTH
Otto Bauer Gasse 20
Tel. 587 12 61
Open Mon.–Fri.
11.30am–2pm, 6–9pm,
Sat. 6–10pm
Closed Sun. and public holidays
Straightforward Austrian cuisine.
350–600 ATS
⓾ ❑

LUDWIG VAN
Laimgrubengasse 22
Tel. 587 13 20
Open Mon.–Sat.
6pm–1am
Closed Sun. and public holidays
In Beethoven's house. Very well-run, Jugendstil appearance.
150–300 ATS
❶ ❑·· ✂ ❑ ♫

HOTELS

HOTEL BEETHOVEN
Millöckergasse 6
Tel. 587 44 820
Fax 587 44 42
Part of the Best Western hotel chain. Irreproachable.
★★★★
1,000–1,700 ATS
❑ ✂ ❑ ☖ ℗

HOTEL SCHNEIDER
Getreidemarkt 5
Tel. 588 380
Fax 588 382 12
200 yards from the center. Apartments available.
★★★★
1,500–1,900 ATS
☖ ⌂ ❑·· ❑ ☖

PENSION ESTERHAZY
Nelkengasse 3
Tel. 5875159
In a small street off Mariahilferstrasse.
450–490 ATS
⌂ ❑··

NIGHTLIFE

BARFLY'S CLUB
In the Hotel Fürst Mettenich
Esterhàzygasse 33
Tel. 58 870
Bar on the ground floor, dancing in the basement.
❑·· ❑ ♫

357

TITANIC
Theobaldgasse 11
Tel. 587 47 58
*Bar on the ground floor,
two dancefloors in the
basement and live
music sometimes. Hot
snacks available.*

7TH DISTRICT
NEUBAU

CULTURAL
ATTRACTIONS

**MUSEUM OF GOLD-
AND SILVERWORK**
Zieglerstrasse 22
Tel. 93 33 88

TABAKMUSEUM
Mariahilferstrasse 2
In the Messepalast
Tel. 961 716
Open Tue. 10am–7pm
Open Wed.–Fri.
10am–3pm
Open Sat., Sun., public
holidays 9am–1pm

SHOWS

**VERANSTALTUNGEN
MESSEPALAST**
Messeplatz 1
Tel. 526 0560

TANZTHEATER
Burggasse 38
Tel. 963 934

VOLKSTHEATER
Neustiftgasse 1
Tel. 932 776

RESTAURANTS

ECK
Neustiftgasse 82
Tel. 931 474
Open Mon.–Thur.
6pm–3am
Open Fri.–Sat.
6pm–4am
Mon.–Sat. 7pm–4am in
summer
Closed Sun., public
holidays
*Viennese food. Fine art
on display.*
250–400 ATS

PLUTZER BRÄU
Schwankgasse 4
Tel. 526 12 15 –
526 87 11
Open Mon.–Sat.
11am–2am
Open Sun. 11am–11pm
*In the narrow streets of
the 7th District. Terrace
for sitting outside in
summer.*
125–250 ATS

**ZU EBENER ERDE UND
ERSTEN STOCK**
Burggasse 13
Tel. 93 62 54
Open Tue.–Sat.
11.30am–2pm and
6pm–midnight
Closed Sun, Mon. and
public holidays
*An excellent choice for
eating after a shopping
trip. Fine food upstairs,
more basic downstairs.*
150–400 ATS

ZUR STADT KREMS
Zieglergasse 37
Tel. 937 200
Open Mon.–Sat.
11am–2pm and
6pm–midnight
Open Sun. 11am-3pm,
Oct.–May

Closed public holidays
*Viennese specialties
available. Pleasant
terrace for eating
outdoors.*
150–250 ATS

HOTELS

**K + K HOTEL MARIA
THERESIA**
Kirchberggasse 6–8
Tel. 52 123
Fax 52 123 70
*The hotel is part of the
Best Western chain,
just outside the Ring in
the old Spittelberg
artists' quarter. Quiet,
good for families.*
****
1,500–2,000 ATS

HOTEL TANGRA
Mariahilferstrasse 58
Tel. 526 13 06
Fax 526 49 29
*Comfortable and
welcoming.*
**
880–980 ATS

PENSION REIMER
Kirchengasse 18
Tel. 936 162
*Small, quiet pension,
15 rooms on several
floors of the building.*
**
350–600 ATS

NIGHTLIFE

DONAU
Karl-Schweighoferg-
gasse 10
Tel. 938 105
*Spacious, polychrome
bar with live music and
a regular crowd.*

8TH DISTRICT
JOSEFSTADT

SHOWS

**KABARETT
NIEDERMAIR**
Lenaugasse 1a
Tel. 408 44 92

KLANGBOGEN
Summer Music
Festival)
Laudongasse 29
Tel. 400 084 10

PALAIS AUERSPERG
Auerspergstrasse 1
Tel. 401 07

**THEATER IN DER
JOSEFSTADT**
Josefstädter Strasse
24–26
Tel. 402 51 27

VEGA
Gonzagagasse 11
Tel. 533 53 14

**VIENNA'S ENGLISH
THEATER**
Josefsgasse 12
Tel. 402 12 60

RESTAURANTS

MARIA TREU
Maria Treu Gasse 8
Tel. 434 709
Open Mon.–Sat.
7.30am–11pm
*Located in the courtyard
of the Piaristenkirche.*
200–300 ATS

LE TUNNEL
Florianigasse 39
Tel. 423 465
Open daily 9am–2am
*Rock concerts in the
basement.*
90–150 ATS

HOTELS

HOTEL JOSEFSHOF
Josefsgasse 4–6
Tel. 438 90 10
Fax 838 901 150
*Apartments and suites
available.*
****

1,500–2,000 ATS
🏠 🍴 🚭 🅿

PENSION ALSERGRUND
Alserstrasse 33
Tel. 512 74 93
*A student residence
used as a pension from
July 1 to Sept. 30.
Recognizable by the
red triangle on its
façade.*
**
350–400 ATS

PENSION AUERSPERG
Auerspergstrasse 9
Tel. 512 74 93
*Close to the center;
recognizable by a red
triangle.*
**
350–400 ATS

PENSION CARINA
Alserstrasse 21
Tel. 42 52 68
Fax 26 90 23–75
**
790–1,090 ATS

PENSION COLUMBIA
Kochgasse 9
Tel. 42 67 57
**
560–650 ATS

PENSION EDELWEISS
Langegasse 61
Tel. 422 306
Fax 424 631-10
900–1,100 ATS
🏠 🚹 🅿

PENSION KOPER
Bennogasse 21
Tel. 403 41 93 –
408 64 43
Fax 402 31 43
*Two buildings in
adjoining streets.*
**
210–220 ATS
🏠 🍴 📧••

**PENSION
LEHRERHEIM DES
LEHRERHAUSVEREINES**
Langegasse 20–22
Tel. 403 23 58 or
402 74 35-0
**
600–500 ATS
🏠 🅿

PENSION WILD
Langegasse 10
Tel. 435 174
*Close to the Ring
and the national
museums.*
*
500–550 ATS
🏠 🍴 C 🅿

CAFÉS

**KLEINES WIENER
CAFÉ**
Kochgasse 18
Tel. 42 79 892
Open 9am–11pm
C 🚭

9TH DISTRICT ALSERGRUND

PRACTICAL INFORMATION

ALLG. KRANKENHAUS
Währingergürtel 18–20
oder Spitalgasse 2/23
Tel. 404 00
Central hospital

**LOST PROPERTY
OFFICE**
Wasagasse 22
Tel. 313 44–92 11
Open Mon.–Fri.
8am–noon

CULTURAL ATTRACTIONS

**MUSEUM MODERNER
KUNST**
Fürstengasse 1
In the Palais
Liechtenstein
Tel. 341 259 or 346 306
Open daily exc. Tue
10am.-6pm
*Contemporary 20th-
century art.*

SCHUBERTMUSEUM
Nussdorferstrasse 54
Tel. 3459924
Open daily. exc Mon.

9am–12.15pm,
1–4.30pm

**SIGMUND FREUD
MUSEUM**
Berggasse 19
Tel. 319 15 96
Open daily 9am–3pm

VOTIVKIRCHE
Rooseveltplatz
*In a small park, set back
from the street.*

SHOWS

**VOLKSOPER (COMIC
OPERA)**
Währingerstrasse 78
Tel. 514 44 33 18

RESTAURANTS

RIEDL'S WIENER BEISL
Schlickgasse 5
Tel. 34 92 49
Open 9am–midnight
Excellent cuisine.

HOTELS

HOTEL ATLANTA
Währingerstrasse 33
Tel. 421 230
*500 yards from the
center of town.*
****
975–1,575 ATS
🏠 🏠 🅿

HOTEL REGINA
Rooseveltplatz 15
Tel. 427 681–0
Fax 408 83 92
*View of the Votivkirche.
Good restaurant for
residents only.*
****

1,500–2,100 ATS
🏠 🍴 C 🚭 🏠 🅿

**HOTEL AM
SCHOTTENPOINT**
Währinger Strasse 22
Tel. 310 87 87
Fax 310 87 87–4
In the center of town.
***
1,240–1,340 ATS
🏠 C 🏠 🅿

PENSION BLECKMANN
Währingerstrasse 15
Tel. 427103
Fax 402 20 24
*Very close to the center
of town.*
***
1,080–1,150 ATS
🏠 🅿

PENSION VERA
Alserstrasse 18
Tel. 4027711-43 25 95
Fax 930213
*In a shopping area
linked to the town
center by tram.*
**
750–800 ATS
🏠 🏠

CAFÉS

CAFÉ STEIN
Währingerstrasse 6
Tel. 317 241
Open Mon.-Sat. 7–1 am
Open Sun. 9–1am
Closed public holidays
*On three floors, facing
the university. Very
stylish café frequented
by intellectuals.*
30–200 ATS
O C 🚭

10TH DISTRICT FAVORITEN

PRACTICAL INFORMATION

REISEBÜRO IM SÜDBAHNHOF
Wiedner Gürtel 1a–1b
Tel. 5800–31050
Open daily 8am–6.30pm
Travel agency in the station; hotel reservations can be made here and train tickets purchased.

TRANSPORT

STATION
SÜDBAHNHOF
Wiedner Gürtel 1a–1b
Tel. 5800–31050
Open daily 6am–midnight

CULTURAL ATTRACTIONS

HORTICULTURE MUSEUM
Parc d'Oberta
Tel. 68 11 70

11TH DISTRICT SIMMERING

CULTURAL ATTRACTIONS

ZENTRALFRIEDHOF
Simmeringer Haupstrasse 234
Tel. 76 55 44
Open Mar., Apr., Sept., Oct. 7am–6pm
Open May–Aug. 7am–7pm
Open Nov.–Feb. 8am–5pm
Tombs of Beethoven, Schubert, Strauss, Schönberg, and Brahms in the musicians' quarter. Jewish cemetery also here.

12TH DISTRICT MEIDLING

NIGHTLIFE

U 4
Schönbrunnerstrasse 222
Tel. 858 318
Mostly rock music.
Admission: 100 ATS

13TH DISTRICT HIETZING

CULTURAL ATTRACTIONS

SCHLOSS SCHÖNBRUNN
Schönbrunner Schloss Strasse. Tel. 811 13
Open Apr.–June, Oct. daily 8.30am–5pm; July–Sept. daily 8.30am–5.30 pm; Nov.–March daily 9am–4pm

TIERGARTEN SCHÖNBRUNN
Schönbrunner
Tel. 877 12 36
Open Apr.–Sept. daily 9am–6pm; Oct.–March daily 9am–4.30pm

14TH DISTRICT PENZING

CULTURAL ATTRACTIONS

ERNST FUCHS PRIVATMUSEUM
Hüttelbergstrasse 26
Tel. 948 575
Open Mon.–Fri. 9am–4pm for organized tours

KIRCHE AM STEINHOF
Baumgartner Höhe 1
Tel. 949 060 23 91
Open for tours Sat. 3pm
Open for organized tours by arrangement.

15TH DISTRICT RUDOLFSHEIM-FÜNFHAUS

PRACTICAL INFORMATION

REISEBÜRO IM WESTBAHNOF
Mariahilferstrasse 132
Tel. 5800–310 60
Open daily 8am–6.30pm

TRAVEL AGENCY.
Zimmernachweis im Westbahnof
Mariahilferstrasse 132
Tel. 835 185
Open daily 6.15am–11pm in summer, 6.15am–10pm in winter
Room reservation service in the West station.

VIKERL'S LOKAL
Würfelgasse 4
Tel. 894 34 30
Open Mon.–Thur.
11.30am–2.30pm,
6pm–11pm
Open Fri.–Sat.
6pm–11pm
Closed Sun. and public
holidays
Good food.
150–500 ATS
◑ ▭•• ▭

Open on the first
Wednesday of each
month 10am–noon

HOTELS

PENSION AM
LERCHENFELD
Hernalser Gürtel 5
Tel. 436 867
Facing the Gürtel.
**
700–750 ATS
⌂ ▭••

Garden.
150–250 ATS
◑ ▭•• ♫

22ND DISTRICT
DONAUSTADT

TRANSPORT

CYCLE RENTAL
FREIZEITZENTRUM
WEIDINGER
Raffineriestrasse
Tel. 220 50 65
Open Sat., Sun.,
holidays 9am–4pm
RADVERLEIH
STEINSPORNBRÜCKE
Am Hubertusdamm
Tel. 223 378
Open Sat., Sun.,
public holidays
9am–7pm
*On the Old Danube
island, near the river.*

RESTAURANT

STRANDCAFÉ
Florian-Berndl Gasse 20
Tel. 236 747
Open from Mar. 15–
Oct. 15 daily
10am–midnight
Open from Oct.
16–Mar.14 Mon.–Fri.
5pm–midnight,
Sat.–Sun.
and public holidays
11am–midnight
*Terrace and landing
stage, with an
outstanding view of
old Vienna.*
200–00 ATS
◑ ▭•• ⚬ ⲡ

TRANSPORT

STATION
WESTBAHNHOF
Mariahilferstrasse 132
Tel. 5800–310 60
Open daily
6am–midnight

RESTAURANTS

ALTWIENERHOF
Herklotzgasse 6
Tel. 892 60 00
Open Mon.–Sat.
noon–2pm,
6.30pm–11pm
Closed Sun. and public
holidays
*French and Viennese
nouvelle cuisine*
1,000–3,000 ATS
⑪ ▭•• ▭

17TH DISTRICT
HEMALS

CULTURAL
ATTRACTIONS

FIAKERMUSEUM
Veronikagasse 12
Tel. 432 60 70

19TH DISTRICT
DOBLING

RESTAURANT

FISCHERBRÄU
Billrothstrasse 17
Tel. 319 62 64
Open daily 11am–1am

"THE MIRAGE OF VIENNA"

WILLIAM SANSOM

APPENDICES

ESSENTIAL READING ◆

◆ CRANKSHAW (E.): *Vienna, the Image of a Culture in Decline*, London and New York, 1938
◆ GRIEBEN GUIDEBOOKS, NO 199: *Vienna and Its Environs*, Vienna, many editions
◆ LEHMAN (J.) and BASSET (R.): *Vienna, a Traveller's Companion*, London, 1988
◆ MICHELIN (PUB): *Austria*, English edition
◆ MEHLING (F .N.): *Austria, Phaidon Cultural Guides*, London, 1985
◆ RICKETT (R.): *A Brief Survey of Austrian History*, London, 1973

GENERAL BOOKS ◆ AND GUIDES ◆

◆ BAREA (I.): *Vienna, Legend and Reality*, London, 1992
◆ CERMAK (A.): *Vienna - A Book of Photographs*, London, 1963
◆ COOK (T.) (PUB): *Traveller's Guide to Venice*, London, 1993
◆ FUERSTEIN (G.): *Vienna Past and Present*, Vienna, 1976
◆ HOOTZ (R.): *Wien*, Munich and Berlin, 1968
◆ MAHAN (J.A.): *Vienna Yesterday and Today*, Vienna, 1928
◆ McGUIGAN (D.): *Vienna Today, a Complete Guide*, New York, 1955
◆ NEUWIRTH (W.), KÖLBEL (A.) and AUBÖCK (M.) : *Die Wiener Porzellan Manufaktur Augarten*, Vienna, 1992
◆ ROBERTSON (I.): *Austria, Blue Guides*, London, 1992
◆ SCHMIED (W.) : *Der Zeicher Alfred Kubin*, éditions Residenz, Salzbourg, 1967
◆ VESTNER (H.): *Vienna, Insight Cityguides*, London 1989
◆ WERKNER (P.): *Austrian Expressionism*, éditions Palo Alto, California, 1993
◆ WILLIAMSON (A.): *The Lure of Vienna*, London, 1926

◆ ART AND ARCHITECTURE ◆

◆ ACADEMY EDITIONS (pub): *Gustav Klimt*, London, 1976
◆ AURENHAMMER (H.): *Fischer von Erlach*, London, 1973
◆ BORSI (F.) and GODOLI (E.): *Vienna 1900, Architecture and Design*, London, 1986
◆ BRANDSTATTER (C): *Vienna*, éditions Molden, Vienna, 1981
◆ BULTMAN (B): *Oskar Kokoschka*, New York, 1961
◆ BUXBAUM (G.): *Mode aus Wien*, éditions Residenz, Salzburg, 1986
◆ COMINI (A.): *Edon Schiele*, London, 1974
◆ GRIESSMAIER (V.): *Austria, Her Landscape and Her Art*, Vienna, 1950
◆ HANSEN (T.): *Wiener Werkstatte*, éditions Brandstatter, Vienna, 1984
◆ HAUSNER (E.): *Wien*, éditions Jugend und Volk, Vienna-Munich, 1975
◆ HOFFMANN (E.): *Kokoschka, Life and Work*, London, 1947
◆ HURLIMANN (M.): *Vienna*, London, 1970
◆ KALLIER (J.): *Viennese Design and the Wiener Werkstatte*, London, 1986
◆ KOMAREK (R.): *Wien*, Éditions Kremayer and Scheriau, Vienna, 1990
◆ KRUCKENHAUSER (S.): *Heritage of Beauty*, Innsbruck, 1965
◆ MANG (K. and E.): *Viennese Architecture, 1860-1930 in Drawings*, New York, 1979
◆ MANG (K.): *Thonet Bugholzmobel*, éditions Brandstatter, Vienna, 1982
◆ MARTINEK (T.): *Kaffehauser in Wien*, éditions Falter, Vienna
◆ MUNZ (L.) AND KUNSTLER (G.): *Adolf Loos, Pioneer of Modern Architecture*, London, 1966
◆ POWELL (N.): *The Sacred Spring, the Arts in Vienna, 1898-1918*, London, 1974
◆ PRINTARIC (V.H.): *Vienna 1900, the Architecture of Otto Wagner*, London, 1989
◆ VERGO (R.): *Art in Vienna, 1898-1918: Klimt, Kokoschka, Schiele and Their Contemporaries*, London, 1975
◆ *Vienna in the Age of Schubert, the Biedermeier Interior*, exhibition catalogue, London, 1979
◆ WEBER (H.): *Wien*, editions Brandstatter, Vienna-Munich, 1984
◆ WEISSENBERGER (R.): *Vienna in the Biedermeier Era, 1815-1848*, New York, 1986
◆ WEISSENBERGER (R.): *Vienna Secession*, London, 1977

◆ WILSON (S.): *Egon Schiele*, Oxford, 1980
◆ WINGLER (H.M.): *Oskar Kokoschka, the Work of the Painter*, London, 1962

◆ HISTORY ◆

◆ BAGGER (E.): *Francis Joseph*, New York, 1927
◆ CRANKSHAW (E.): *Maria Theresa*, London, 1989
◆ CRANKSHAW (E.): *The Fall of the House of Hapsburg*, London, 1963
◆ HASLIP (J.): *The Emperor and the Actress*, London, 1982
◆ JOHNSTON (W.H.): *Vienna, the Golden Age, 1815-1914*, New York, 1981
◆ LEVETUS (A.S.): *Imperial Vienna*, London and New York, 1905
◆ LEHNE (I.) and JOHNSON (L.): *Vienna, the Past in the Present*, Vienna, 1985
◆ LONYAY (C.): *Rudolf, the Tragedy of Mayerling*, London, 1950
◆ MUSULIN (S.): *Vienna in the Age of Metternich*, London, 1975
◆ REDLICH (O.): *Emperor Francis Joseph of Austria*, London, 1929
◆ RUMBOLD (SIR H.): *The Austrian Court in the Nineteenth Century*, London, 1909
◆ SPEIL (H.): *Vienna's Golden Autumn, 1866-1938*, London, 1987
◆ TAYLOR (A.J.P.): *The Hapsburg Monarchy*, Harmondsworth, 1976
◆ TSCHUPPIK (K.): *The Reign of the Emperor Franz Joseph*, 1930

HISTORY ◆ OF IDEAS ◆

◆ BARTLEY (W. W.): *Wittgenstein*, London, 1974
◆ BROME (V.): *Freud*, London, 1984
◆ CLARK (R. W.): *Freud*, London, 1980
◆ FRANCIS (M.) (ED.): *The Viennese Enlightenment*, London, 1985
◆ GAL (H.): *The Golden Age of Vienna*, New York, 1948
◆ GRIFFIN (R.A.): *High Baroque Culture and Theatre in Vienna*, New York, 1972
◆ GRIMSTAD (K.): *Masks of the Prophet: the Theatrical World of Karl Kraus*, Toronto and London, 1982
◆ JANIK (A.) and TOULMIN (S.): *Wittgenstein's Vienna*, London, 1973

◆ JONES (E.): *The Life and Times of Sigmund Freud*, London, 1962
◆ McGUINESS (B.) (ed.): *Wittgenstein and His Times*, Oxford, 1982
◆ PEARS (D.): *Wittgenstein*, London, 1971
◆ RHEES (R.) (ed.): *Ludwig Wittgenstein*, Oxford, 1981
◆ SZASZ (T.): *Karl Kraus and the Soul Doctor*, London, 1977
◆ TIMMS (E.): *Karl Kraus, Apocalyptic Satirist: Culture and Catastrophe in Habsburg Vienna*, New Haven and London, 1986
◆ WIJDEVELD (P.): *Ludwig Wittgenstein, Architect*, London, 1994
◆ YATES (W.E.) and McKENZIE (J.R.P.): *Viennese Popular Theatre*, Exeter, 1985
◆ ZWEIG (S.): *The World of Yesterday* London, 1943

◆ LITERATURE ◆

◆ BRIGHT (R.): *Travels from Vienna in the Year 1814*, Edinburgh and London, 1818
◆ CASANOVA (G.): *History of My Life*, Eng. trans. London, 1970 (especially Volume 10).
◆ DODERER (H. VON): *The Waterfalls of Slunj*, London, 1966
◆ GREENE (G.): *The Third Man*, London, 1950
◆ KRAUS (K.): *In These Great Times*, Manchester, 1984
◆ KRAUS (K.): *Half-Truths and One-and-a-half Truths*, Manchester, 1986
◆ MUSIL (R.): *The Man without Qualities*, London, 1953
◆ SCHNITZLER (A.): *Vienna 1900, Games with Love and Death*, London, 1985
◆ SCHNITZLER (A.):*My Youth in Vienna*, London, 1971
◆ TROLLOPE (F.): *Vienna and the Austrians*, London, 1838
◆ WORTLEY-MONTAGUE (LADY M.): *Letters* (many editions)

◆ MUSIC ◆

◆ ABRAHAM (G.) (ed.): *Schubert, A Symposium*, London, 1947
◆ ANDERSON (E.) (ed. and trans.): *The Letters of Beethoven*, London, 1961
◆ BORY (R.): *Ludwig van Beethoven, His Life and*

His Work in Pictures,
New York, 1960
◆ BRION (M.): *Daily Life
in the Vienna of Mozart
and Schubert,* London,
1961
◆ BROWN (M.J.E.):
*Schubert, a Critical
Biography,* London
1958
◆ BURNEY (C.): *Musical
Tours in Europe, 1772*
ed. Scholes, London,
1959
◆ CARNER (M.): *Alban
Berg,* London, 1975
◆ COOPER (M.):
*Beethoven, the Last
Decade, 1817-1827,*
London, 1970
◆ DA PONTE (L.):
Memoirs, New York,
1929 (reprinted)
◆ ENDLER (F.): *Vienna,
a Guide to its Music
and Musicians,*
Portland, Oregon,
1989
◆ FLOWER (N.): *Franz
Schubert, the Man and
His Circle,* London,
1928
◆ GRAF (M.): *Legend of
a Musical City,* New
York, 1945
◆ HAMBURGER (M.) (ed.
and trans.): *Beethoven:
Letters, Journals and
Conversations,* London,
1966
◆ HANSLICK (E.):
*Vienna's Golden Years
of Music, 1850-1900,*
London, 1951
◆ HUGHES (R.) (ed.): *A
Mozart Pilgrimage,
Being the Travel Diaries
of Vincent and Mary
Novello,* London, 1955
◆ KELLY (M.):
Reminiscences,
London, 1826
◆ LANDON (H.C.R.):
Mozart and Vienna,
London, 1991
◆ LANDON (H.C.R.):
*Mozart, the Golden
Years,* London, 1989
◆ LANDON (H.C.R.):
*1791, Mozart's Last
Year,* London and New
York, 1988
◆ LANDON (H.C.R.):
*Essays in the Viennese
Classical Style,* London,
1970
◆ MITTAG (E.): *The
Vienna Philharmonic,*
Vienna, 1954
◆ MOLDENHAUER (H.):
*Anton von Webern,
Chronicles of His Life
and Works,* London,
and New York, 1978
◆ MOZART (W.A.): *Letters*
(many editions)
◆ NEWLIN (D.): *Bruckner,
Mahler, Schoenberg,*
New York, 1947
◆ PAYNE (A.):
Schoenberg, London,
1968
◆ REDLICH (H.): *Alban
Berg, the Man and His
Music,* London, 1951
◆ REICH (W.): *Alban
Berg,* London, 1965
◆ RICKETT (R.): *Music
and Musicians in
Vienna,* London, 1973
◆ WELLESZ (E.): *Arnold
Schoenberg,* London,
1925
◆ WIESMAN (S.) (ed.):
*Gustav Mahler in
Vienna,* New York, 1976
◆ WILDGANS (F.): *Anton
Webern,* London, 1966

◆ **MISCELLANEOUS** ◆

◆ BRAUNEIS and
ROSENER: *Die
Umgebungen Wiens,*
editions P. Zsolnay,
Vienna, 1978
◆ COLLECT.F: *Wien
Wirklich,* editions
Gesellschaftskritik,
Vienna, 1992
◆ GRUNAUER (G.), KISLER
(A.) and FRIEDMAN (D.F.):
*Viennese Cuisine, the
New Approach,*
London, 1989
◆ SINHUBER (B.F.): *Das
Grosse Buch vom
Wiener Heuriger,*
editions Orac Pietsch,
Vienna, 1980

◆ **ACKNOWLEDGEMENTS** ◆

**The Architectural
Review**: Excerpt from
Mackintosh and Vienna,
article by E. Seckler
published in the
Architectural Review,
London, in 1967.
Reprinted in the UK and
US by permission of the
Architectural Review,
London.

Faber & Faber:
Excerpt from
Nightwood by Djuna
Barnes, published by
Faber & Faber in 1956.
Reprinted in the UK by
permission of Faber &
Faber Ltd, London.

**J. M. Dent & Sons
Ltd**: Diary entry of
Franz Schubert on June
14, 1816, from *Schubert
– A Documentary
Biography* by Eric
Deutsch, translated by
Eric Blom (J. M. Dent &
Sons, London 1946).
Reprinted by
permission of J. M. Dent
& Sons Ltd.

**Northern Illinois
University Press**:
Excerpt from *The Travel
Diary of Peter Tolstoi,*
translated by Max J.
Okenfuss, copyright ©
1987 by Northern Illinois
University Press.
Reprinted in the UK and
US by permission of
Northern Illinois
University Press.

**Penguin Books
USA, Inc**: Excerpt
from March 20, 1891,
letter of Anton Chekhov
from *The Letters of
Anton Chekhov,* by
Anton Chekhov,
translated by Avraham
Yarmolinsky, translation
copyright © 1947, 1968
by the Viking Press.
Reprinted by
permission of Viking
Penguin, a division of
Penguin Books USA,
Inc.

**Penguin Books
USA, Inc. and John
Murray (Publishers)
Ltd**: Excerpt from *A
Time of Gifts* by Patrick
Leigh Fermor. Copyright
© 1977 by Patrick Leigh
Fermor. Rights outside
the U.S. administered
by John Murray
(Publishers) Ltd,
London. Reprinted by
permission of Viking
Penguin, a division of
Penguin Books USA,
Inc., and John Murray
(Publishers) Ltd.

Vanguard Press:
Excerpt from *Sigmund
Freud: Father and Man*
by Martin Freud,
copyright © 1958 by
Vanguard Press, Inc.
Reprinted by
permission of Vanguard
Press, a division of
Random House, Inc.

**W. W. Norton & Co.,
Inc**: Excerpts from
letters of August 22,
1781, and May 3, 1783,
from Mozart to his
father, and excerpt from
letter of December 5,
1791, from Sophie
Haibel to Georg
Nikolaus von Nissen
from *The Letters of
Mozart and His Family,
3rd Edition,* edited by
Emily Anderson,
copyright © 1966, 1985,
1989 by The Executors
of the late Miss Emily
Anderson. Reprinted by
permission of W. W.
Norton & Co., Inc.

INDEX

◆ Index